Norihiro Yagi won the 32nd Akatsuka Award for his debut work, *UNDEADMAN*, which appeared in *Monthly Shonen Jump* magazine and produced two sequels. His first serialized manga was his comedy *Angel Densetsu* (Angel Legend), which appeared in *Monthly Shonen Jump* from 1992 to 2000. His epic saga, *Claymore*, has been running in the magazine since 2001.

In his spare time, Yagi enjoys things like the Japanese comedic duo Downtown, martial arts, games, driving, and hard rock music, but he doesn't consider these actual hobbies.

CLAYMORE VOL. 4
SHONEN JUMP ADVANCED Manga Edition

STORY AND ART BY
NORIHIRO YAGI

English Adaptation & Translation/Jonathan Tarbox
Touch-up Art & Lettering/Sabrina Heep
Design/Izumi Evers
Editor/Yuki Takagaki

Published by VIZ Media, LLC
P.O. Box 77010
San Francisco, CA 94107

10 9 8 7 6
First printing, August 2006
Sixth printing, September 2011

PARENTAL ADVISORY
CLAYMORE is rated T+ for Older
Teen and is recommended for
ages 16 and up. This volume
contains realistic violence.
ratings.viz.com

SHONEN JUMP ADVANCED Manga Edition

Claymore

クレイモア

Vol. 4
Marked for Death

Story and Art by **Norihiro Yagi**

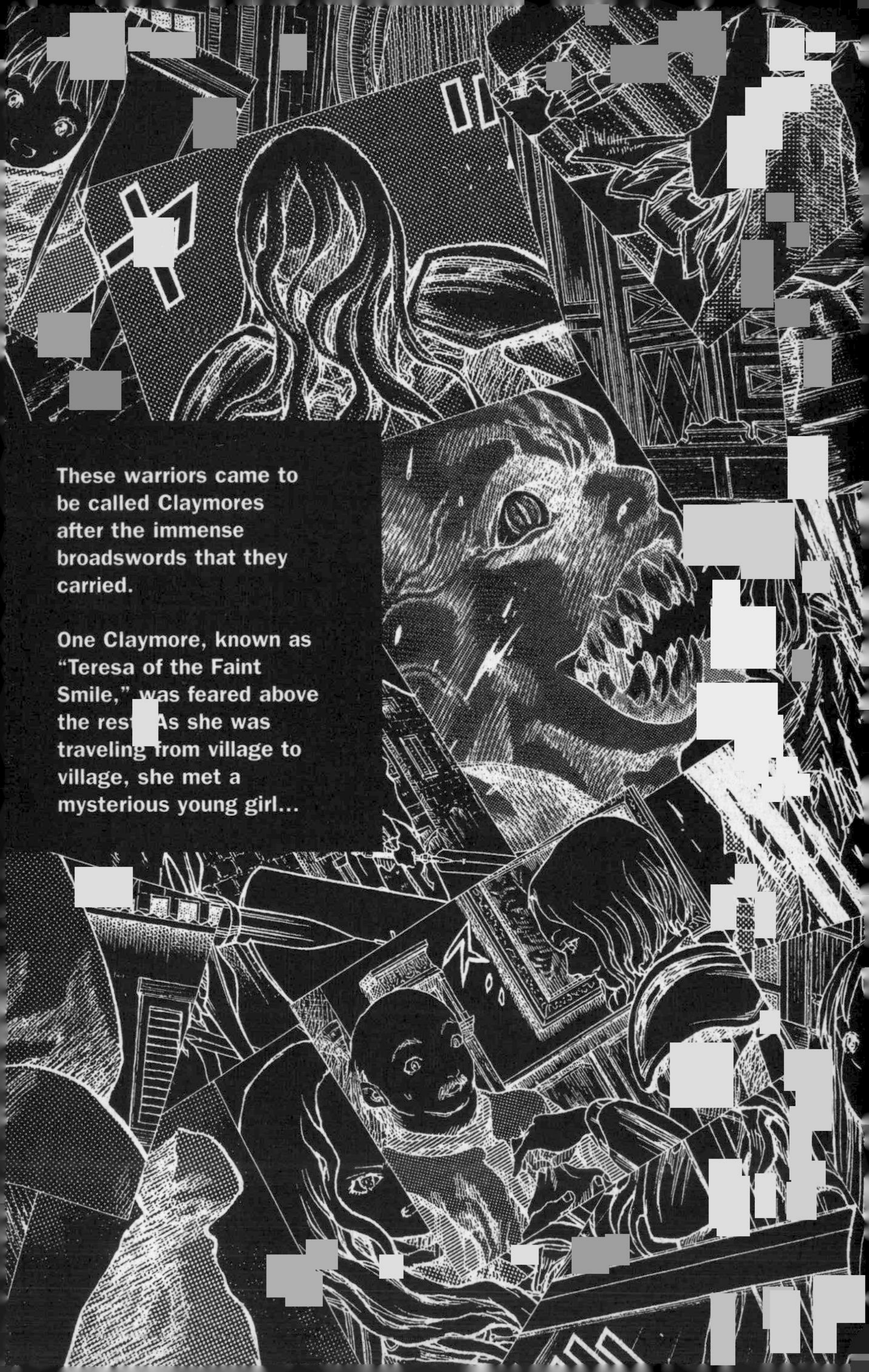
These warriors came to be called Claymores after the immense broadswords that they carried.
One Claymore, known as "Teresa of the Faint Smile," was feared above the rest. As she was traveling from village to village, she met a mysterious young girl...

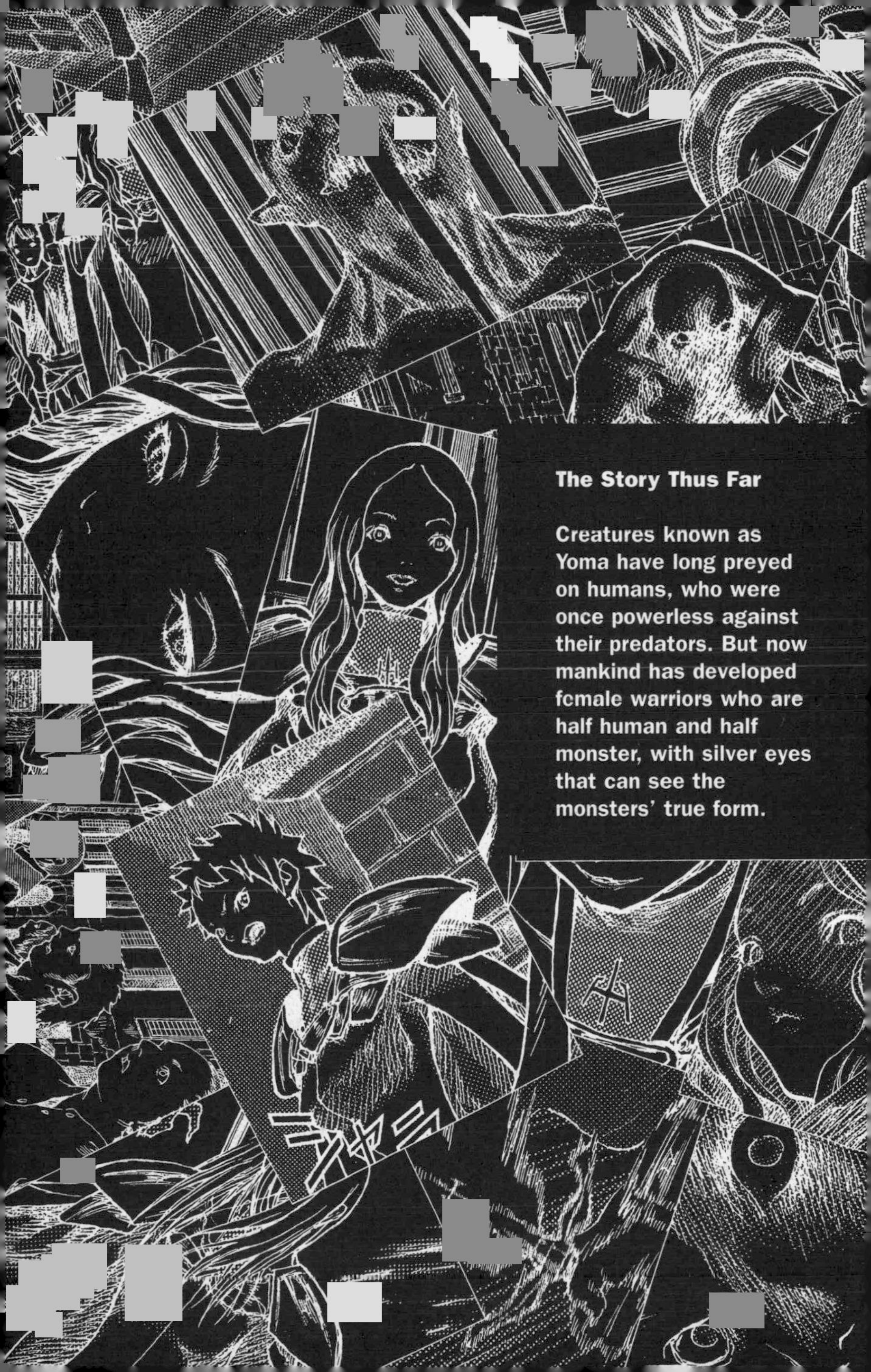

The Story Thus Far

Creatures known as Yoma have long preyed on humans, who were once powerless against their predators. But now mankind has developed female warriors who are half human and half monster, with silver eyes that can see the monsters' true form.

Claymore

クレイモア

Vol. 4

CONTENTS

Scene 16: Teresa of the Faint Smile, Part 5

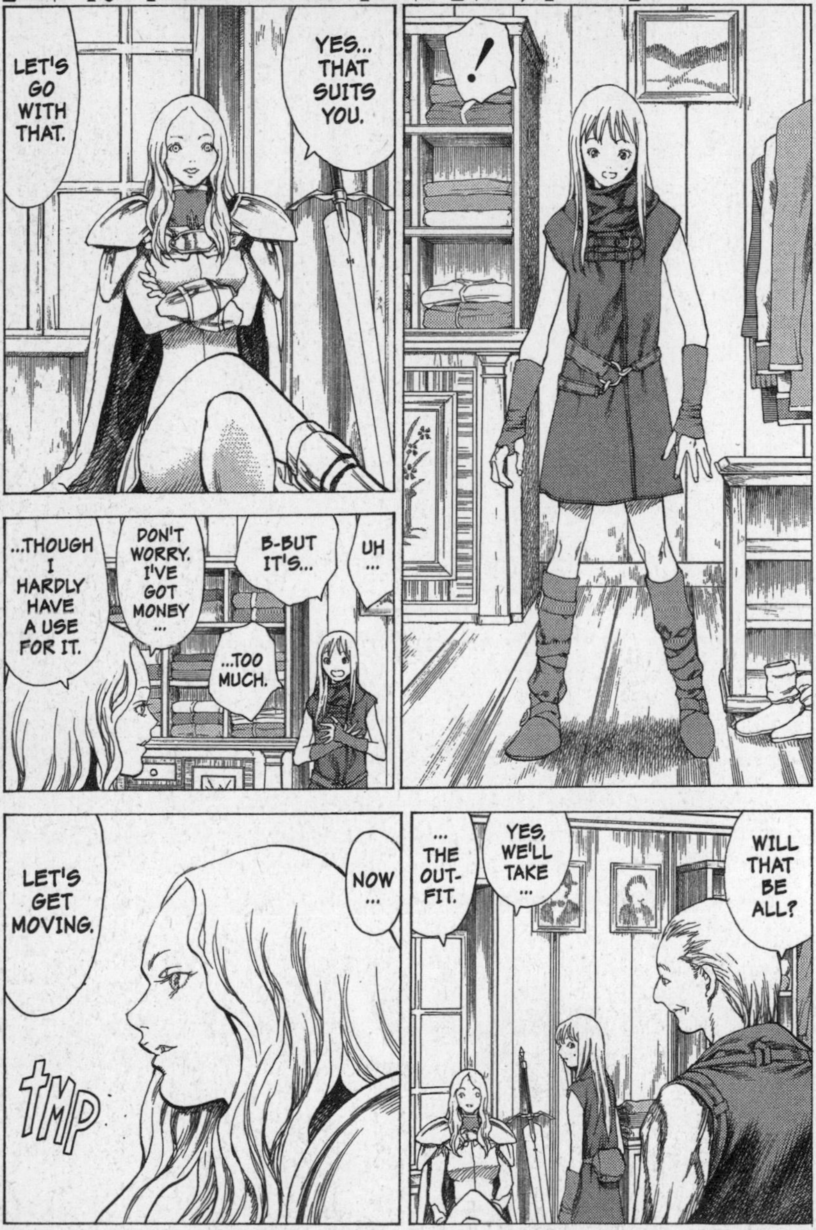
!
YES... THAT SUITS YOU.
LET'S GO WITH THAT.
UH...
B-BUT IT'S...
...TOO MUCH.
DON'T WORRY. I'VE GOT MONEY...
...THOUGH I HARDLY HAVE A USE FOR IT.
WILL THAT BE ALL?
YES, WE'LL TAKE...
...THE OUT-FIT.
NOW...
LET'S GET MOVING.
TMP

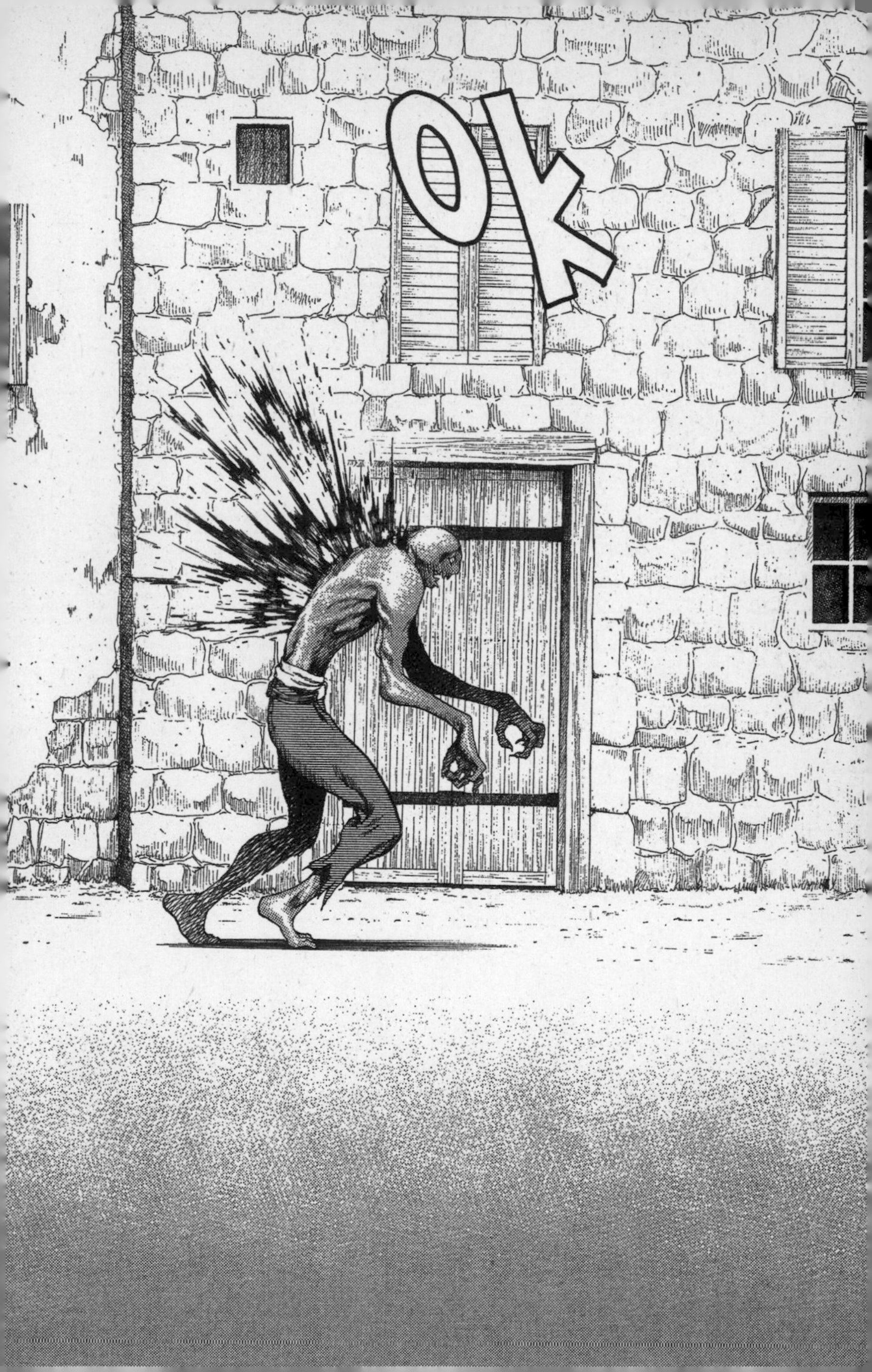

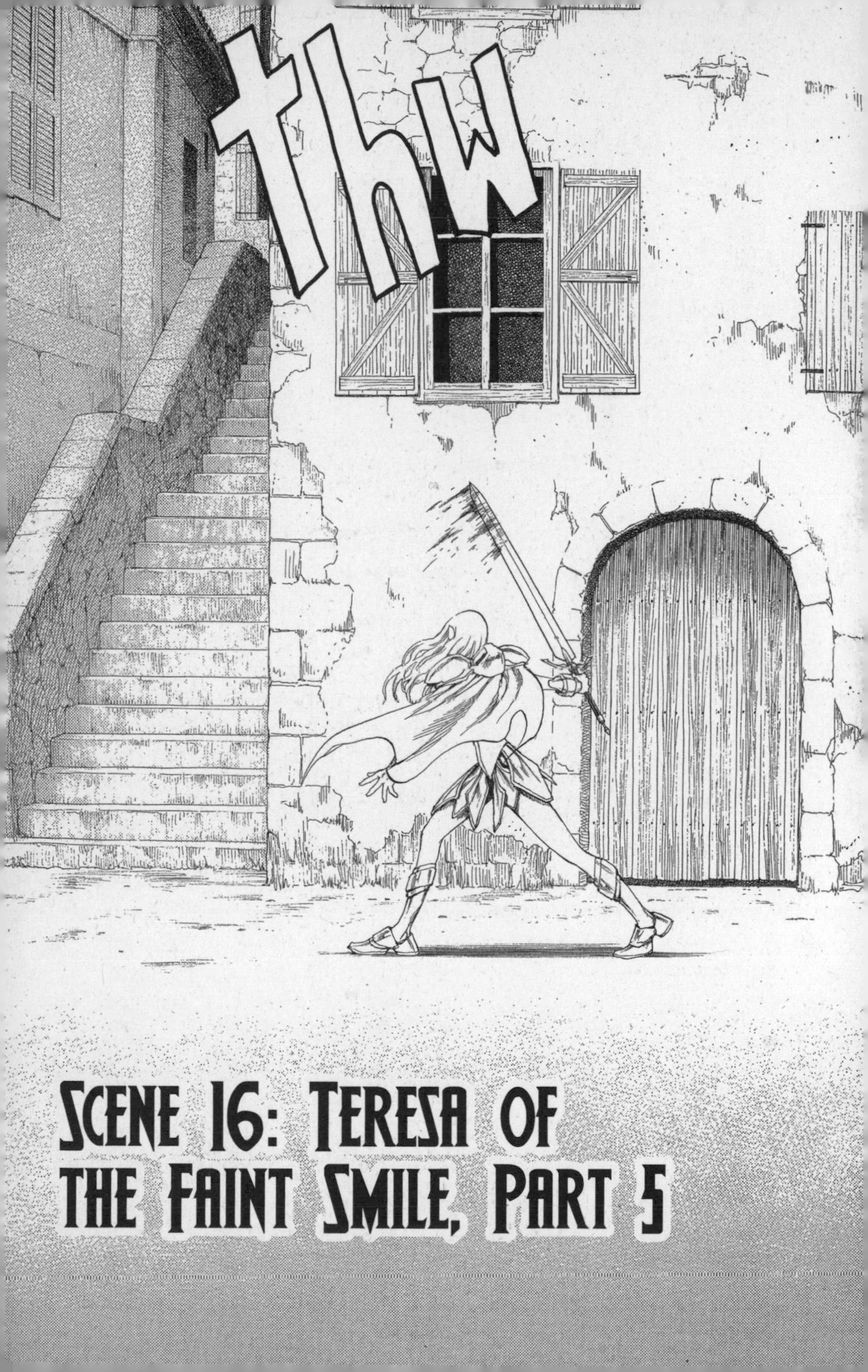
thw

Scene 16: Teresa of the Faint Smile, Part 5

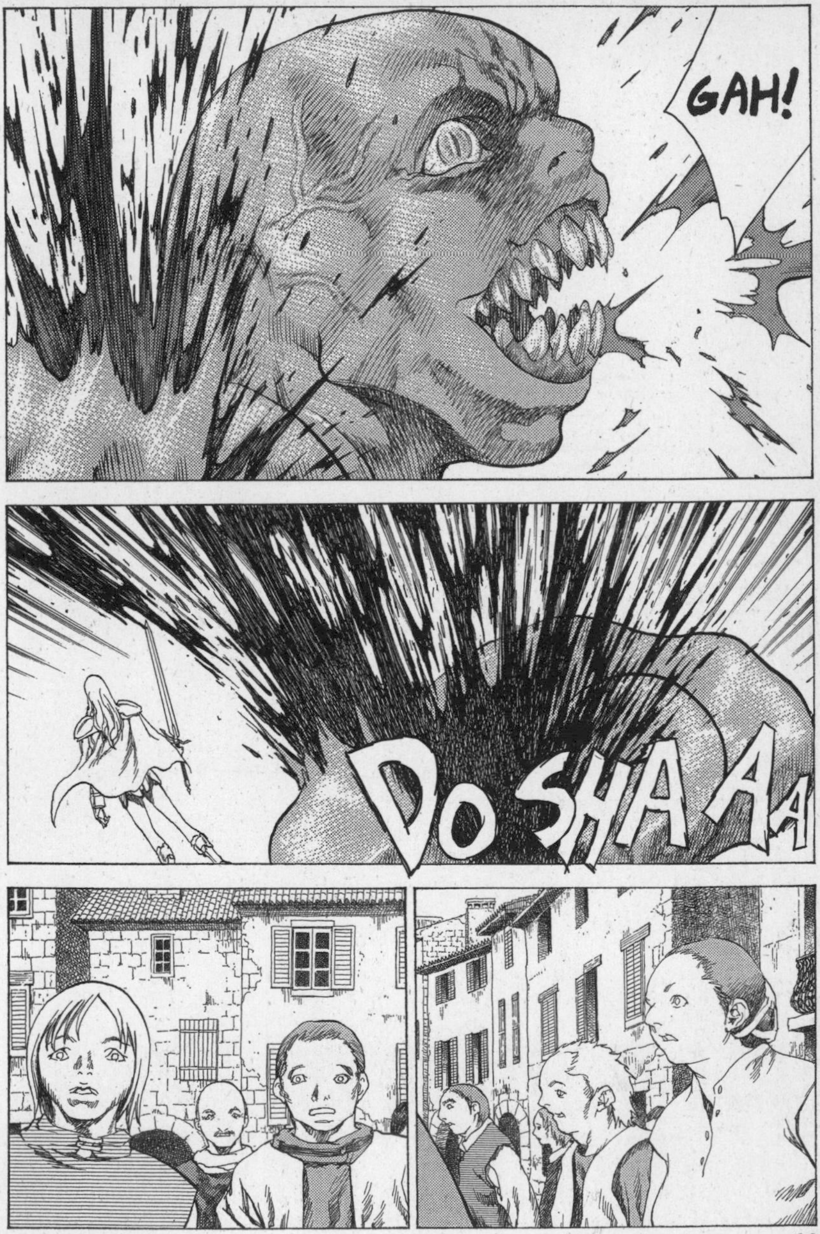
GAH!
DO SHA AA

READ THIS WAY

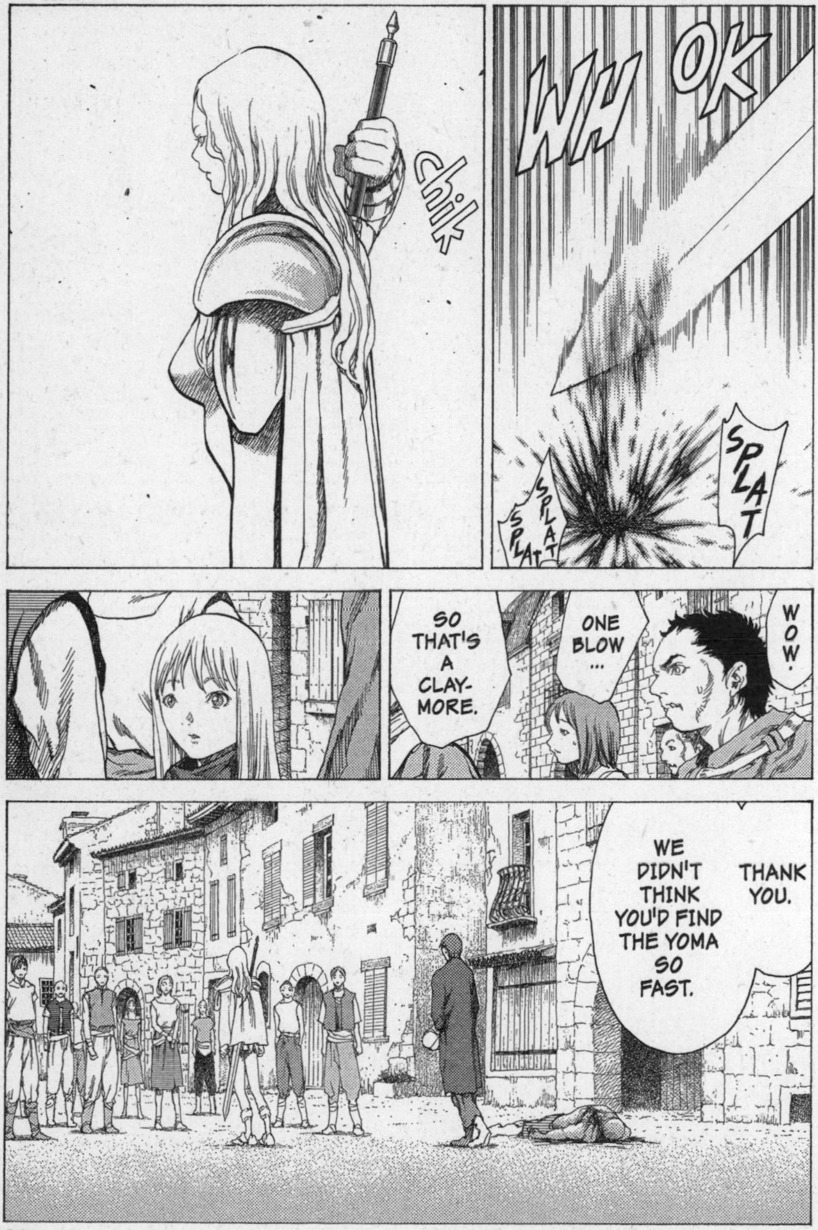
WH OK
SPLAT
SPLAT
SPLAT
chik
WOW.
ONE BLOW ...
SO THAT'S A CLAY-MORE.
THANK YOU.
WE DIDN'T THINK YOU'D FIND THE YOMA SO FAST.

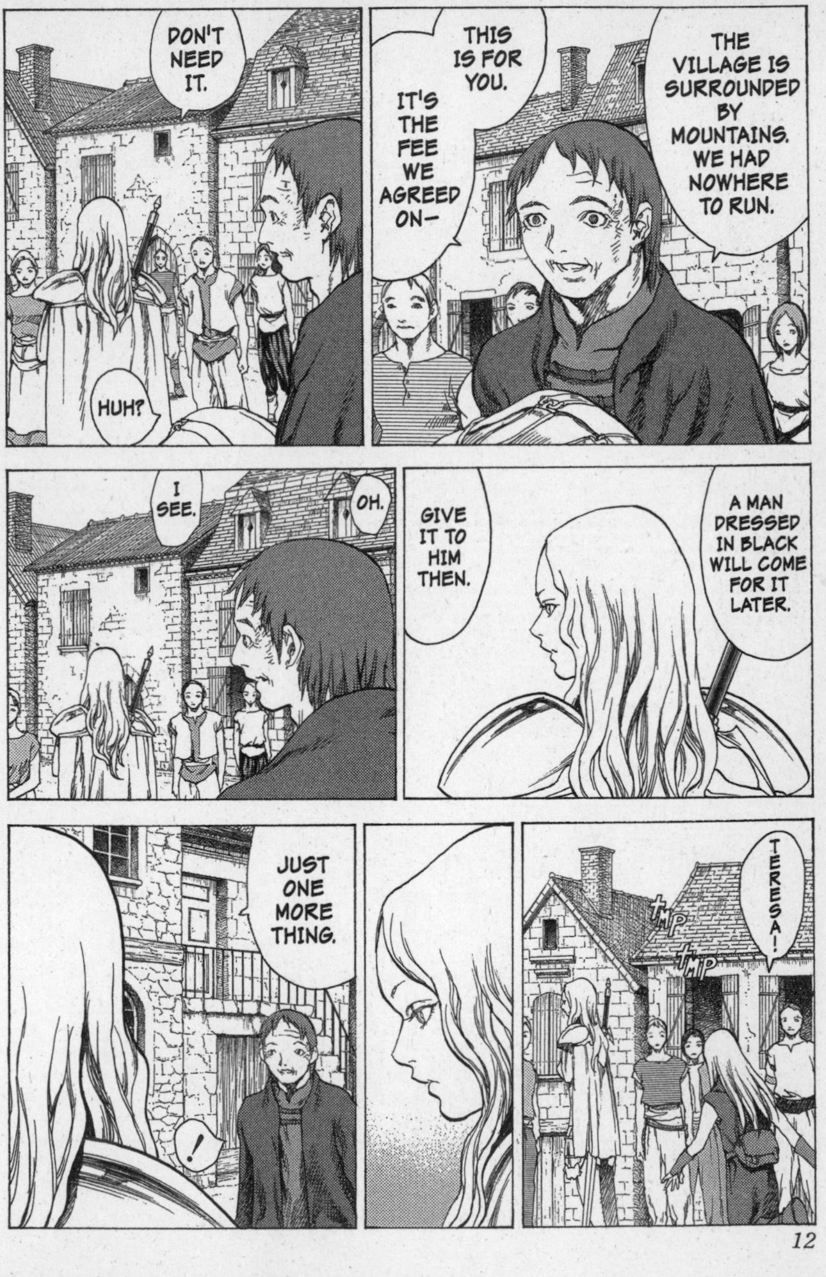
THE VILLAGE IS SURROUNDED BY MOUNTAINS. WE HAD NOWHERE TO RUN.
THIS IS FOR YOU.
IT'S THE FEE WE AGREED ON—
DON'T NEED IT.
HUH?
A MAN DRESSED IN BLACK WILL COME FOR IT LATER.
GIVE IT TO HIM THEN.
OH.
I SEE.
TERESA!
TMP
TMP
JUST ONE MORE THING.
!

READ THIS WAY

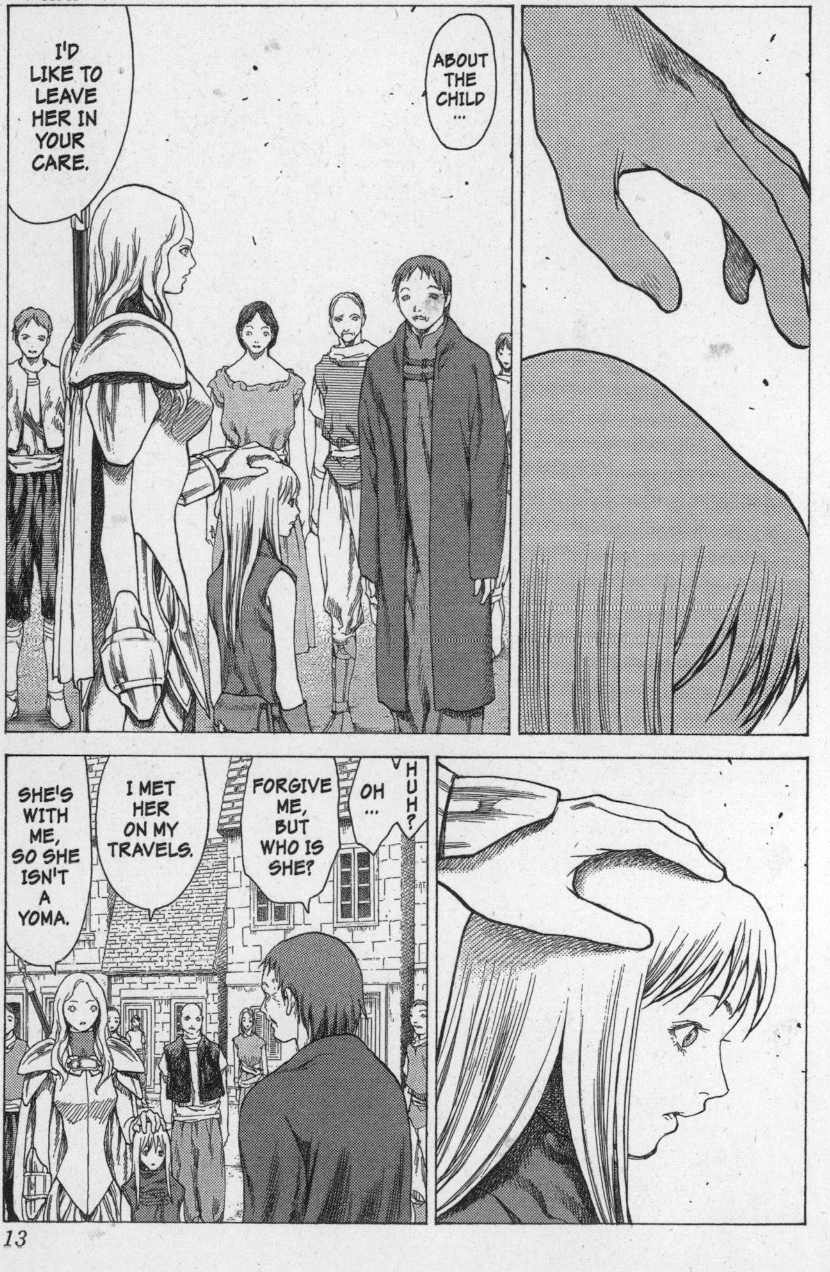
ABOUT THE CHILD ...
I'D LIKE TO LEAVE HER IN YOUR CARE.
HUH?
OH ...
FORGIVE ME, BUT WHO IS SHE?
I MET HER ON MY TRAVELS.
SHE'S WITH ME, SO SHE ISN'T A YOMA.

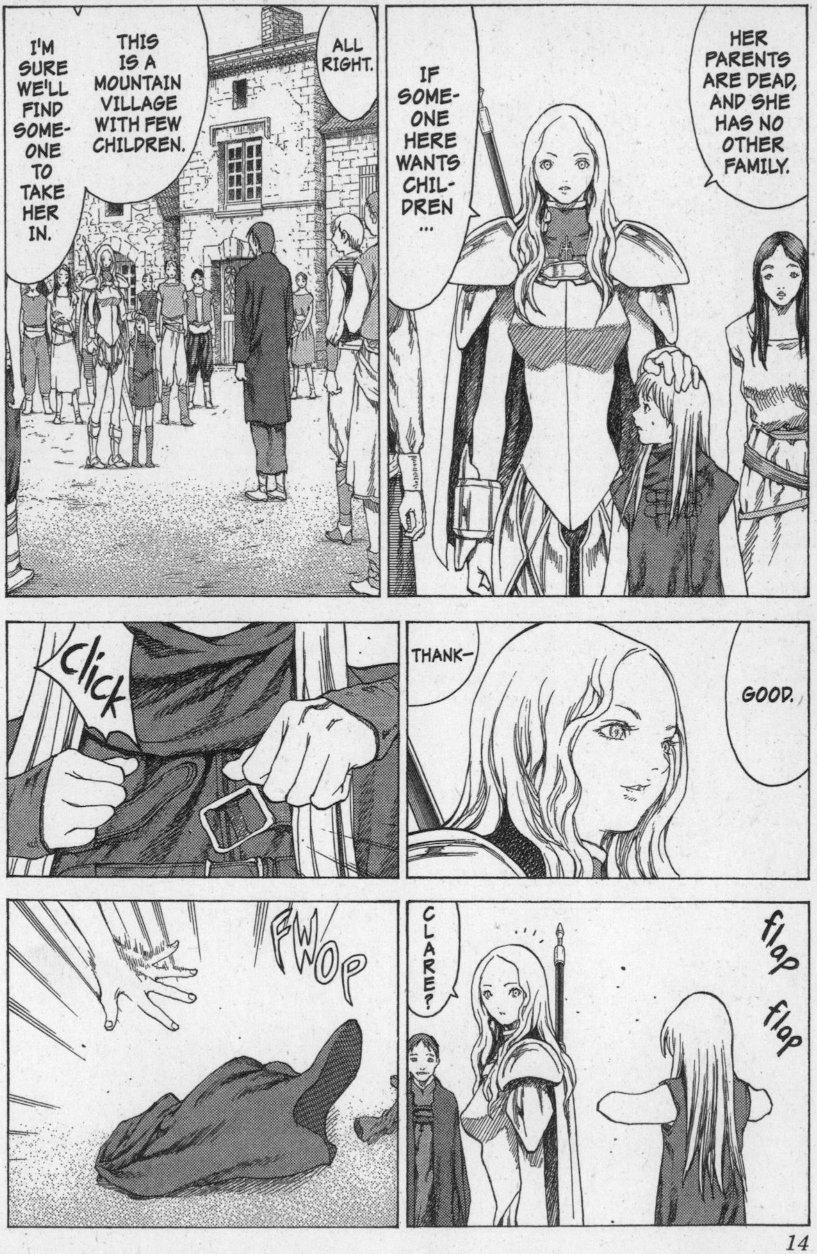
HER PARENTS ARE DEAD, AND SHE HAS NO OTHER FAMILY.
IF SOMEONE HERE WANTS CHILDREN...
ALL RIGHT.
THIS IS A MOUNTAIN VILLAGE WITH FEW CHILDREN.
I'M SURE WE'LL FIND SOMEONE TO TAKE HER IN.
GOOD.
THANK—
Click
flap flap
CLARE?
FWOP

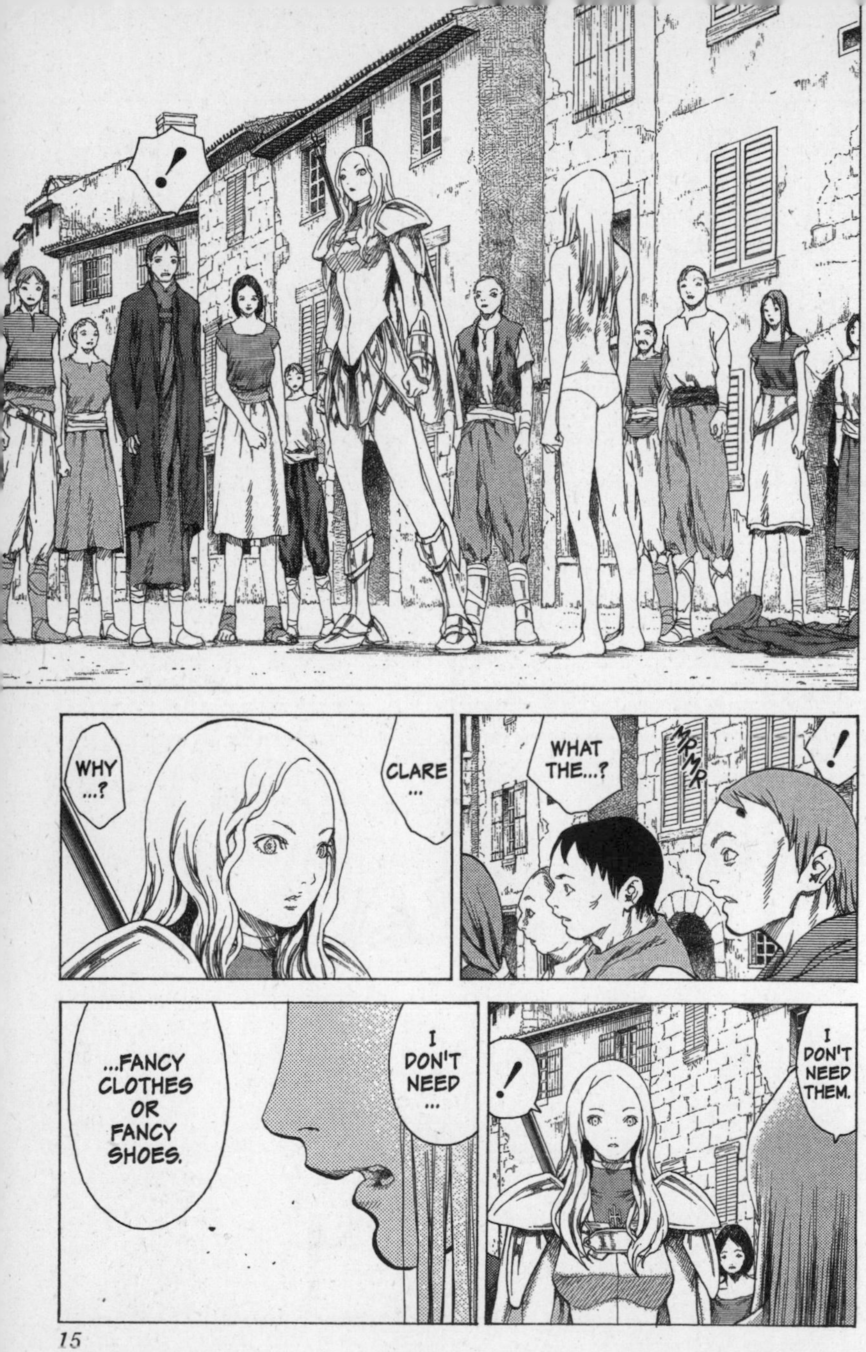
!
!
MRMR
WHAT THE...?
CLARE ...
WHY ...?
I DON'T NEED THEM.
!
I DON'T NEED ...
...FANCY CLOTHES OR FANCY SHOES.

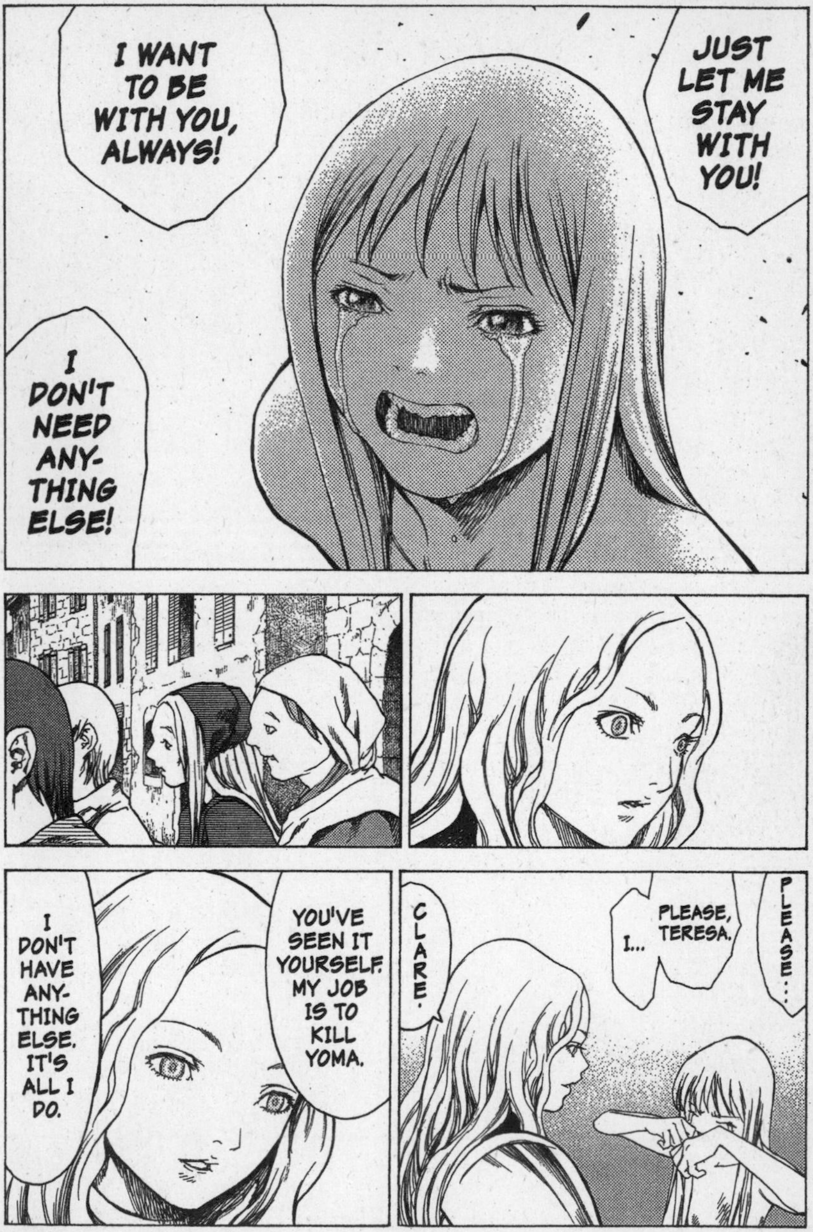
JUST LET ME STAY WITH YOU!
I WANT TO BE WITH YOU, ALWAYS!
I DON'T NEED ANY-THING ELSE!
PLEASE...
PLEASE, TERESA.
I...
CLARE.
YOU'VE SEEN IT YOURSELF. MY JOB IS TO KILL YOMA.
I DON'T HAVE ANY-THING ELSE. IT'S ALL I DO.

READ THIS WAY

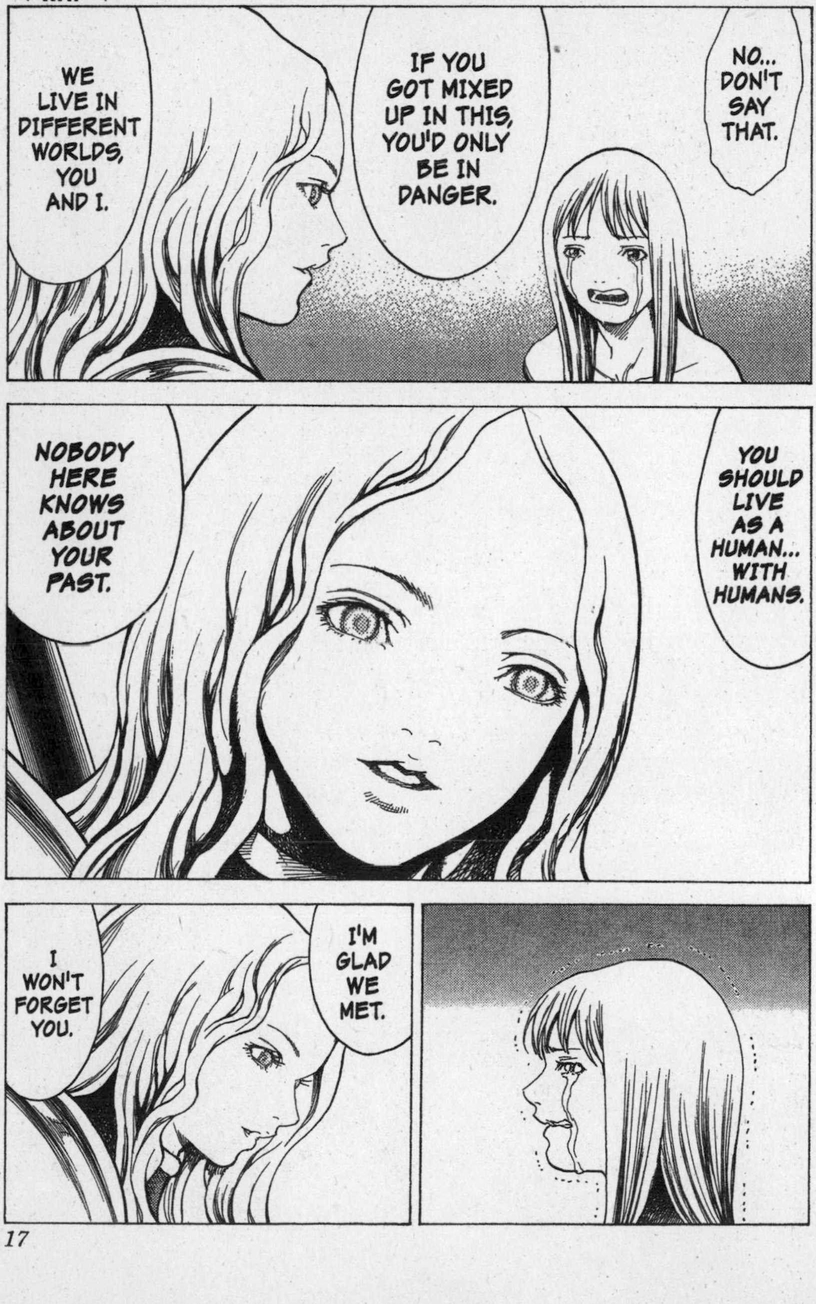
NO... DON'T SAY THAT.
IF YOU GOT MIXED UP IN THIS, YOU'D ONLY BE IN DANGER.
WE LIVE IN DIFFERENT WORLDS, YOU AND I.
YOU SHOULD LIVE AS A HUMAN... WITH HUMANS.
NOBODY HERE KNOWS ABOUT YOUR PAST.
I'M GLAD WE MET.
I WON'T FORGET YOU.

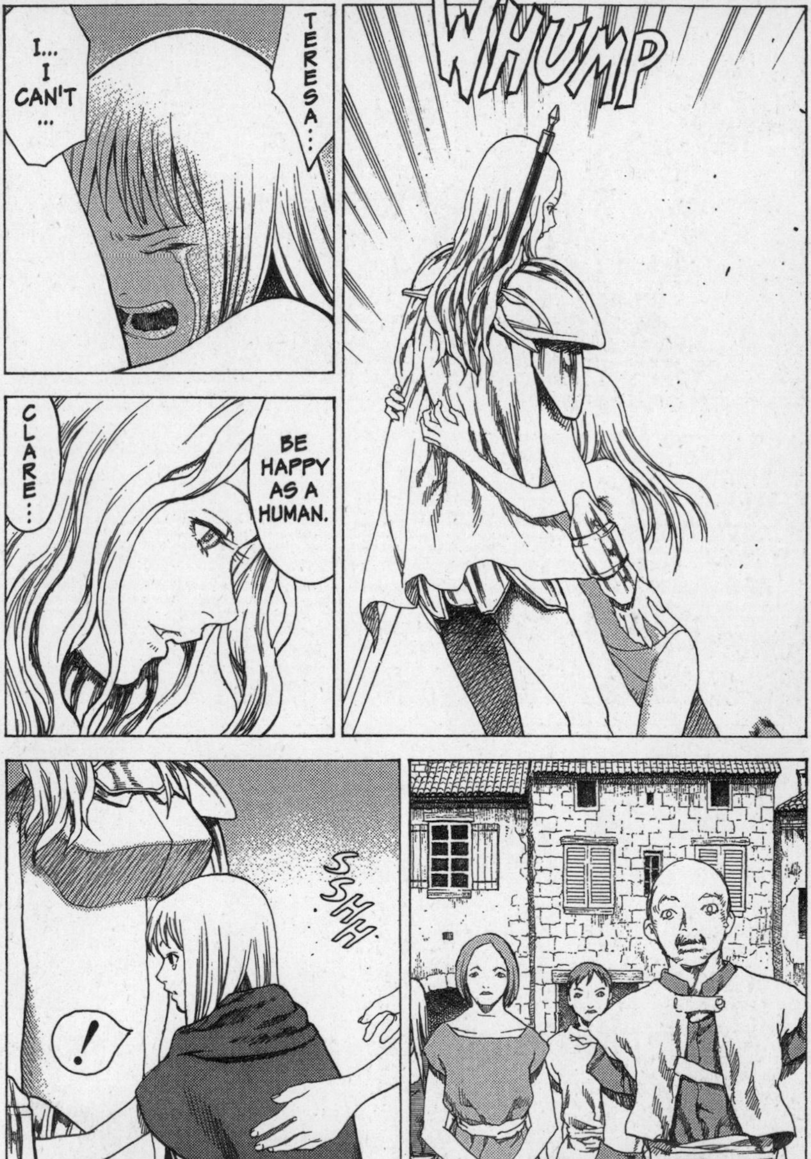
WHUMP
TERESA...
I... I CAN'T ...
BE HAPPY AS A HUMAN.
CLARE...
SSHH
!

READ THIS WAY

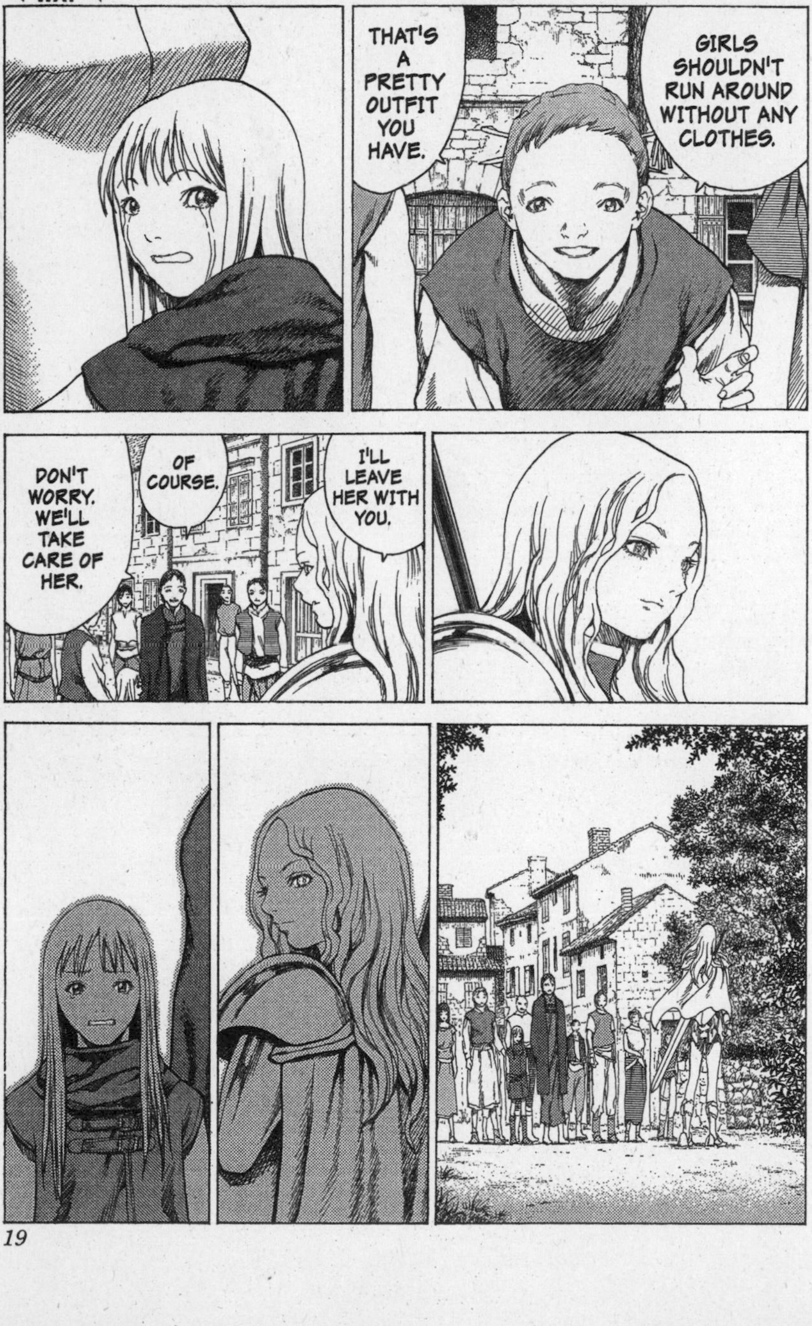
GIRLS SHOULDN'T RUN AROUND WITHOUT ANY CLOTHES.
THAT'S A PRETTY OUTFIT YOU HAVE.
I'LL LEAVE HER WITH YOU.
OF COURSE.
DON'T WORRY. WE'LL TAKE CARE OF HER.

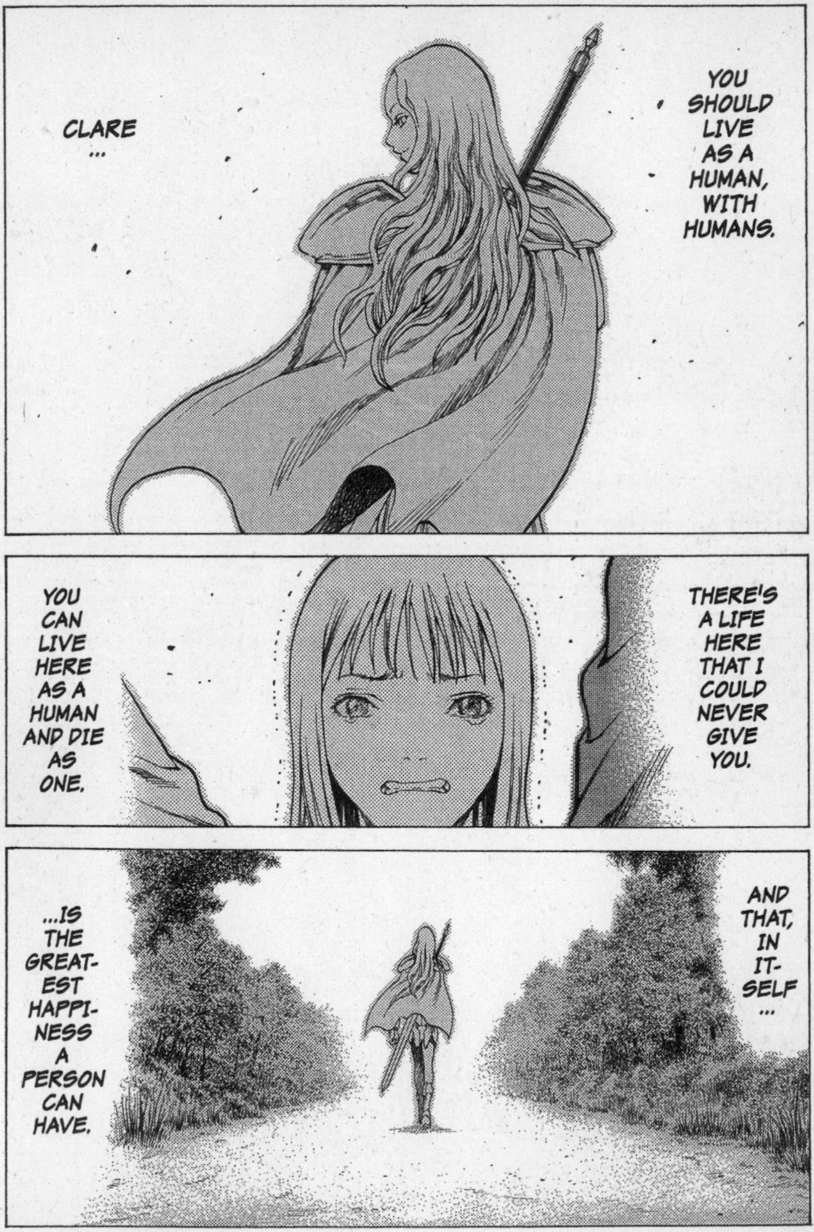
YOU SHOULD LIVE AS A HUMAN, WITH HUMANS.
CLARE ...
THERE'S A LIFE HERE THAT I COULD NEVER GIVE YOU.
YOU CAN LIVE HERE AS A HUMAN AND DIE AS ONE.
AND THAT, IN IT-SELF ...
...IS THE GREAT-EST HAPPI-NESS A PERSON CAN HAVE.

FAREWELL,
CLARE.

KA-CLOP KA-CLOP

KA-CLOP

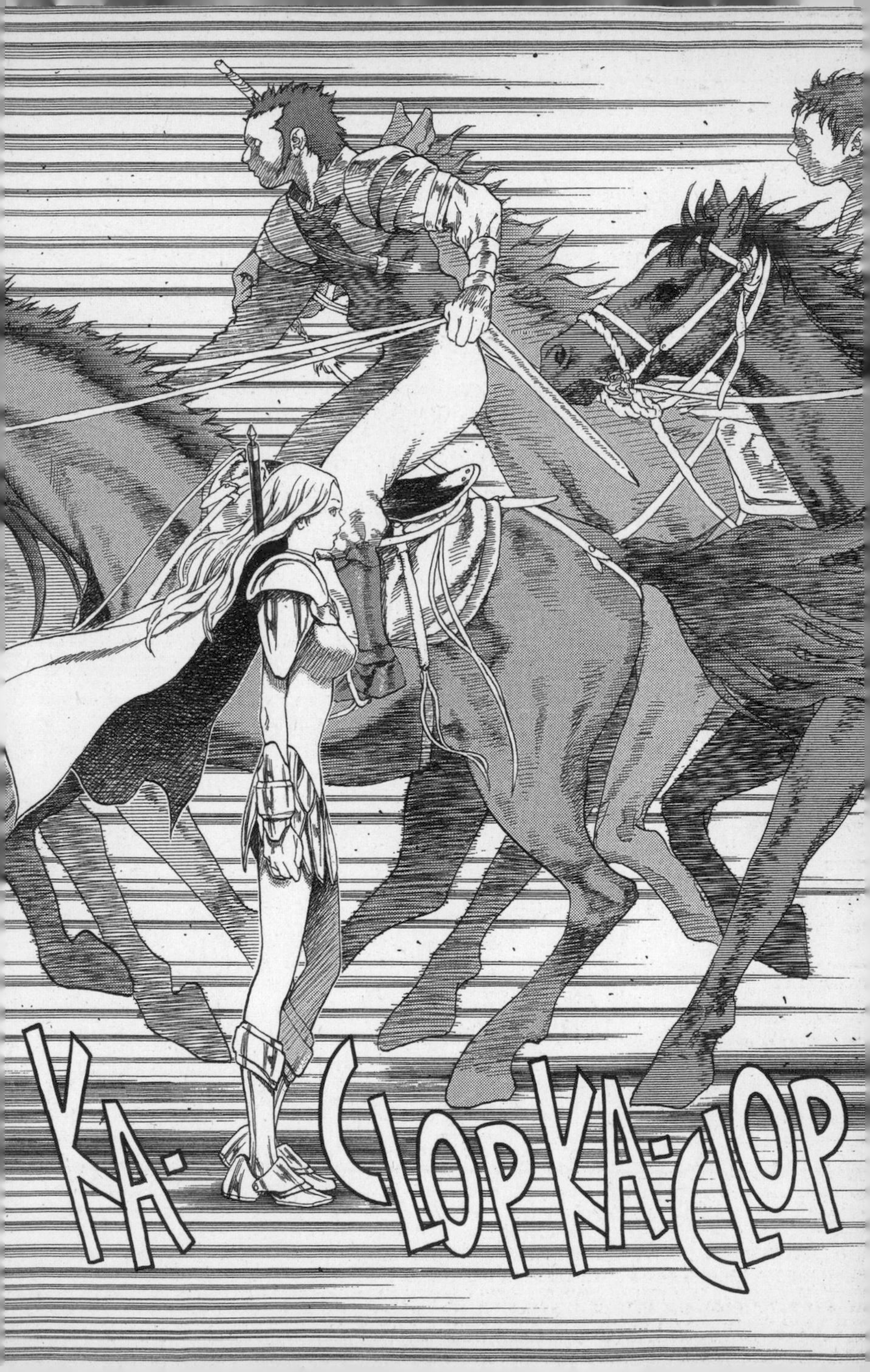
KA-CLOP KA-CLOP

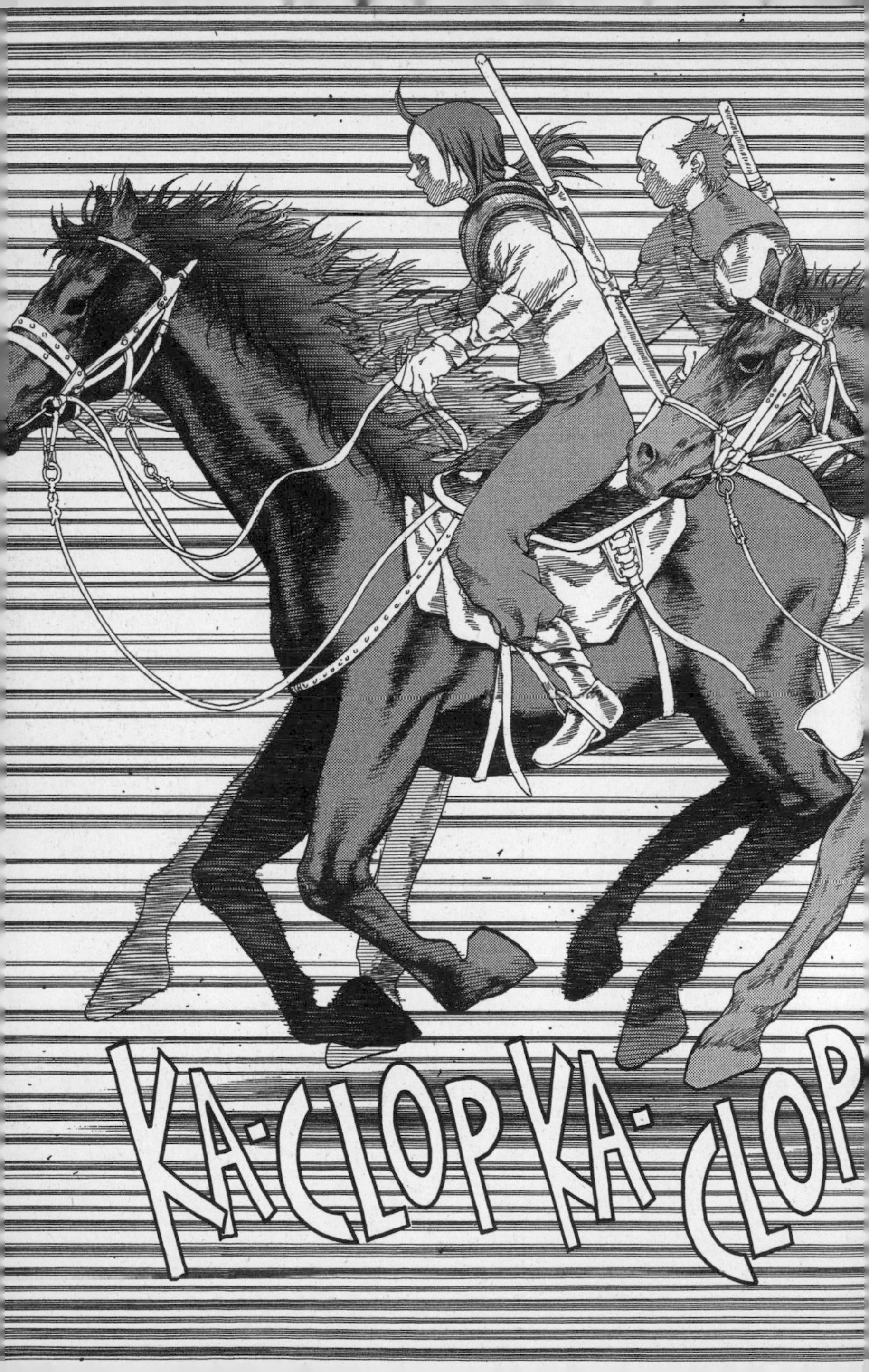
KA-CLOP KA-CLOP

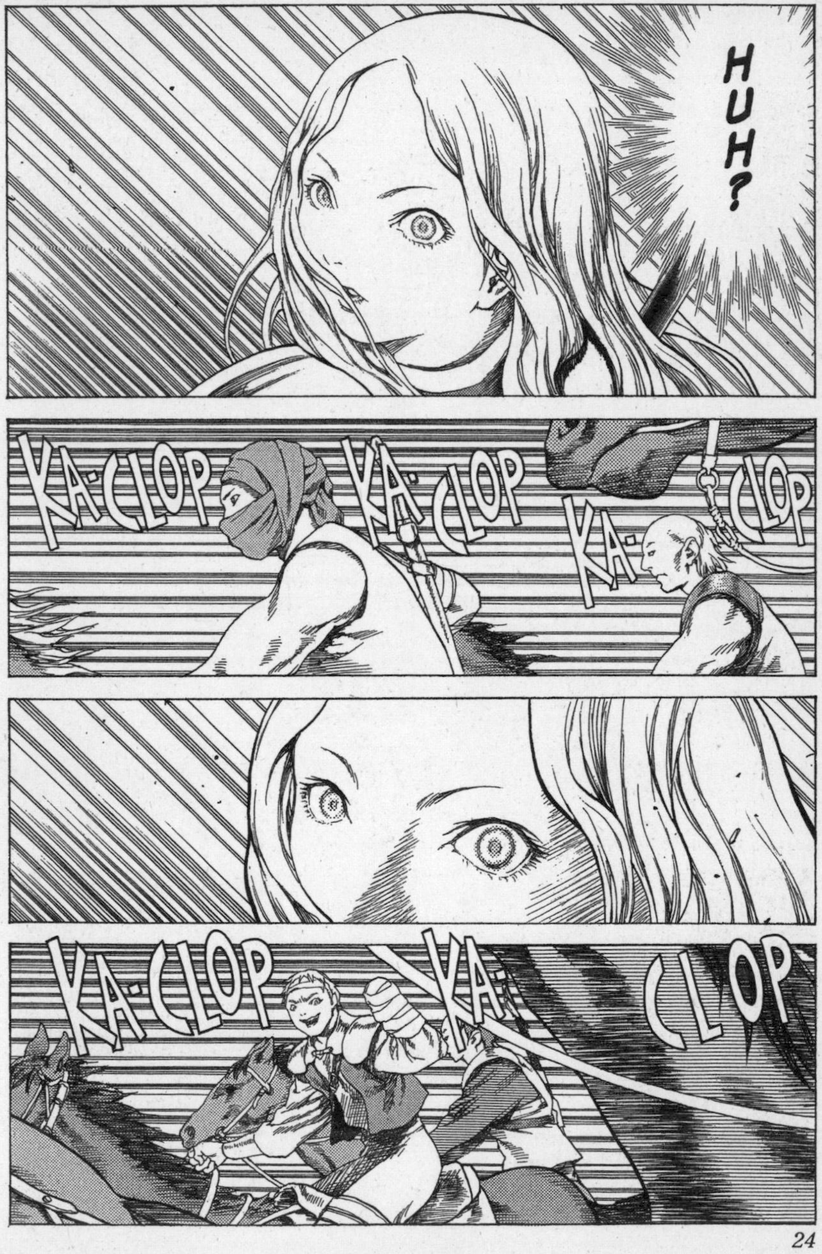
HUH?
KA-CLOP
KA-CLOP
KA-CLOP
KA-CLOP
KA-CLOP

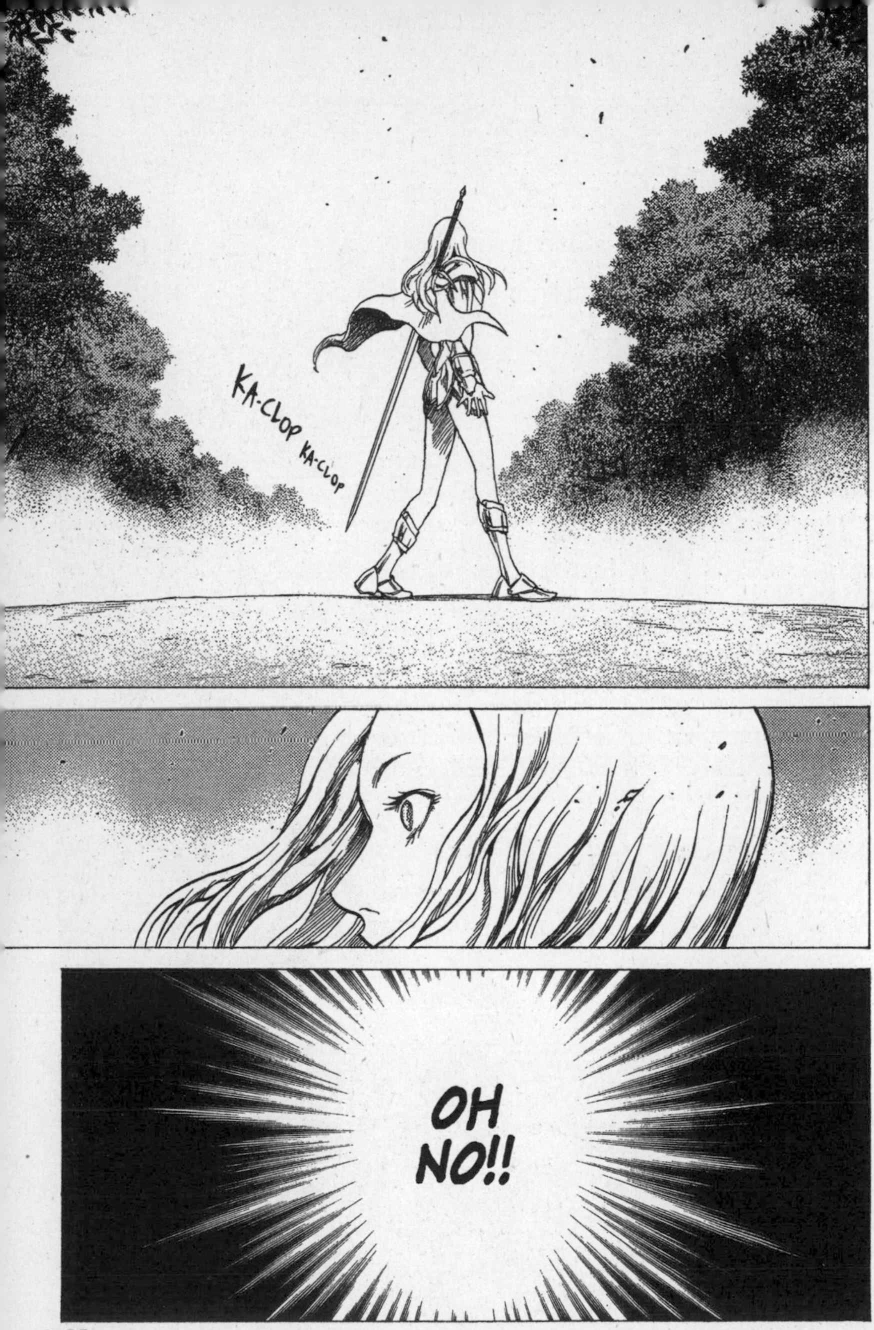
KA-CLOP KA-CLOP
OH NO!!

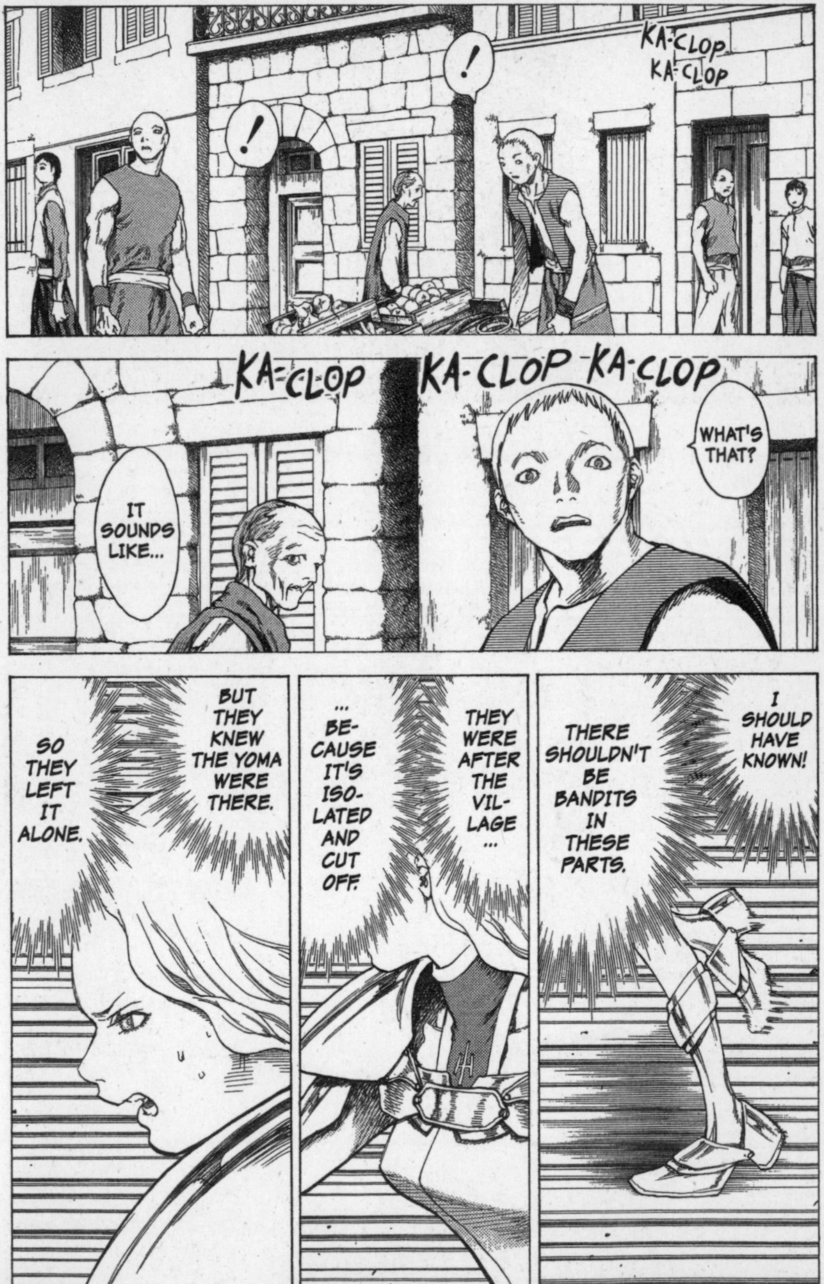
KA-CLOP KA-CLOP
!
!
KA-CLOP KA-CLOP
WHAT'S THAT?
KA-CLOP
IT SOUNDS LIKE...
I SHOULD HAVE KNOWN!
THERE SHOULDN'T BE BANDITS IN THESE PARTS.
THEY WERE AFTER THE VILLAGE...
...BECAUSE IT'S ISOLATED AND CUT OFF.
BUT THEY KNEW THE YOMA WERE THERE.
SO THEY LEFT IT ALONE.

READ THIS WAY

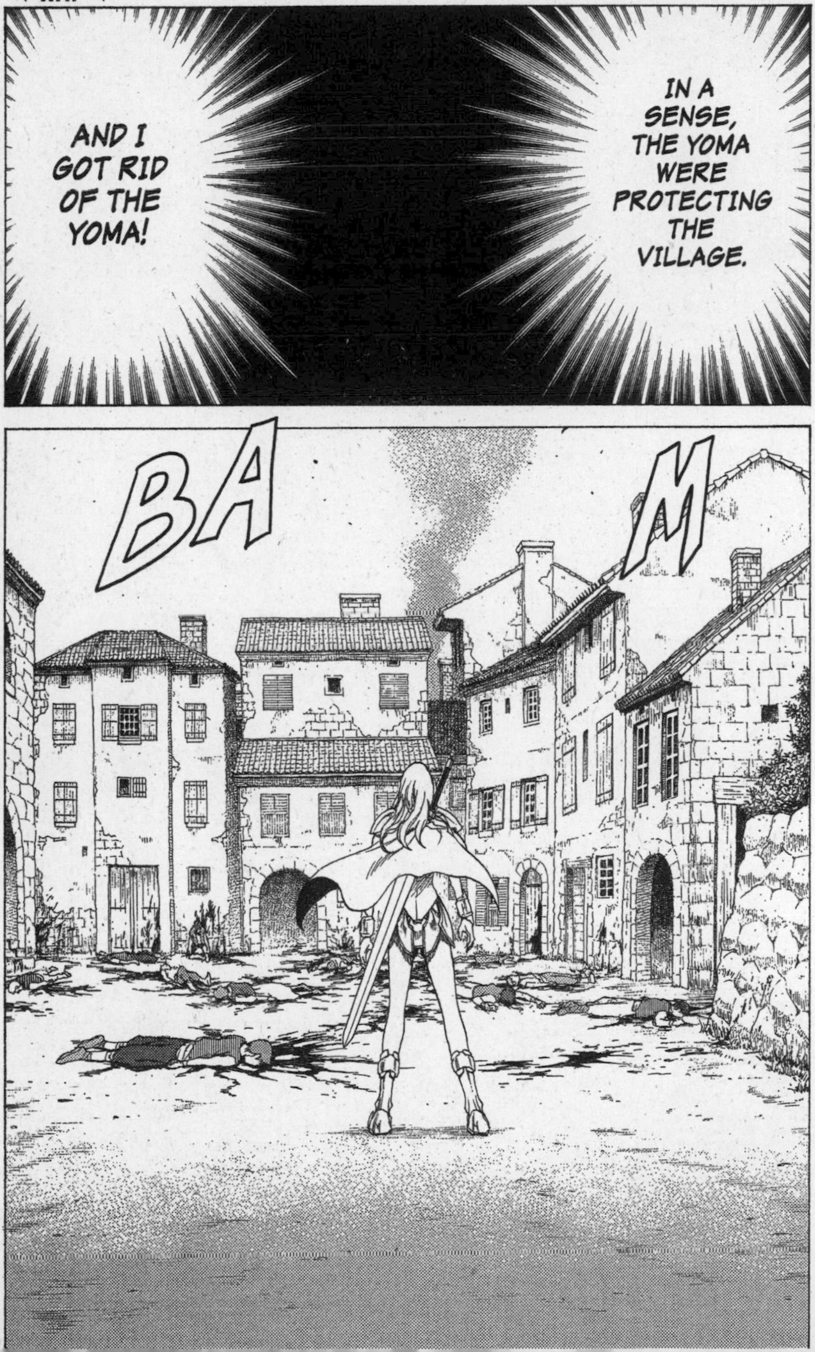

IN A SENSE, THE YOMA WERE PROTECTING THE VILLAGE.
AND I GOT RID OF THE YOMA!
BAM

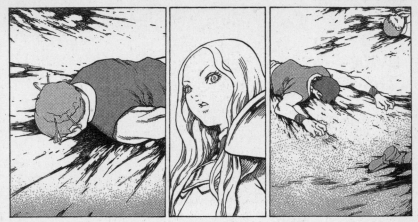

CLARE
...

CLARE!

READ THIS WAY

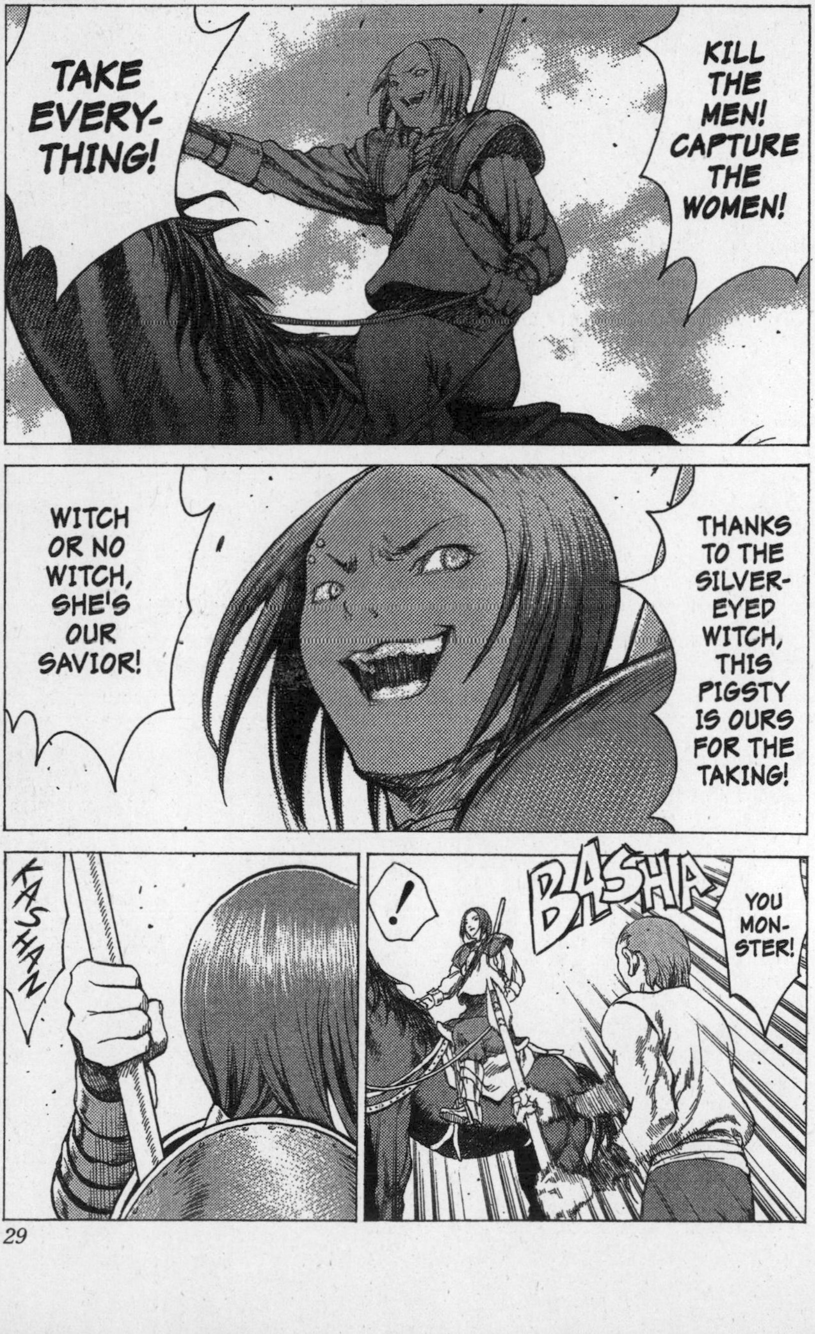

KILL THE MEN! CAPTURE THE WOMEN!
TAKE EVERY-THING!
THANKS TO THE SILVER-EYED WITCH, THIS PIGSTY IS OURS FOR THE TAKING!
WITCH OR NO WITCH, SHE'S OUR SAVIOR!
YOU MON-STER!
BASHA
!
KASHAN

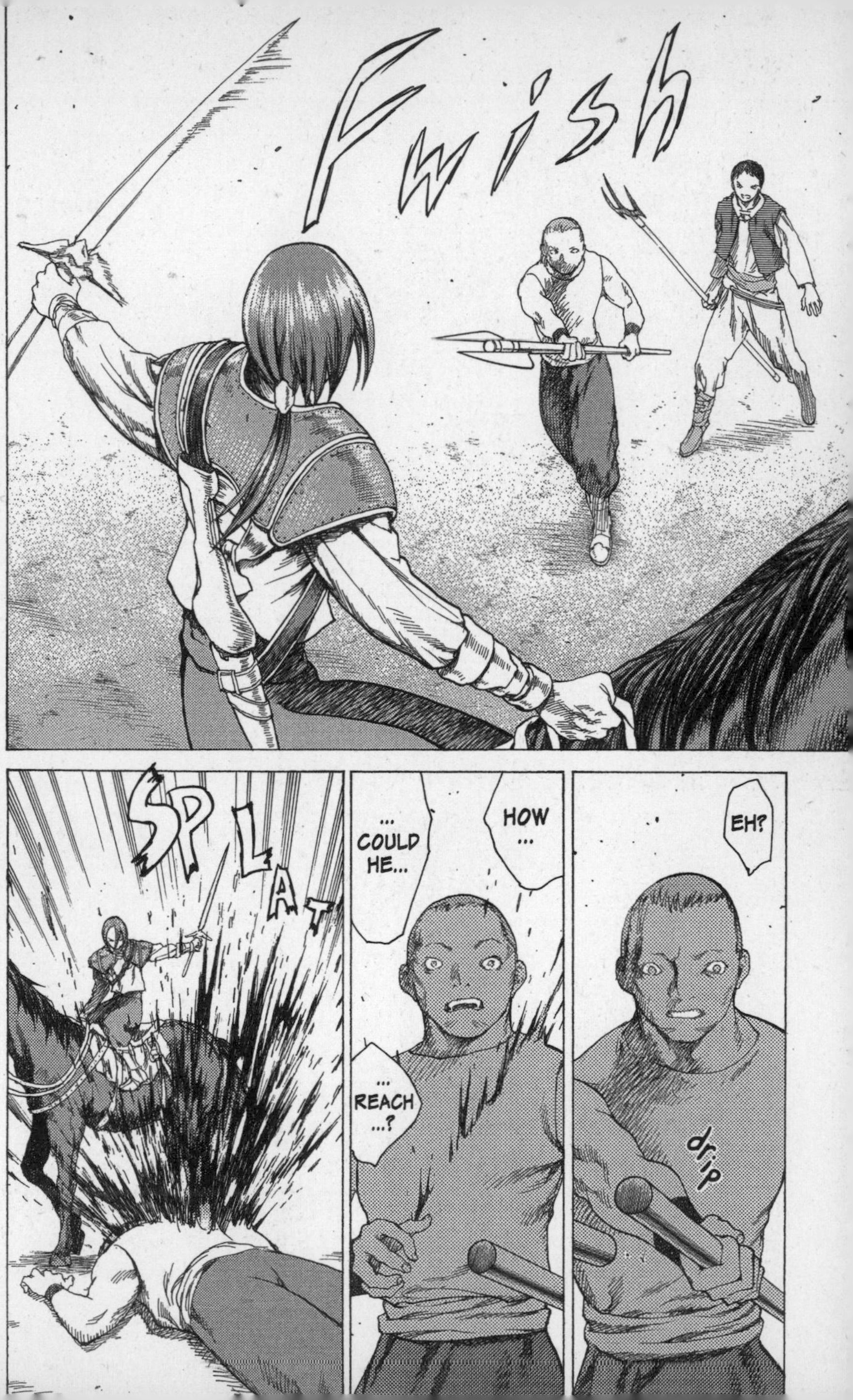
Fwish
EH?
drip
HOW ...
... COULD HE...
... REACH ...?
SPLAT

READ THIS WAY

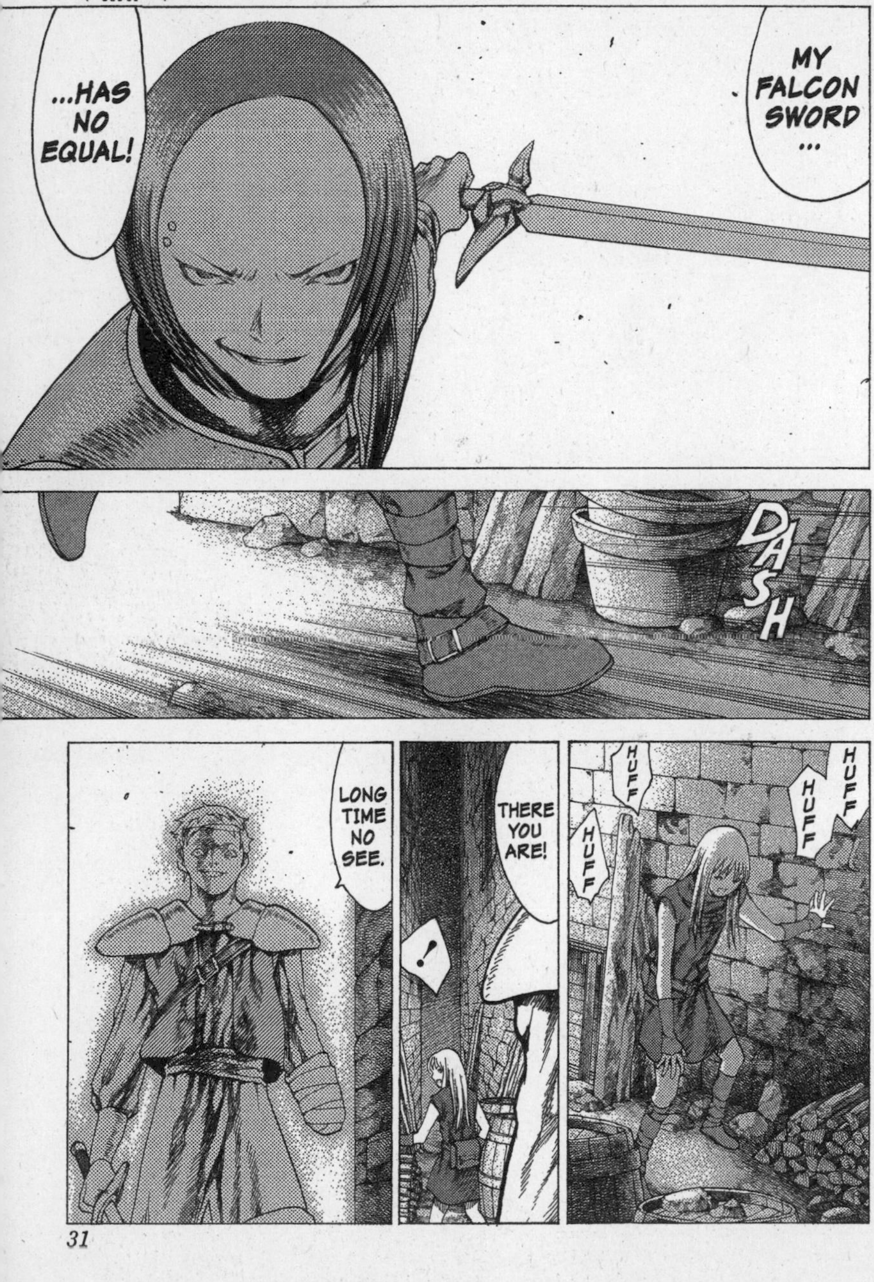
MY FALCON SWORD ...
...HAS NO EQUAL!
DASH
HUFF HUFF
HUFF HUFF
HUFF
HUFF
THERE YOU ARE!
!
LONG TIME NO SEE.

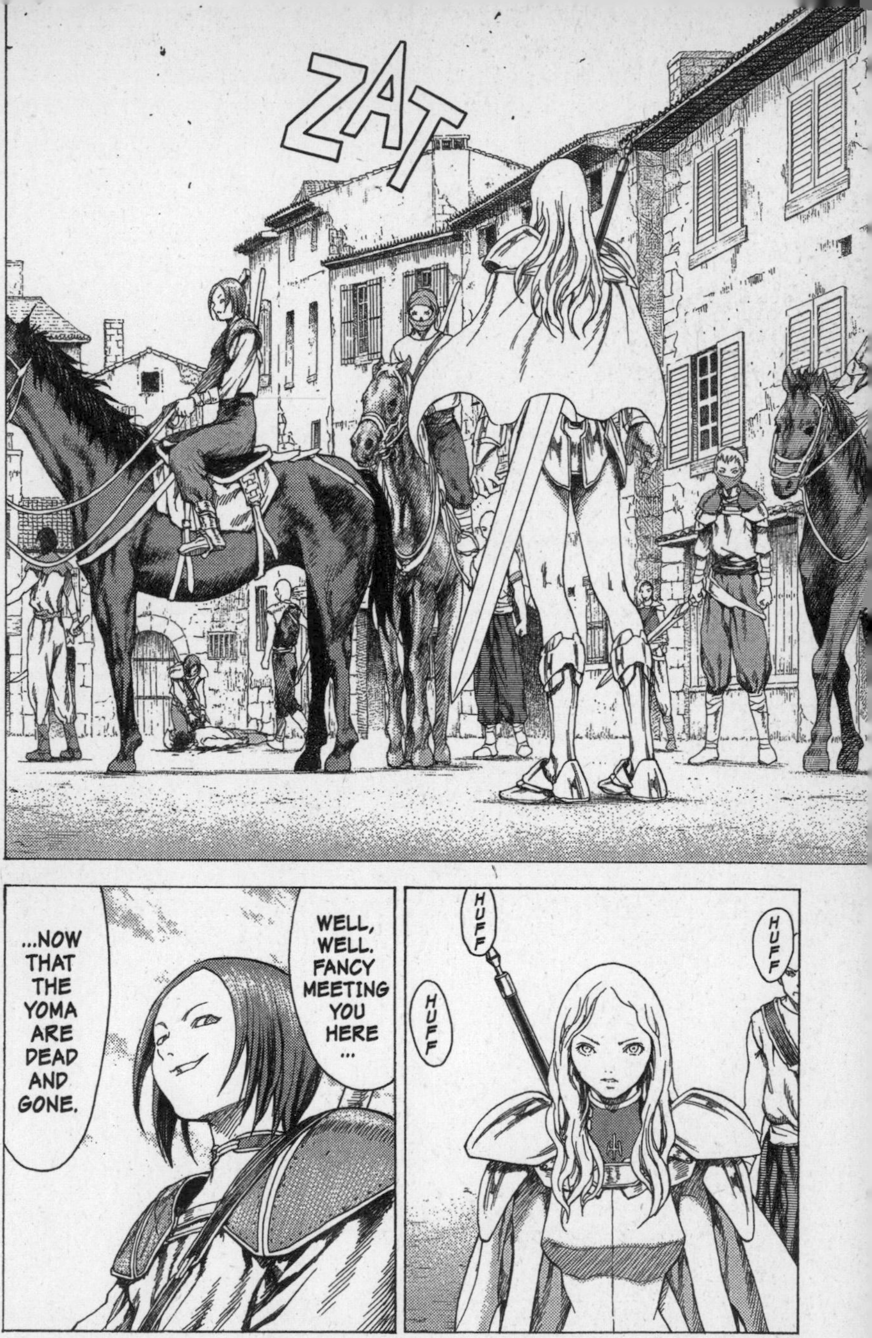
ZAT
HUFF
HUFF
HUFF
WELL, WELL. FANCY MEETING YOU HERE...
...NOW THAT THE YOMA ARE DEAD AND GONE.

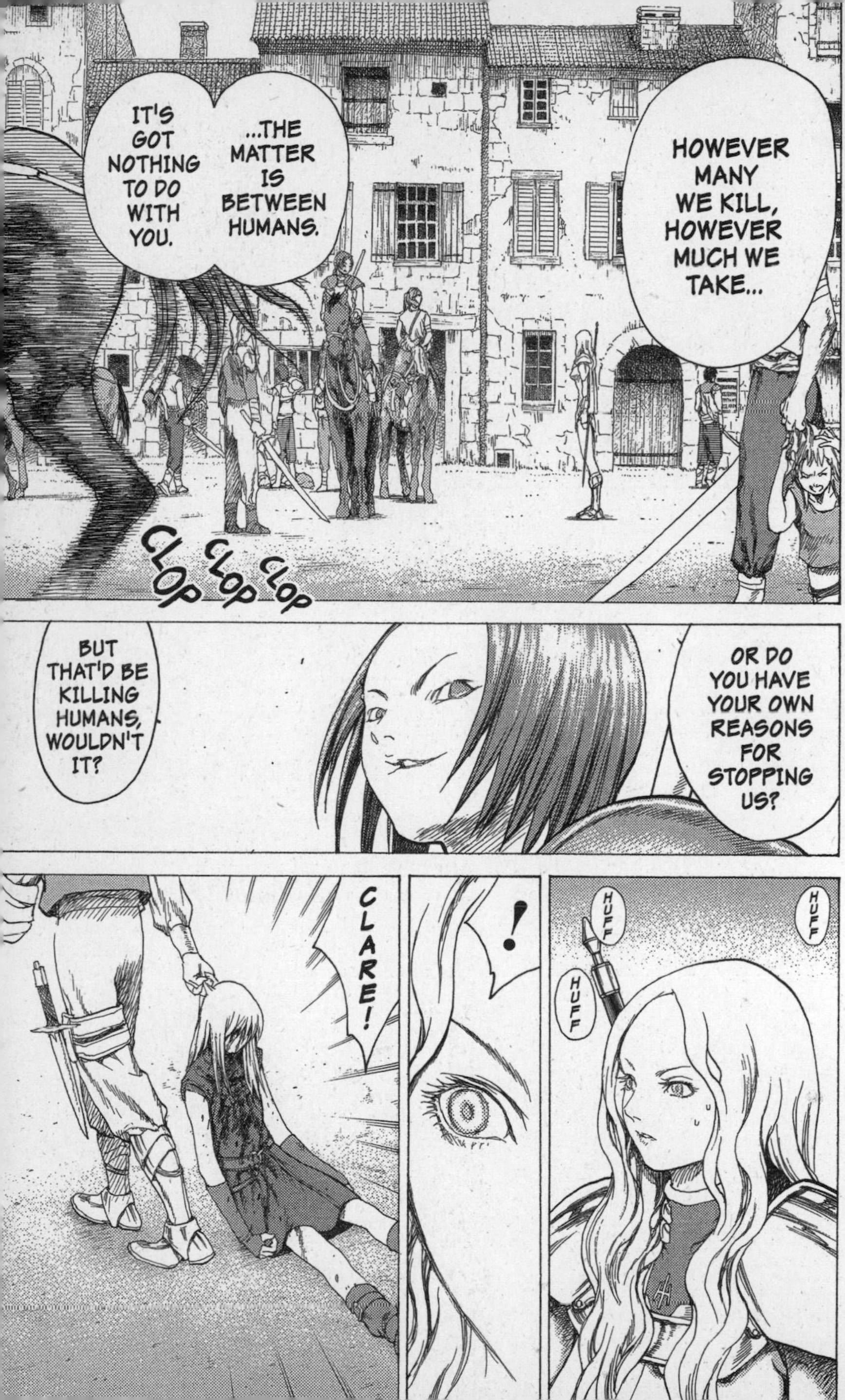
HOWEVER MANY WE KILL, HOWEVER MUCH WE TAKE...
...THE MATTER IS BETWEEN HUMANS.
IT'S GOT NOTHING TO DO WITH YOU.
CLOP CLOP CLOP
OR DO YOU HAVE YOUR OWN REASONS FOR STOPPING US?
BUT THAT'D BE KILLING HUMANS, WOULDN'T IT?
HUFF
HUFF
HUFF
!
CLARE!

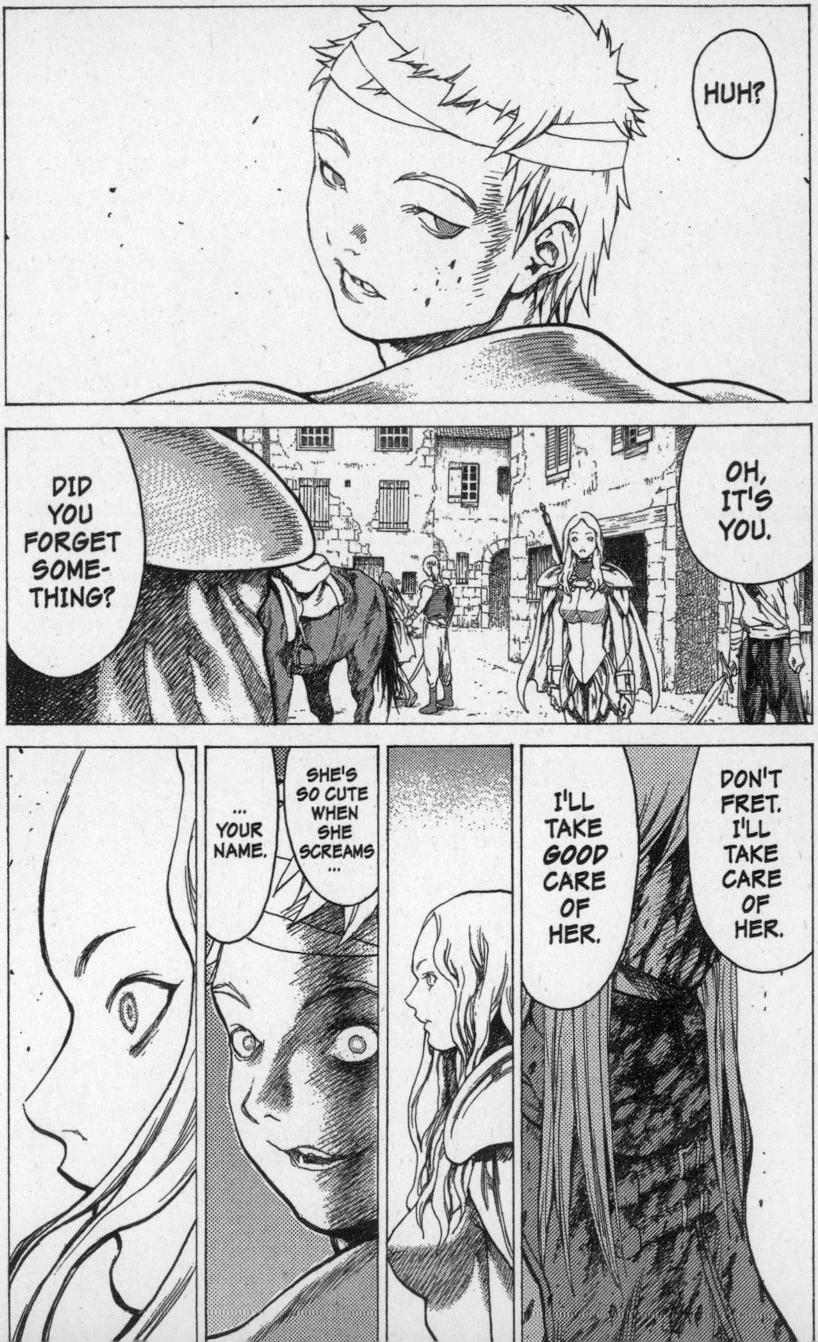
HUH?
OH, IT'S YOU.
DID YOU FORGET SOME-THING?
DON'T FRET. I'LL TAKE CARE OF HER.
I'LL TAKE GOOD CARE OF HER.
SHE'S SO CUTE WHEN SHE SCREAMS ...
... YOUR NAME.

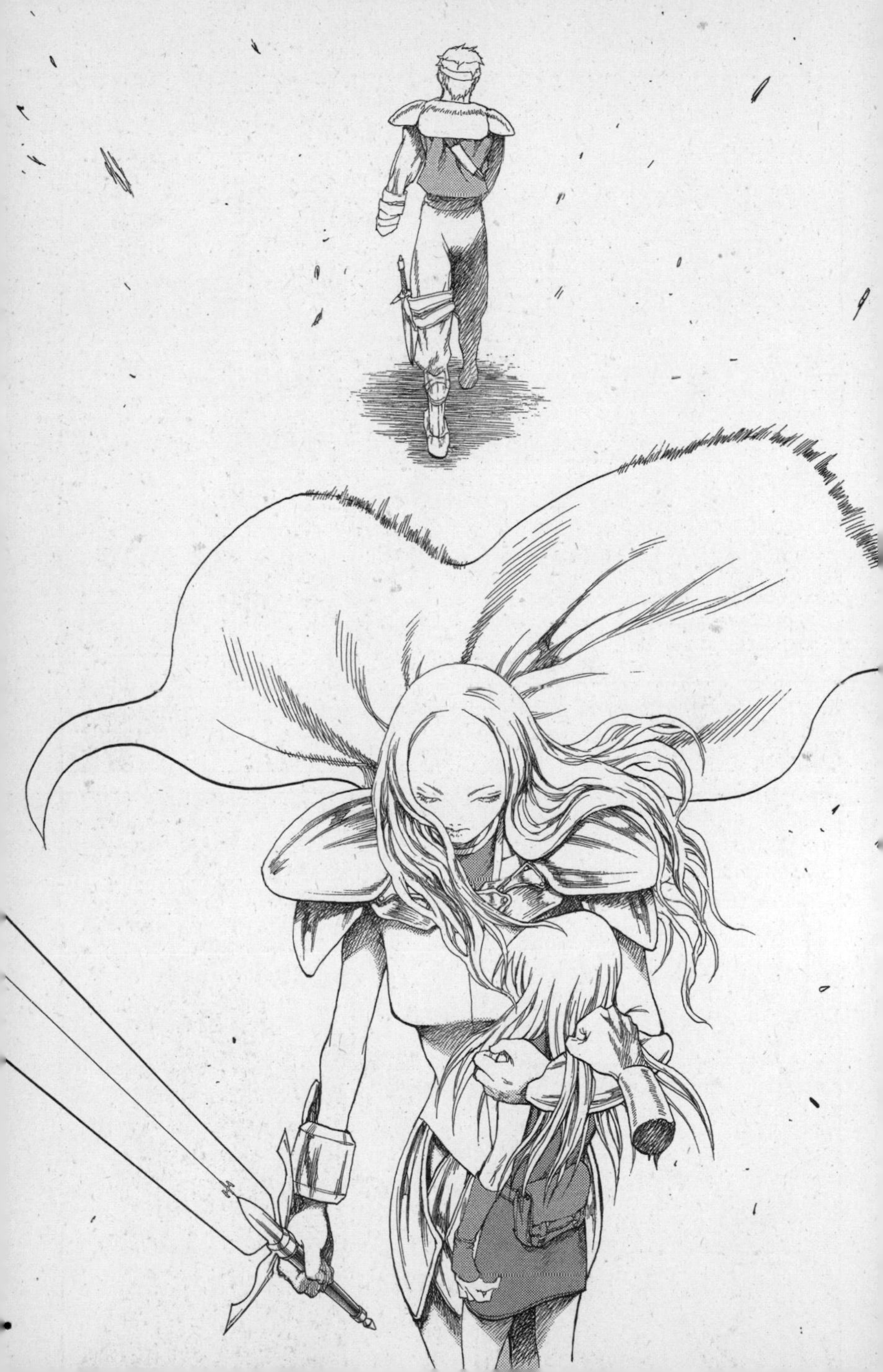

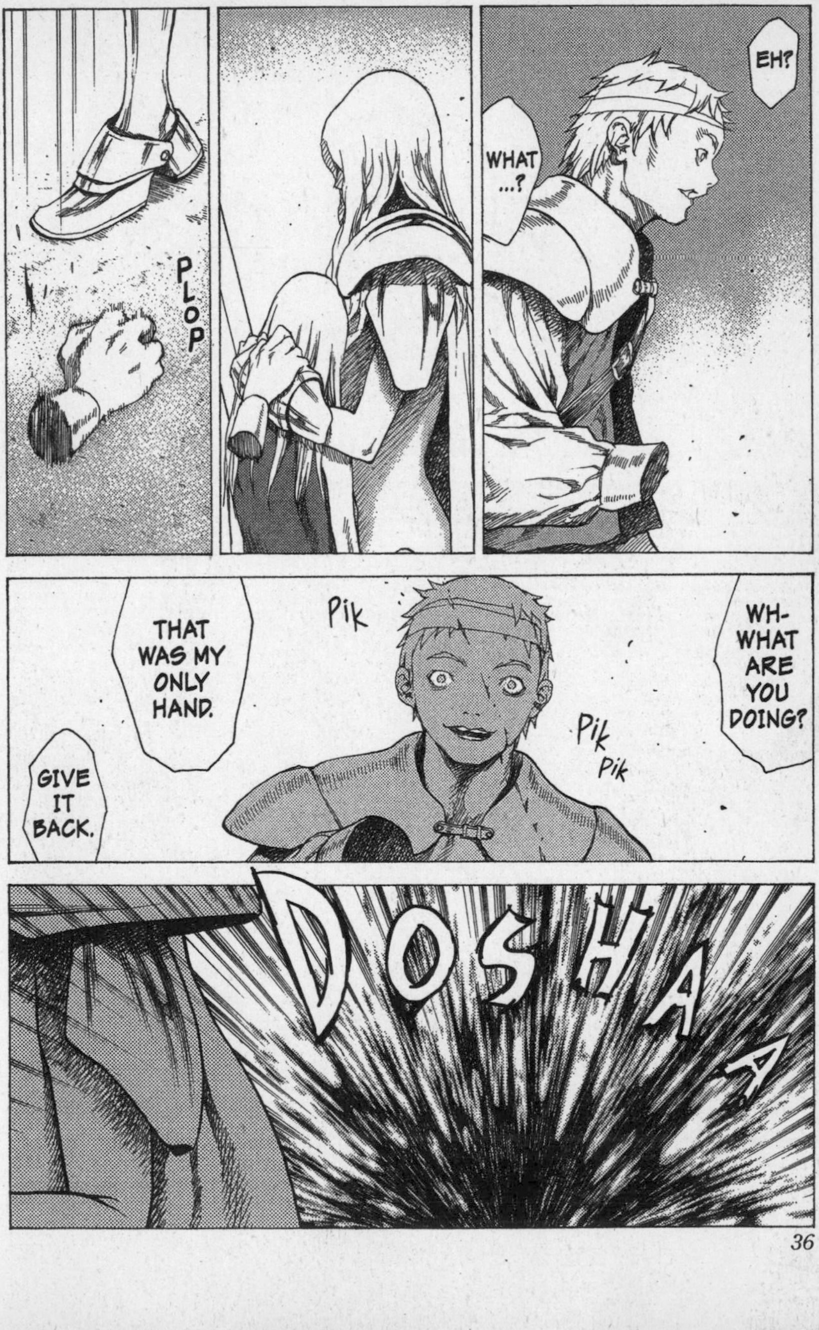
EH?
WHAT ...?
PLOP
WH- WHAT ARE YOU DOING?
Pik pik
Pik
THAT WAS MY ONLY HAND.
GIVE IT BACK.
DOSHAA

READ THIS WAY

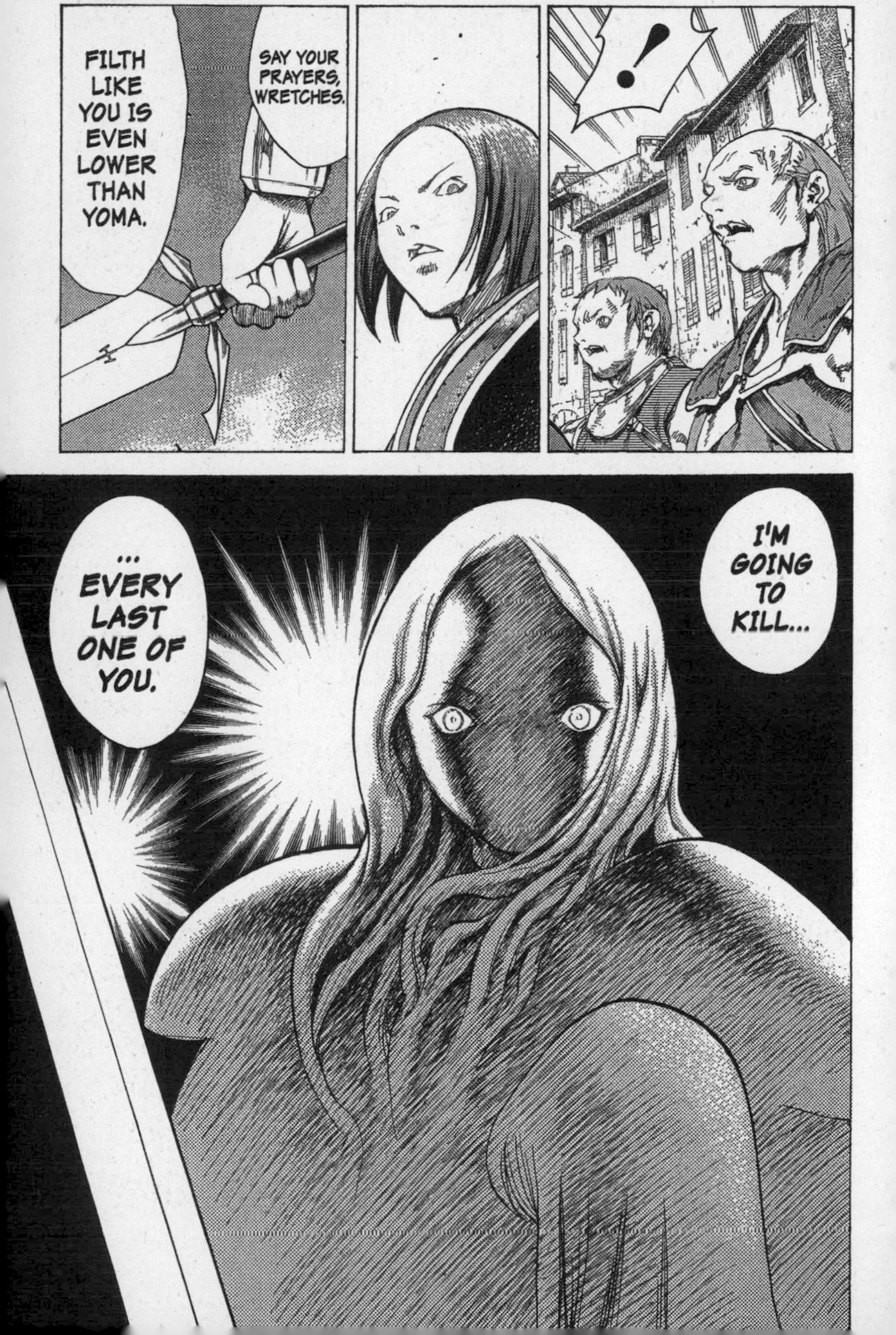
!
SAY YOUR PRAYERS, WRETCHES.
FILTH LIKE YOU IS EVEN LOWER THAN YOMA.
I'M GOING TO KILL...
... EVERY LAST ONE OF YOU.

クレイモア
Claymore™

Scene 17: Teresa of the Faint Smile, Part 6

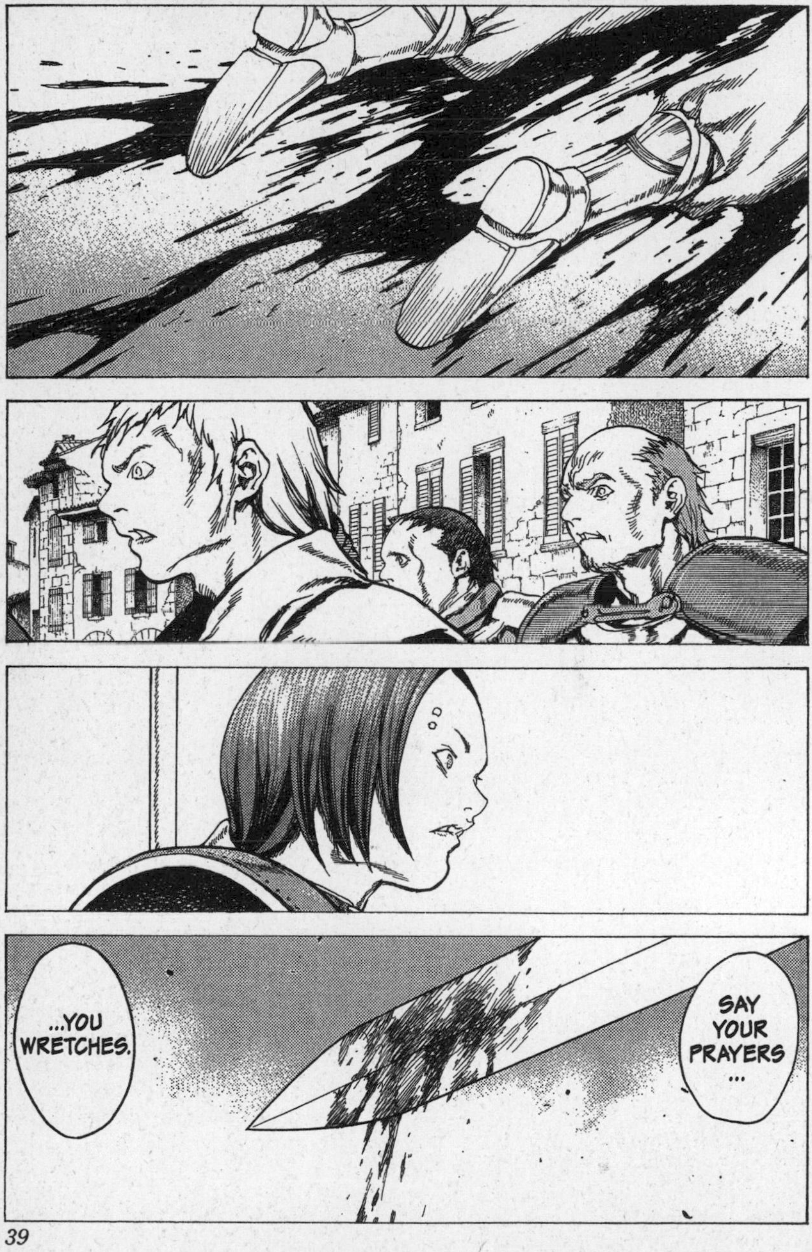
SAY YOUR PRAYERS ...
...YOU WRETCHES.

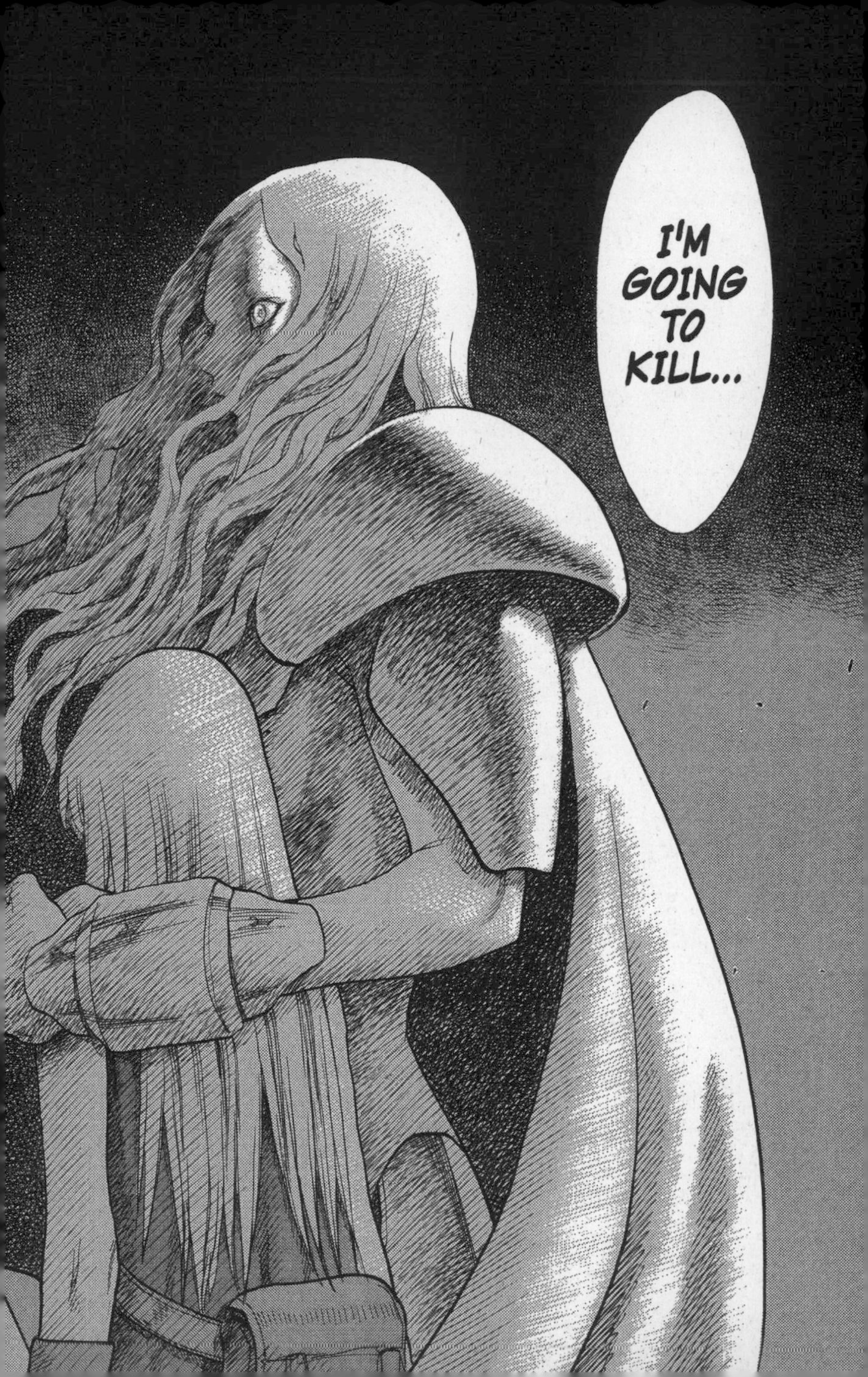
I'M GOING TO KILL...

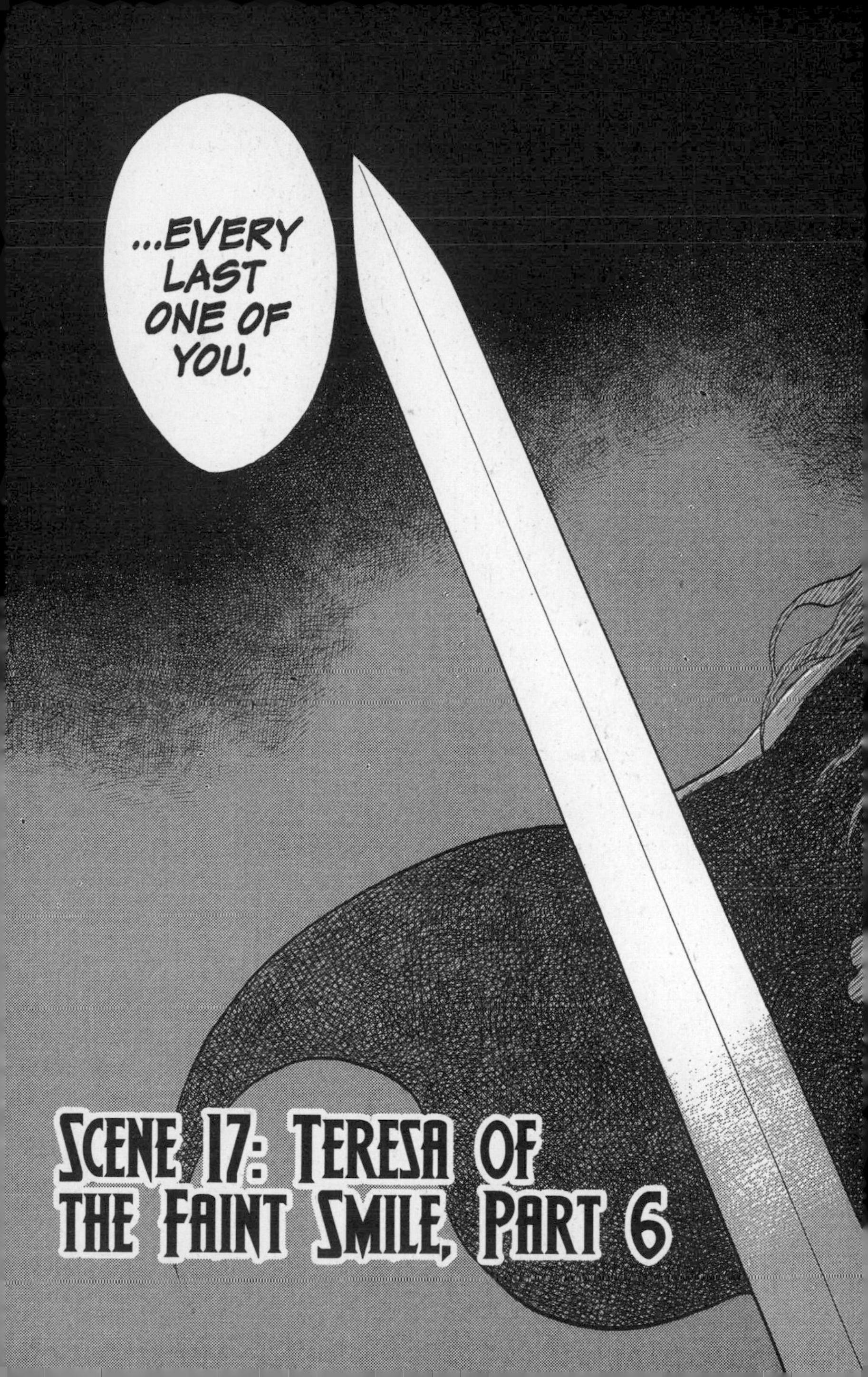
...EVERY LAST ONE OF YOU.
SCENE 17: TERESA OF THE FAINT SMILE, PART 6

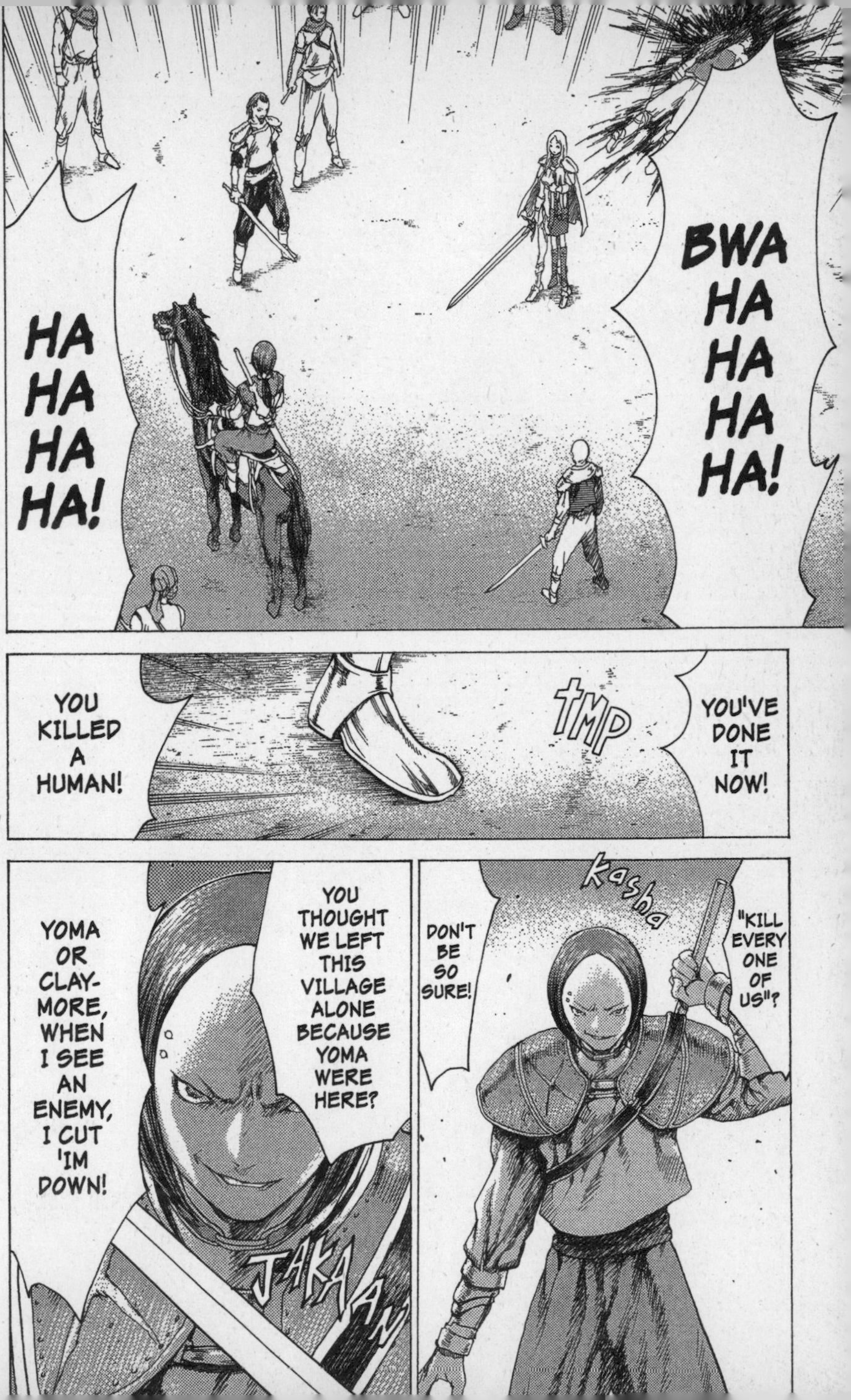
BWA HA HA HA HA!
HA HA HA HA!
YOU'VE DONE IT NOW!
TMP
YOU KILLED A HUMAN!
kasha
"KILL EVERY ONE OF US"?
DON'T BE SO SURE!
YOU THOUGHT WE LEFT THIS VILLAGE ALONE BECAUSE YOMA WERE HERE?
YOMA OR CLAY-MORE, WHEN I SEE AN ENEMY, I CUT 'IM DOWN!
JAKAAN

READ THIS WAY

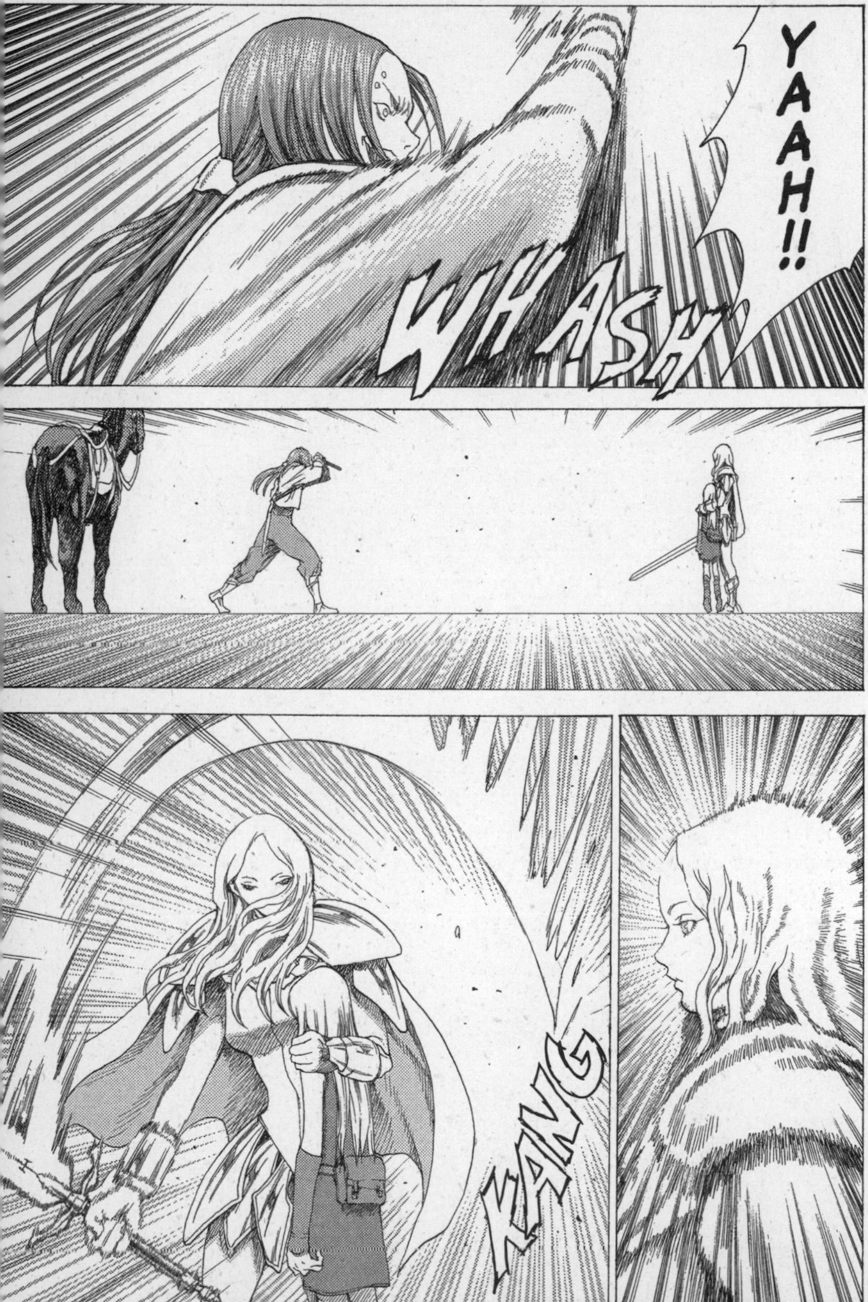
YAAH!!
WHASH
KANG

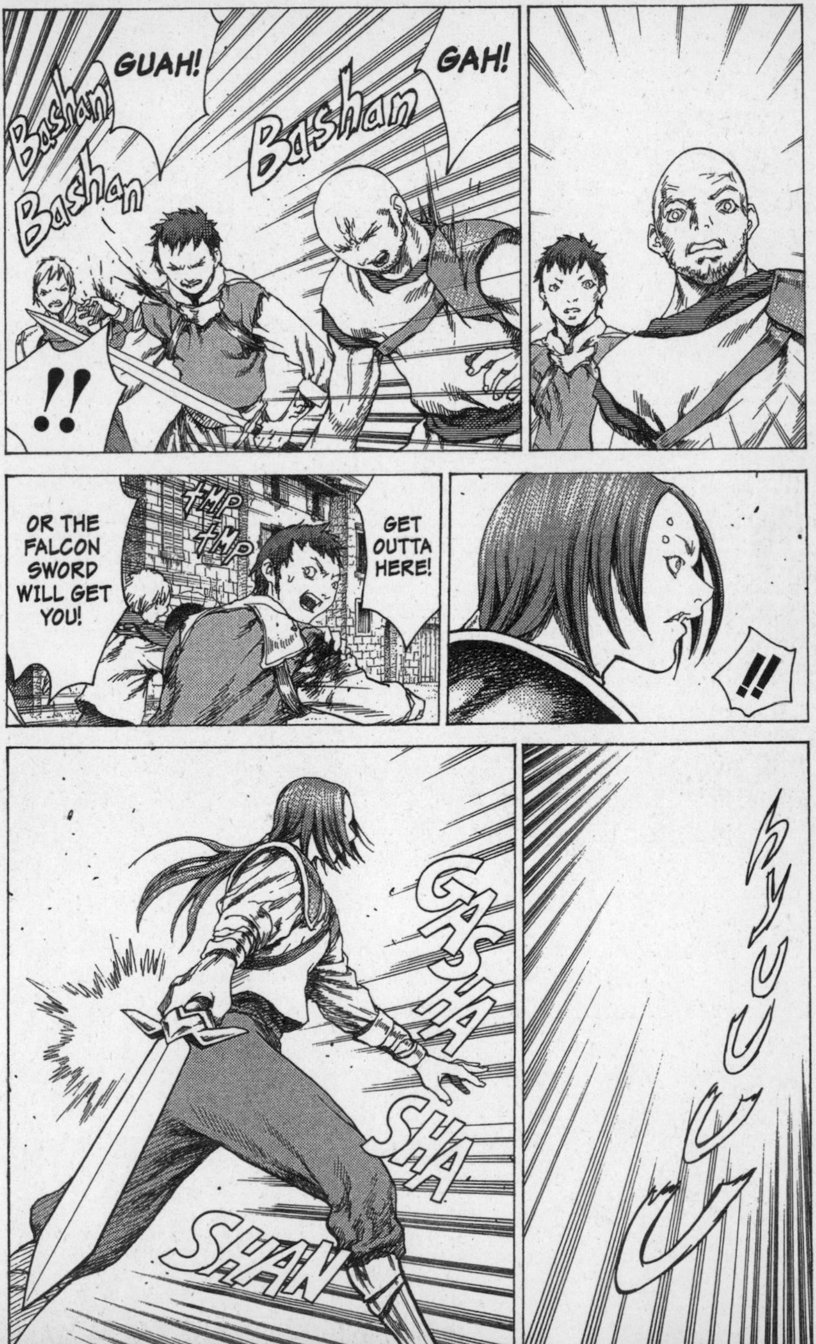
GAH!
Bashan
GUAH!
Bashan
Bashan
!!
!!
GET OUTTA HERE!
tmp
tmp
OR THE FALCON SWORD WILL GET YOU!
hyuuuuu
GASHA
SHA
SHAN

READ THIS WAY

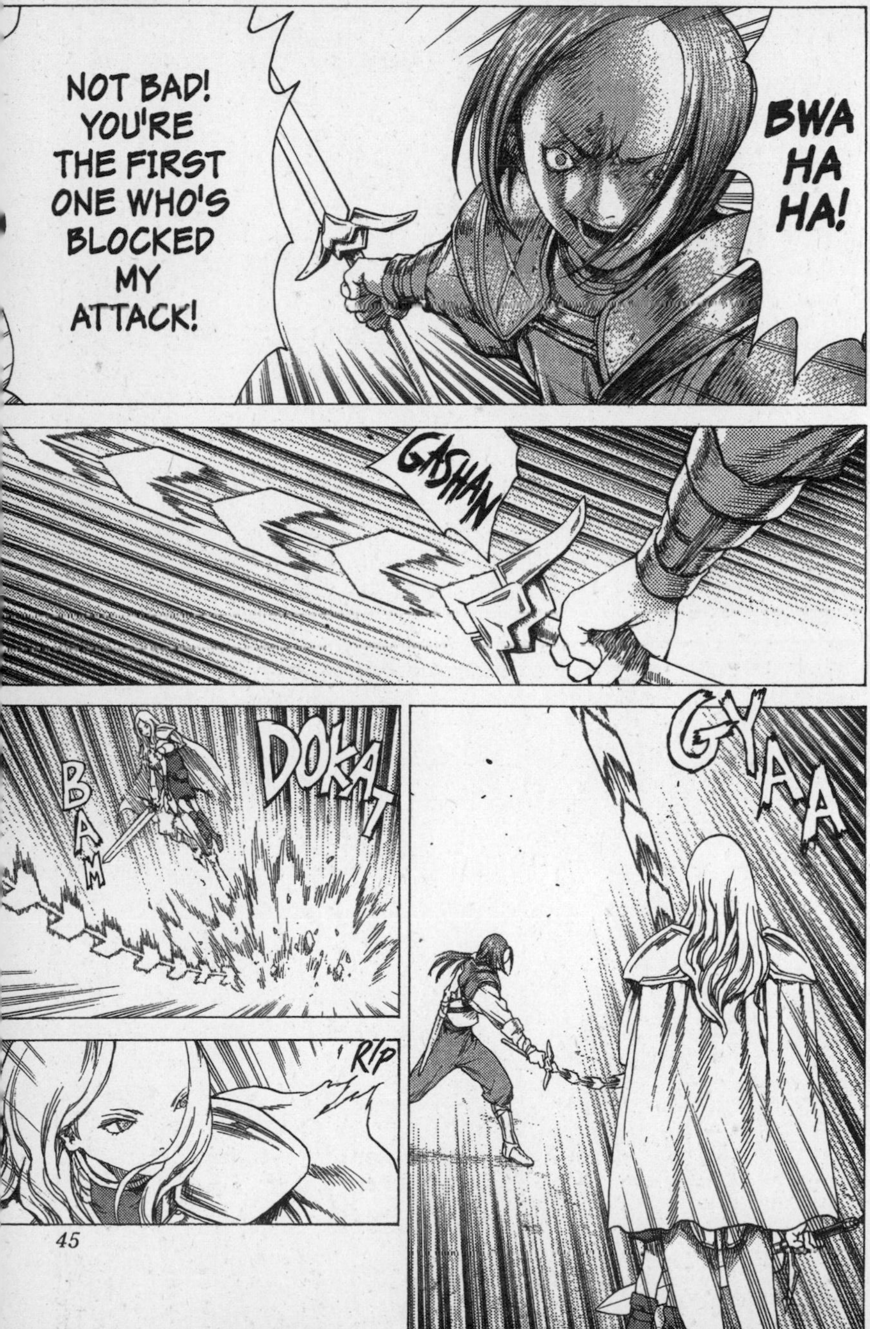

BWA HA HA!
NOT BAD! YOU'RE THE FIRST ONE WHO'S BLOCKED MY ATTACK!
GASHAN
GYAA
DOKAT
BAM
Rip

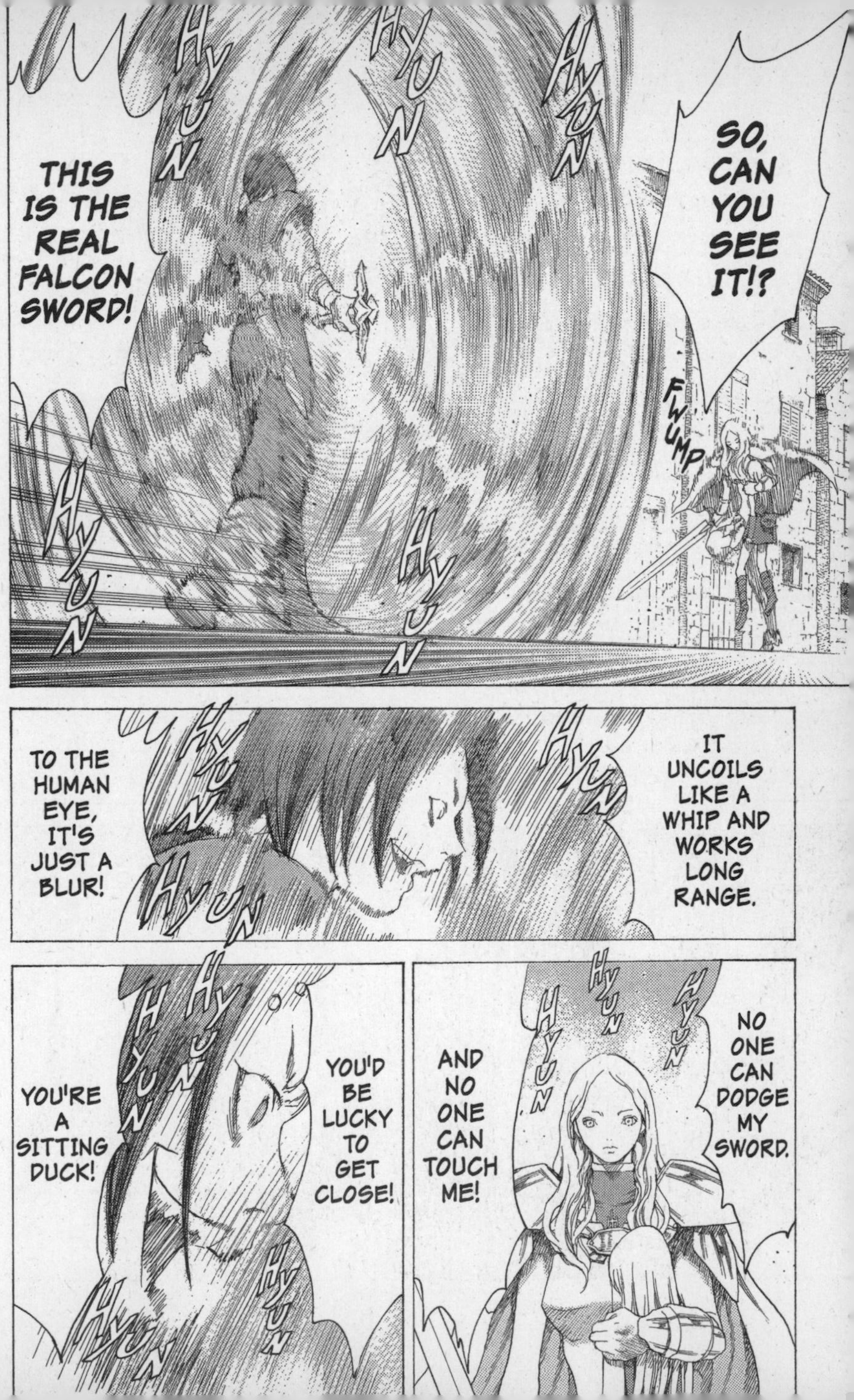
SO, CAN YOU SEE IT!?
HYUN
HYUN
HYUN
FWUMP
THIS IS THE REAL FALCON SWORD!
HYUN
HYUN
HYUN
IT UNCOILS LIKE A WHIP AND WORKS LONG RANGE.
HYUN
HYUN
HYUN
TO THE HUMAN EYE, IT'S JUST A BLUR!
HYUN
HYUN
HYUN
NO ONE CAN DODGE MY SWORD.
AND NO ONE CAN TOUCH ME!
HYUN
HYUN
YOU'D BE LUCKY TO GET CLOSE!
HYUN
HYUN
YOU'RE A SITTING DUCK!
HYUN
HYUN

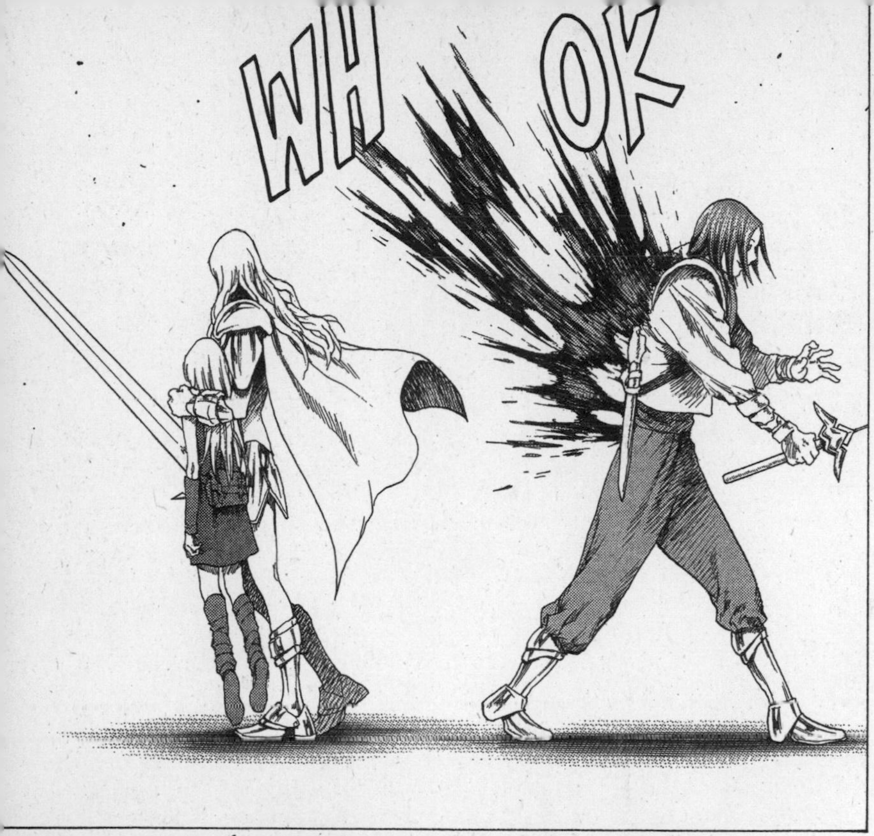
WH OK

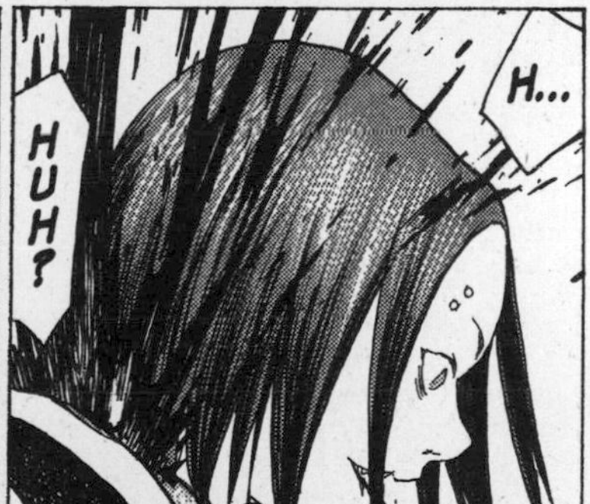
H...
HUH?

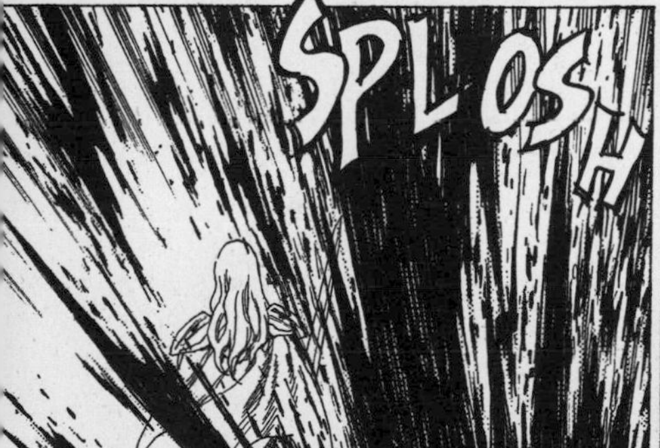
SPLOSH

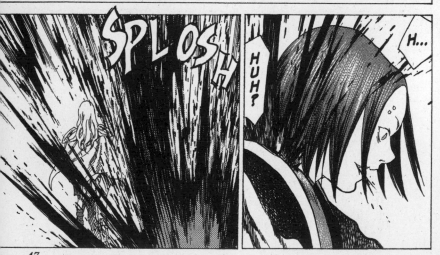

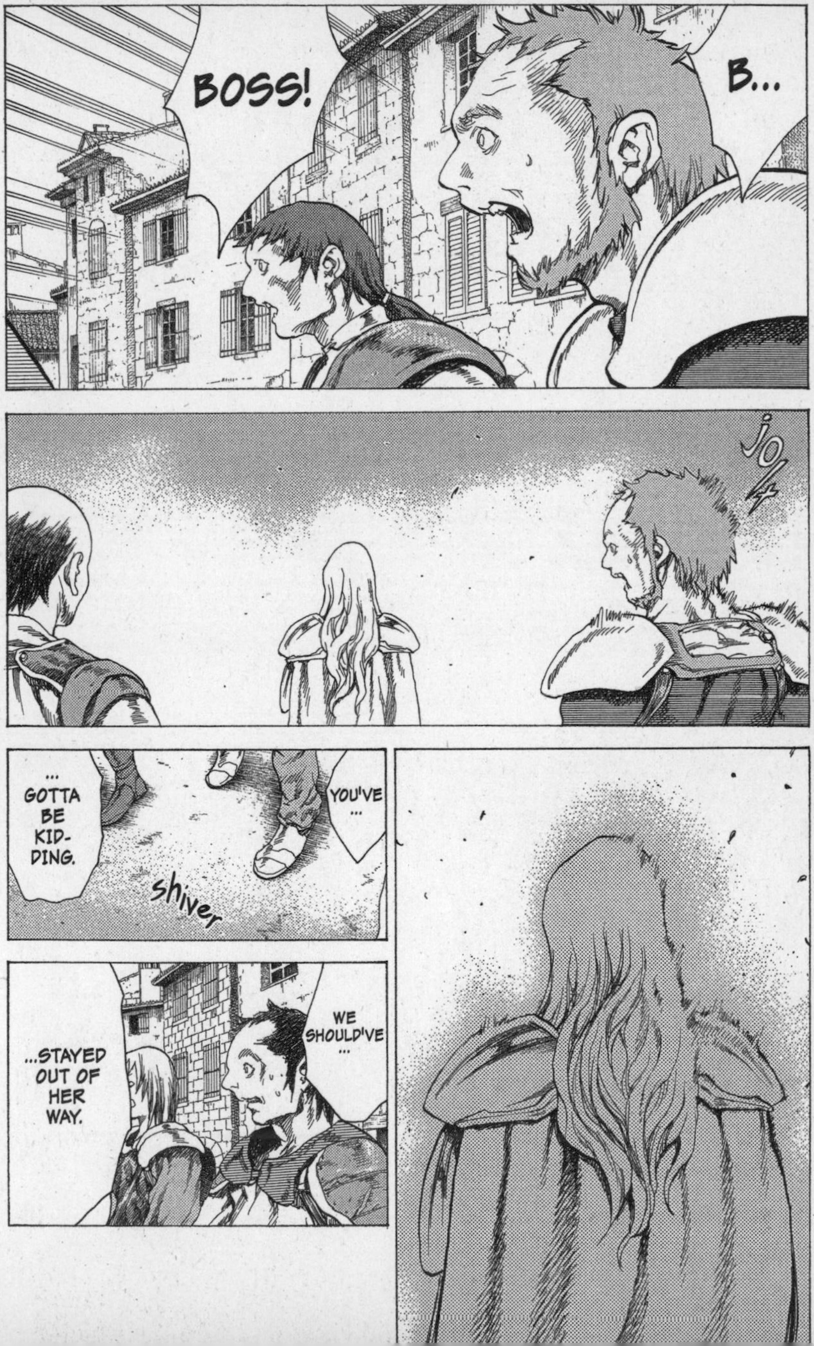
B...
BOSS!
jolt
YOU'VE ...
...GOTTA BE KID-DING.
shiver
WE SHOULD'VE ...
...STAYED OUT OF HER WAY.

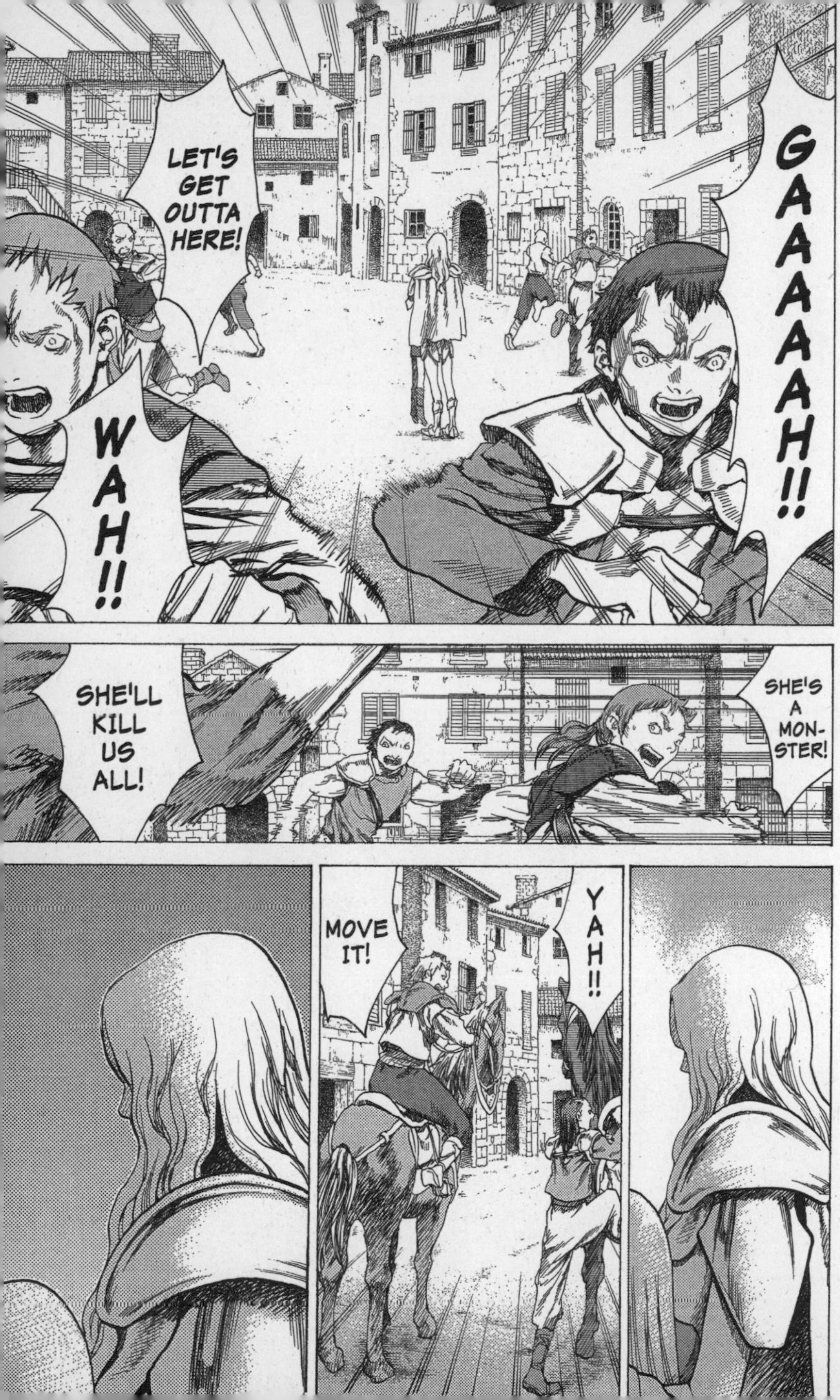
GAAAAAH!!
LET'S GET OUTTA HERE!
WAH!!
SHE'S A MON-STER!
SHE'LL KILL US ALL!
YAH!!
MOVE IT!

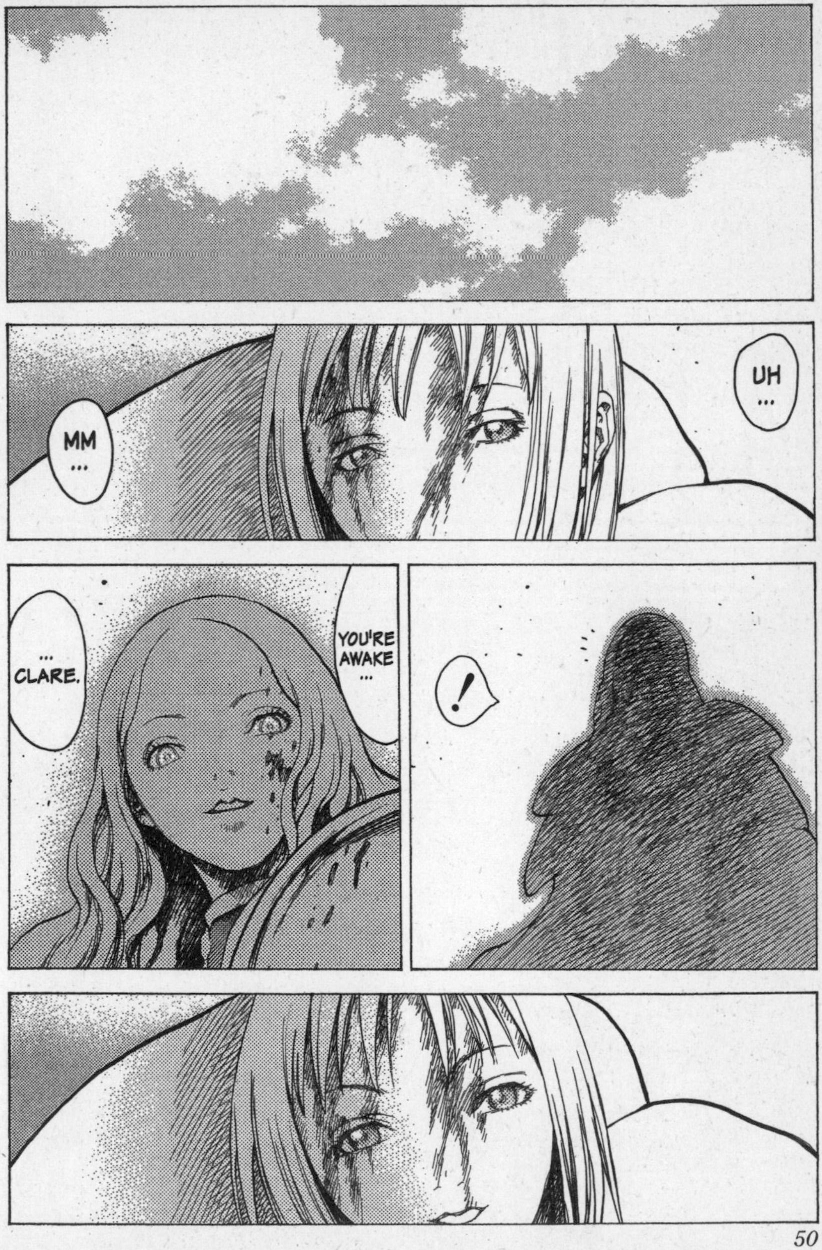
UH ...
MM ...
!
YOU'RE AWAKE ...
... CLARE.

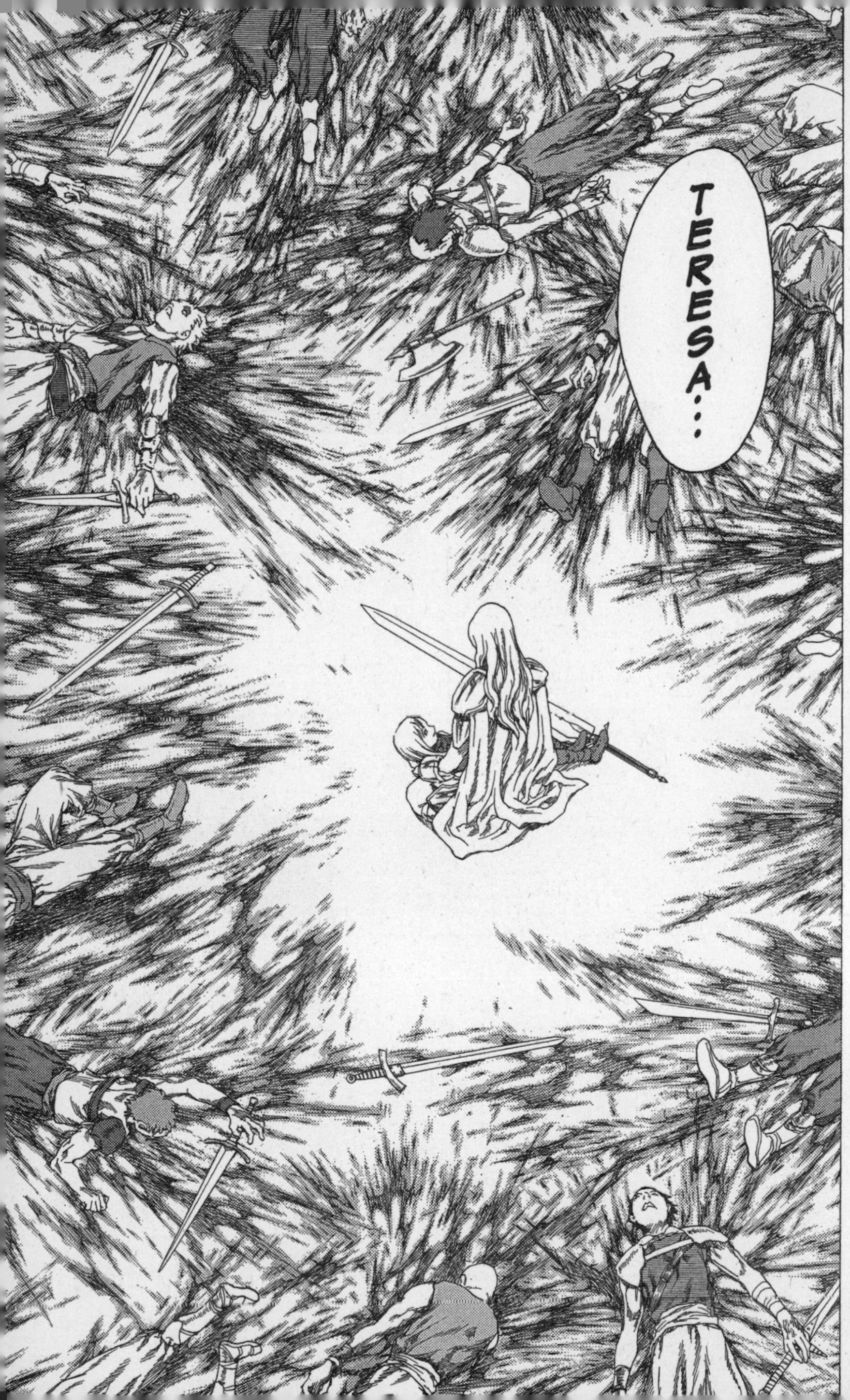
TERESA...

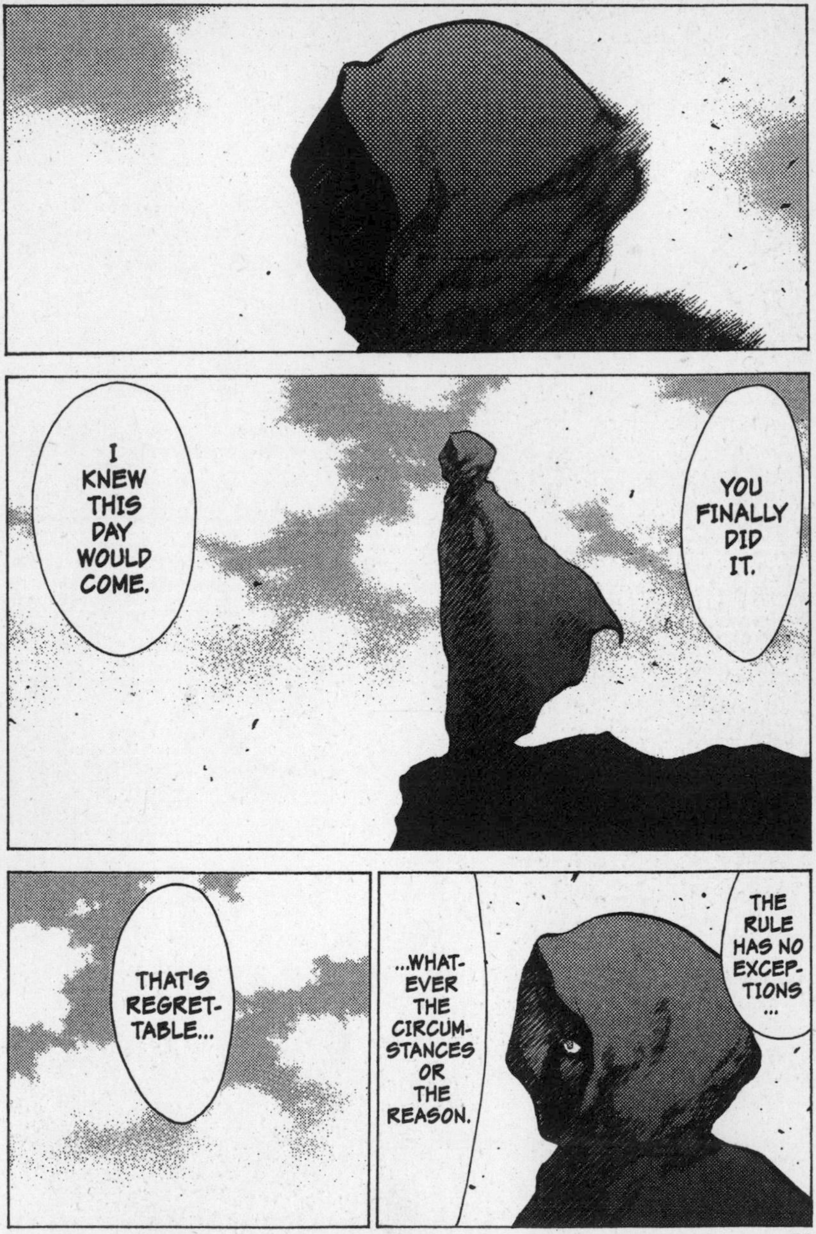
YOU FINALLY DID IT.
I KNEW THIS DAY WOULD COME.
THE RULE HAS NO EXCEPTIONS...
...WHATEVER THE CIRCUMSTANCES OR THE REASON.
THAT'S REGRETTABLE...

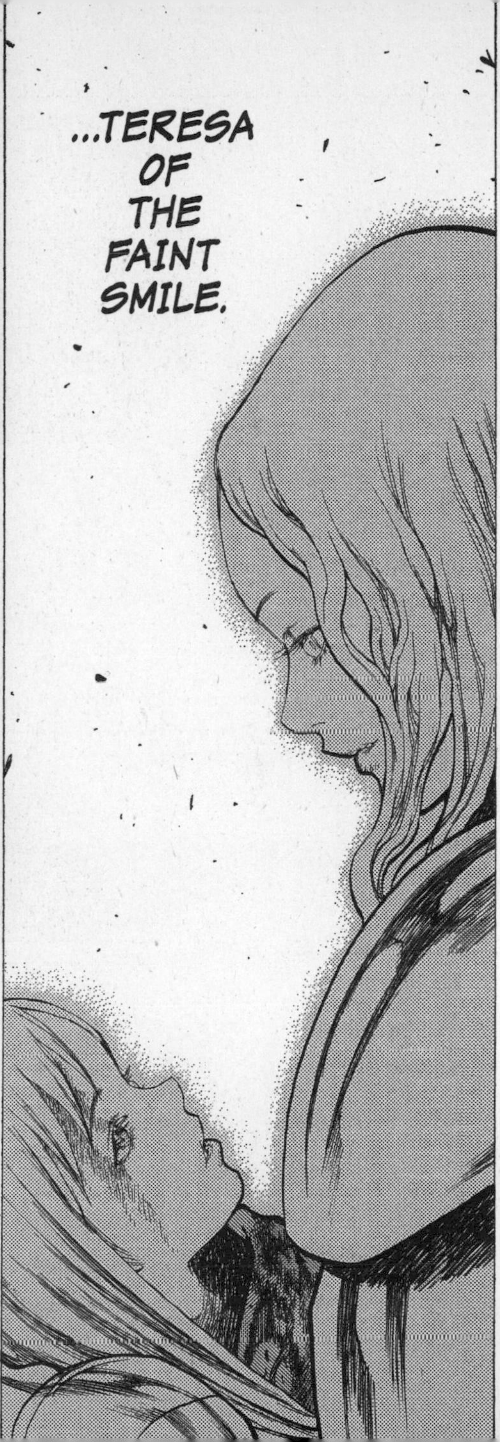
...TERESA OF THE FAINT SMILE.
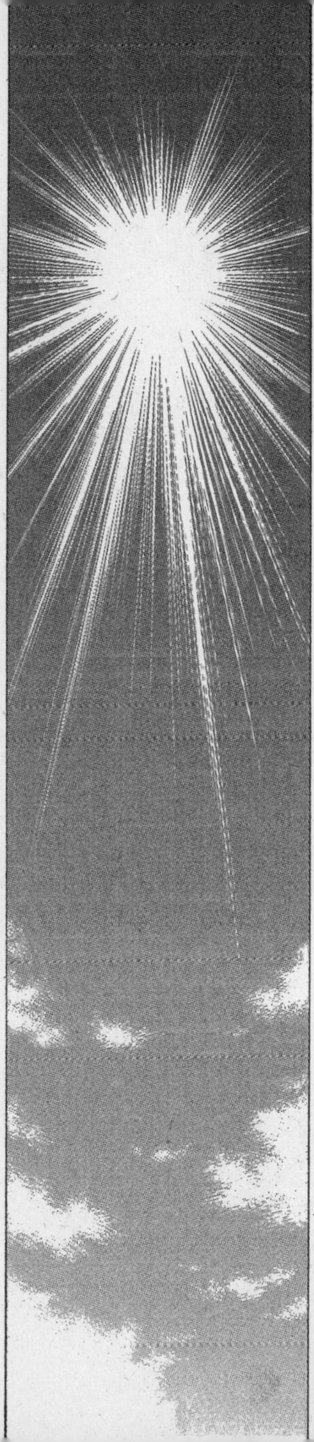

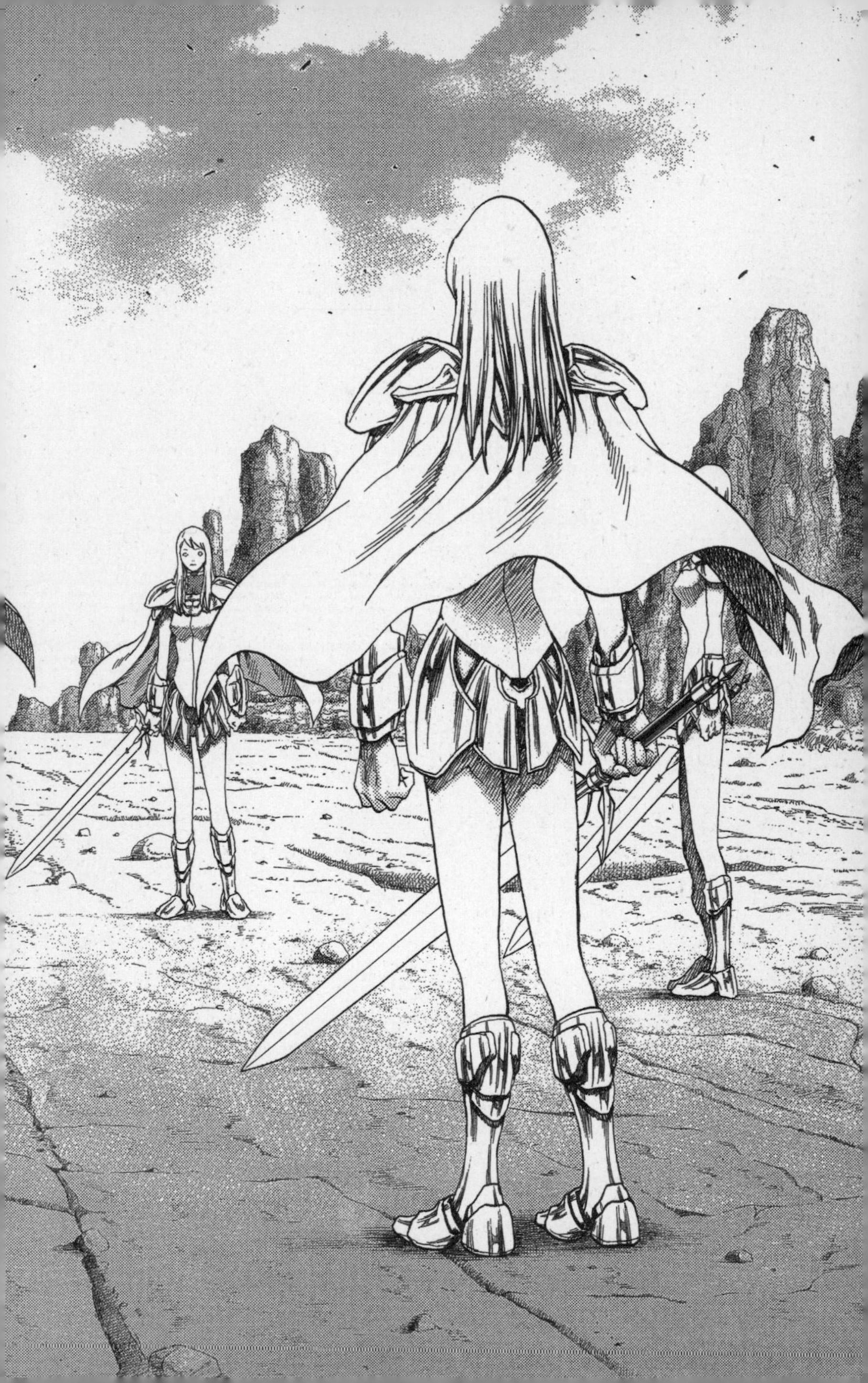

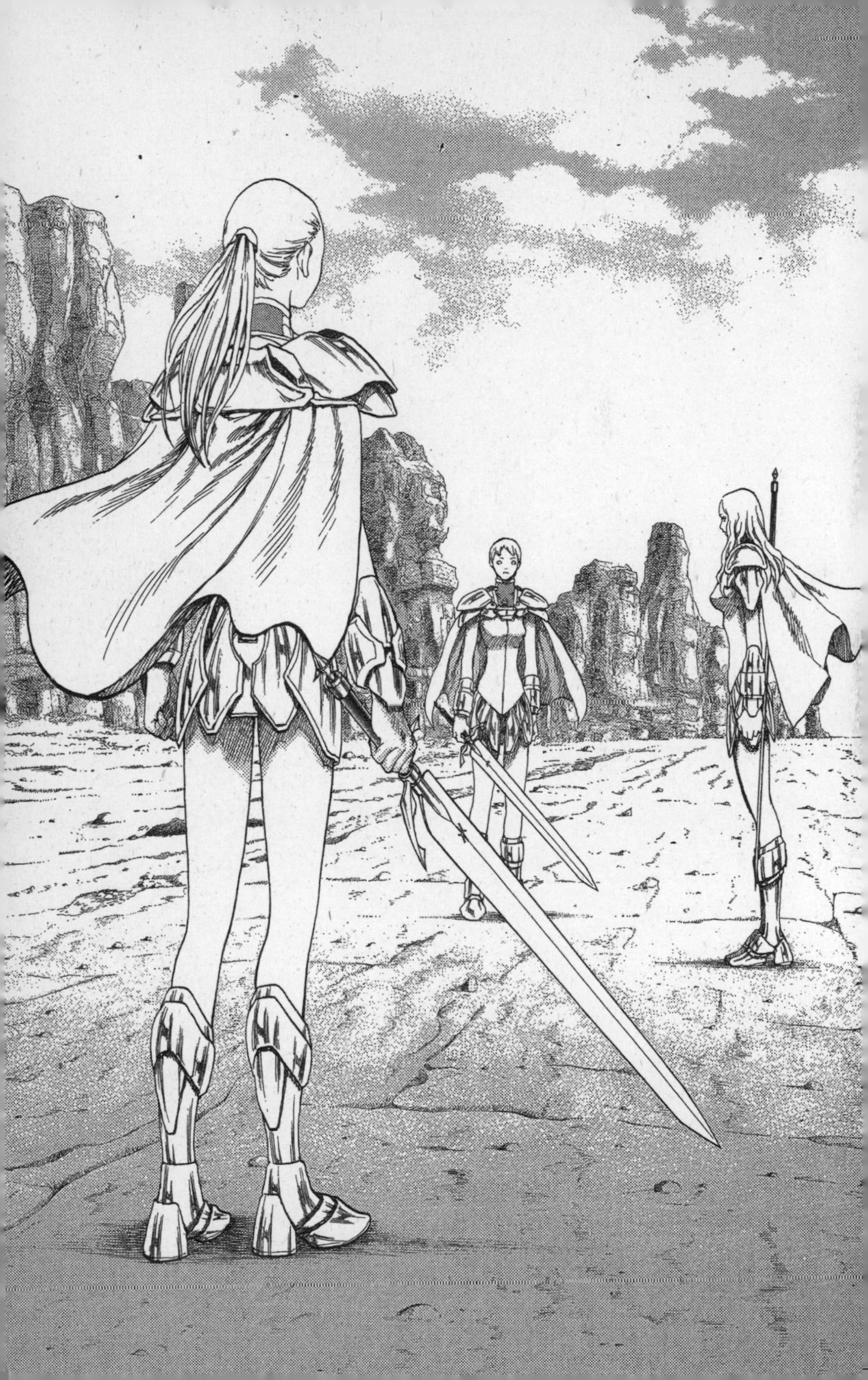

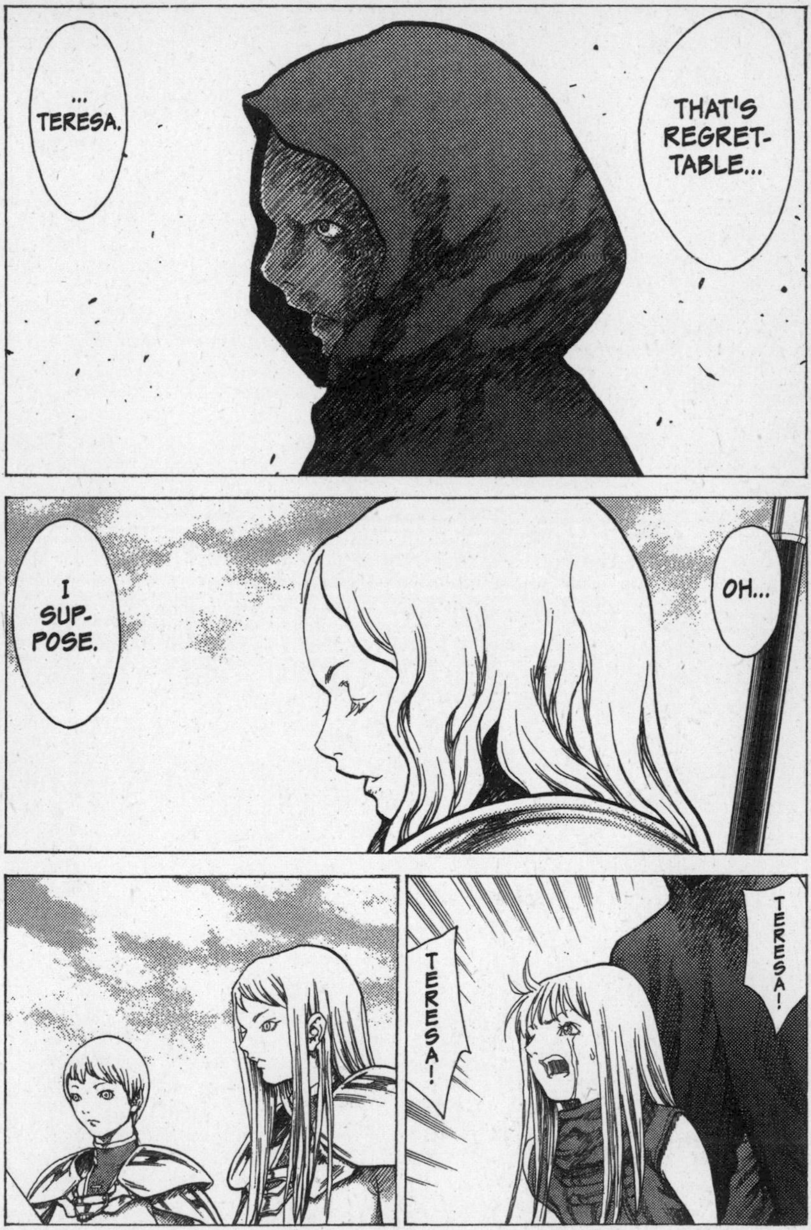
THAT'S REGRET-TABLE...
... TERESA.
OH...
I SUP-POSE.
TERESA!
TERESA!

READ THIS WAY

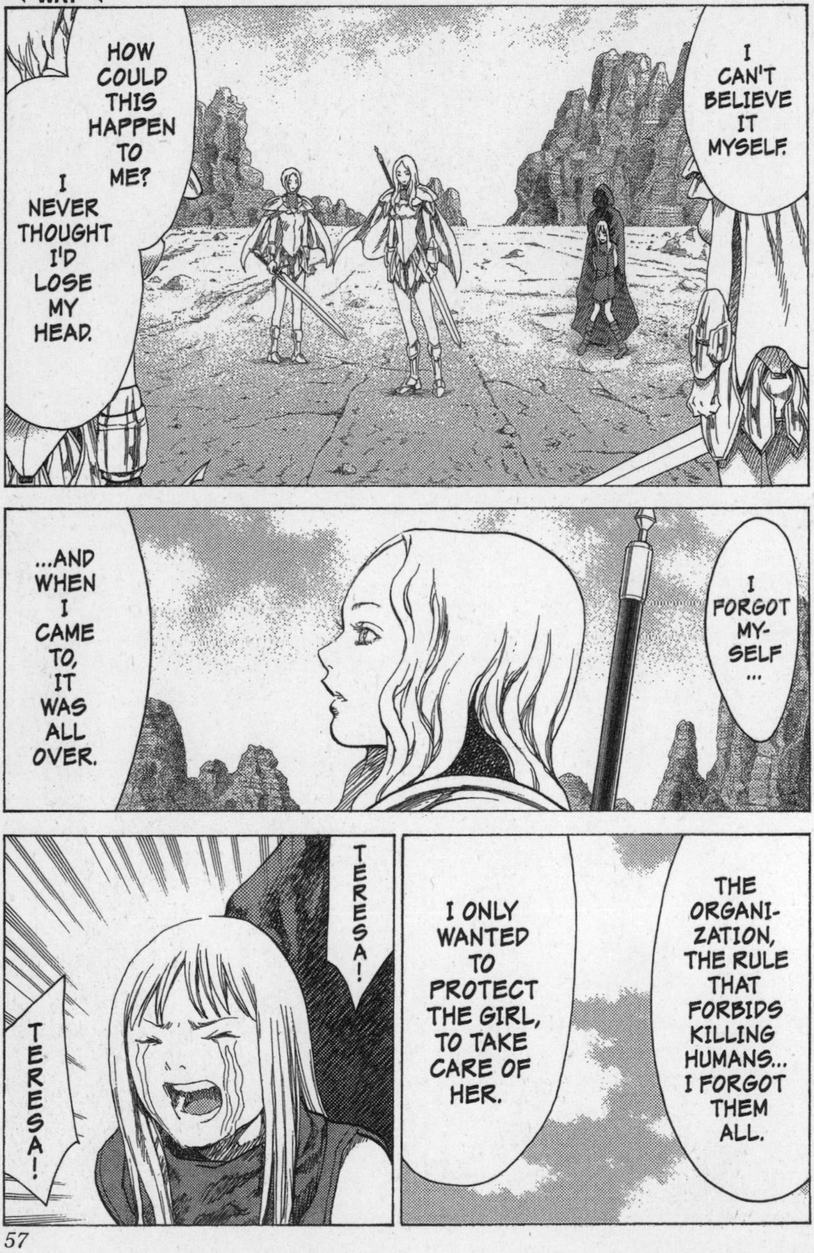

I CAN'T BELIEVE IT MYSELF.
HOW COULD THIS HAPPEN TO ME?
I NEVER THOUGHT I'D LOSE MY HEAD.
I FORGOT MY-SELF...
...AND WHEN I CAME TO, IT WAS ALL OVER.
THE ORGANI-ZATION, THE RULE THAT FORBIDS KILLING HUMANS... I FORGOT THEM ALL.
I ONLY WANTED TO PROTECT THE GIRL, TO TAKE CARE OF HER.
TERESA!
TERESA!

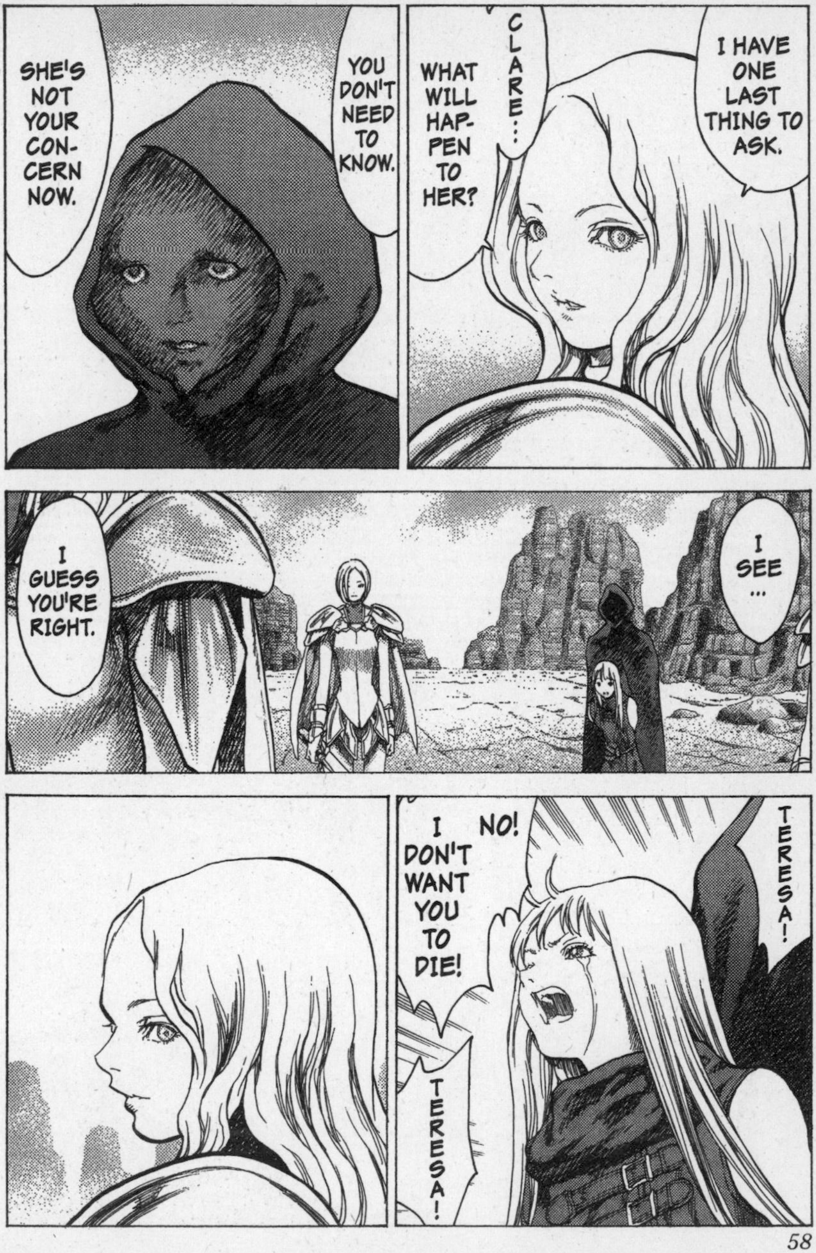
I HAVE ONE LAST THING TO ASK.
CLARE...
WHAT WILL HAP-PEN TO HER?
YOU DON'T NEED TO KNOW.
SHE'S NOT YOUR CON-CERN NOW.
I SEE...
I GUESS YOU'RE RIGHT.
TERESA!
NO!
I DON'T WANT YOU TO DIE!
TERESA!

READ THIS WAY

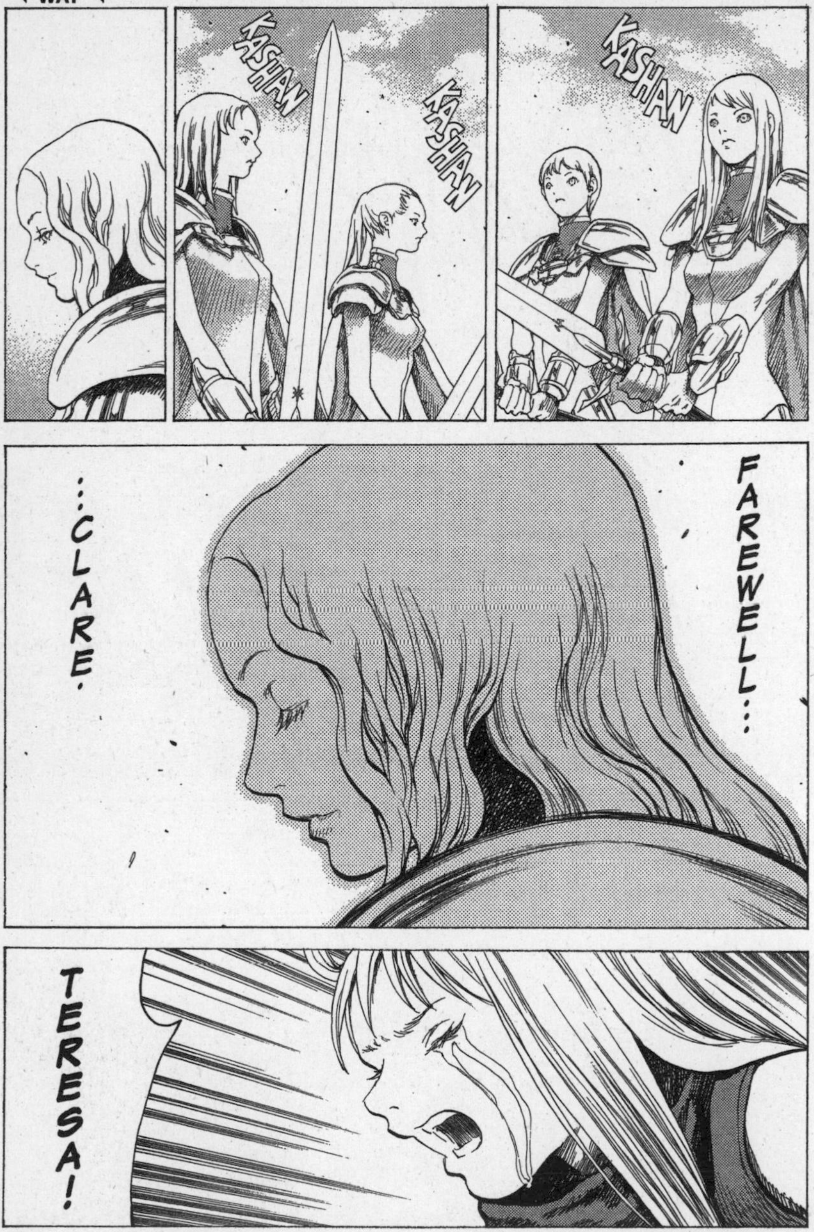

KASHAN
KASHAN
KASHAN
FAREWELL...
...CLARE.
TERESA!

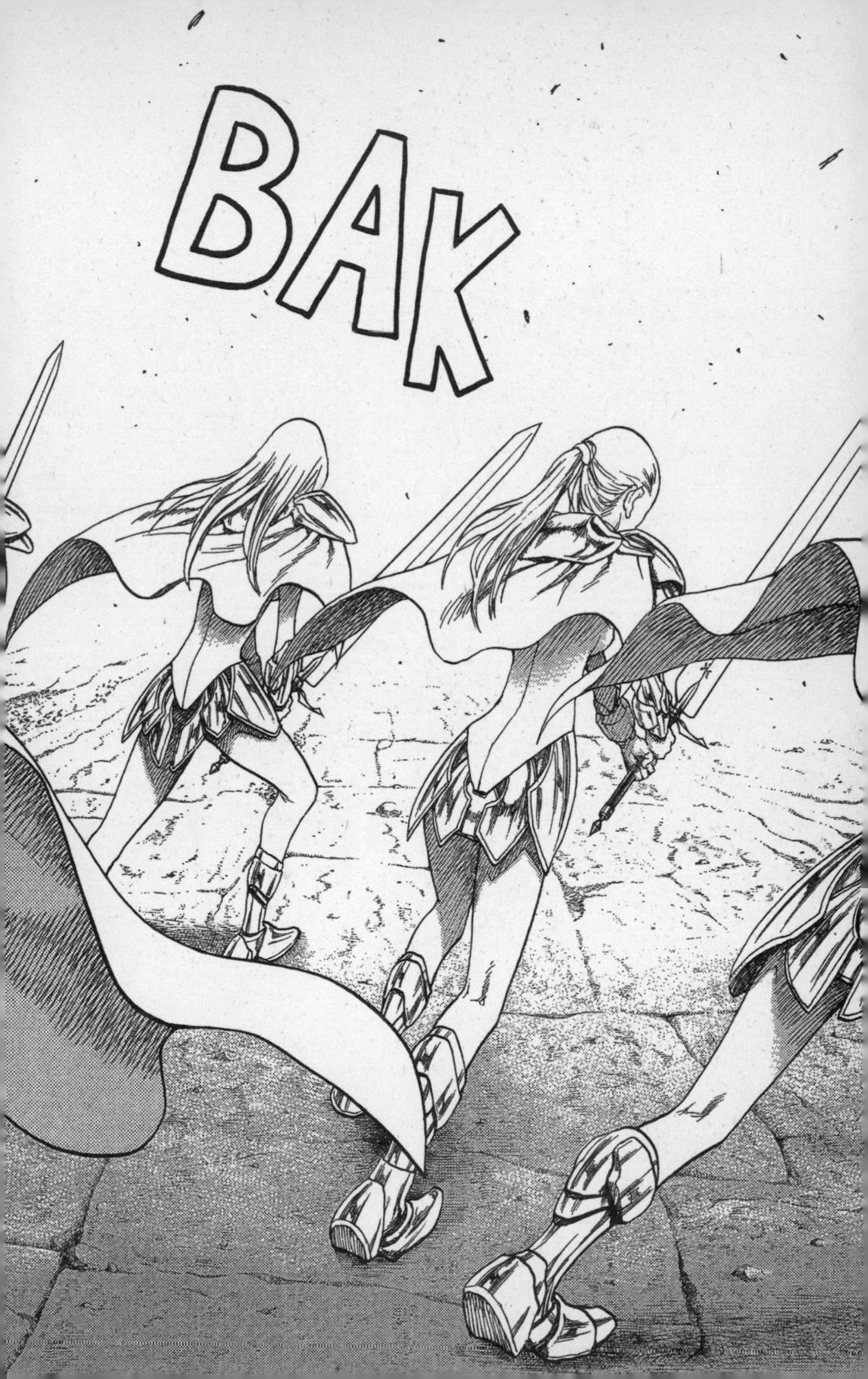
BAK

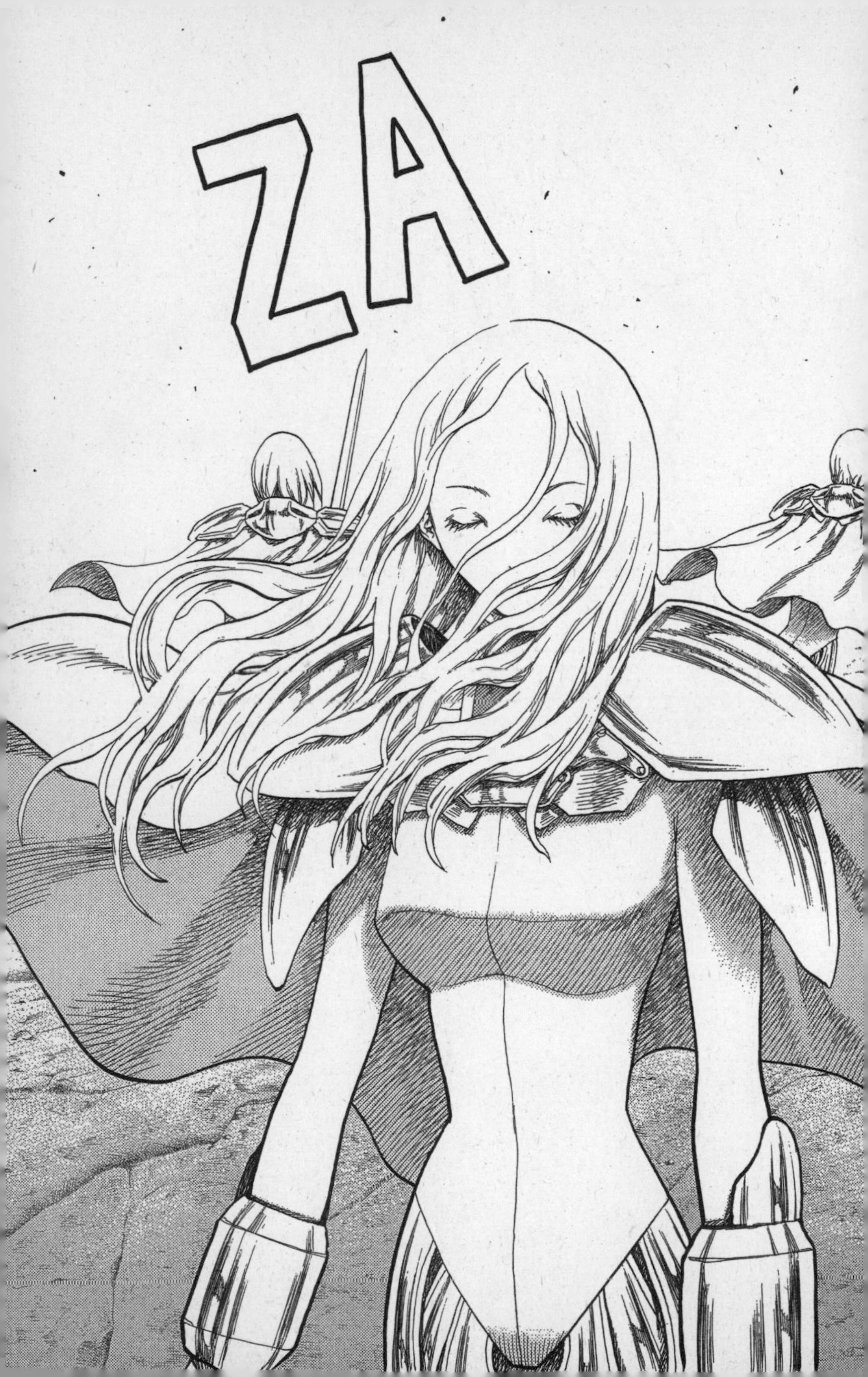
ZA

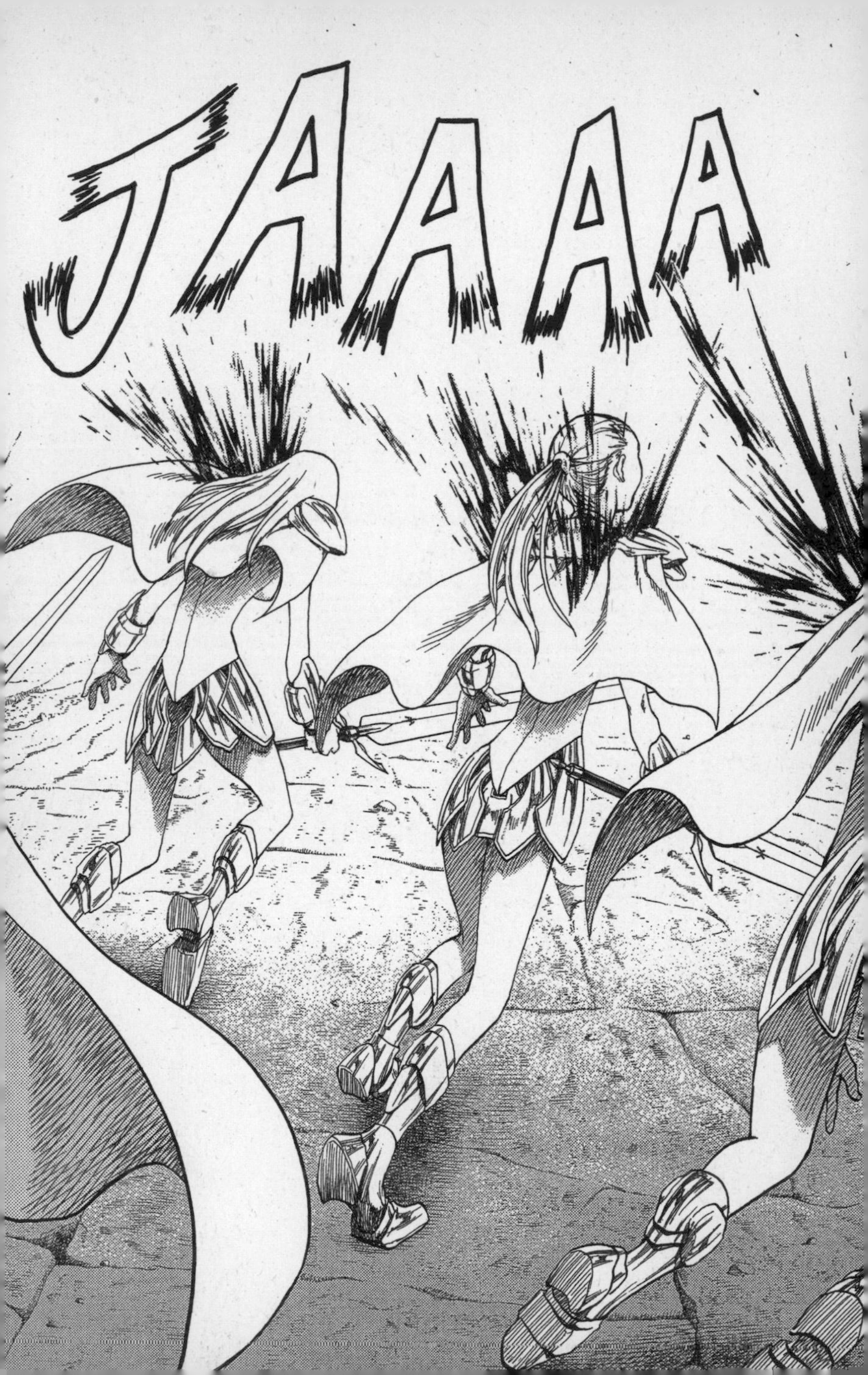
JAAAA

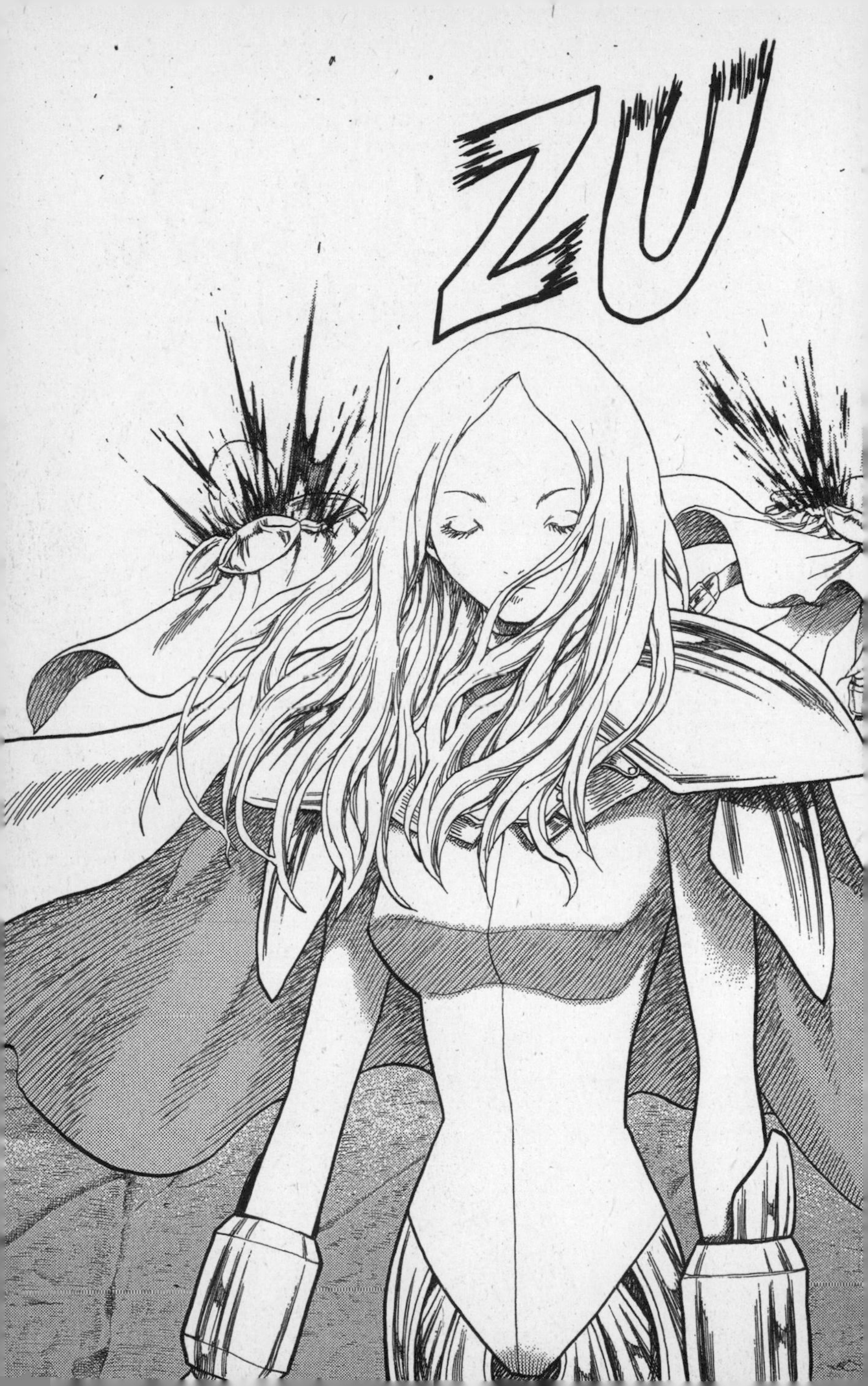
ZU

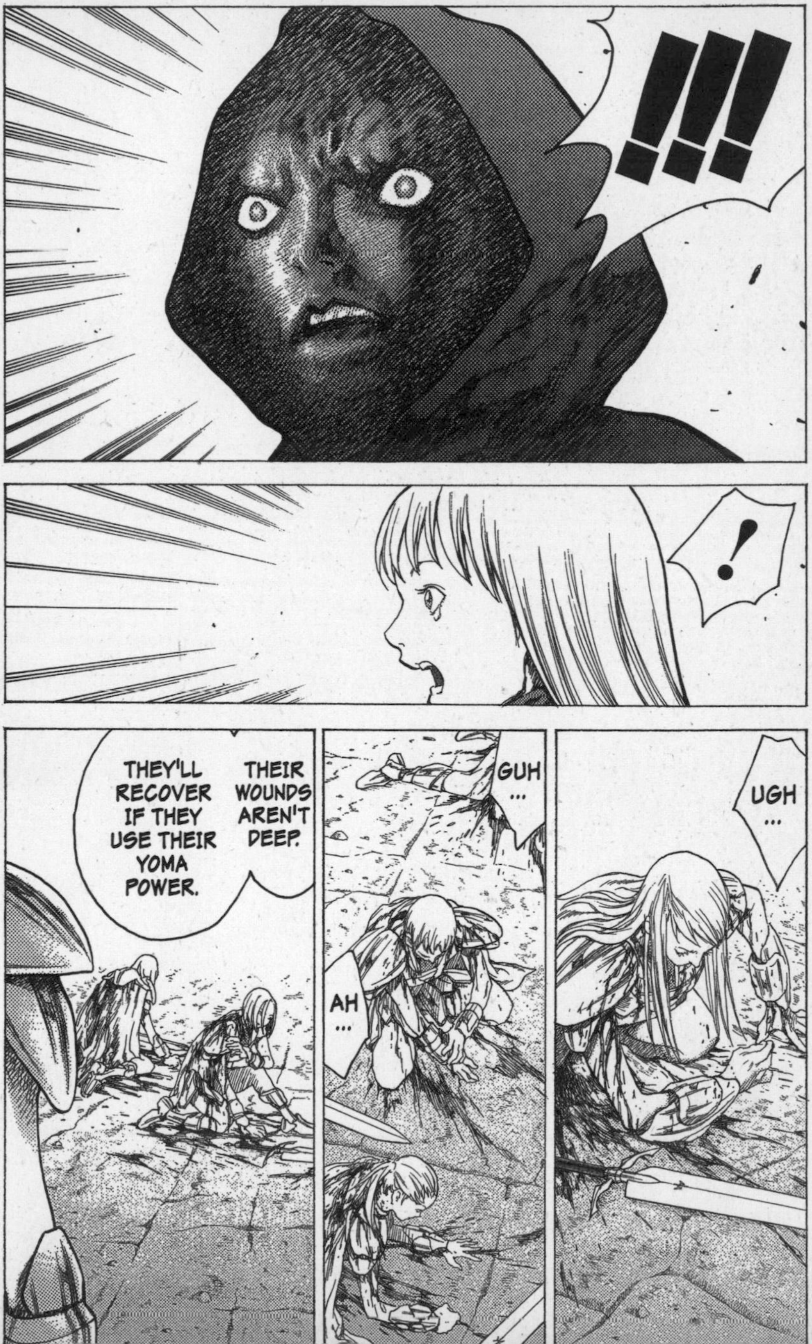
!!!
!
UGH ...
GUH ...
AH ...
THEIR WOUNDS AREN'T DEEP.
THEY'LL RECOVER IF THEY USE THEIR YOMA POWER.

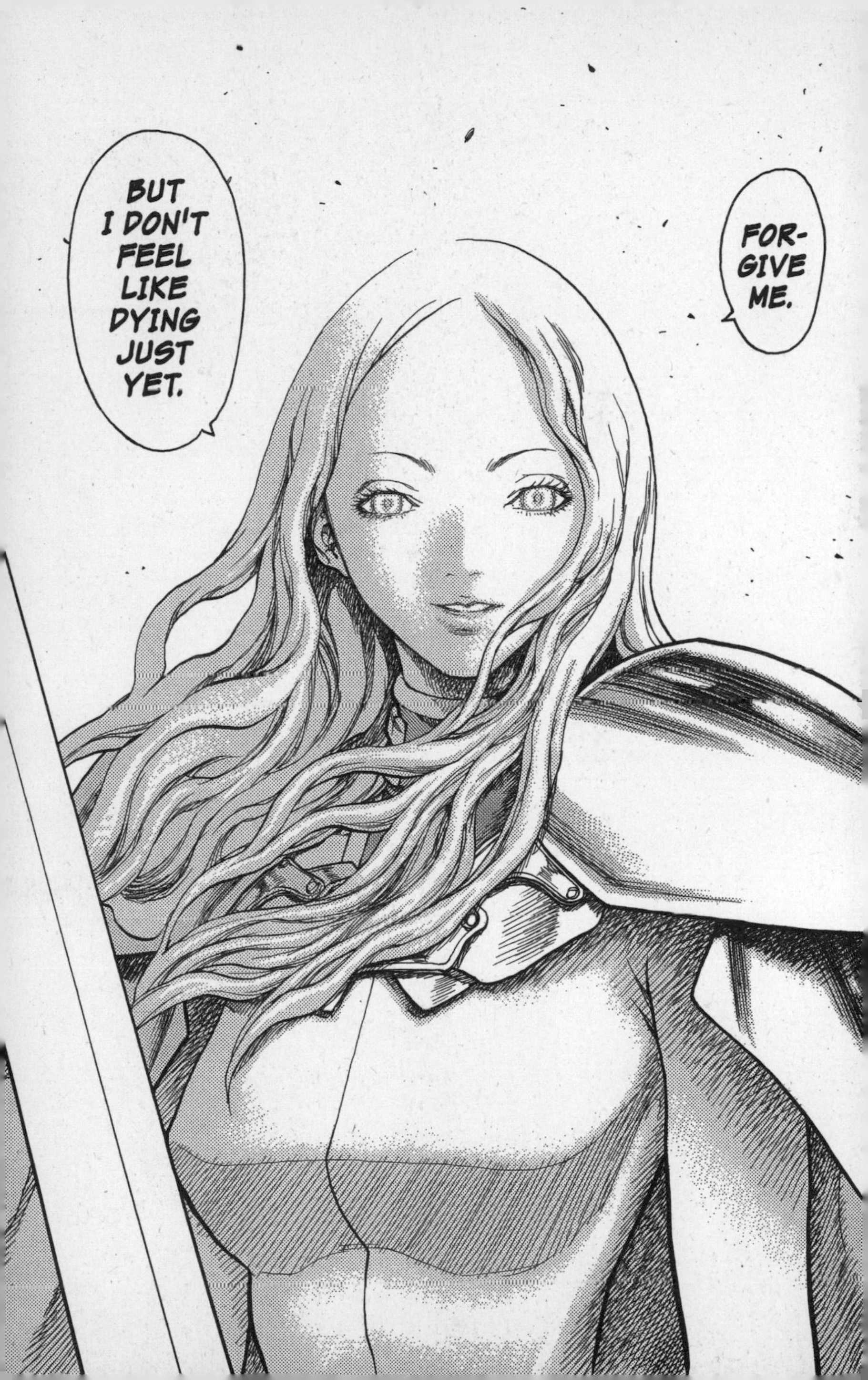
FOR-GIVE ME.
BUT I DON'T FEEL LIKE DYING JUST YET.

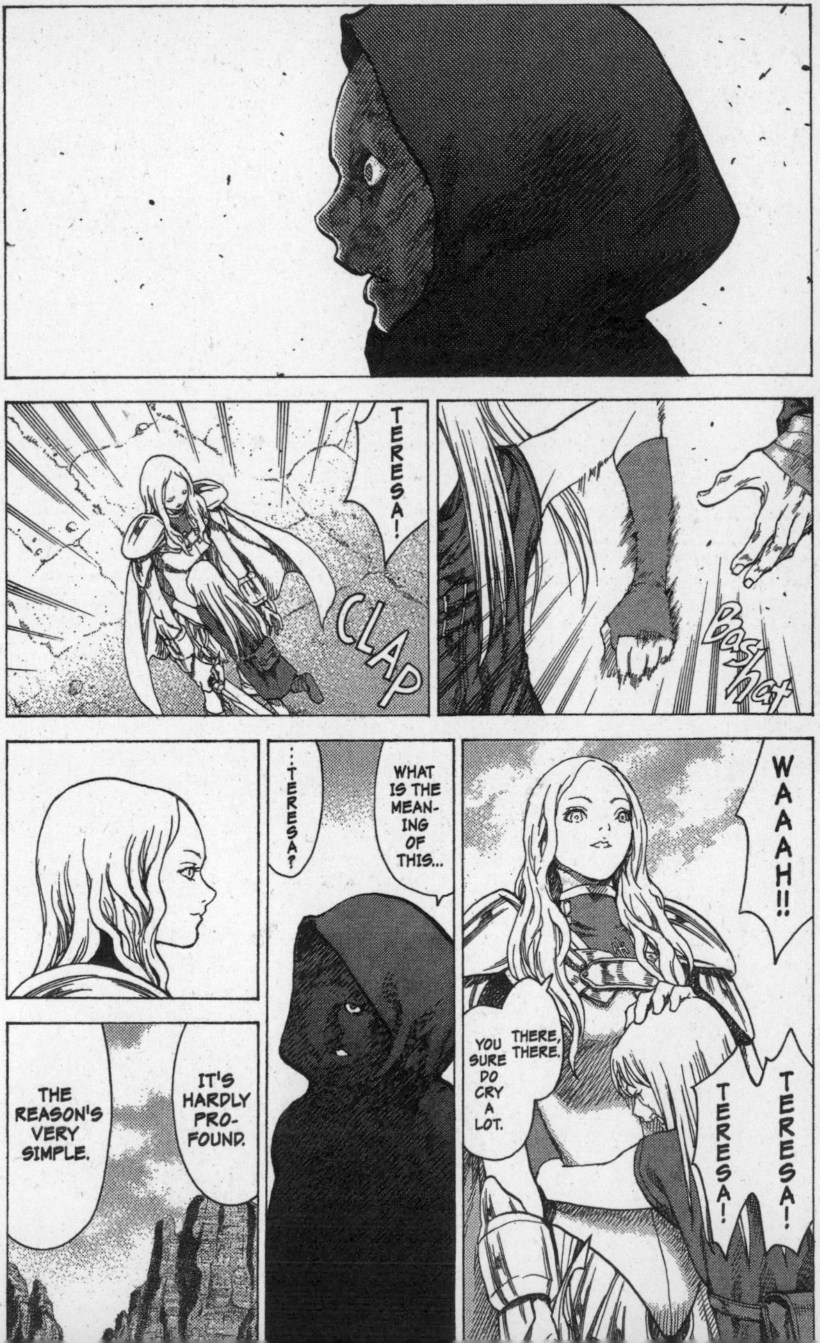
Bashax
TERESA!
CLAP
WAAAAH!!
THERE, THERE.
YOU SURE DO CRY A LOT.
TERESA!
TERESA!
WHAT IS THE MEANING OF THIS...
...TERESA?
IT'S HARDLY PRO-FOUND.
THE REASON'S VERY SIMPLE.

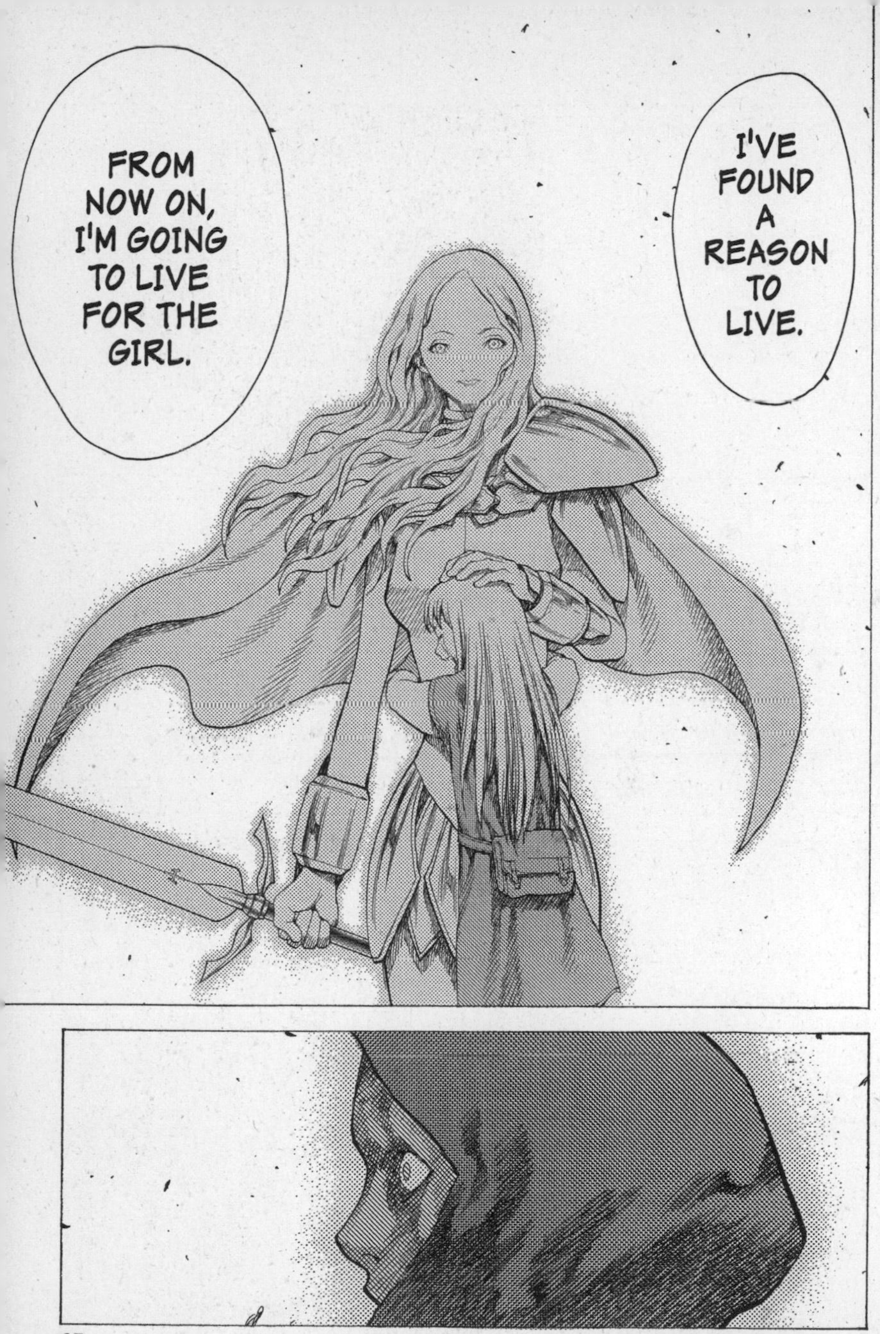
I'VE FOUND A REASON TO LIVE.
FROM NOW ON, I'M GOING TO LIVE FOR THE GIRL.

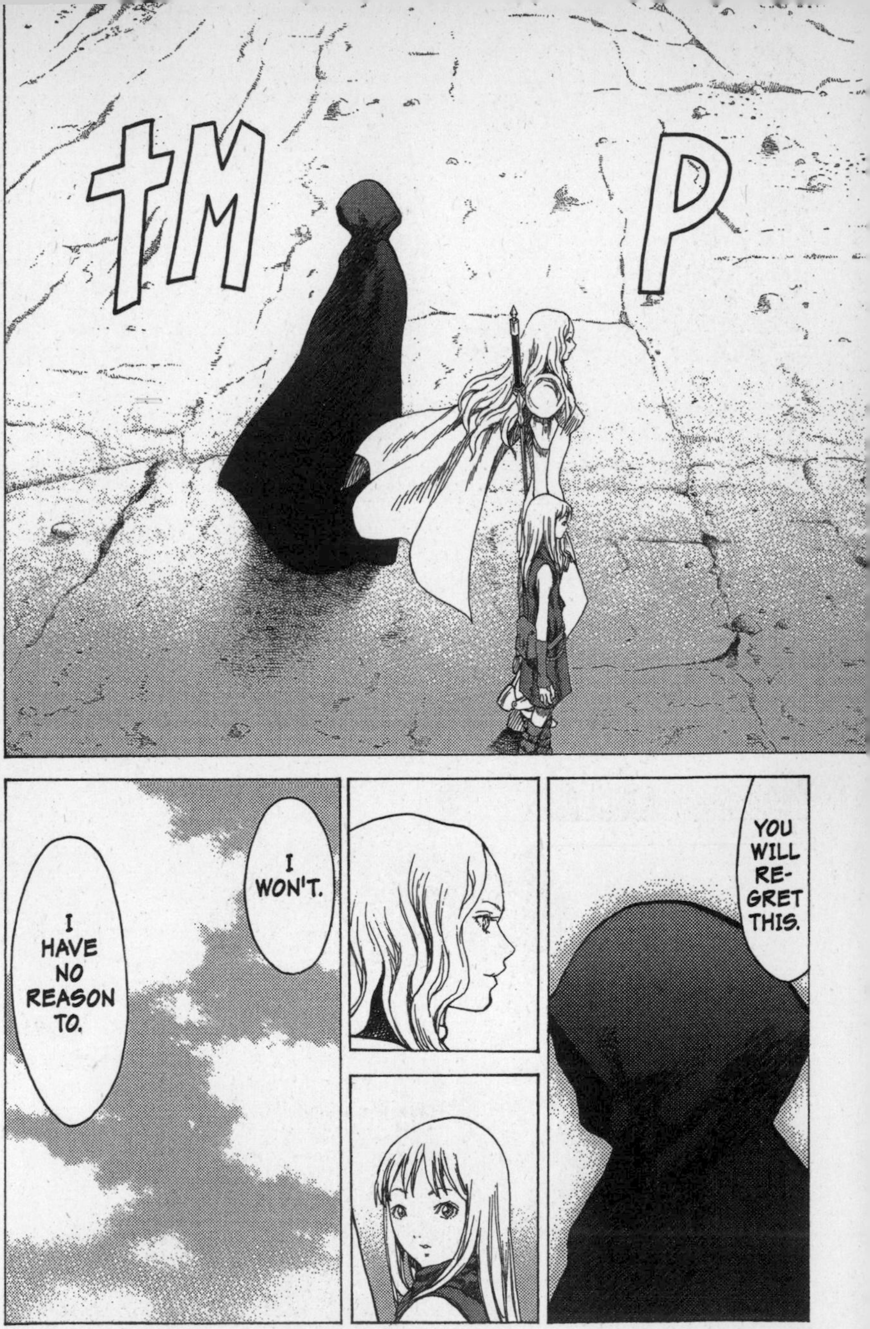
TMP
YOU WILL REGRET THIS.
I WON'T.
I HAVE NO REASON TO.

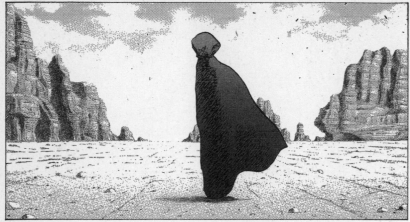

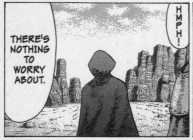

READ THIS WAY

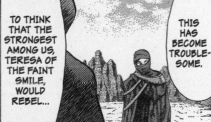

THIS HAS BECOME TROUBLE-SOME.
TO THINK THAT THE STRONGEST AMONG US, TERESA OF THE FAINT SMILE, WOULD REBEL...
HMPH!
THERE'S NOTHING TO WORRY ABOUT.
SUMMON NUMBERS TWO THROUGH FIVE...
...AND HAVE THEM SUBDUE TERESA.

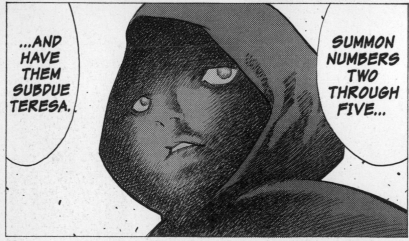

クレイモア
Claymore™

Scene 18: Marked for Death, Part 1

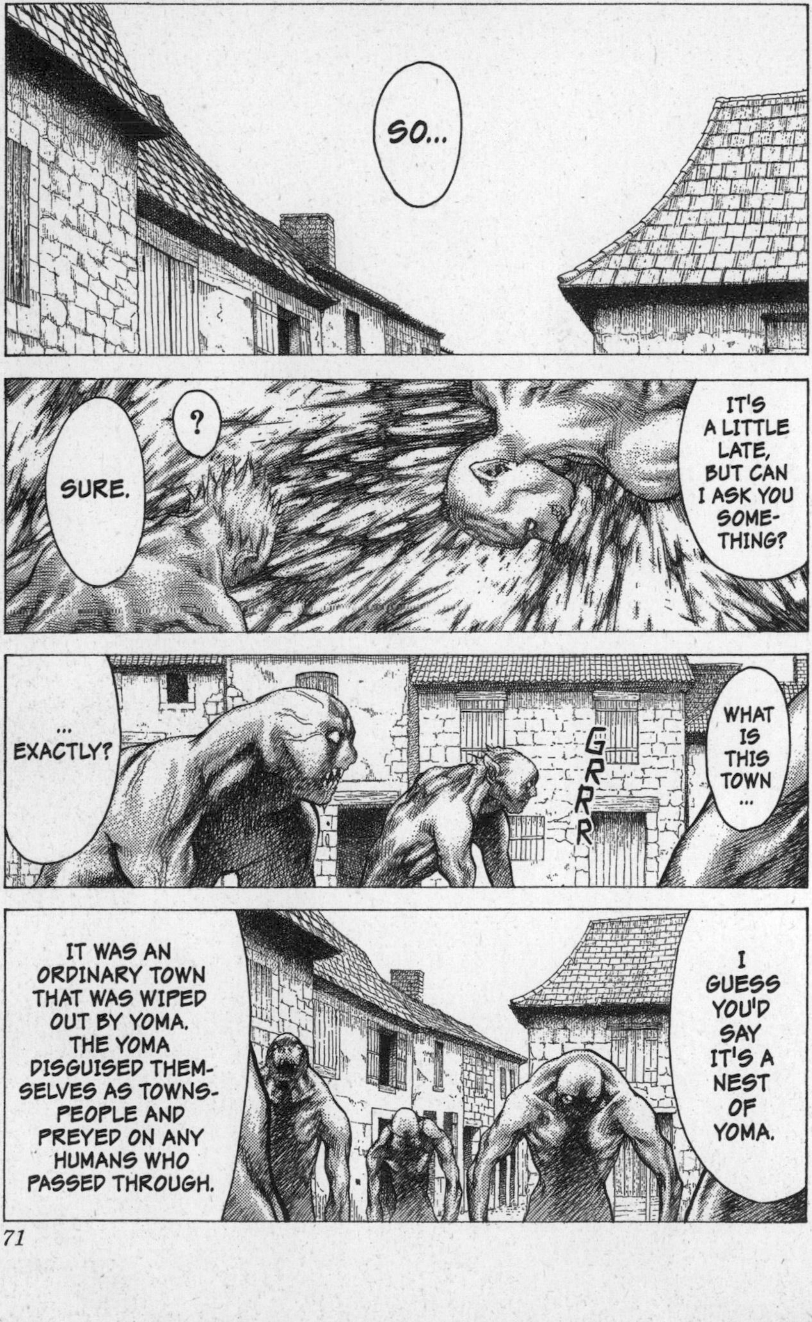
SO...
IT'S A LITTLE LATE, BUT CAN I ASK YOU SOME-THING?
?
SURE.
WHAT IS THIS TOWN ...
GRRR
... EXACTLY?
I GUESS YOU'D SAY IT'S A NEST OF YOMA.
IT WAS AN ORDINARY TOWN THAT WAS WIPED OUT BY YOMA. THE YOMA DISGUISED THEM-SELVES AS TOWNS-PEOPLE AND PREYED ON ANY HUMANS WHO PASSED THROUGH.

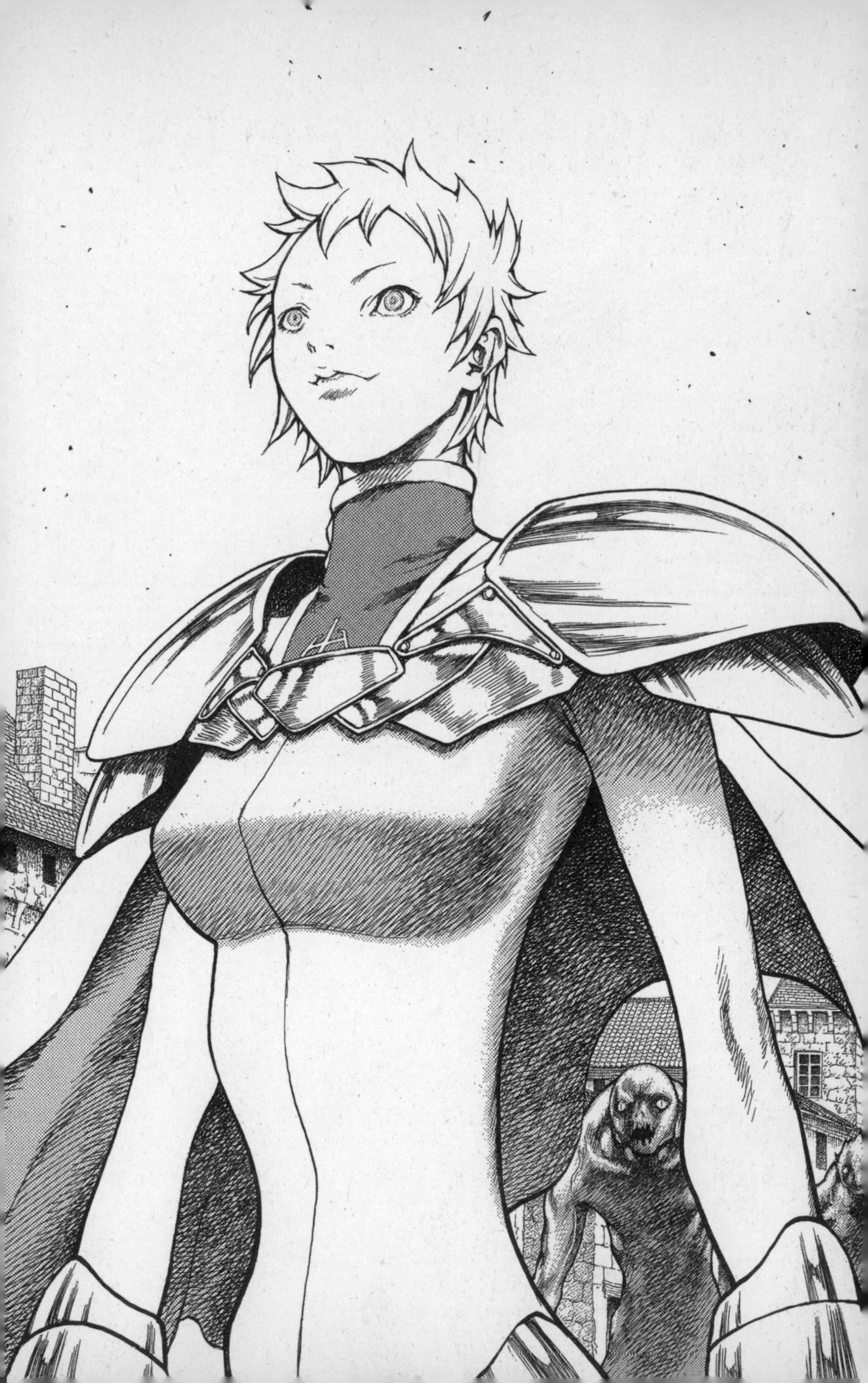

Scene 18: Marked for Death, Part 1

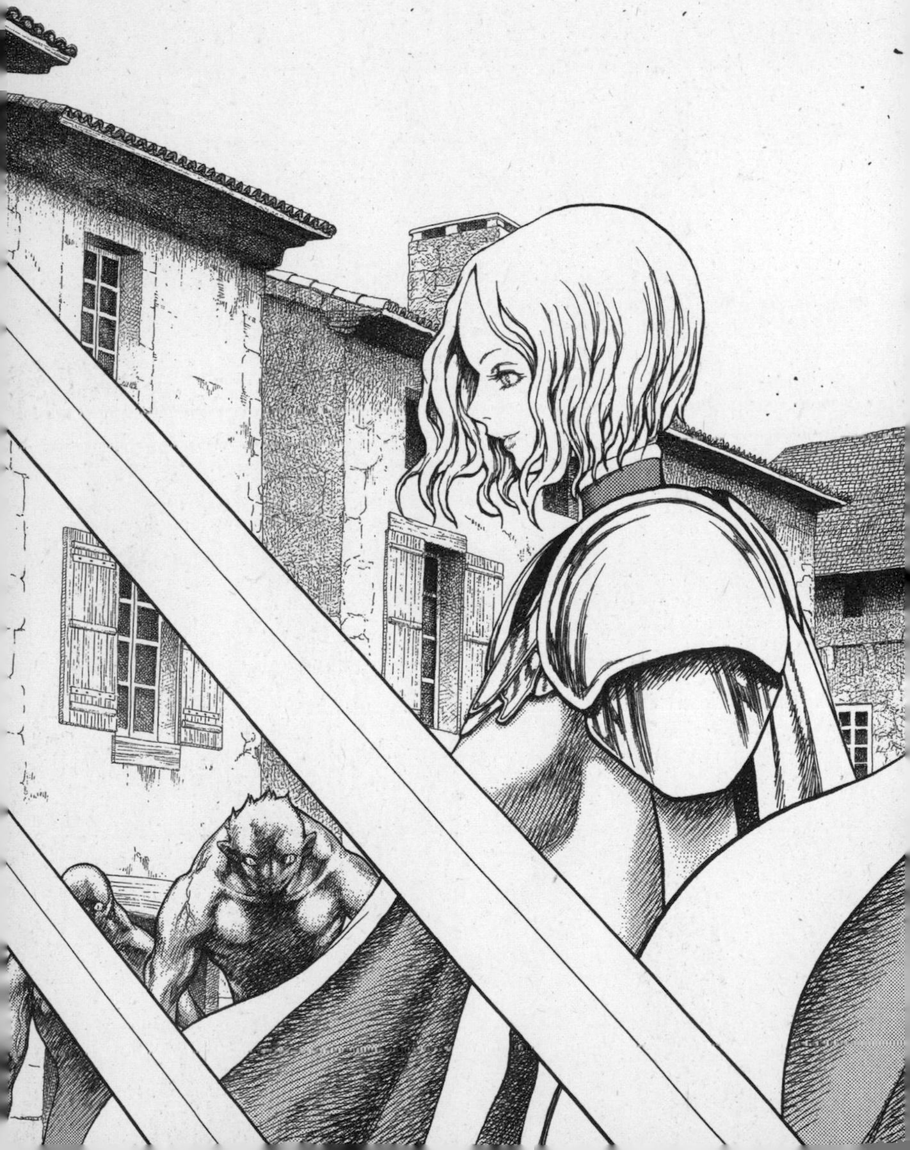

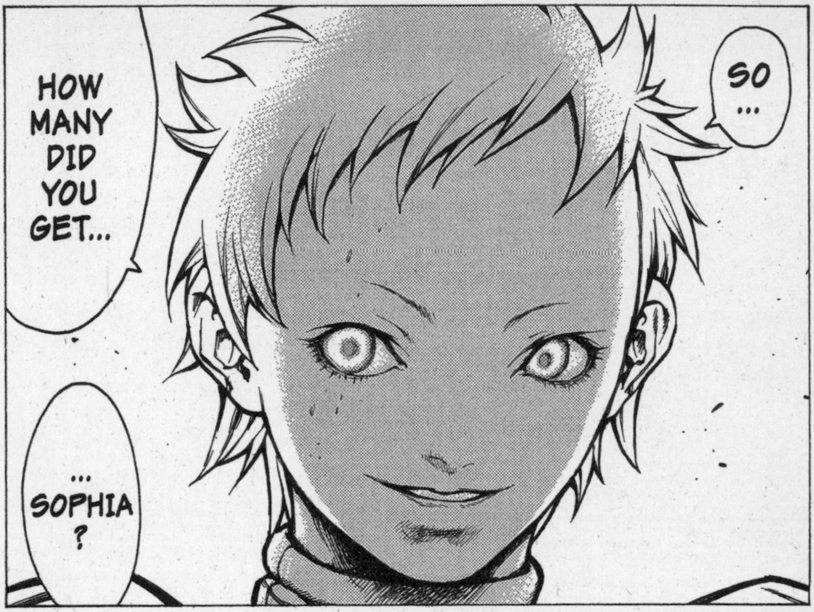
SO ...
HOW MANY DID YOU GET...
... SOPHIA?

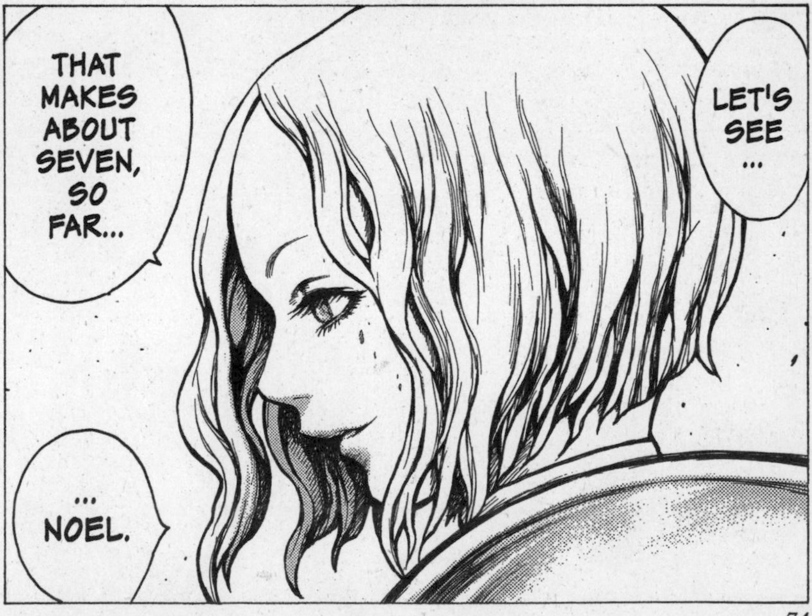
LET'S SEE ...
THAT MAKES ABOUT SEVEN, SO FAR...
... NOEL.

READ THIS WAY

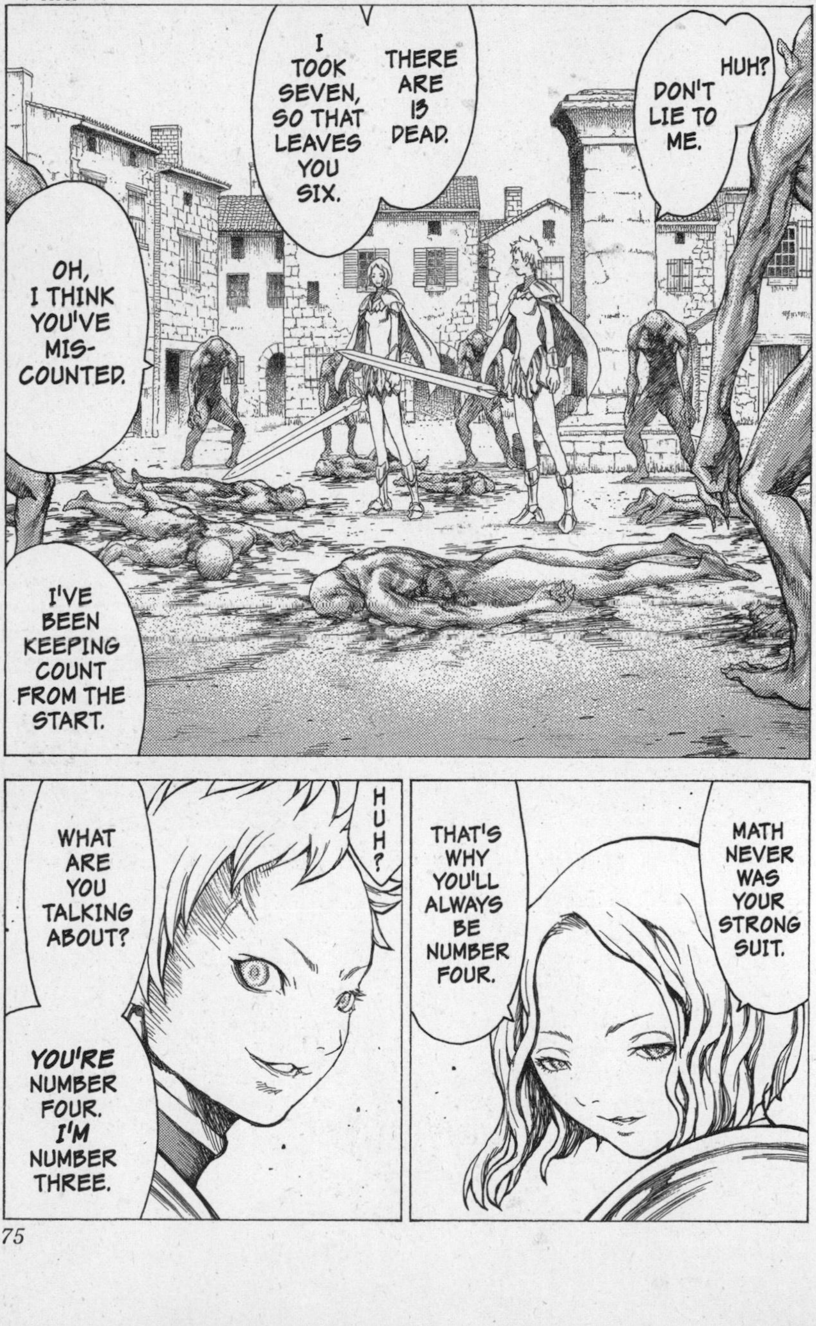
HUH? DON'T LIE TO ME.
THERE ARE 13 DEAD.
I TOOK SEVEN, SO THAT LEAVES YOU SIX.
OH, I THINK YOU'VE MIS-COUNTED.
I'VE BEEN KEEPING COUNT FROM THE START.
MATH NEVER WAS YOUR STRONG SUIT.
THAT'S WHY YOU'LL ALWAYS BE NUMBER FOUR.
HUH?
WHAT ARE YOU TALKING ABOUT?
YOU'RE NUMBER FOUR. I'M NUMBER THREE.

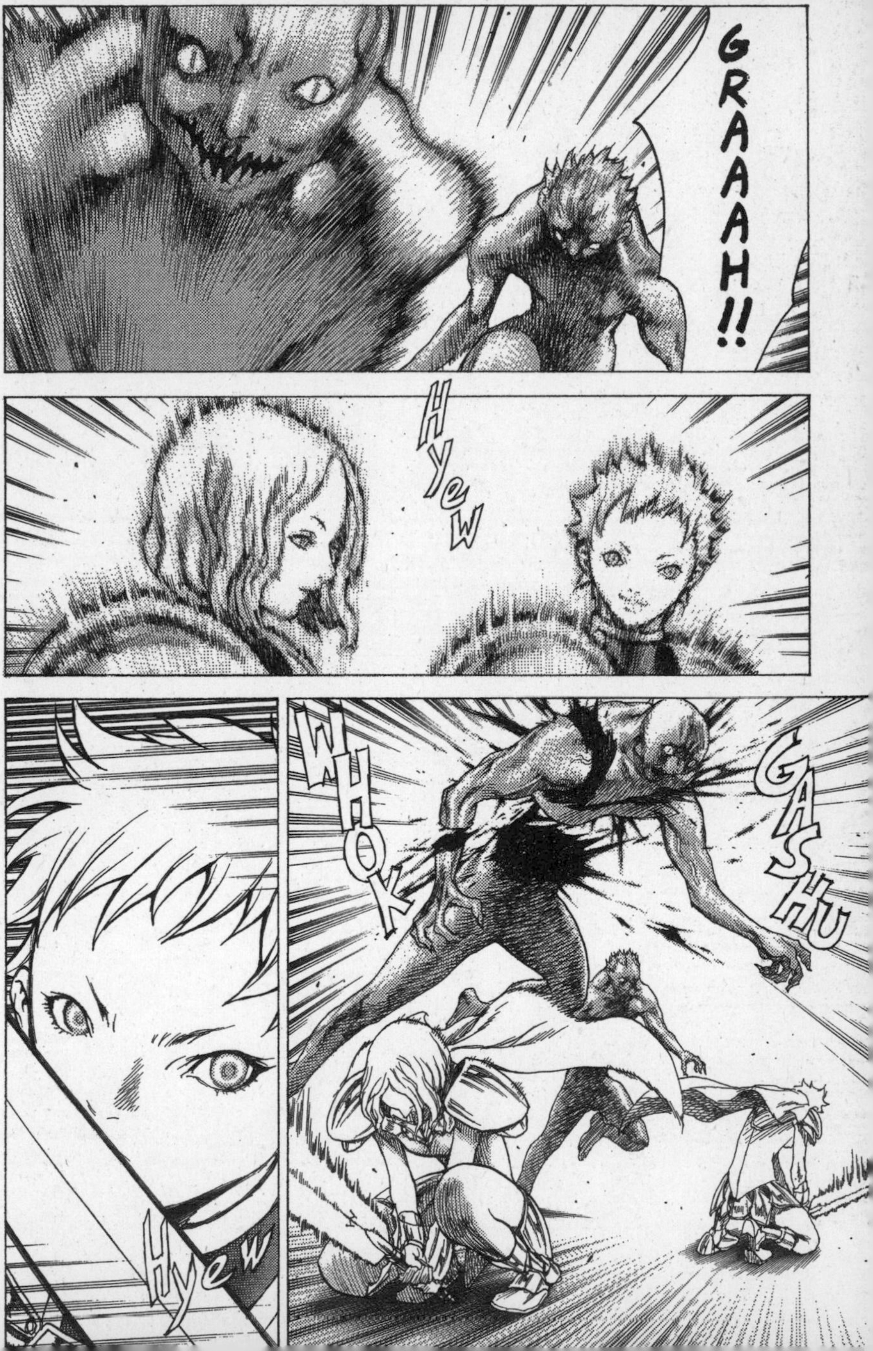
GRAAAAH!!
Hyew
GASHU
WHOK
Hyew

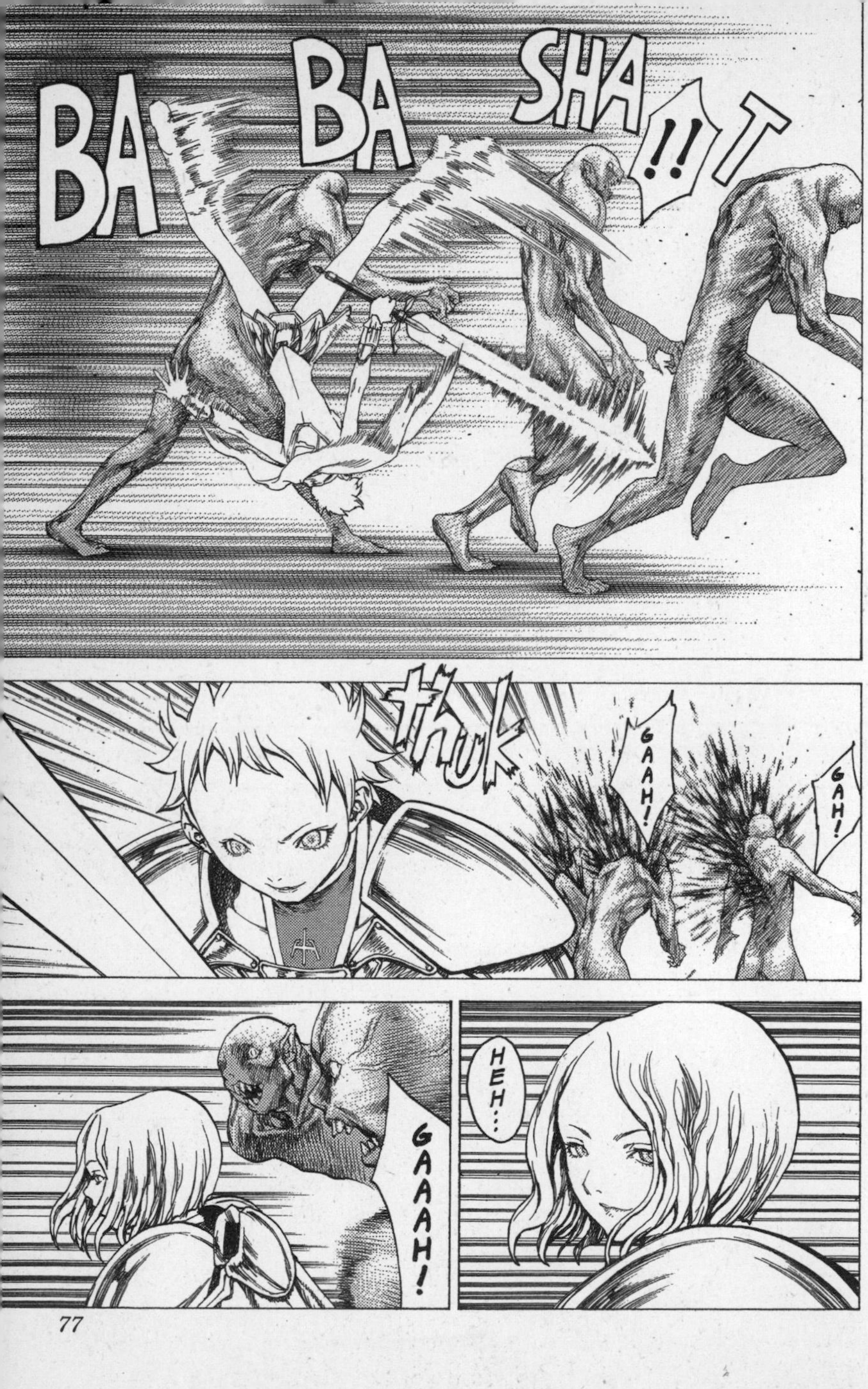
SHA!!T
BA
BA
GAH!
GAAAH!
thuk
HEH...
GAAAAH!

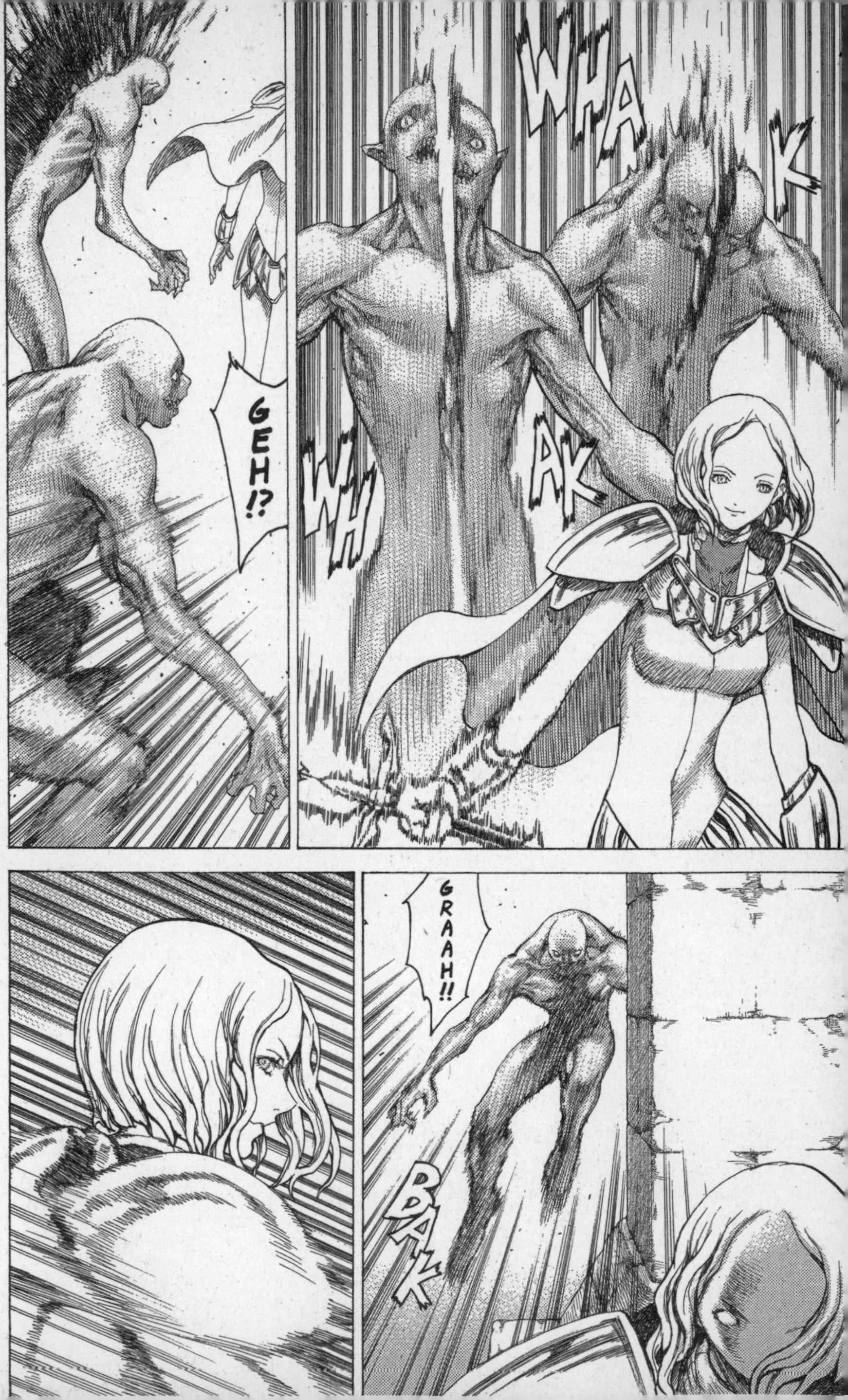
WHAK
WHAK
GEH!?
GRAAAH!!
BAK

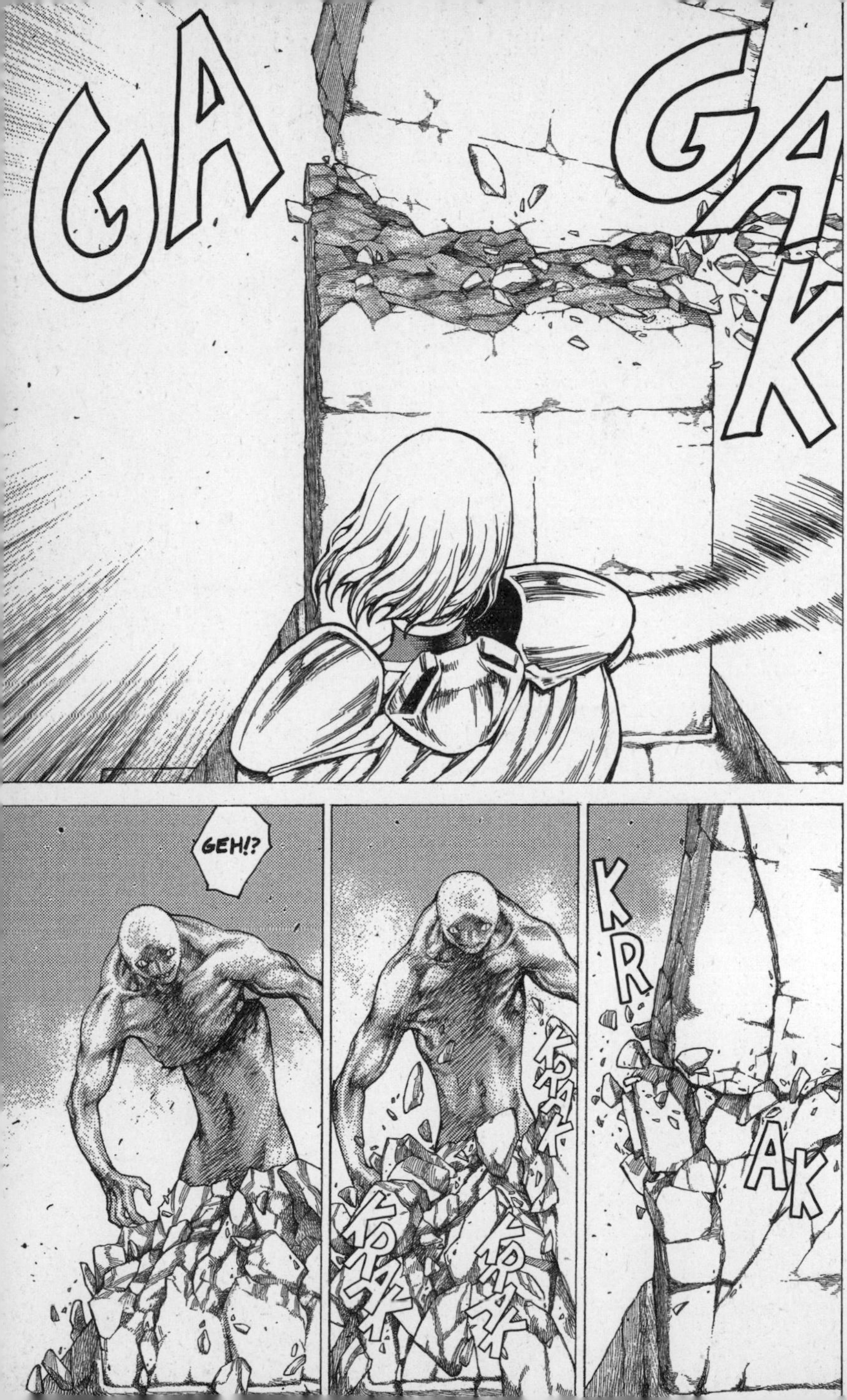
GAK
GA
KR
AK
KRAK
KRAK
KRAK
GEH!?

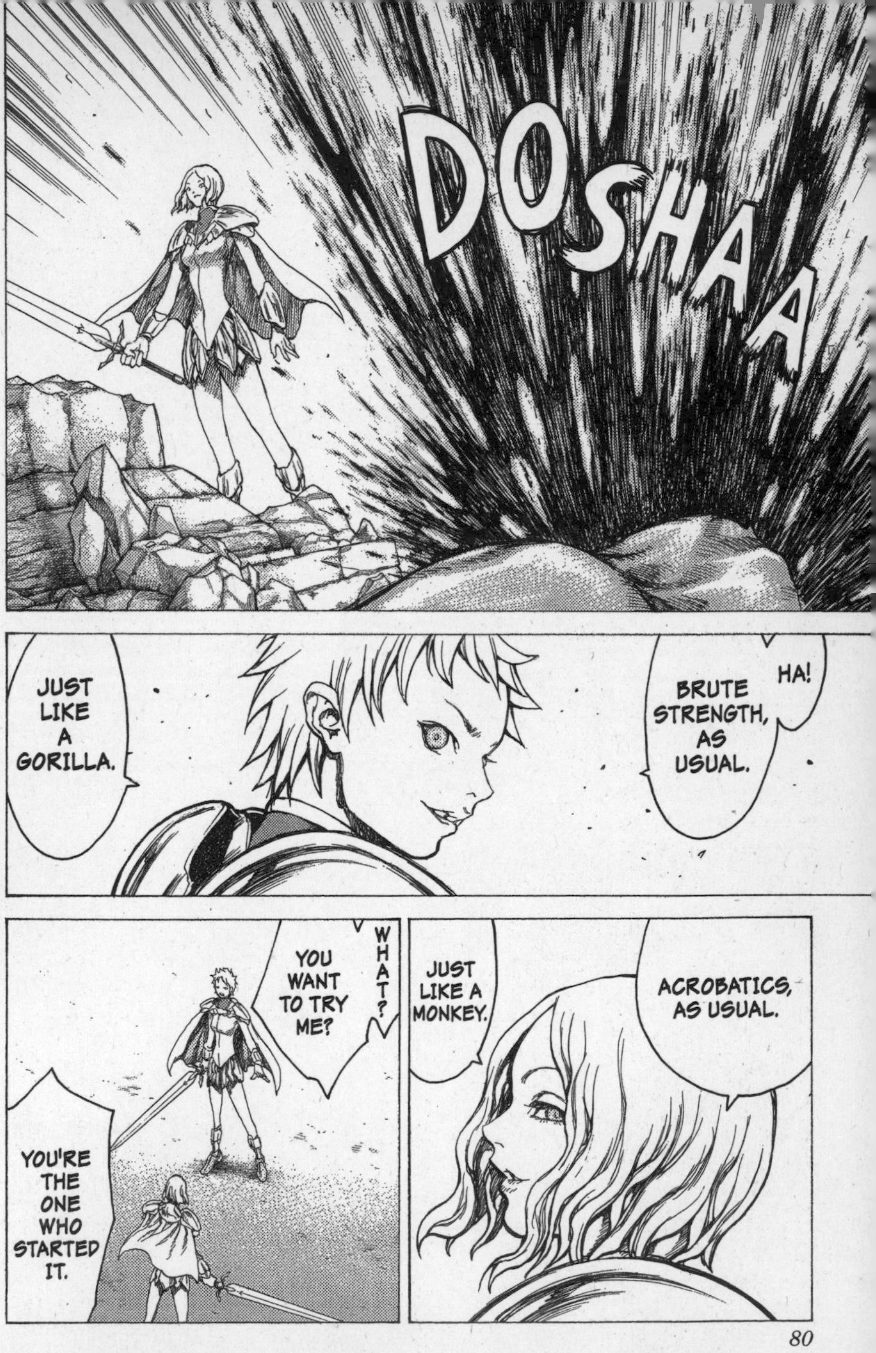
DOSHAA
HA!
BRUTE STRENGTH, AS USUAL.
JUST LIKE A GORILLA.
ACROBATICS, AS USUAL.
JUST LIKE A MONKEY.
WHAT?
YOU WANT TO TRY ME?
YOU'RE THE ONE WHO STARTED IT.

READ THIS WAY

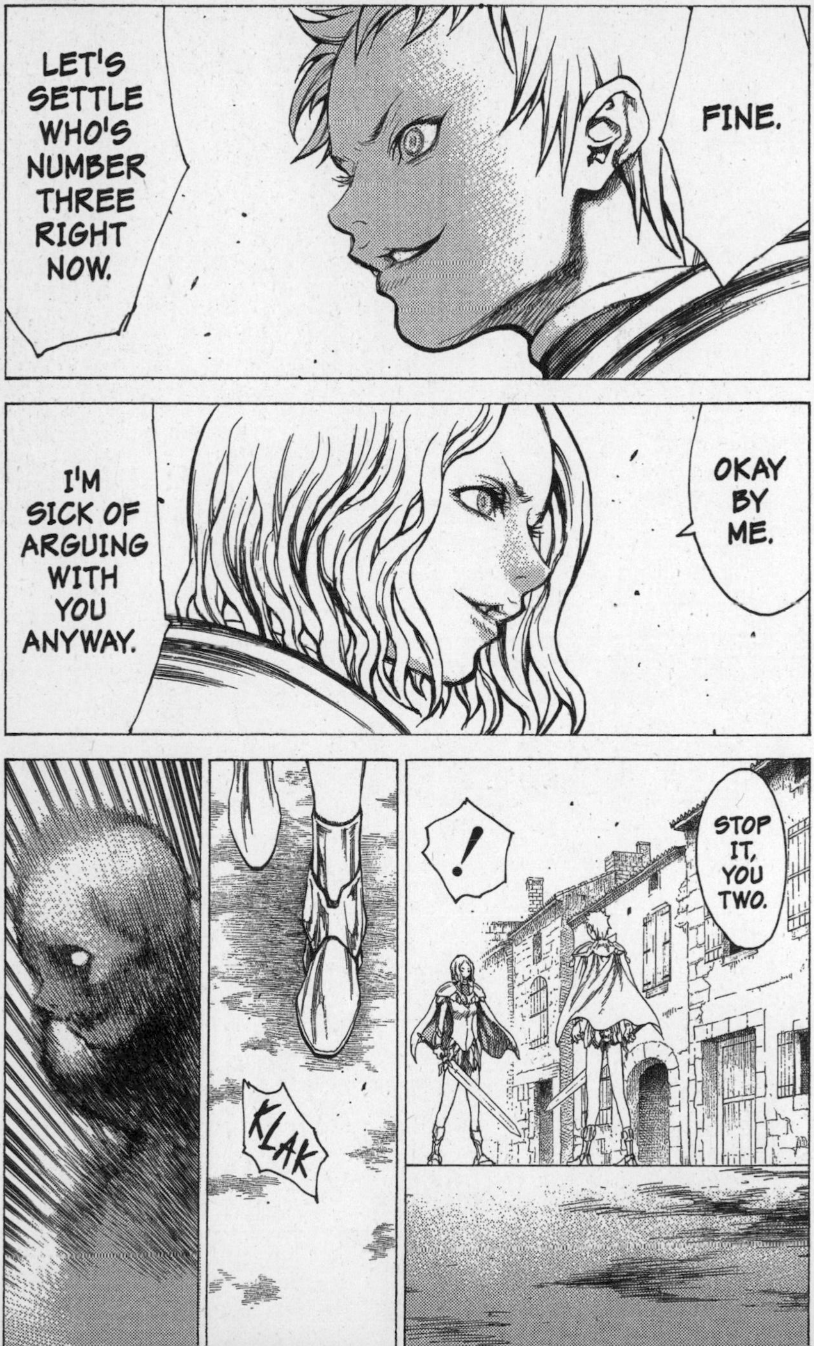
FINE.
LET'S SETTLE WHO'S NUMBER THREE RIGHT NOW.
OKAY BY ME.
I'M SICK OF ARGUING WITH YOU ANYWAY.
STOP IT, YOU TWO.
!
KLAK

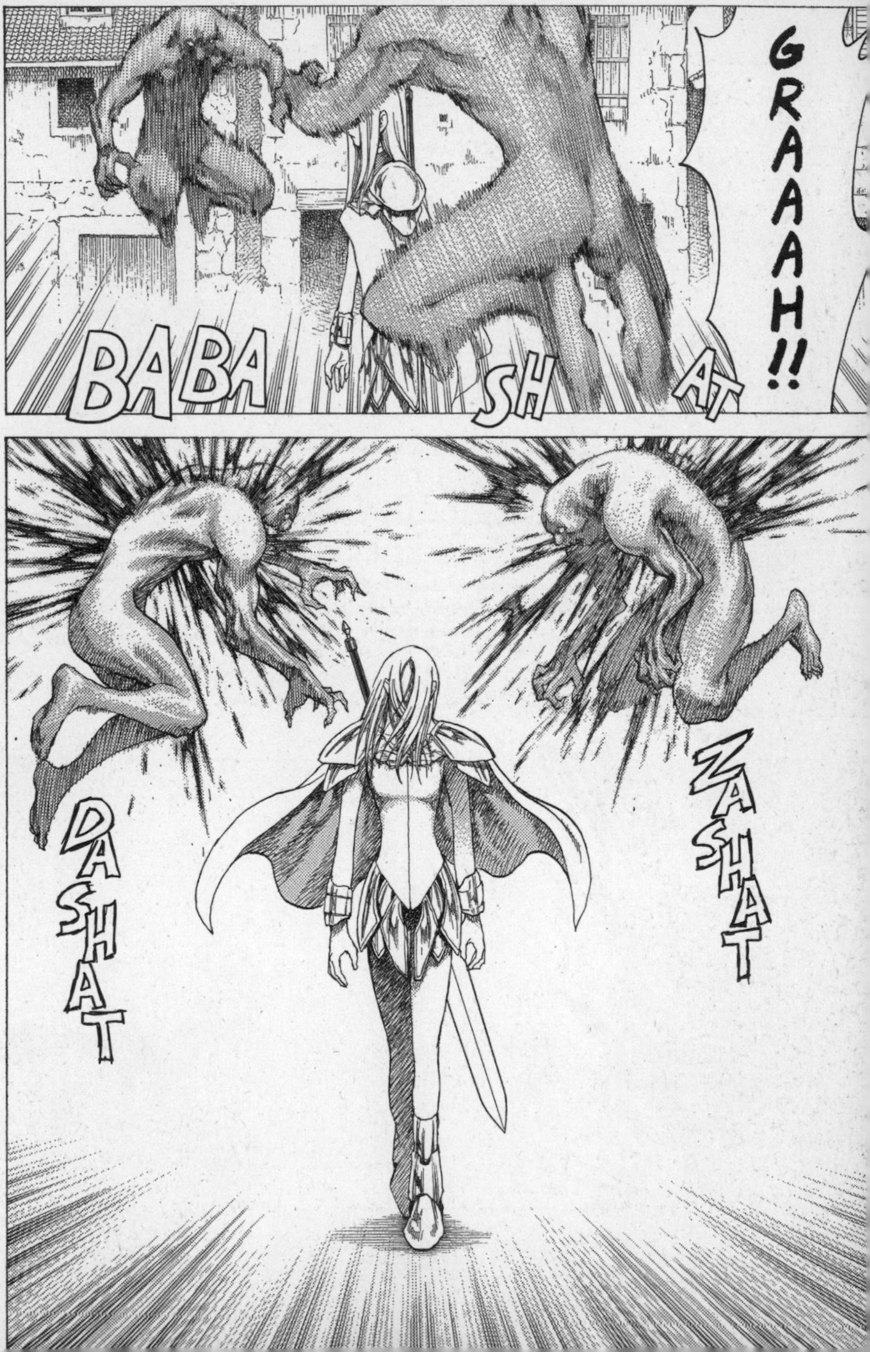
GRAAAH!!
BABA SH AT
ZASHAT
DASHAT

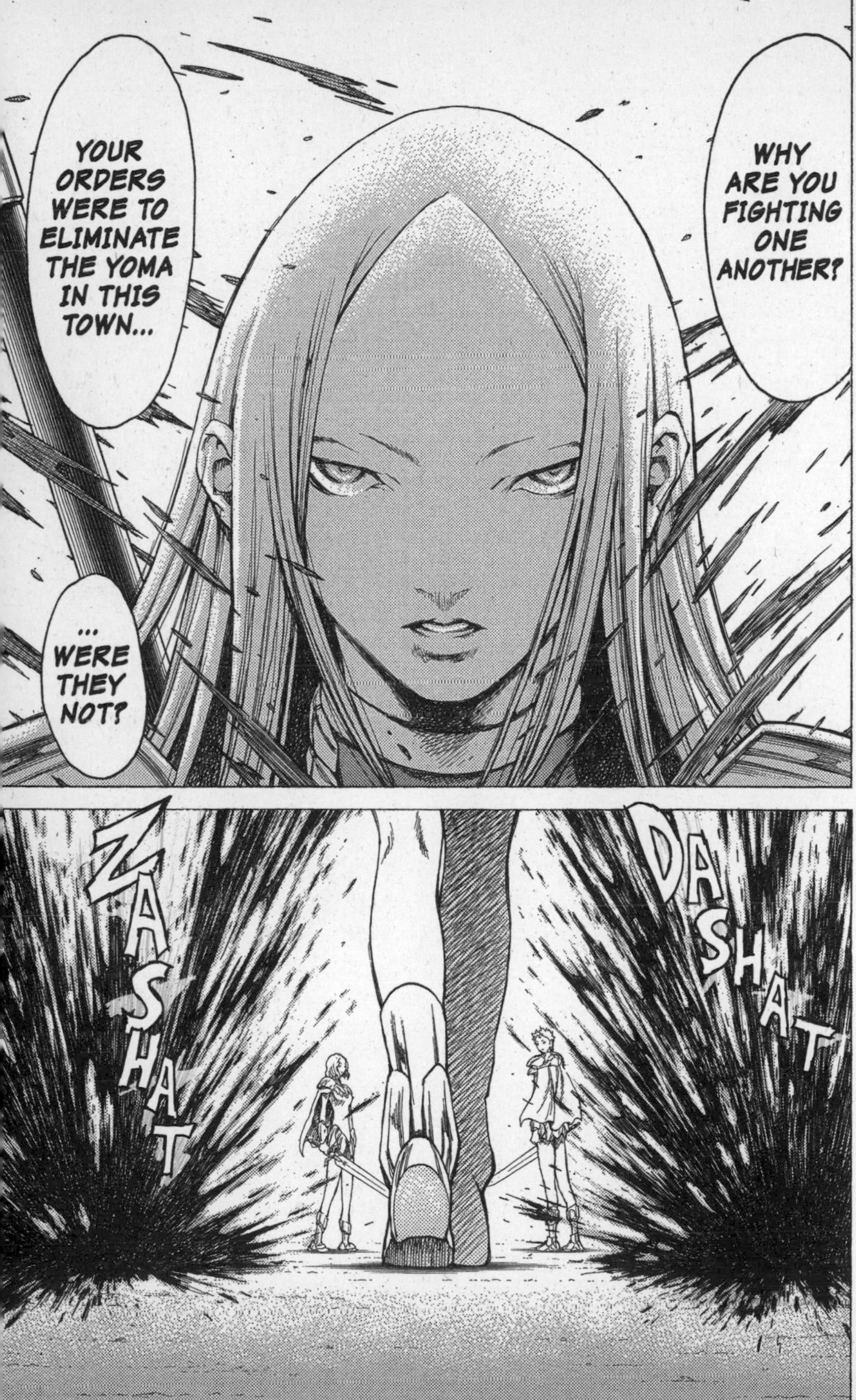
WHY ARE YOU FIGHTING ONE ANOTHER?
YOUR ORDERS WERE TO ELIMINATE THE YOMA IN THIS TOWN...
... WERE THEY NOT?
DASHAT
ZASHAT

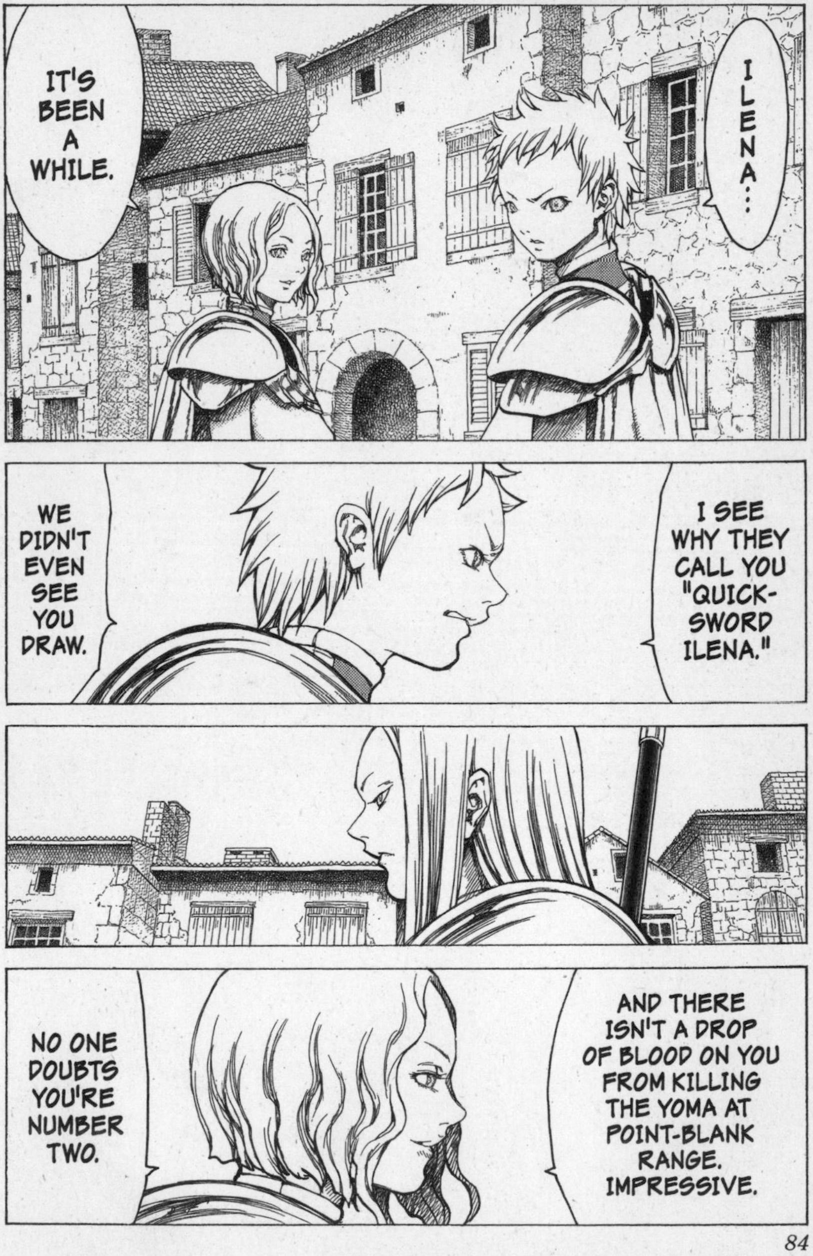
ILENA...
IT'S BEEN A WHILE.
I SEE WHY THEY CALL YOU "QUICK-SWORD ILENA."
WE DIDN'T EVEN SEE YOU DRAW.
AND THERE ISN'T A DROP OF BLOOD ON YOU FROM KILLING THE YOMA AT POINT-BLANK RANGE. IMPRESSIVE.
NO ONE DOUBTS YOU'RE NUMBER TWO.

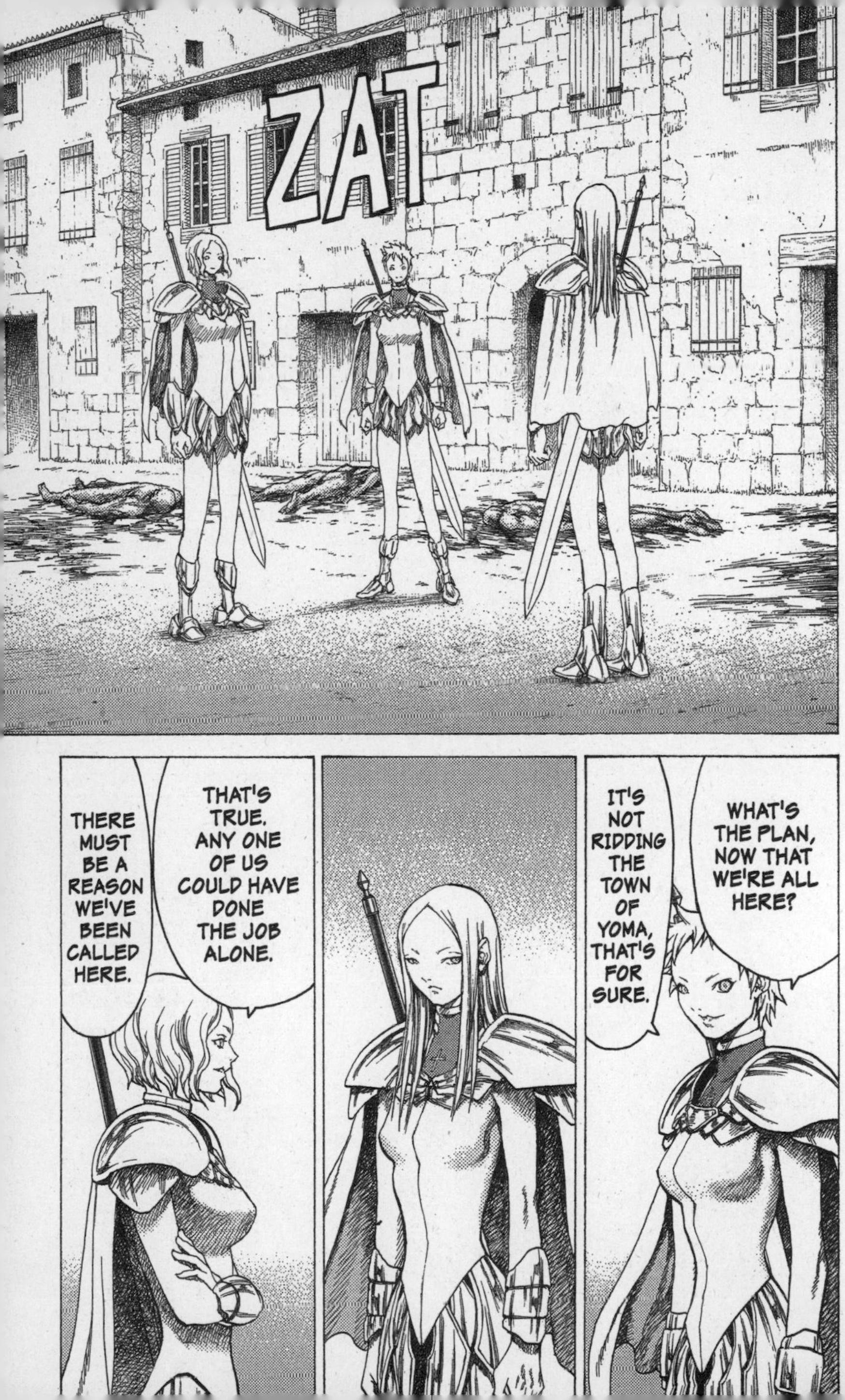
ZAT
WHAT'S THE PLAN, NOW THAT WE'RE ALL HERE?
IT'S NOT RIDDING THE TOWN OF YOMA, THAT'S FOR SURE.
THAT'S TRUE. ANY ONE OF US COULD HAVE DONE THE JOB ALONE.
THERE MUST BE A REASON WE'VE BEEN CALLED HERE.

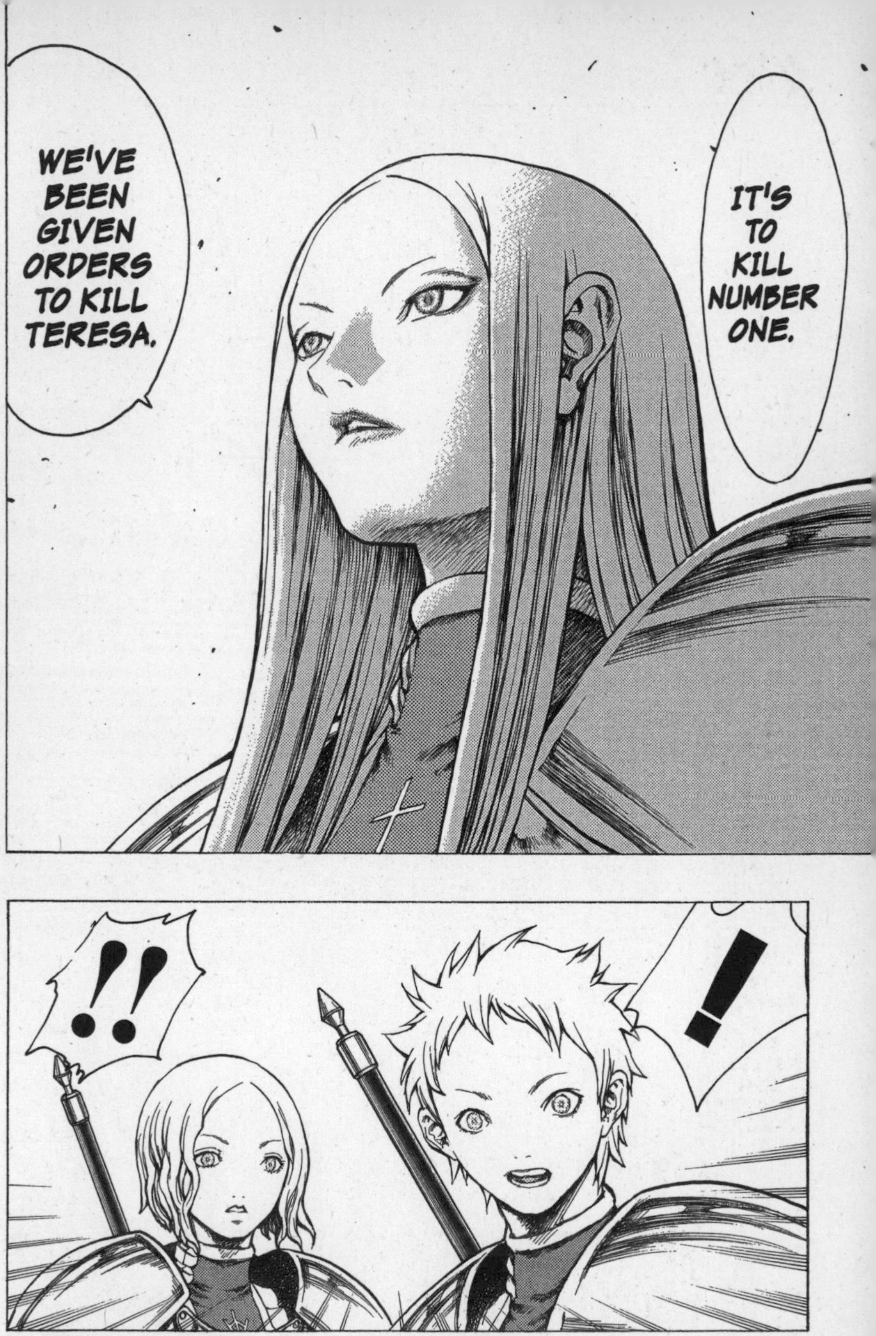
IT'S TO KILL NUMBER ONE.
WE'VE BEEN GIVEN ORDERS TO KILL TERESA.
!
!!

READ THIS WAY

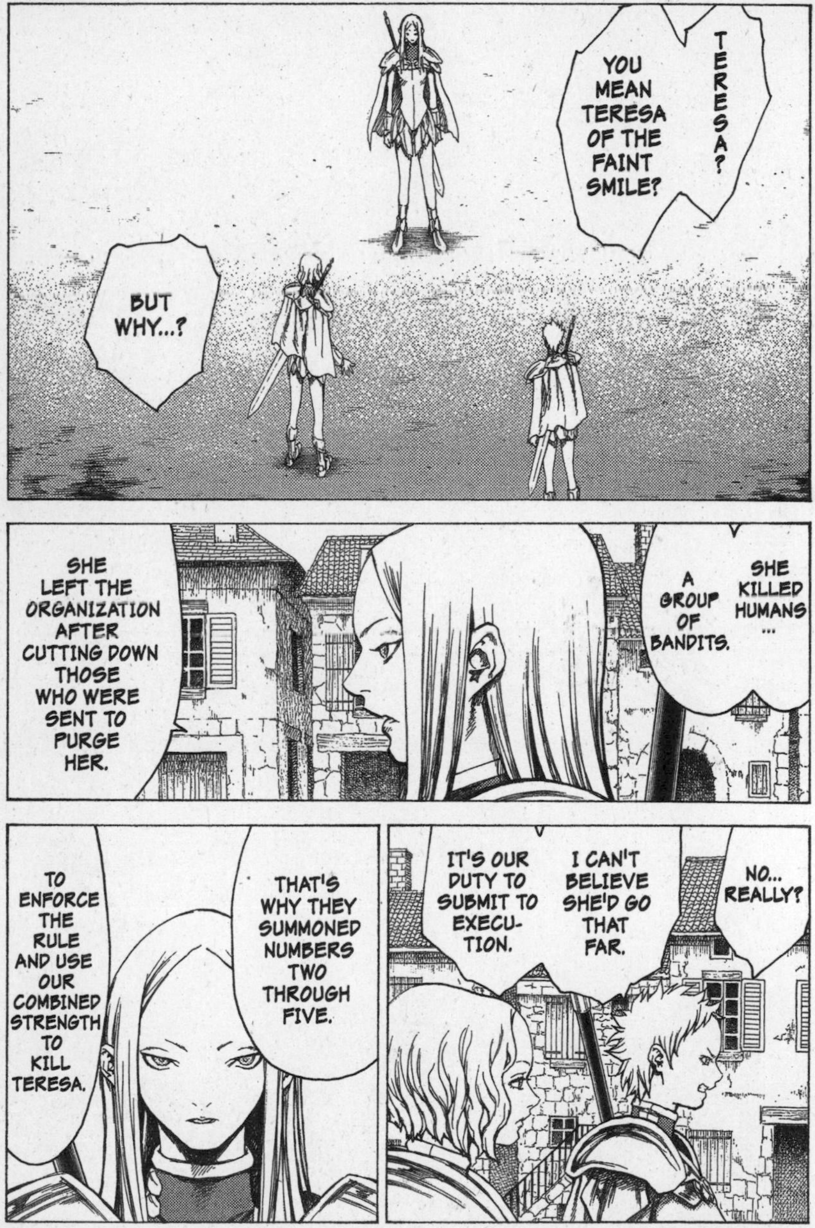
TERESA?
YOU MEAN TERESA OF THE FAINT SMILE?
BUT WHY...?
SHE KILLED HUMANS...
A GROUP OF BANDITS.
SHE LEFT THE ORGANIZATION AFTER CUTTING DOWN THOSE WHO WERE SENT TO PURGE HER.
NO... REALLY?
I CAN'T BELIEVE SHE'D GO THAT FAR.
IT'S OUR DUTY TO SUBMIT TO EXECU-TION.
THAT'S WHY THEY SUMMONED NUMBERS TWO THROUGH FIVE.
TO ENFORCE THE RULE AND USE OUR COMBINED STRENGTH TO KILL TERESA.

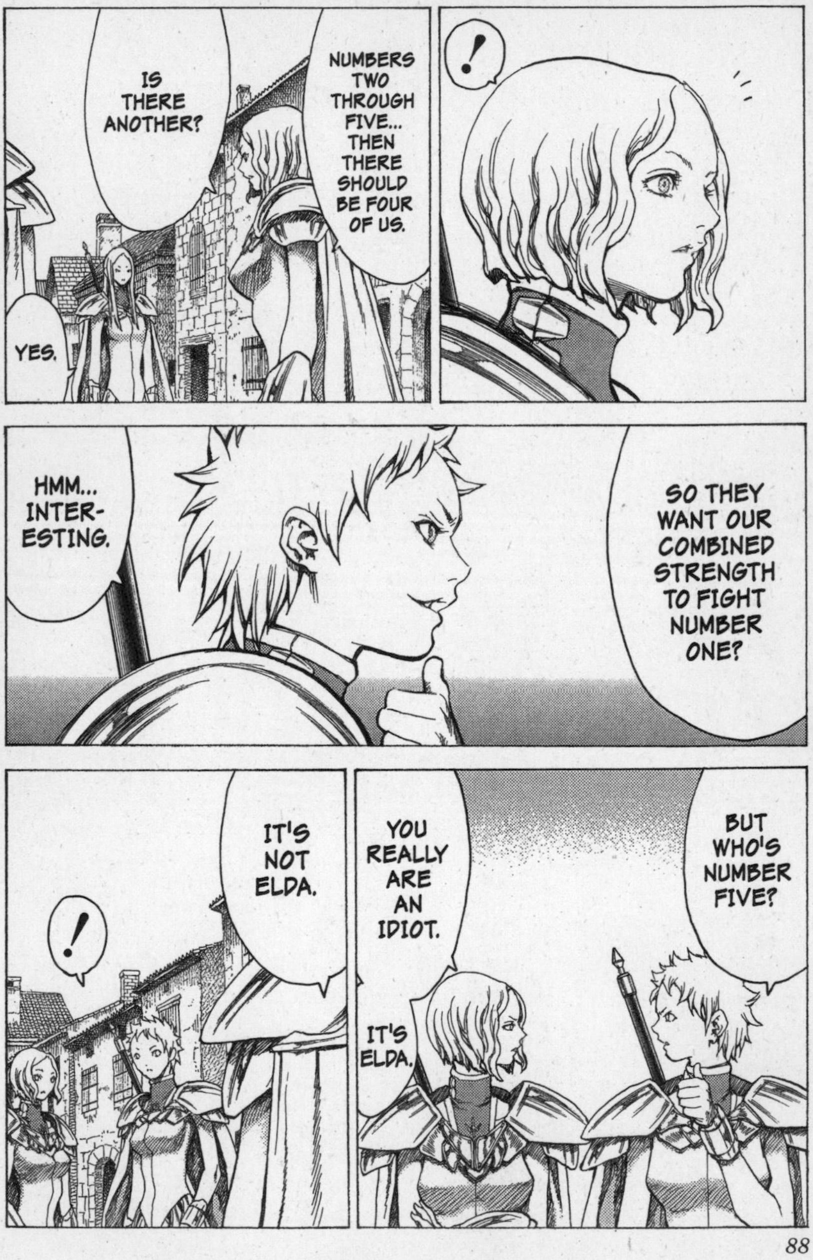
!
NUMBERS TWO THROUGH FIVE... THEN THERE SHOULD BE FOUR OF US.
IS THERE ANOTHER?
YES.
SO THEY WANT OUR COMBINED STRENGTH TO FIGHT NUMBER ONE?
HMM... INTER-ESTING.
BUT WHO'S NUMBER FIVE?
YOU REALLY ARE AN IDIOT.
IT'S ELDA.
IT'S NOT ELDA.
!

READ THIS WAY

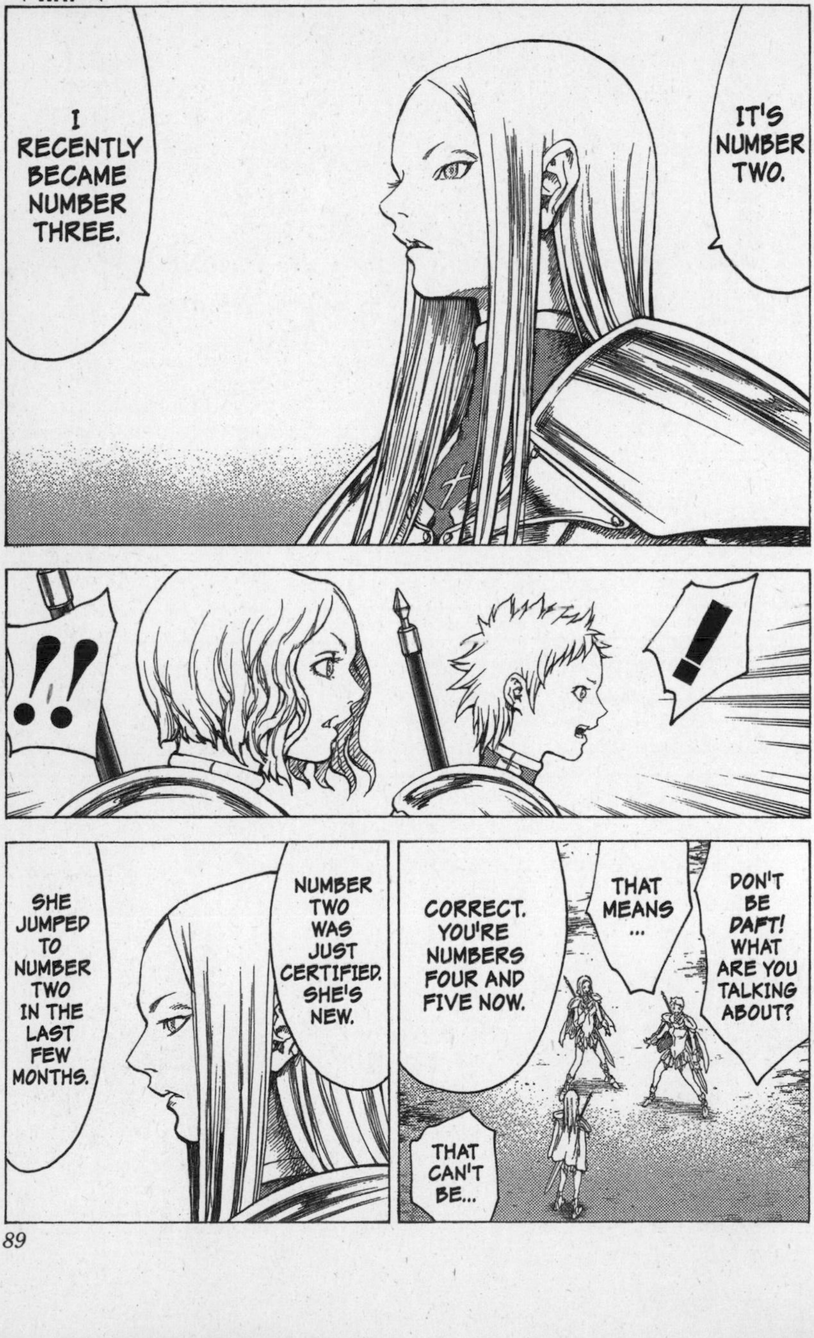
IT'S NUMBER TWO.
I RECENTLY BECAME NUMBER THREE.
!
!!
DON'T BE DAFT! WHAT ARE YOU TALKING ABOUT?
THAT MEANS ...
CORRECT. YOU'RE NUMBERS FOUR AND FIVE NOW.
THAT CAN'T BE...
NUMBER TWO WAS JUST CERTIFIED. SHE'S NEW.
SHE JUMPED TO NUMBER TWO IN THE LAST FEW MONTHS.

A NOVICE? HOW DOES SOMEONE LIKE THAT GET MADE NUMBER TWO!?
DON'T MAKE ME LAUGH!
IF YOU HAVE A PROBLEM WITH IT, TAKE THE NUMBER TWO SPOT YOUR-SELF.
ONE LOOK WAS ENOUGH TO SATISFY ME.
HUH?
!
EEEK!!
thump

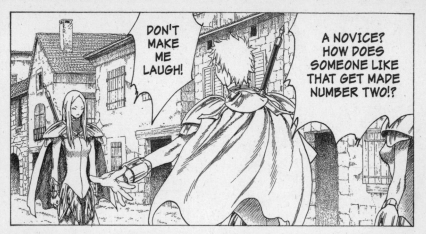

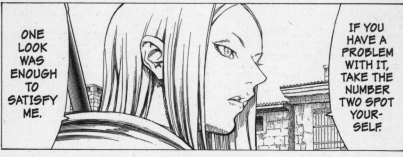

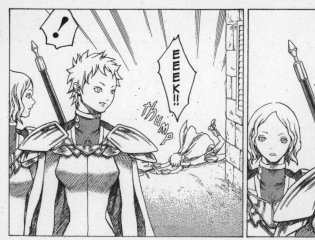

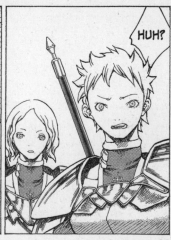

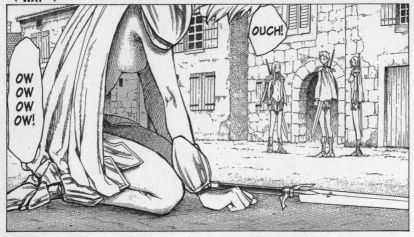

OUCH!

OW OW OW OW!

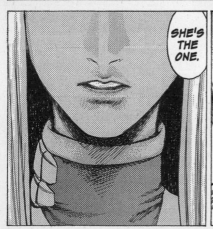

THERE WERE MORE OF US?

WHAT AN IDIOT!

WHO'S THAT?

SHE'S THE ONE.

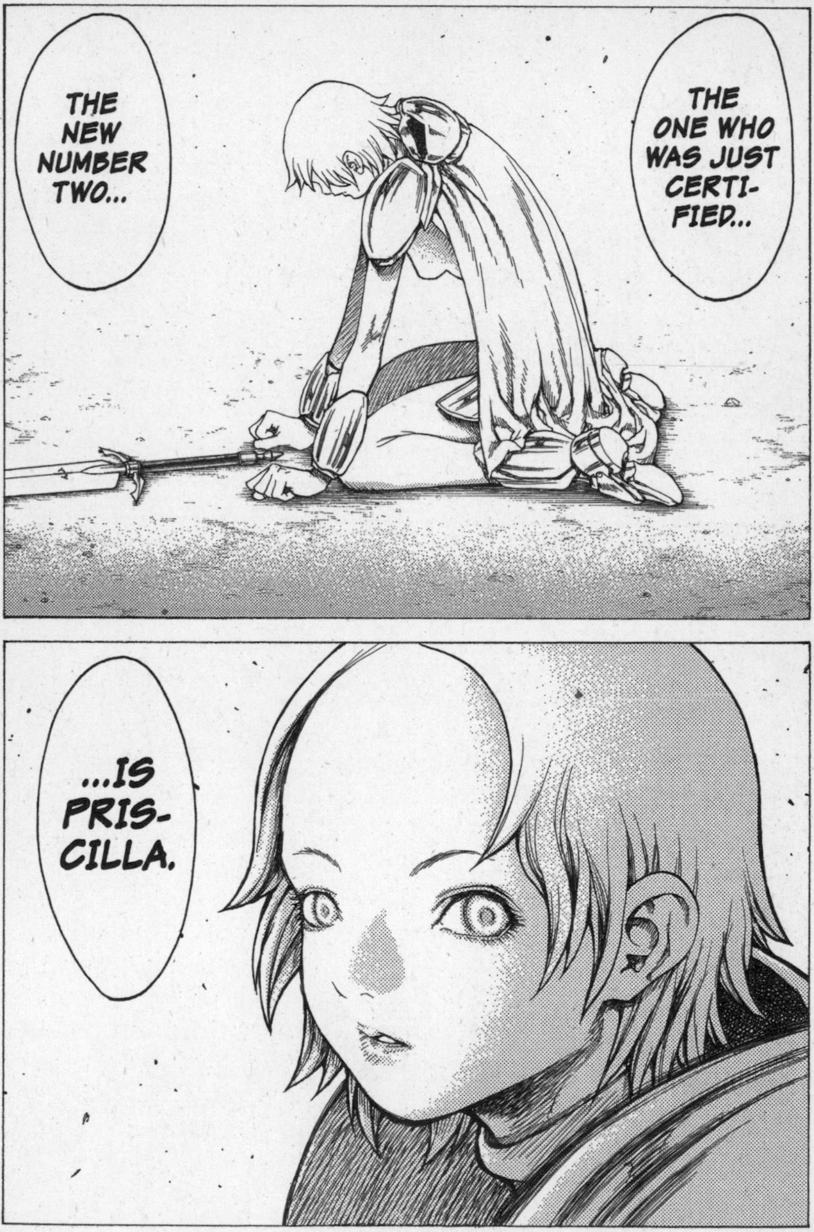
THE ONE WHO WAS JUST CERTI-FIED...
THE NEW NUMBER TWO...
...IS PRIS-CILLA.

READ THIS WAY

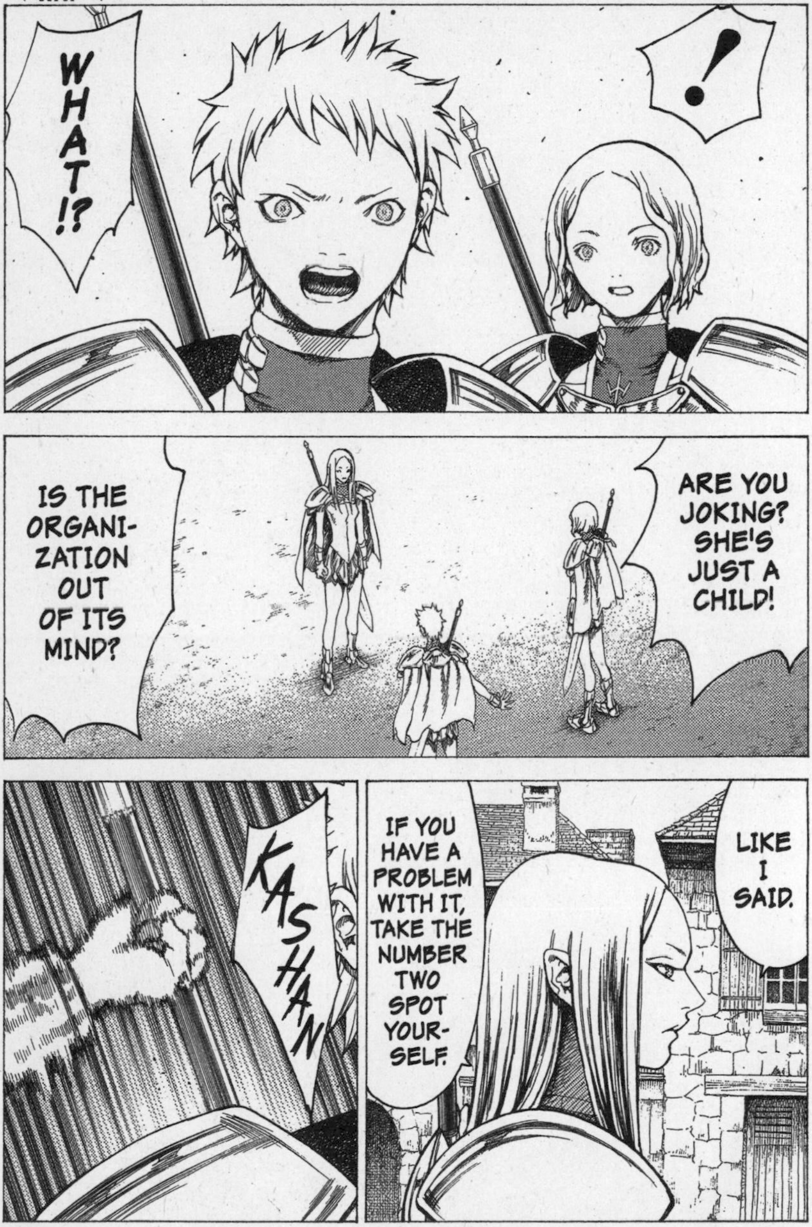
!
WHAT!?
ARE YOU JOKING? SHE'S JUST A CHILD!
IS THE ORGANIZATION OUT OF ITS MIND?
LIKE I SAID.
IF YOU HAVE A PROBLEM WITH IT, TAKE THE NUMBER TWO SPOT YOURSELF.
KASHAN

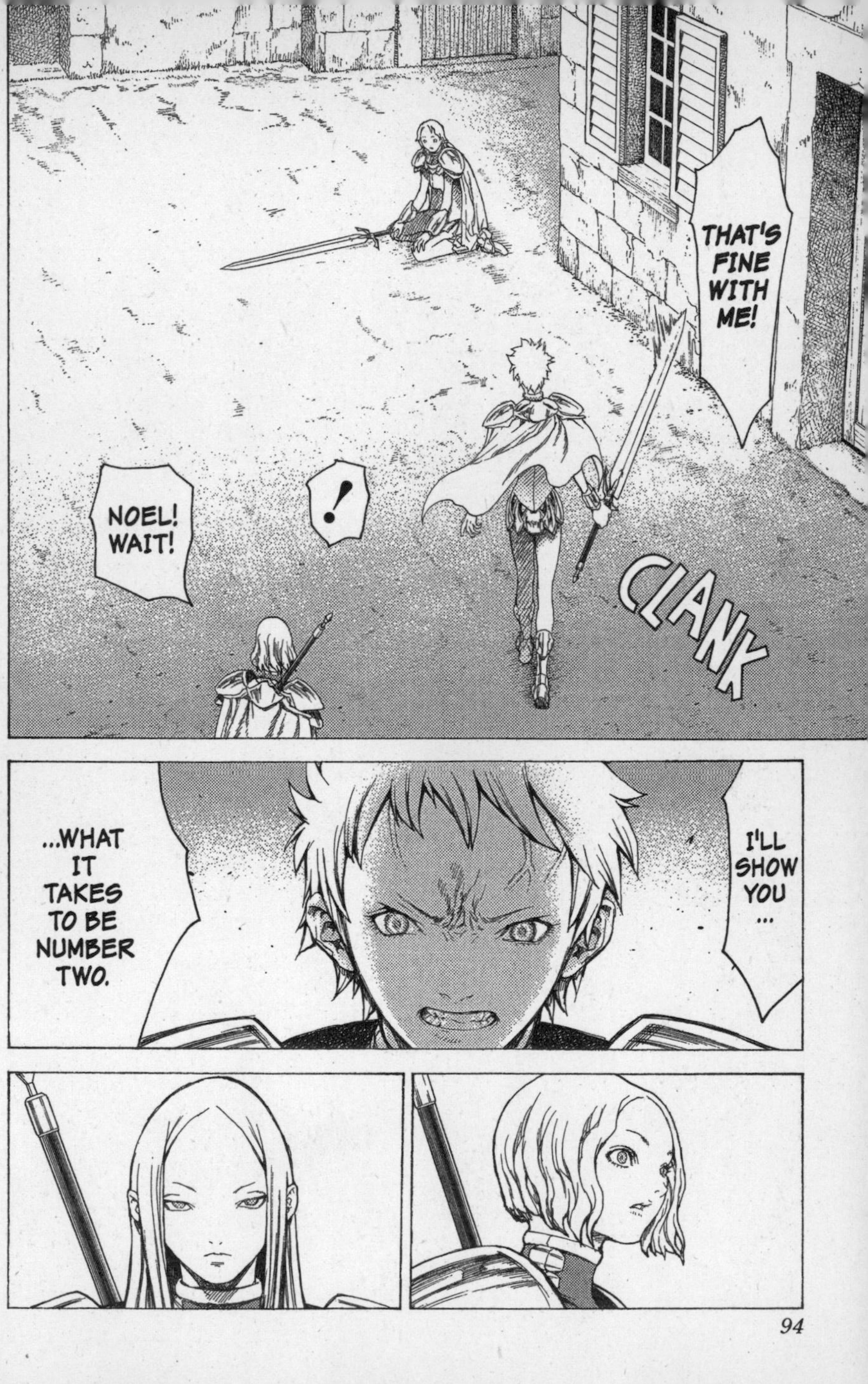
THAT'S FINE WITH ME!
CLANK
!
NOEL! WAIT!
I'LL SHOW YOU ...
...WHAT IT TAKES TO BE NUMBER TWO.

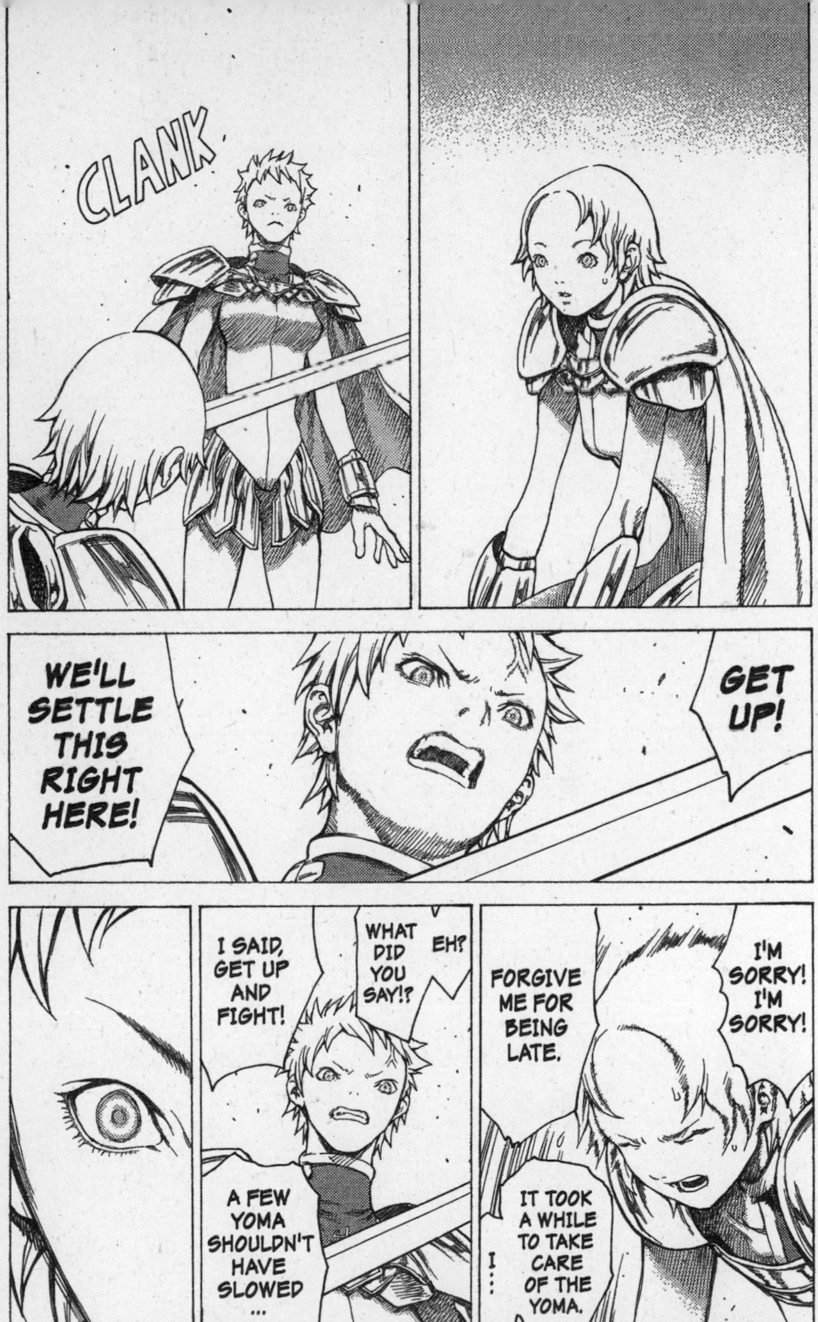
CLANK
GET UP!
WE'LL SETTLE THIS RIGHT HERE!
I'M SORRY! I'M SORRY!
FORGIVE ME FOR BEING LATE.
IT TOOK A WHILE TO TAKE CARE OF THE YOMA.
I...
EH?
WHAT DID YOU SAY!?
I SAID, GET UP AND FIGHT!
A FEW YOMA SHOULDN'T HAVE SLOWED ...

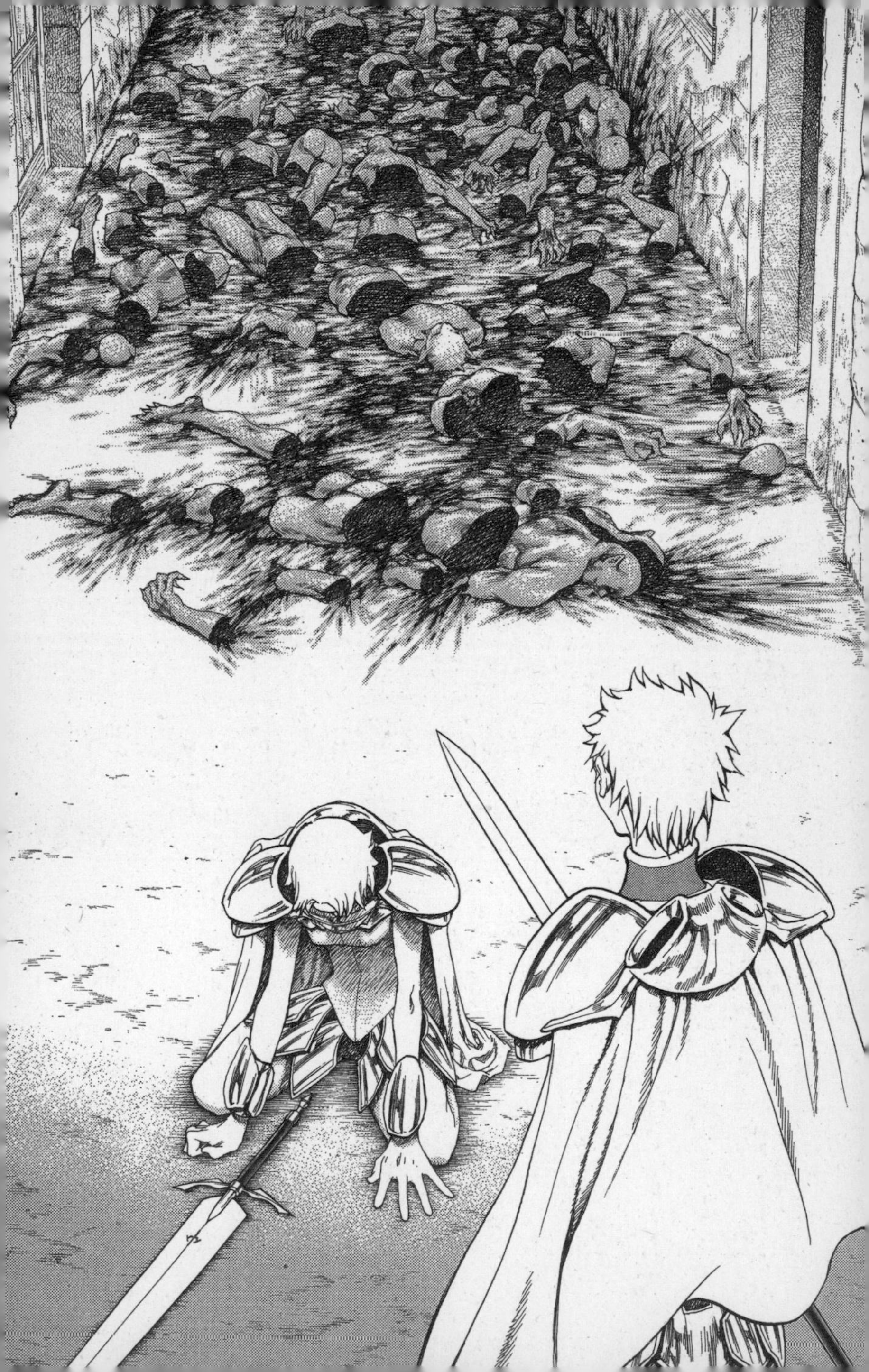

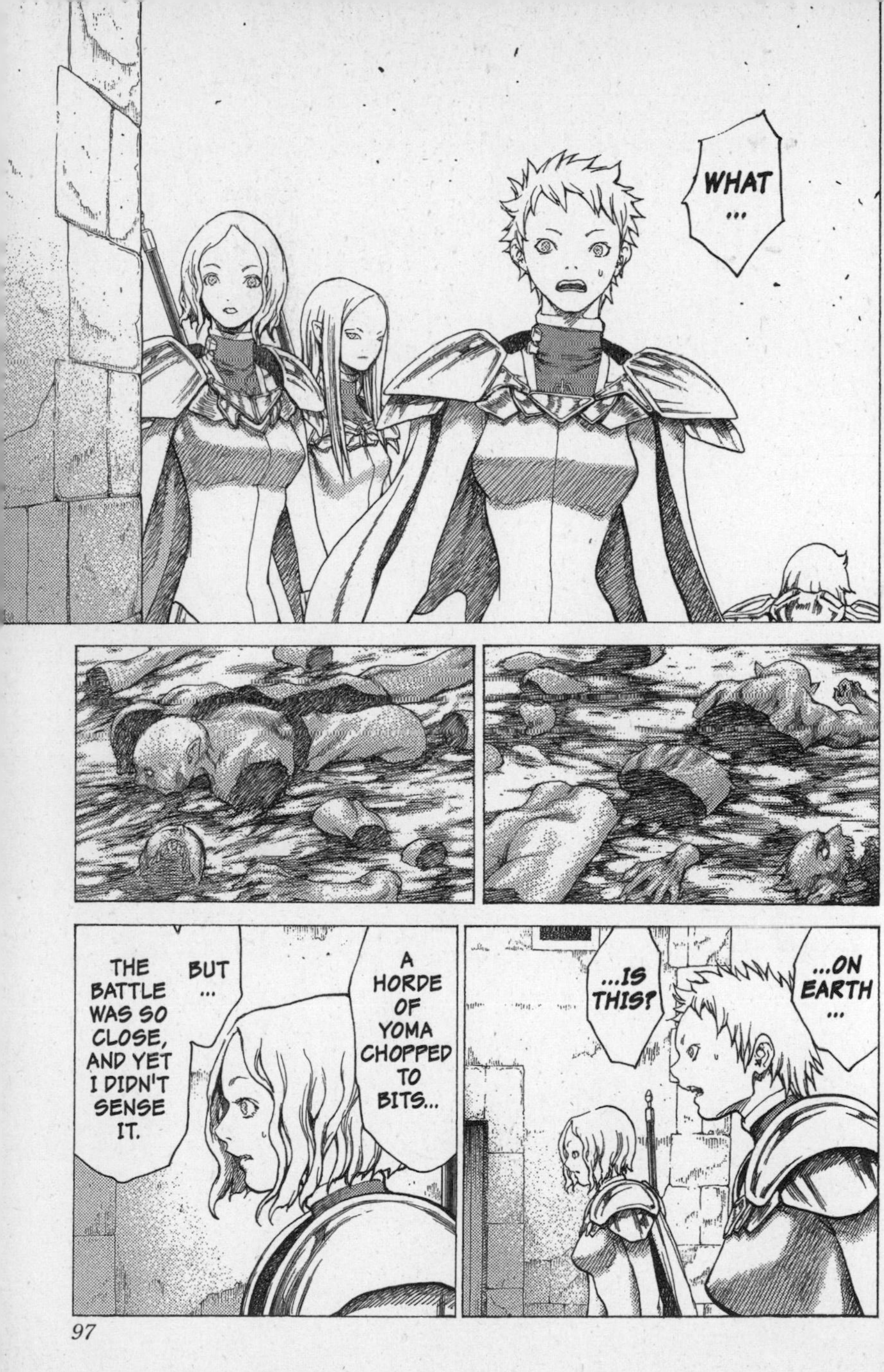
WHAT ...
...ON EARTH ...
...IS THIS?
A HORDE OF YOMA CHOPPED TO BITS...
BUT ...
THE BATTLE WAS SO CLOSE, AND YET I DIDN'T SENSE IT.

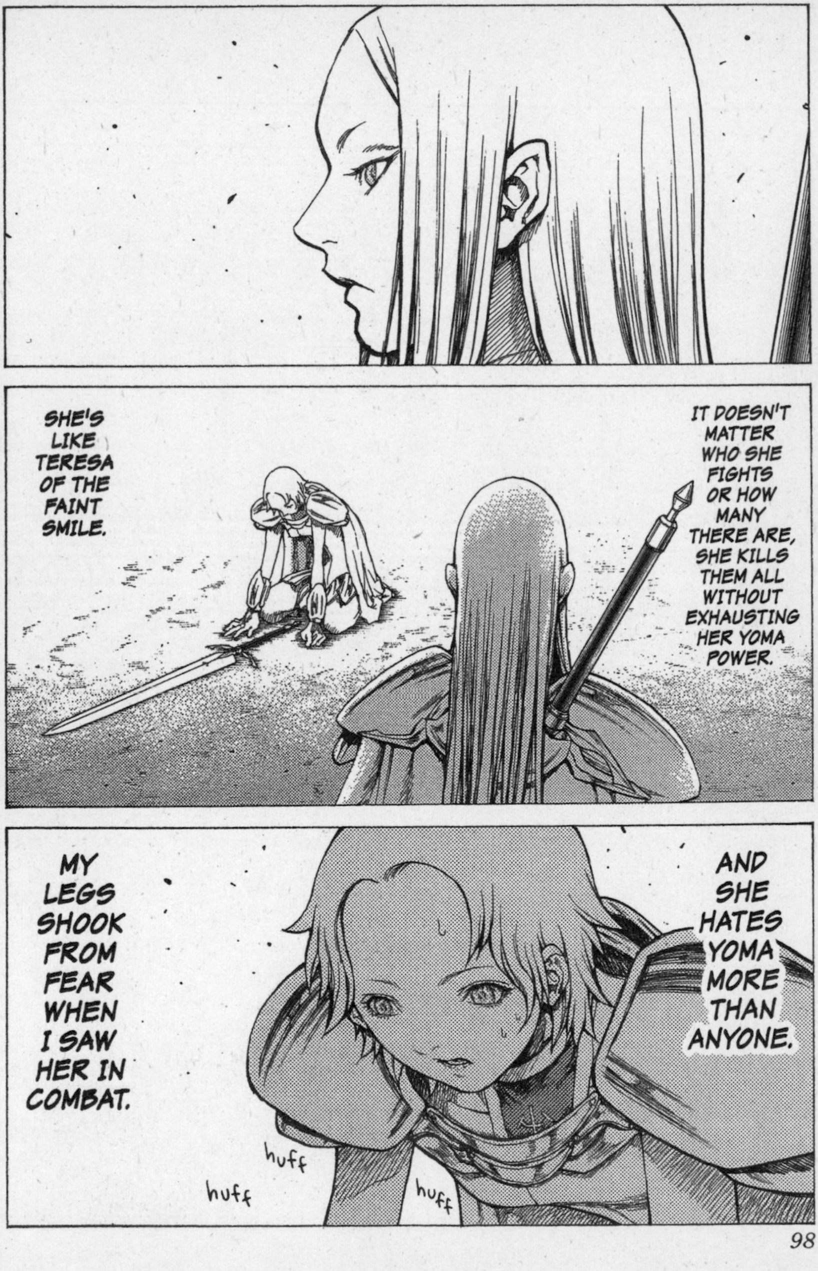
IT DOESN'T MATTER WHO SHE FIGHTS OR HOW MANY THERE ARE, SHE KILLS THEM ALL WITHOUT EXHAUSTING HER YOMA POWER.
SHE'S LIKE TERESA OF THE FAINT SMILE.
AND SHE HATES YOMA MORE THAN ANYONE.
MY LEGS SHOOK FROM FEAR WHEN I SAW HER IN COMBAT.
huff
huff
huff

READ THIS WAY

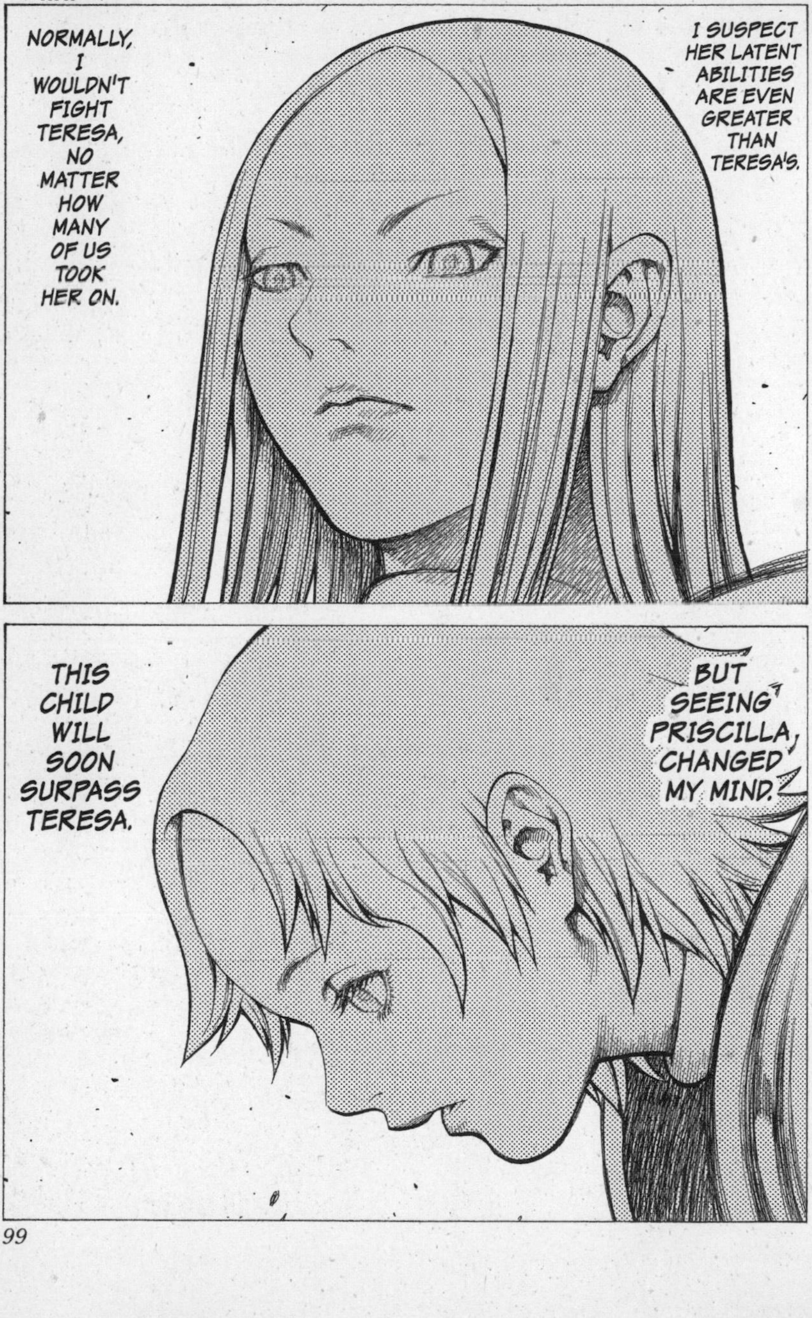
I SUSPECT HER LATENT ABILITIES ARE EVEN GREATER THAN TERESA'S.
NORMALLY, I WOULDN'T FIGHT TERESA, NO MATTER HOW MANY OF US TOOK HER ON.
BUT SEEING PRISCILLA, CHANGED MY MIND.
THIS CHILD WILL SOON SURPASS TERESA.

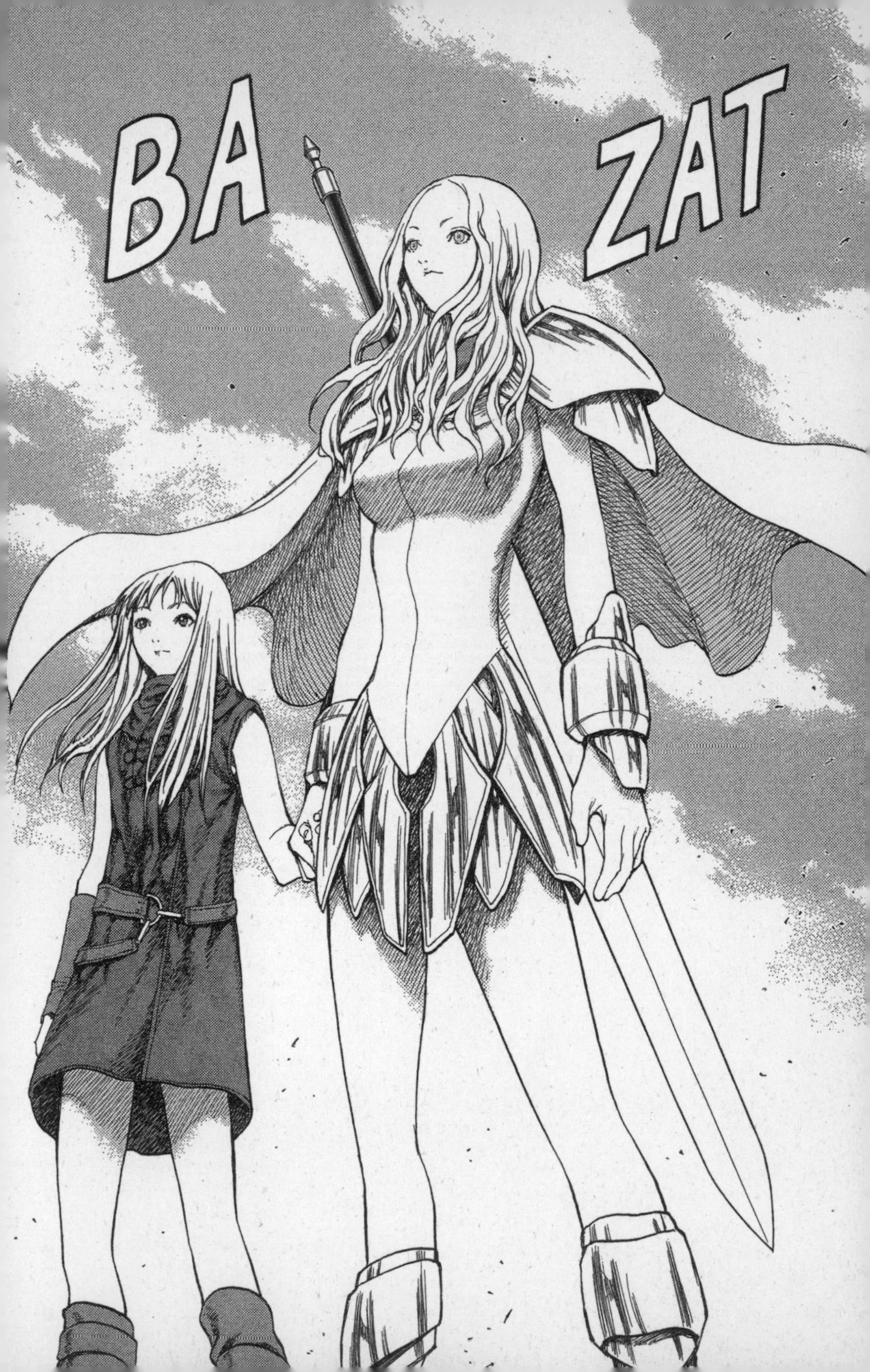
BA ZAT

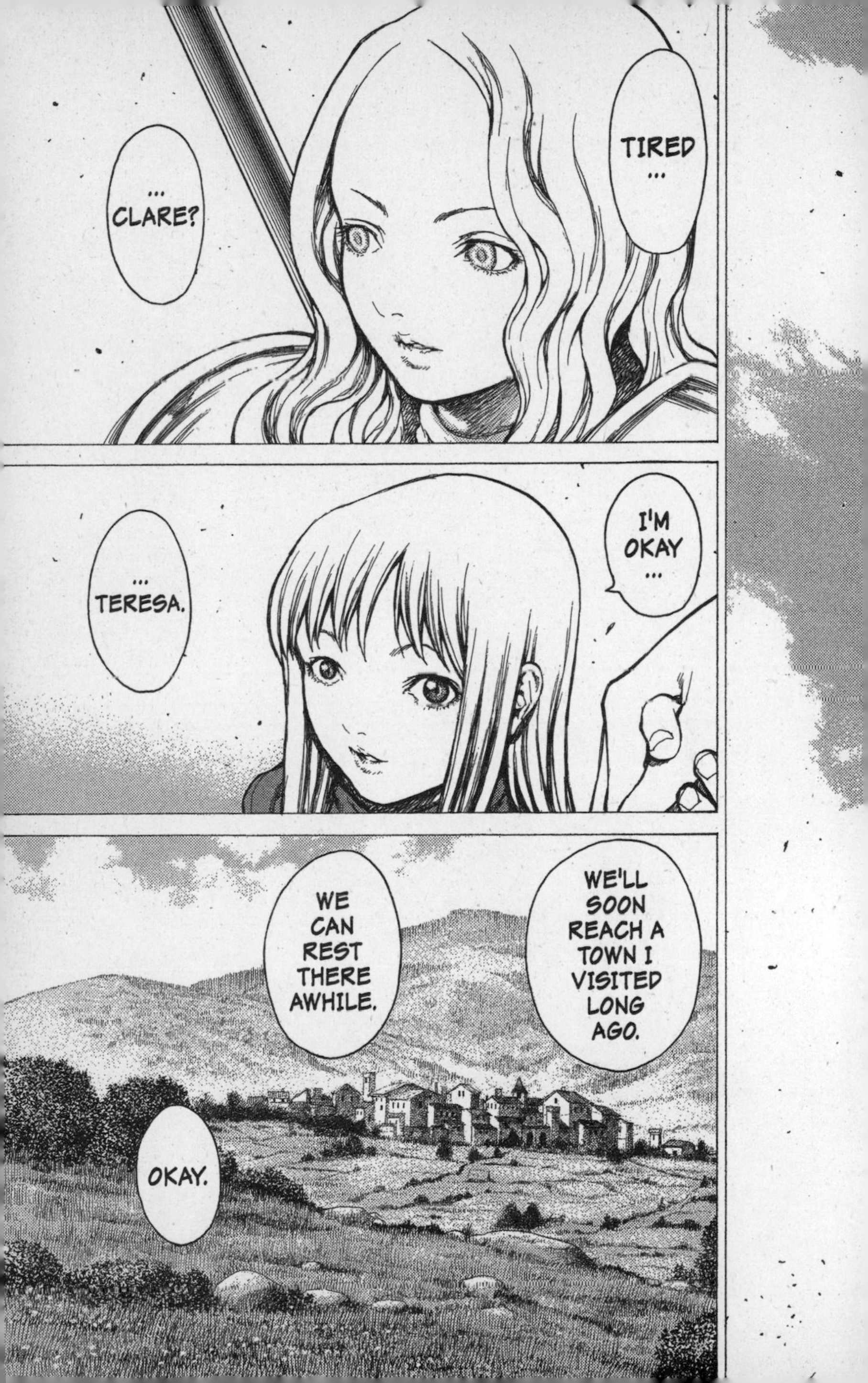
TIRED ...
... CLARE?
I'M OKAY ...
... TERESA.
WE'LL SOON REACH A TOWN I VISITED LONG AGO.
WE CAN REST THERE AWHILE.
OKAY.

クレイモア

Claymore™

Scene 19: Marked for Death, Part 2

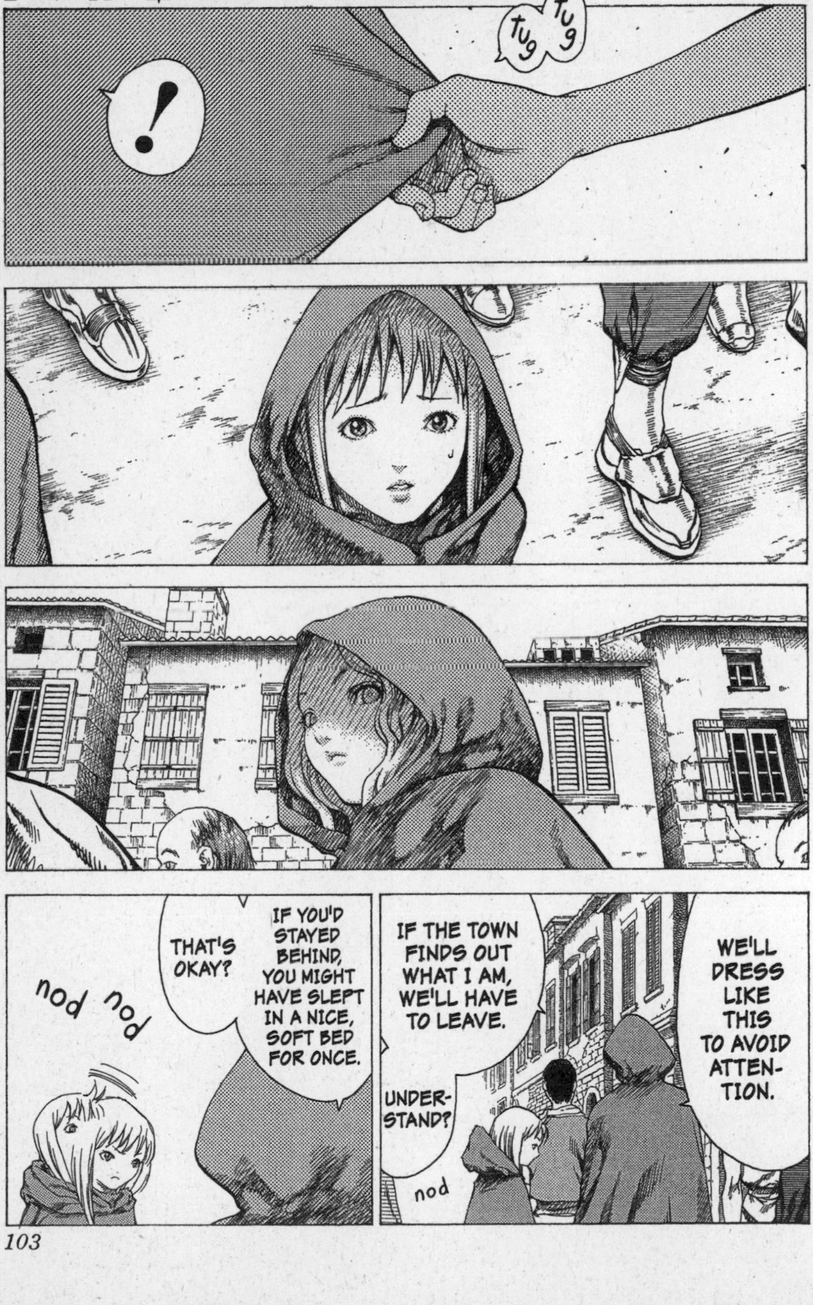
tug tug
!
WE'LL DRESS LIKE THIS TO AVOID ATTEN-TION.
IF THE TOWN FINDS OUT WHAT I AM, WE'LL HAVE TO LEAVE.
UNDER-STAND?
nod
IF YOU'D STAYED BEHIND, YOU MIGHT HAVE SLEPT IN A NICE, SOFT BED FOR ONCE.
THAT'S OKAY?
nod nod

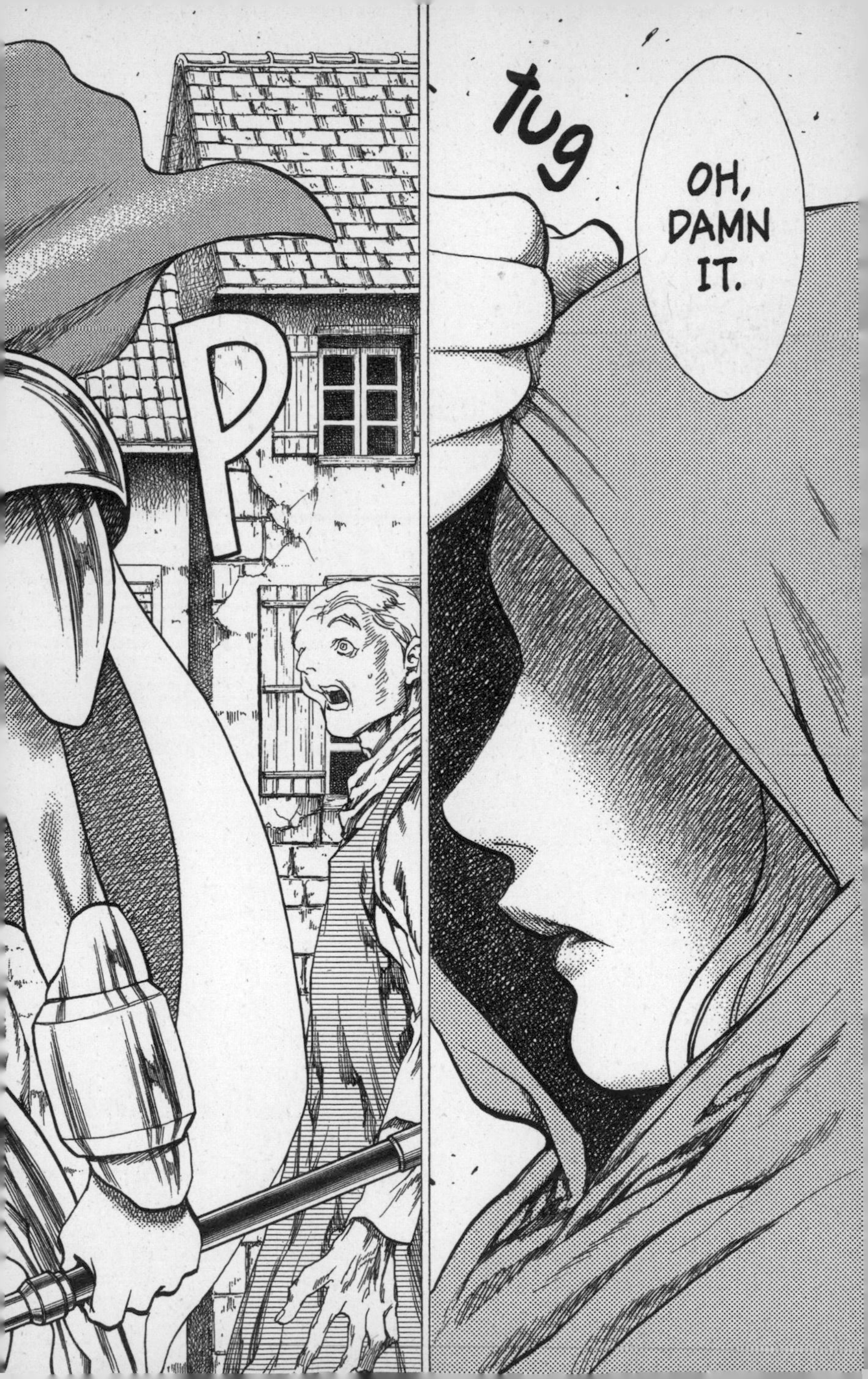
tug
OH, DAMN IT.
P

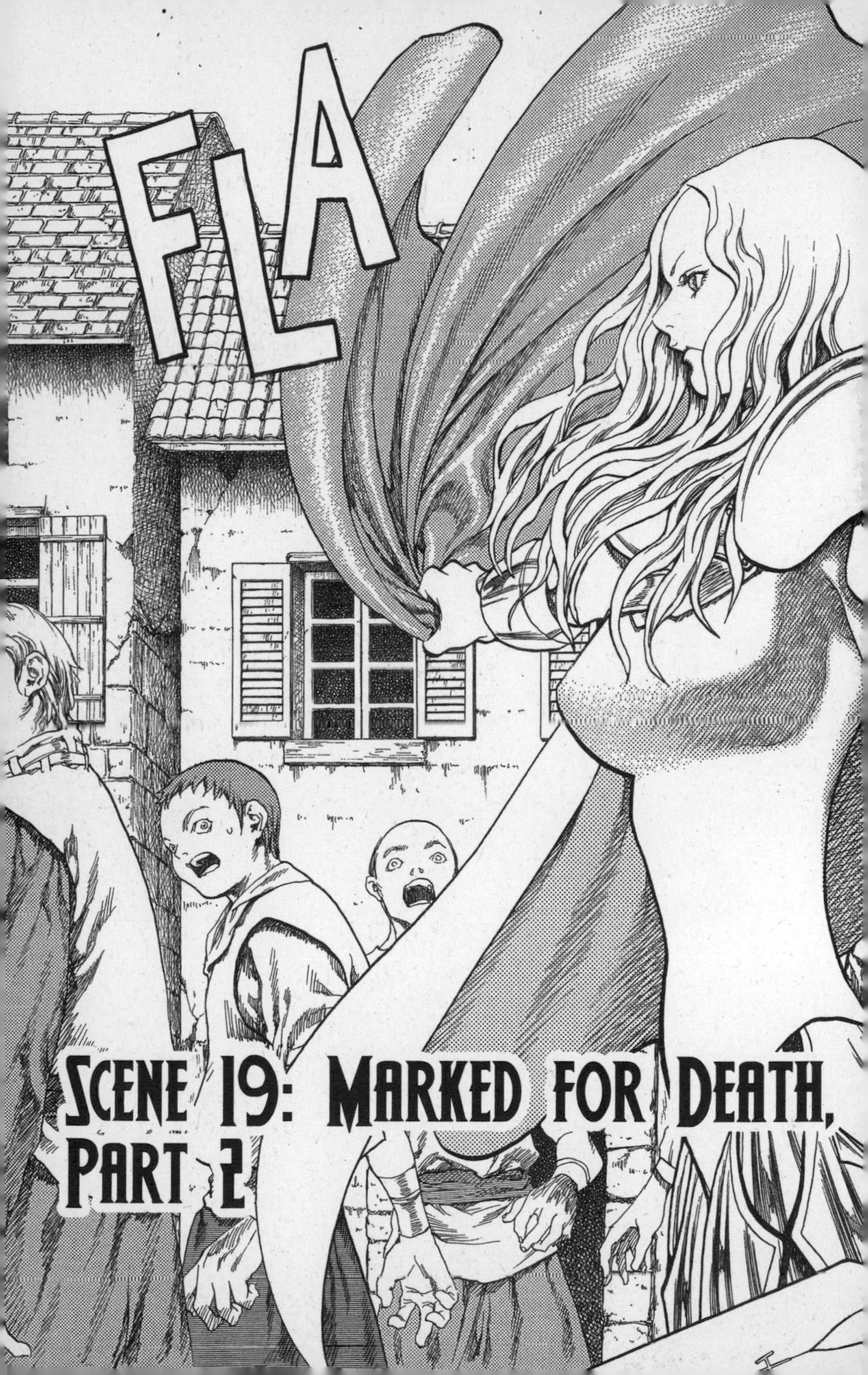
FLA
SCENE 19: MARKED FOR DEATH, PART 2

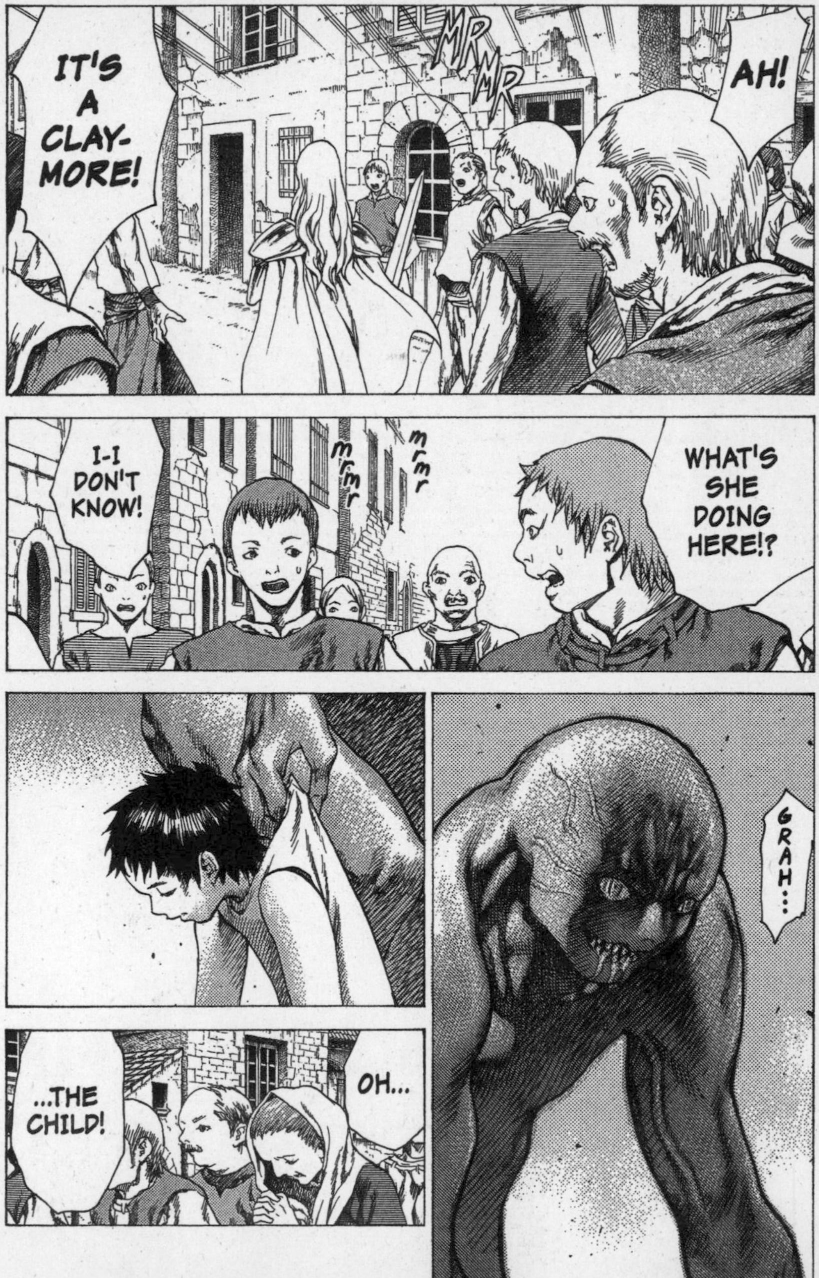
AH!
MR MR
IT'S A CLAYMORE!
WHAT'S SHE DOING HERE!?
mrmr
mrmr
I-I DON'T KNOW!
GRAH...
OH...
...THE CHILD!

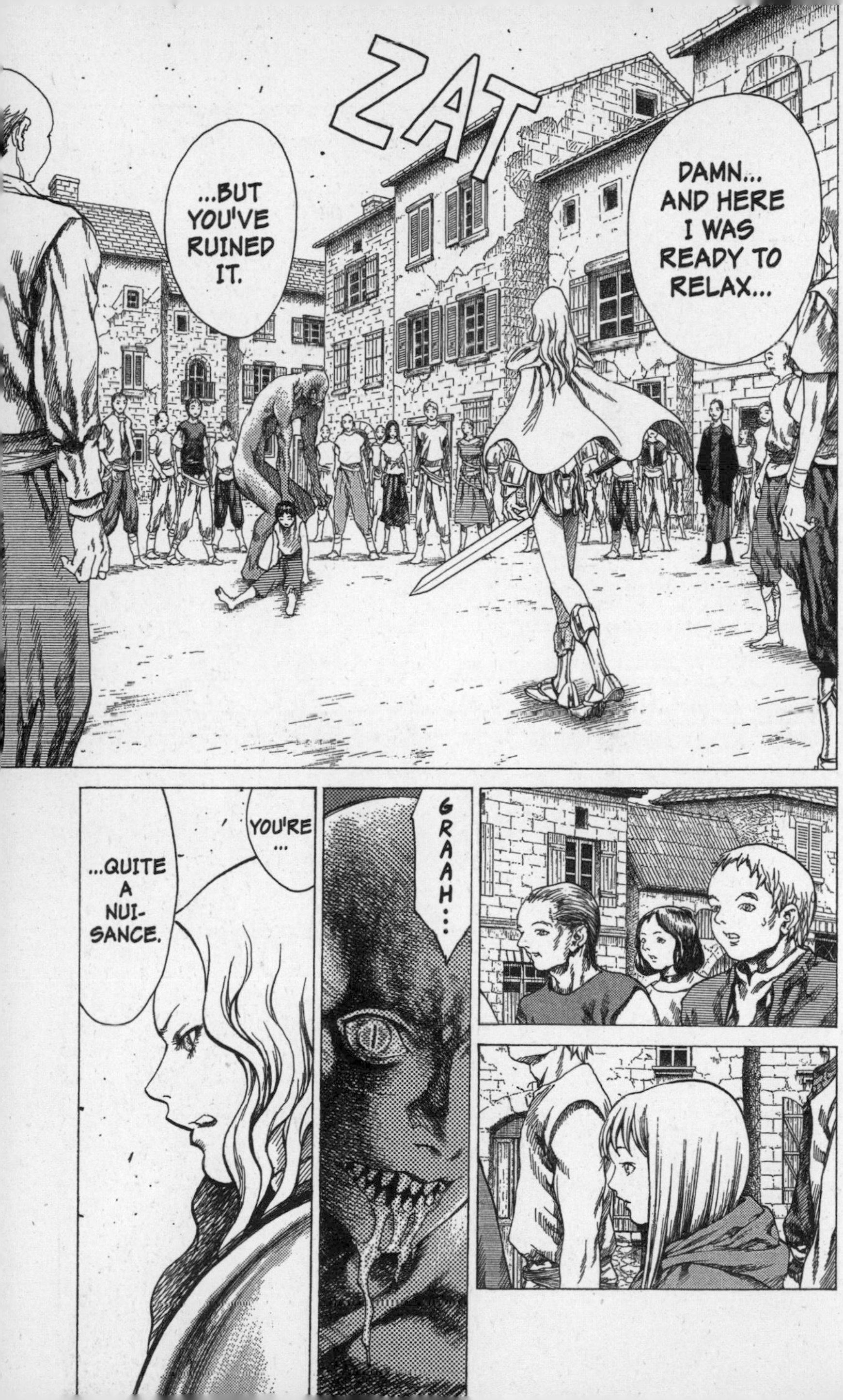
ZAT
DAMN... AND HERE I WAS READY TO RELAX...
...BUT YOU'VE RUINED IT.
GRAAAH...
YOU'RE ...
...QUITE A NUI-SANCE.

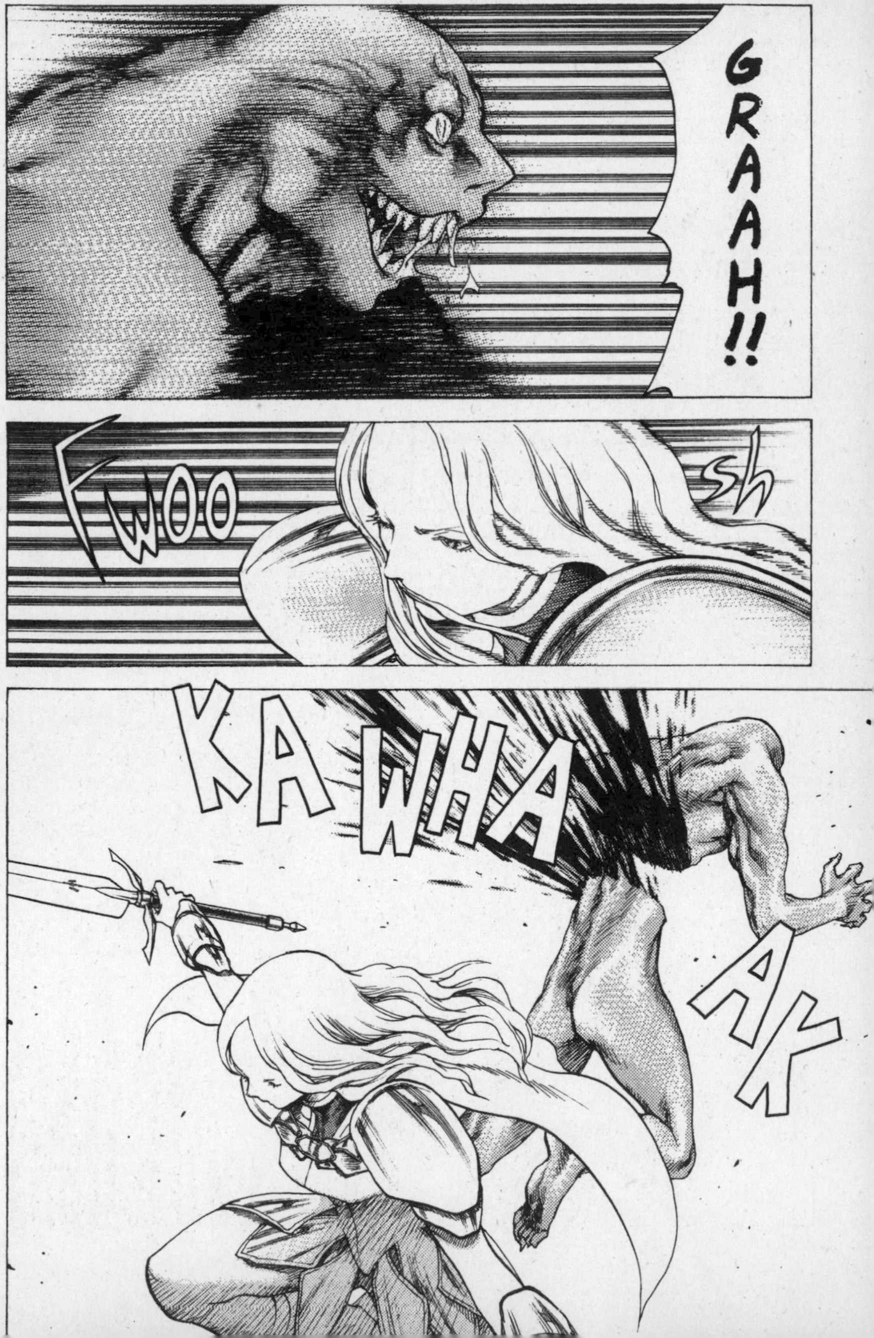
GRAAAH!!
FWOOsh
KAWHAAK

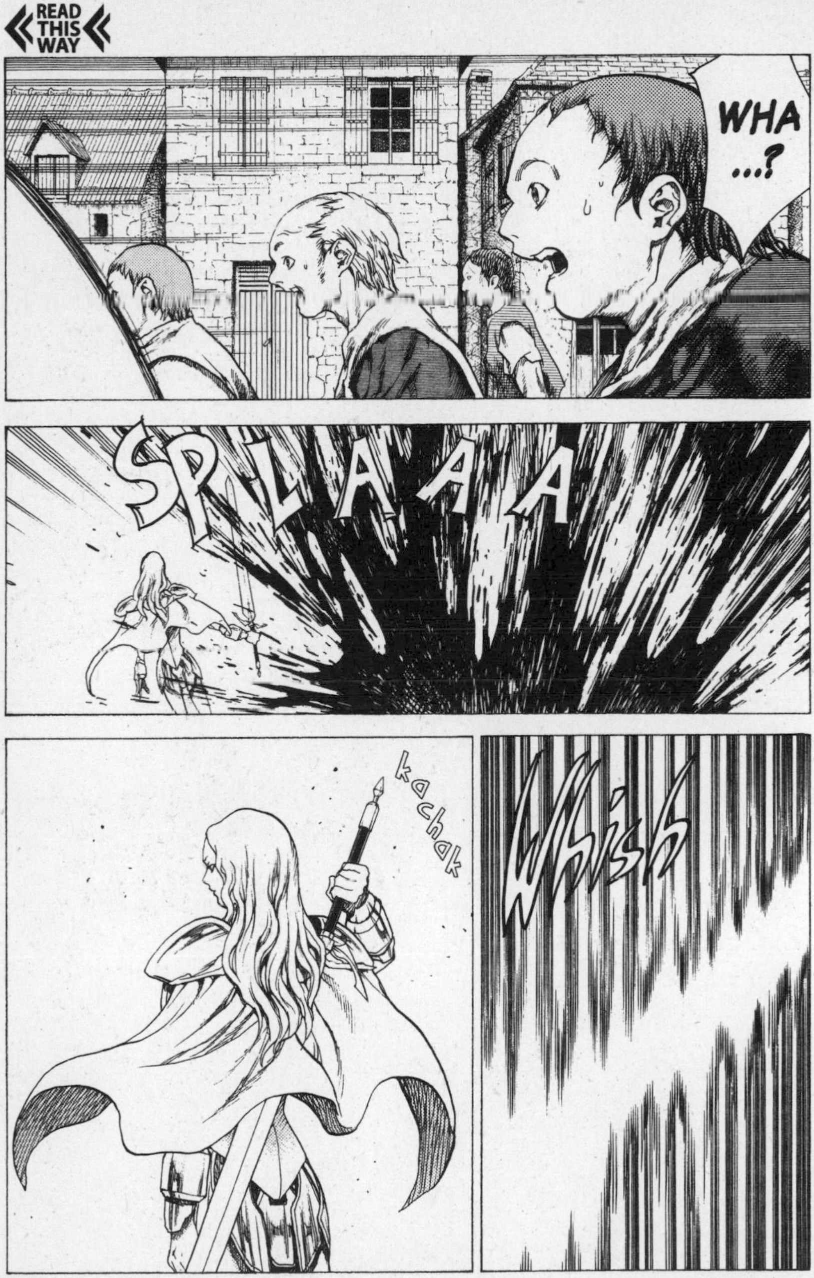
READ THIS WAY
WHA ...?
SPLAAA
kachak
Whish

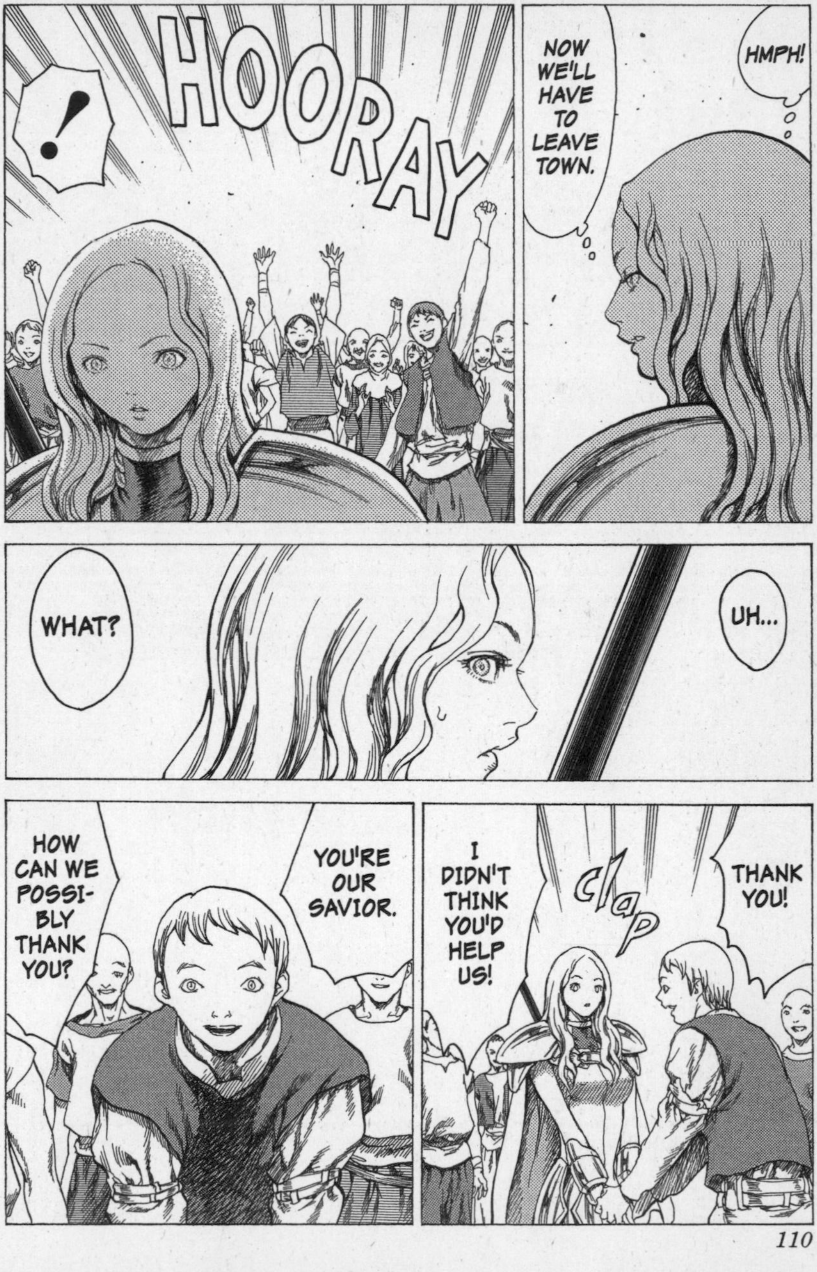
HMPH!
NOW WE'LL HAVE TO LEAVE TOWN.
HOORAY
!
UH...
WHAT?
THANK YOU!
CLAP
I DIDN'T THINK YOU'D HELP US!
YOU'RE OUR SAVIOR.
HOW CAN WE POSSI-BLY THANK YOU?

READ THIS WAY

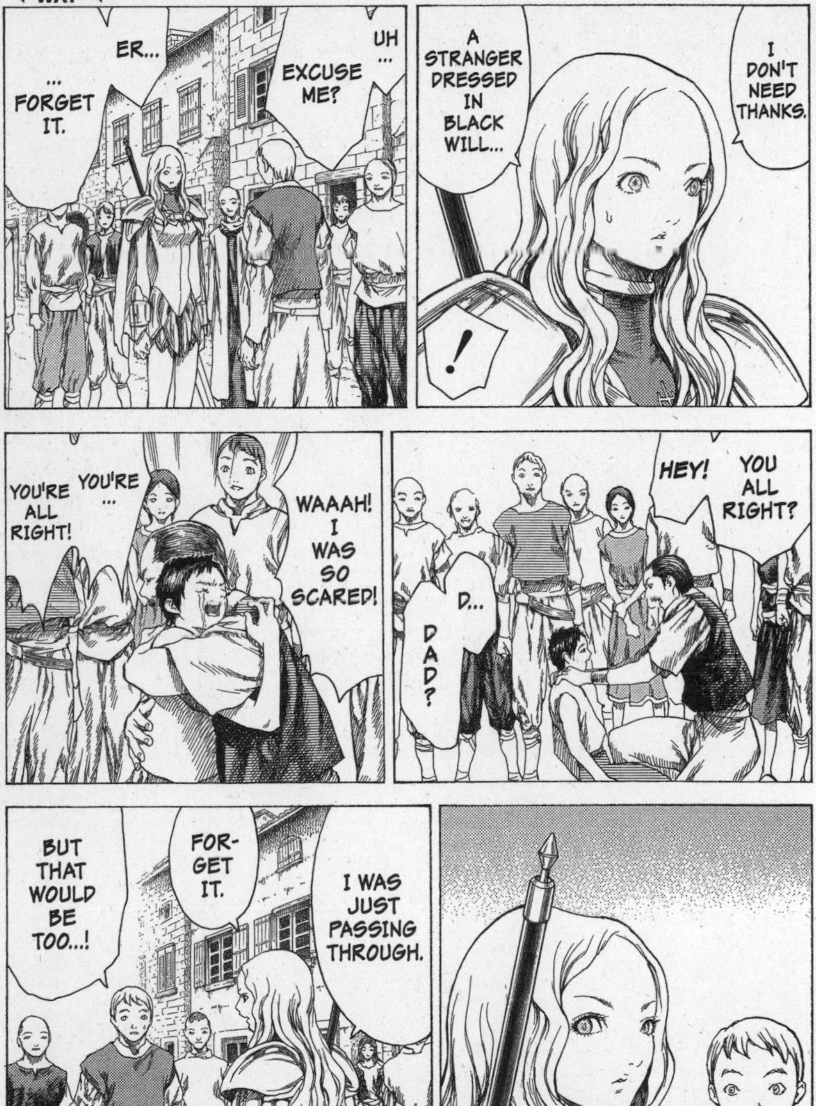
I DON'T NEED THANKS.
A STRANGER DRESSED IN BLACK WILL...
!
UH ...
EXCUSE ME?
ER...
... FORGET IT.
YOU ALL RIGHT?
HEY!
D... DAD?
WAAAH! I WAS SO SCARED!
YOU'RE ...
YOU'RE ALL RIGHT!
I WAS JUST PASSING THROUGH.
FOR-GET IT.
BUT THAT WOULD BE TOO...!

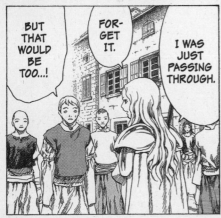

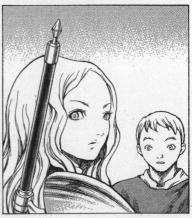

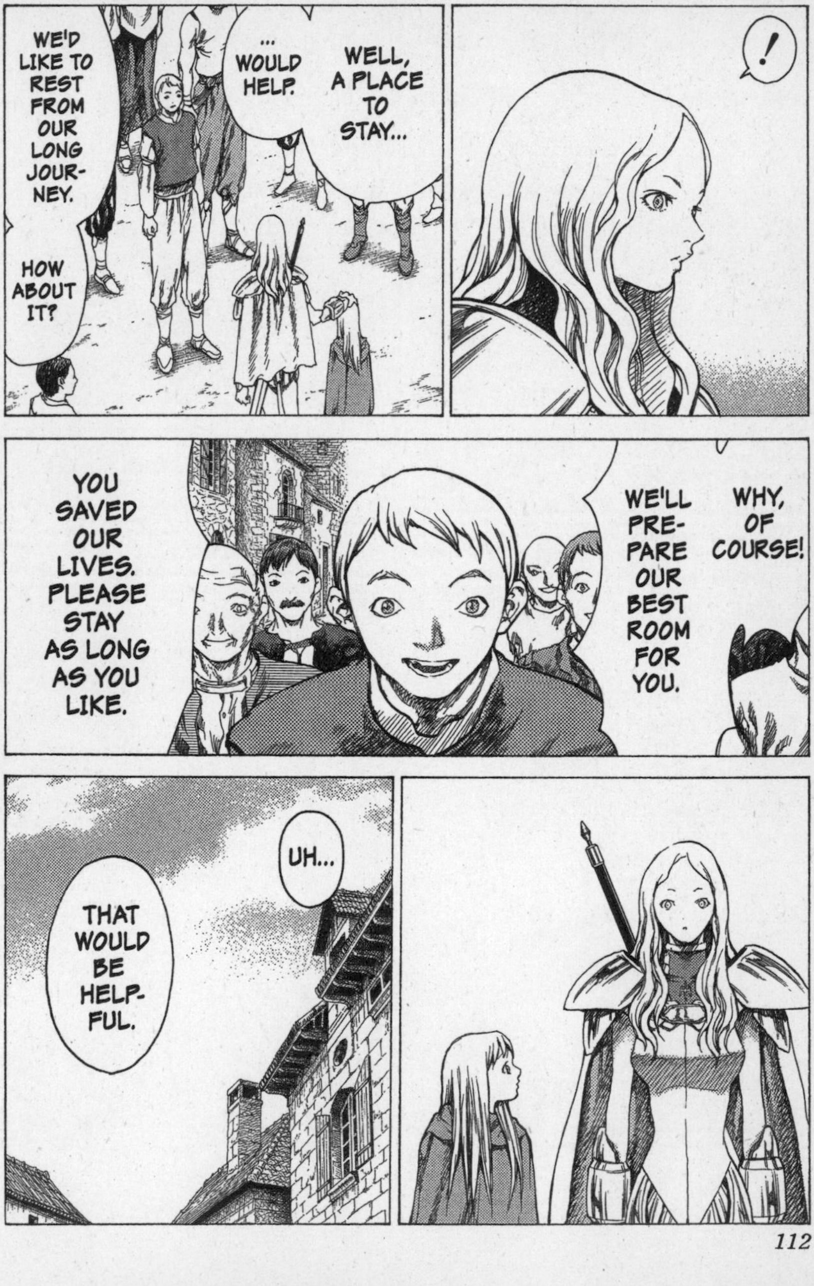
!
WELL, A PLACE TO STAY...
... WOULD HELP.
WE'D LIKE TO REST FROM OUR LONG JOURNEY.
HOW ABOUT IT?
WHY, OF COURSE!
WE'LL PREPARE OUR BEST ROOM FOR YOU.
YOU SAVED OUR LIVES. PLEASE STAY AS LONG AS YOU LIKE.
UH...
THAT WOULD BE HELPFUL.

READ THIS WAY

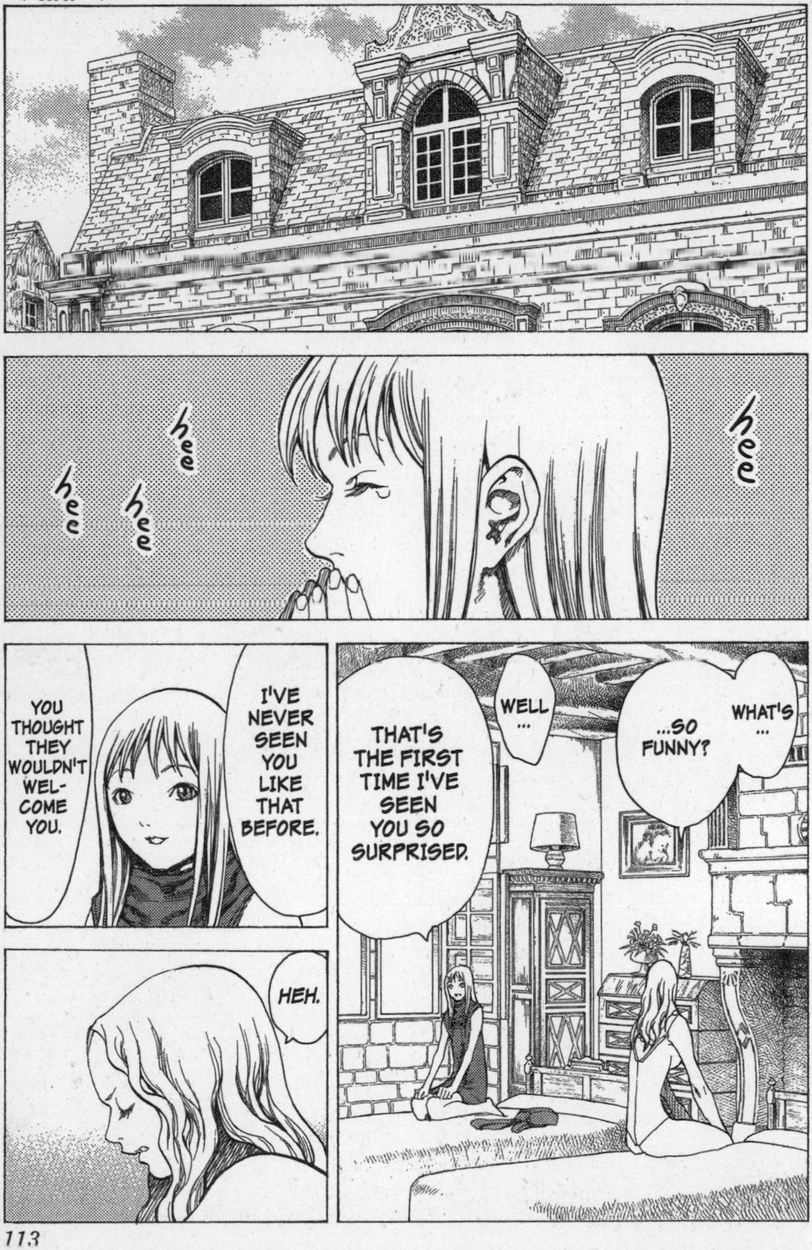
hee
hee
hee
hee
WHAT'S ...
...SO FUNNY?
WELL ...
THAT'S THE FIRST TIME I'VE SEEN YOU SO SURPRISED.
I'VE NEVER SEEN YOU LIKE THAT BEFORE.
YOU THOUGHT THEY WOULDN'T WEL-COME YOU.
HEH.

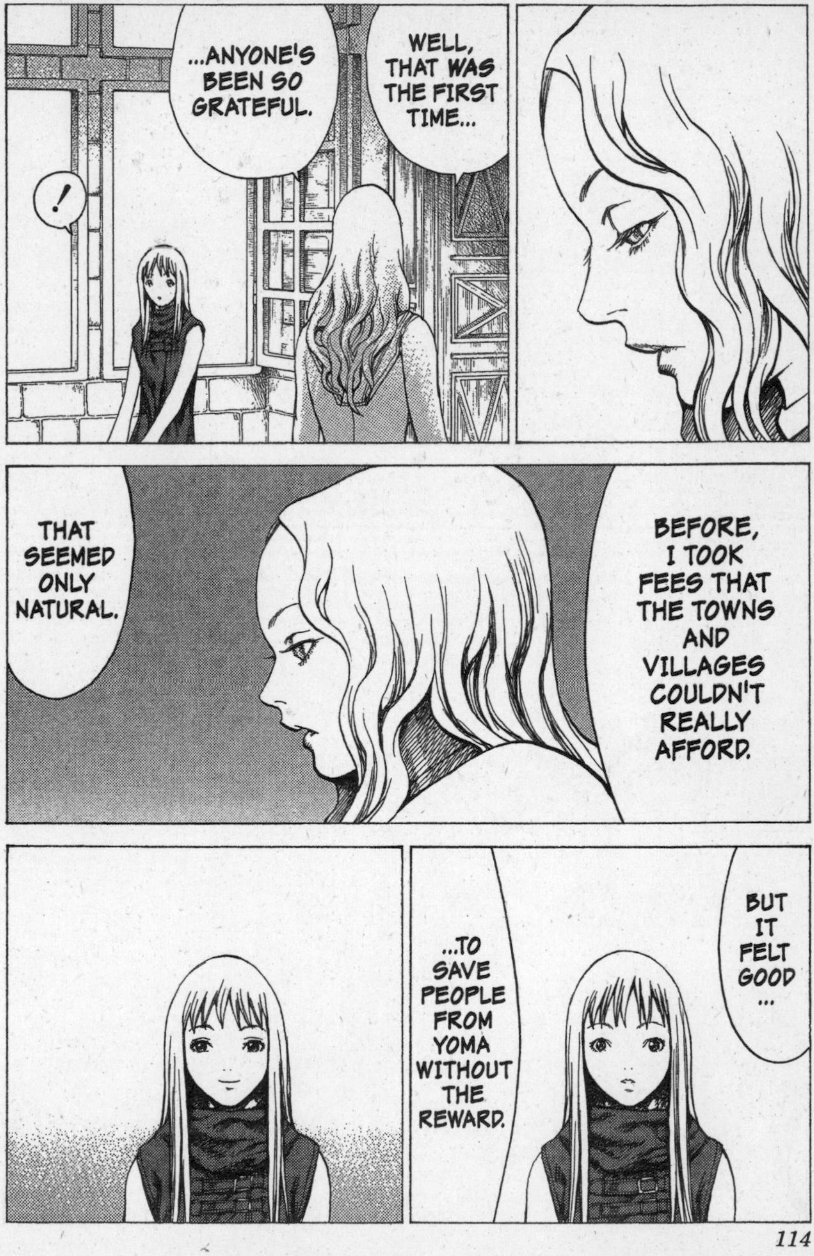
WELL, THAT WAS THE FIRST TIME...
...ANYONE'S BEEN SO GRATEFUL.
!
BEFORE, I TOOK FEES THAT THE TOWNS AND VILLAGES COULDN'T REALLY AFFORD.
THAT SEEMED ONLY NATURAL.
BUT IT FELT GOOD ...
...TO SAVE PEOPLE FROM YOMA WITHOUT THE REWARD.

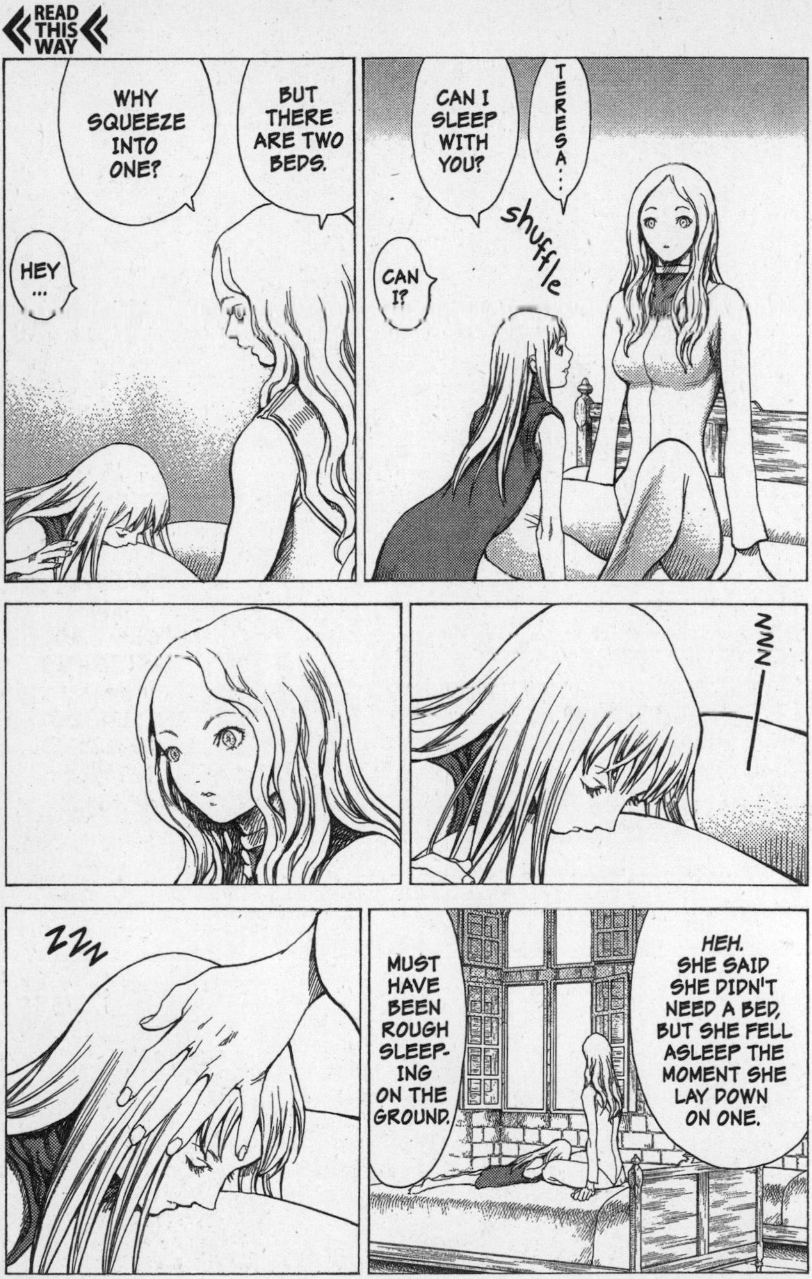
READ THIS WAY
TERESA...
CAN I SLEEP WITH YOU?
shuffle
CAN I?
BUT THERE ARE TWO BEDS.
WHY SQUEEZE INTO ONE?
HEY...
ZZZ—
HEH. SHE SAID SHE DIDN'T NEED A BED, BUT SHE FELL ASLEEP THE MOMENT SHE LAY DOWN ON ONE.
MUST HAVE BEEN ROUGH SLEEP-ING ON THE GROUND.
ZZZ

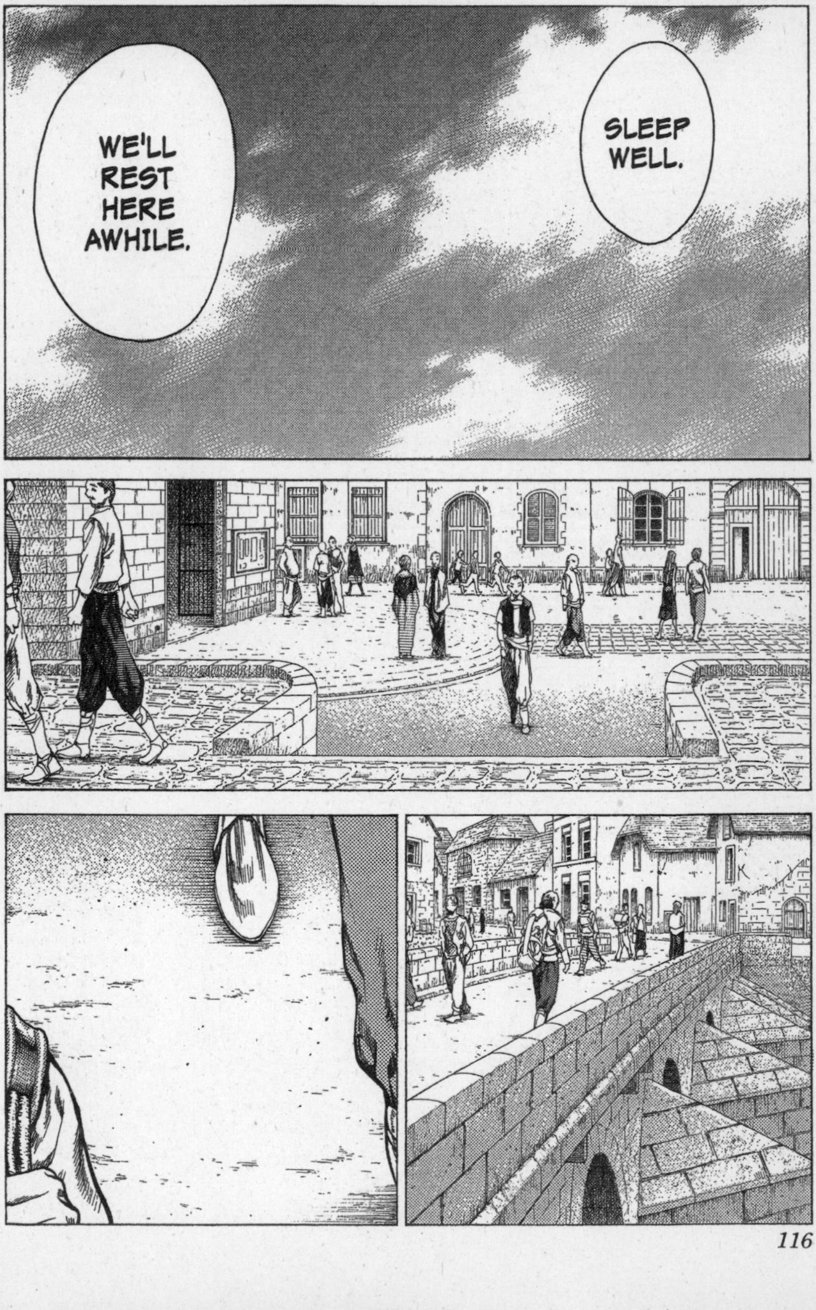
SLEEP WELL.
WE'LL REST HERE AWHILE.

READ THIS WAY

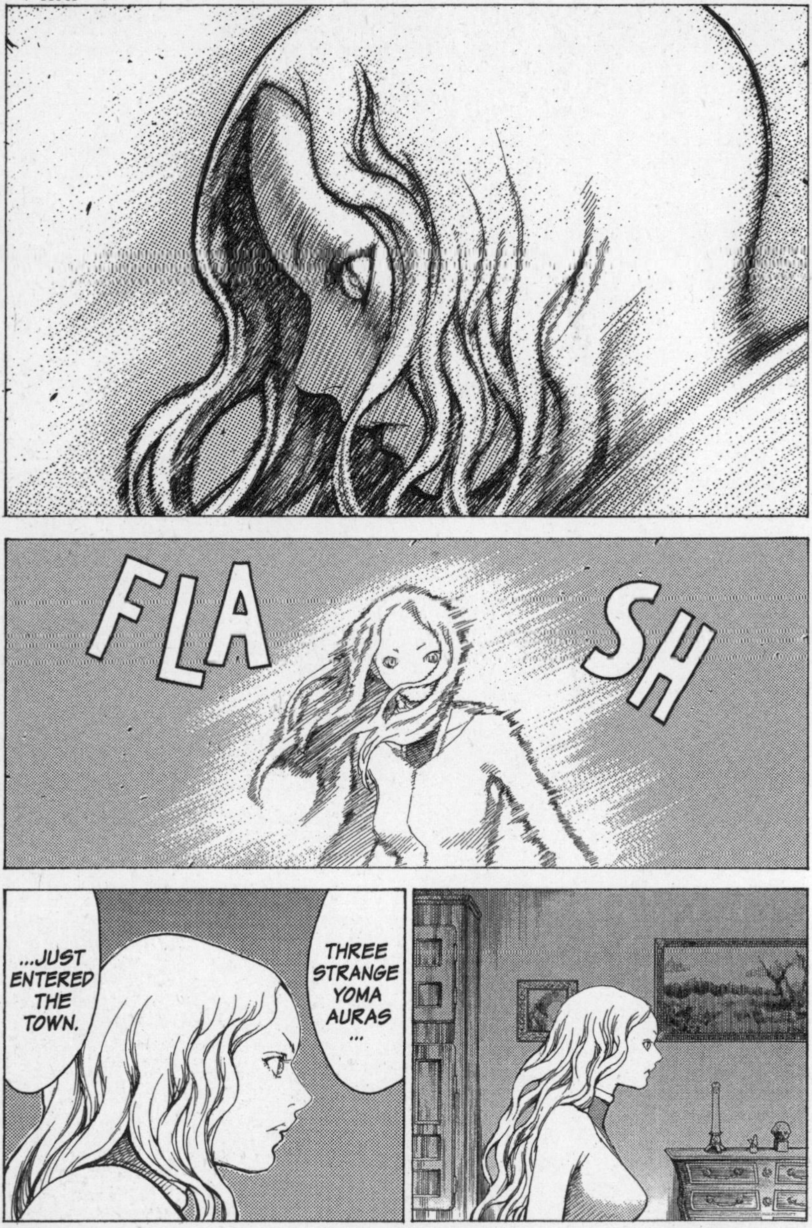
FLA SH
THREE STRANGE YOMA AURAS ...
...JUST ENTERED THE TOWN.

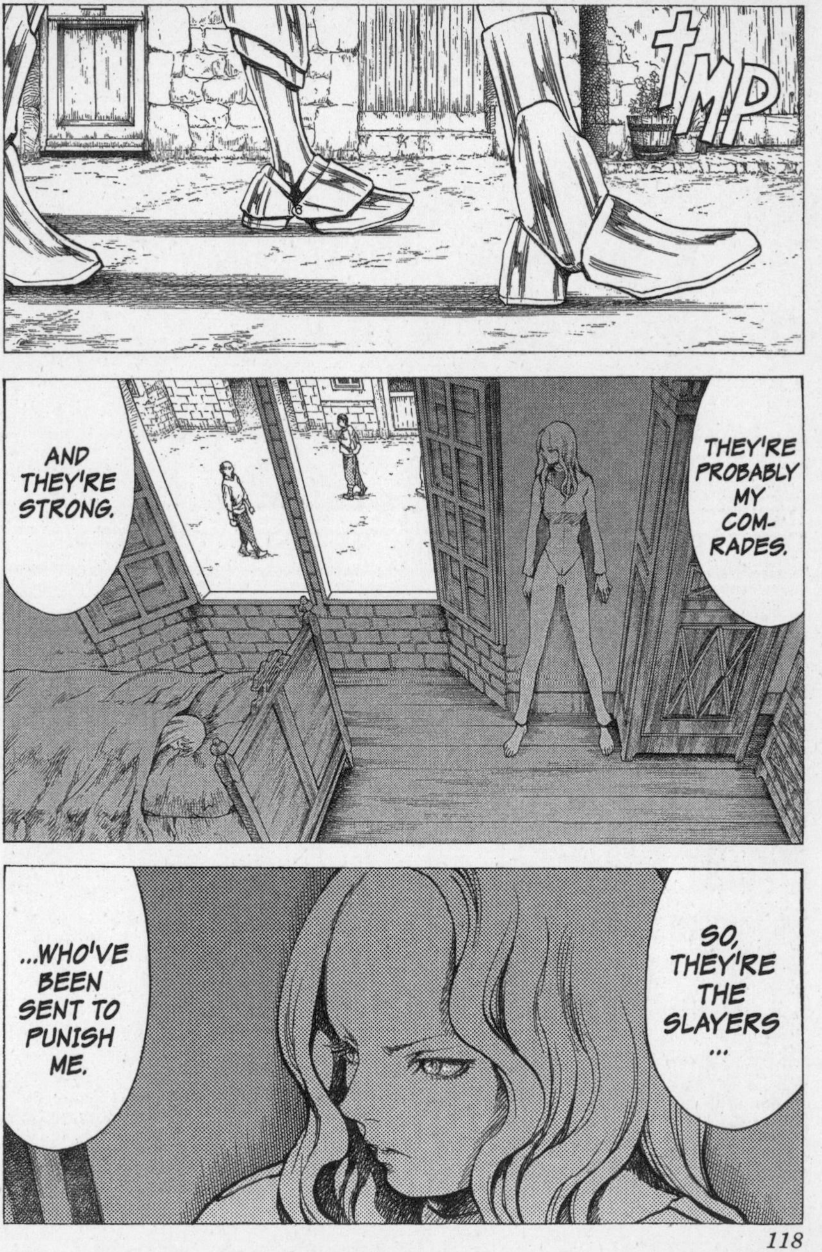
TMP
THEY'RE PROBABLY MY COM-RADES.
AND THEY'RE STRONG.
SO, THEY'RE THE SLAYERS ...
...WHO'VE BEEN SENT TO PUNISH ME.

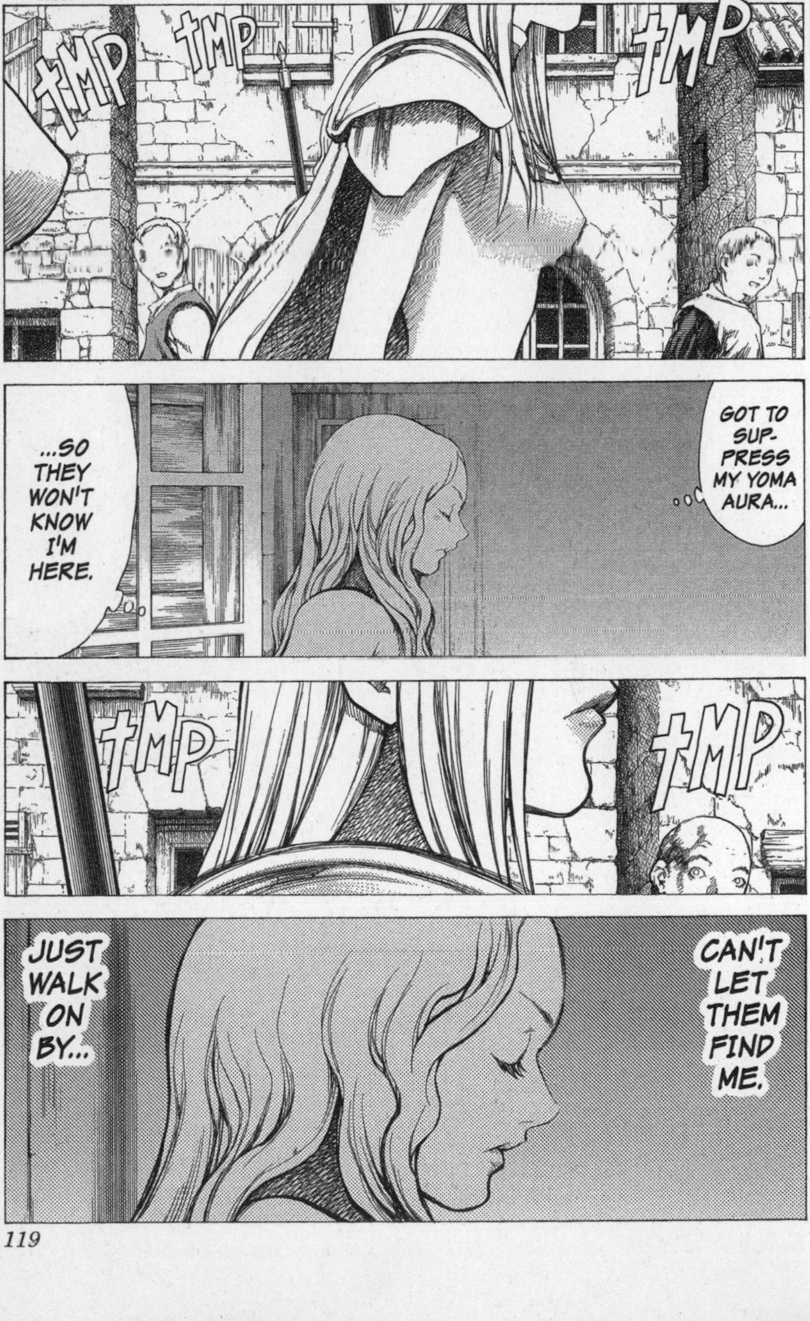
TMP
TMP
TMP
GOT TO SUP-PRESS MY YOMA AURA...
...SO THEY WON'T KNOW I'M HERE.
TMP
TMP
CAN'T LET THEM FIND ME.
JUST WALK ON BY...

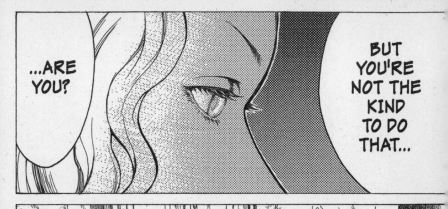

...ARE YOU?

BUT YOU'RE NOT THE KIND TO DO THAT...

TMP

TMP

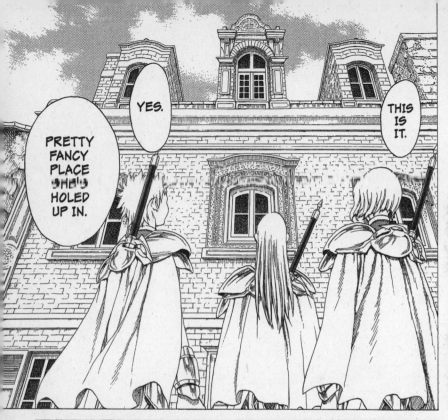

PRETTY FANCY PLACE SHE'S HOLED UP IN.

YES.

THIS IS IT.

CREAK

!

LET'S GO.

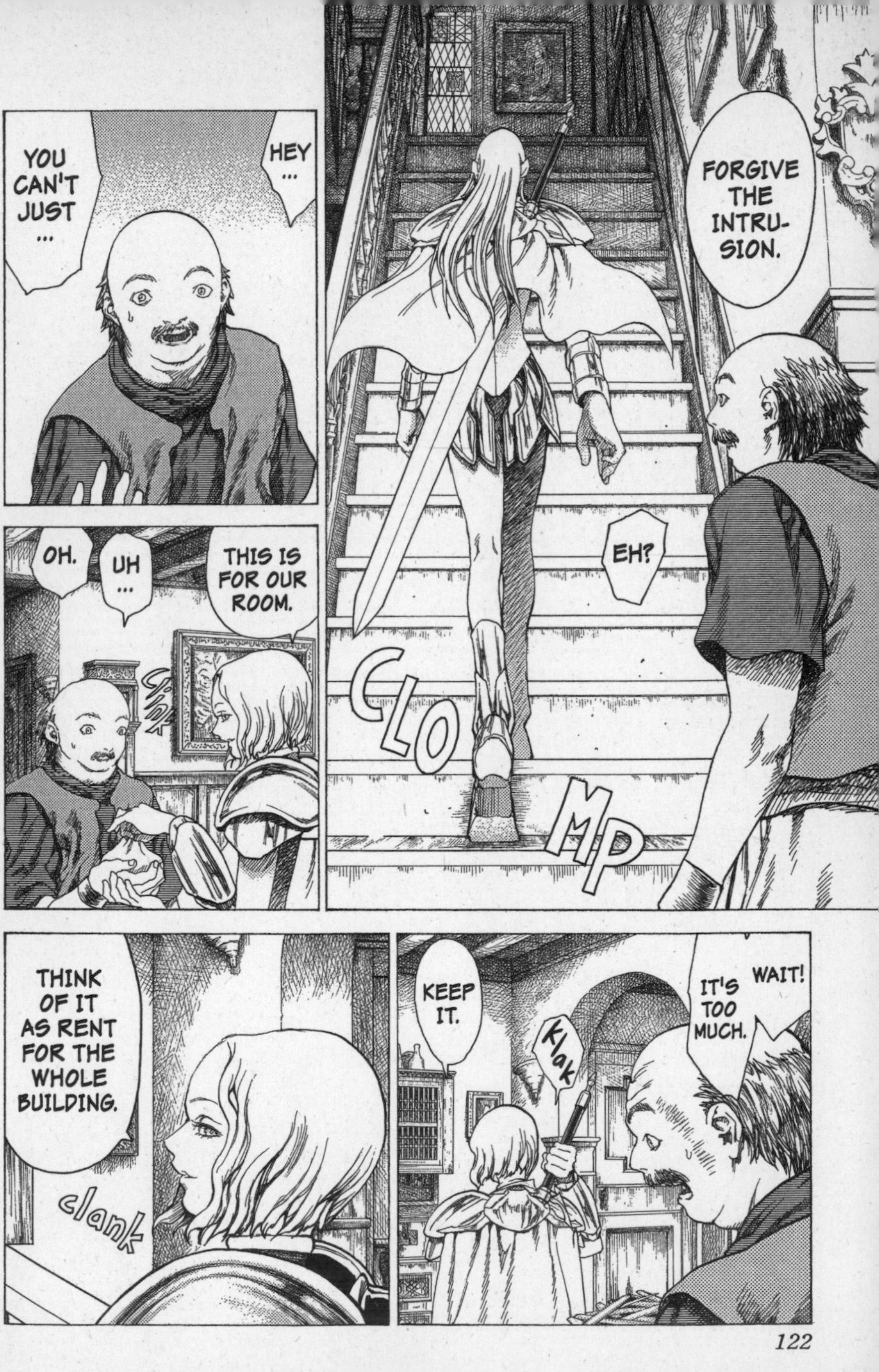
FORGIVE THE INTRUSION.
EH?
CLOMP
HEY ...
YOU CAN'T JUST ...
THIS IS FOR OUR ROOM.
UH ...
OH.
clink
WAIT!
IT'S TOO MUCH.
KEEP IT.
klak
THINK OF IT AS RENT FOR THE WHOLE BUILDING.
clank

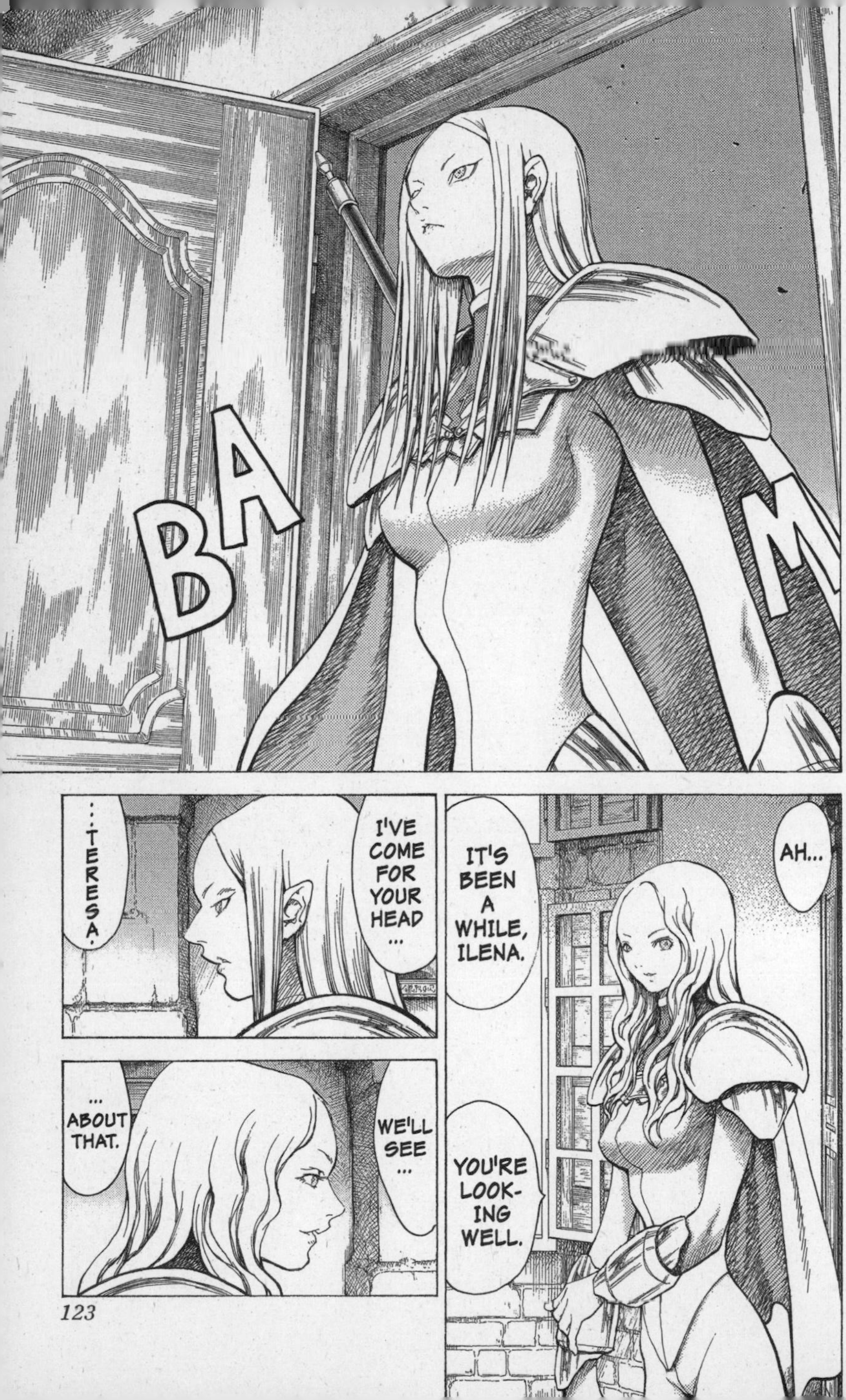
BAM
AH...
IT'S BEEN A WHILE, ILENA.
YOU'RE LOOKING WELL.
I'VE COME FOR YOUR HEAD...
...TERESA.
WE'LL SEE...
...ABOUT THAT.

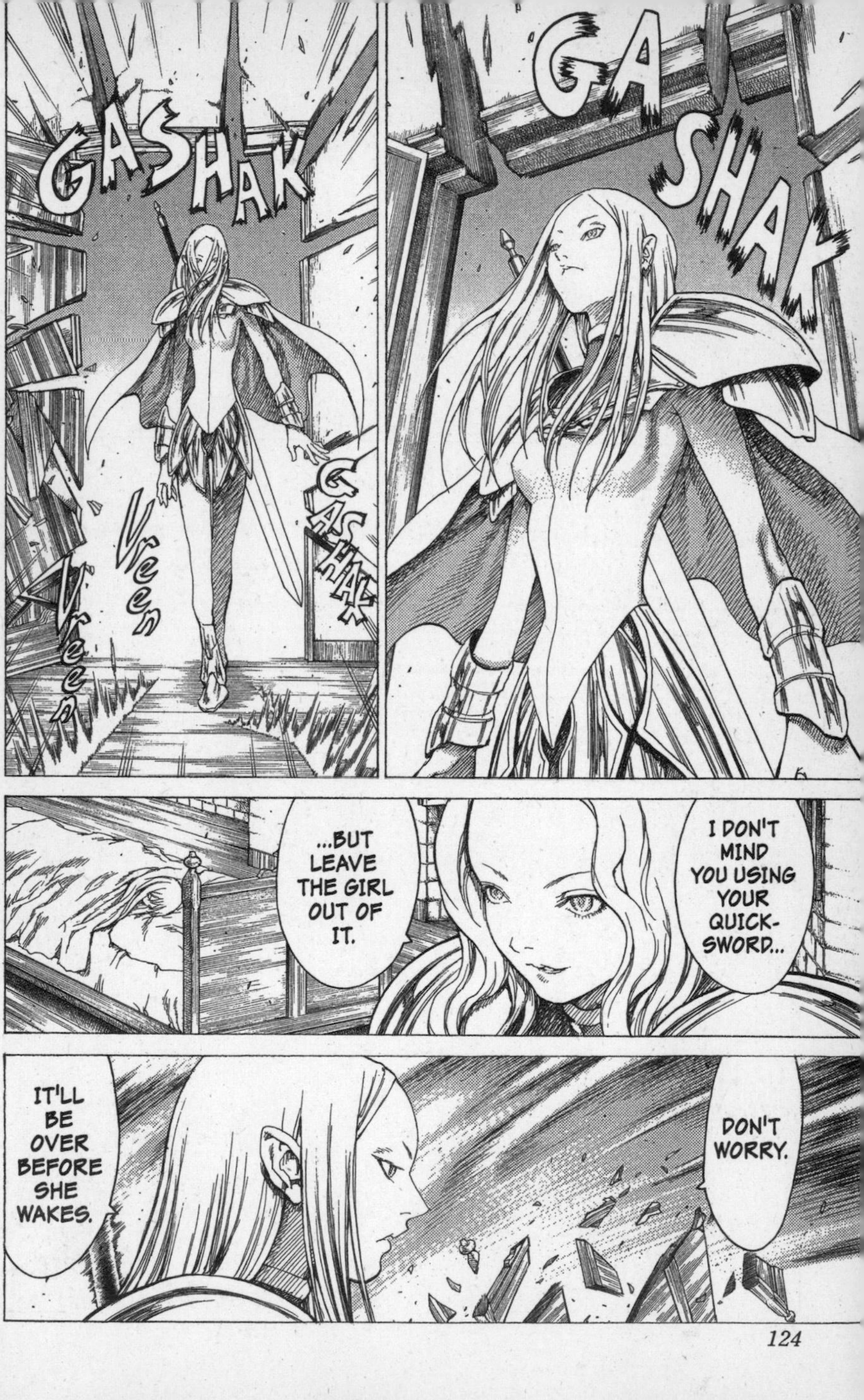
GASHAK
GASHAK
GASHAK
Vreen
Vreen
I DON'T MIND YOU USING YOUR QUICK-SWORD...
...BUT LEAVE THE GIRL OUT OF IT.
DON'T WORRY.
IT'LL BE OVER BEFORE SHE WAKES.

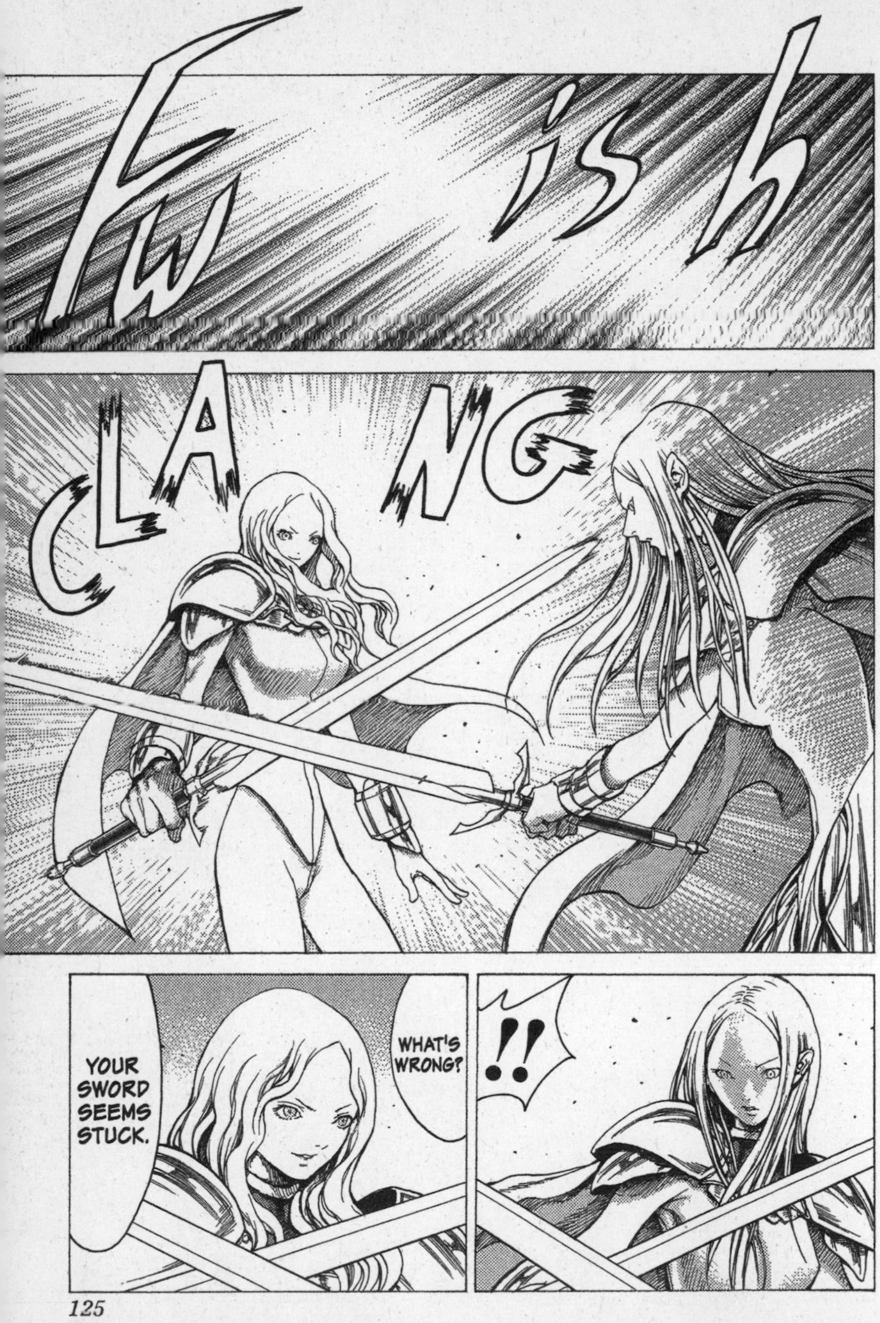
FWISH
CLANG
!!
WHAT'S WRONG?
YOUR SWORD SEEMS STUCK.

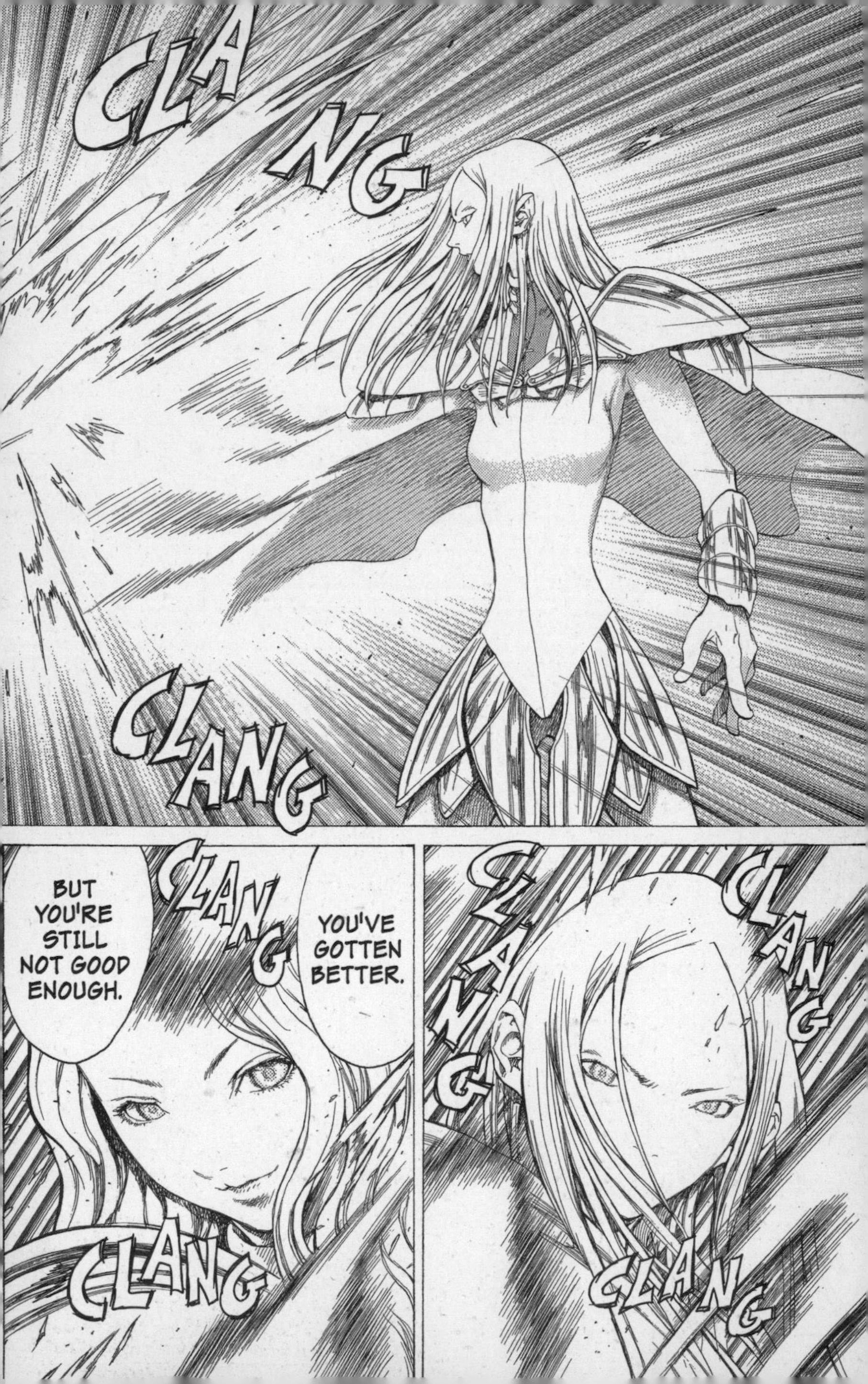
CLANG
CLANG
CLANG
CLANG
CLANG
YOU'VE GOTTEN BETTER.
BUT YOU'RE STILL NOT GOOD ENOUGH.
CLANG
CLANG

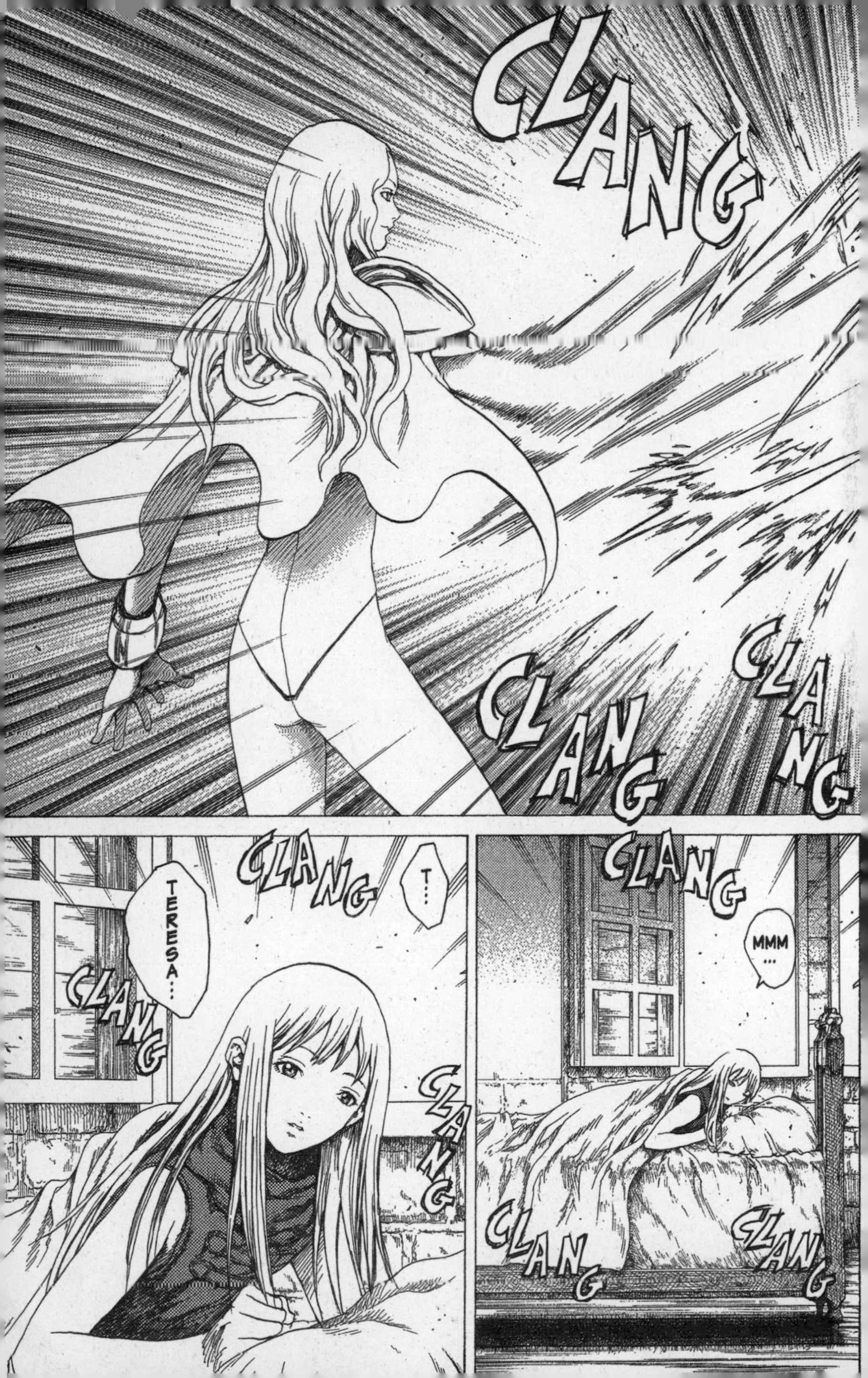
CLANG
CLANG
CLANG
CLANG
MMM...
CLANG
CLANG
T...
CLANG
TERESA...
CLANG
CLANG

LET'S SEE.

... HERE.

CLANG CLANG CLANG CLANG

SOUNDS LIKE THEY'RE RIGHT ABOUT ...

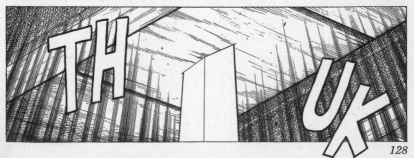

TH UK

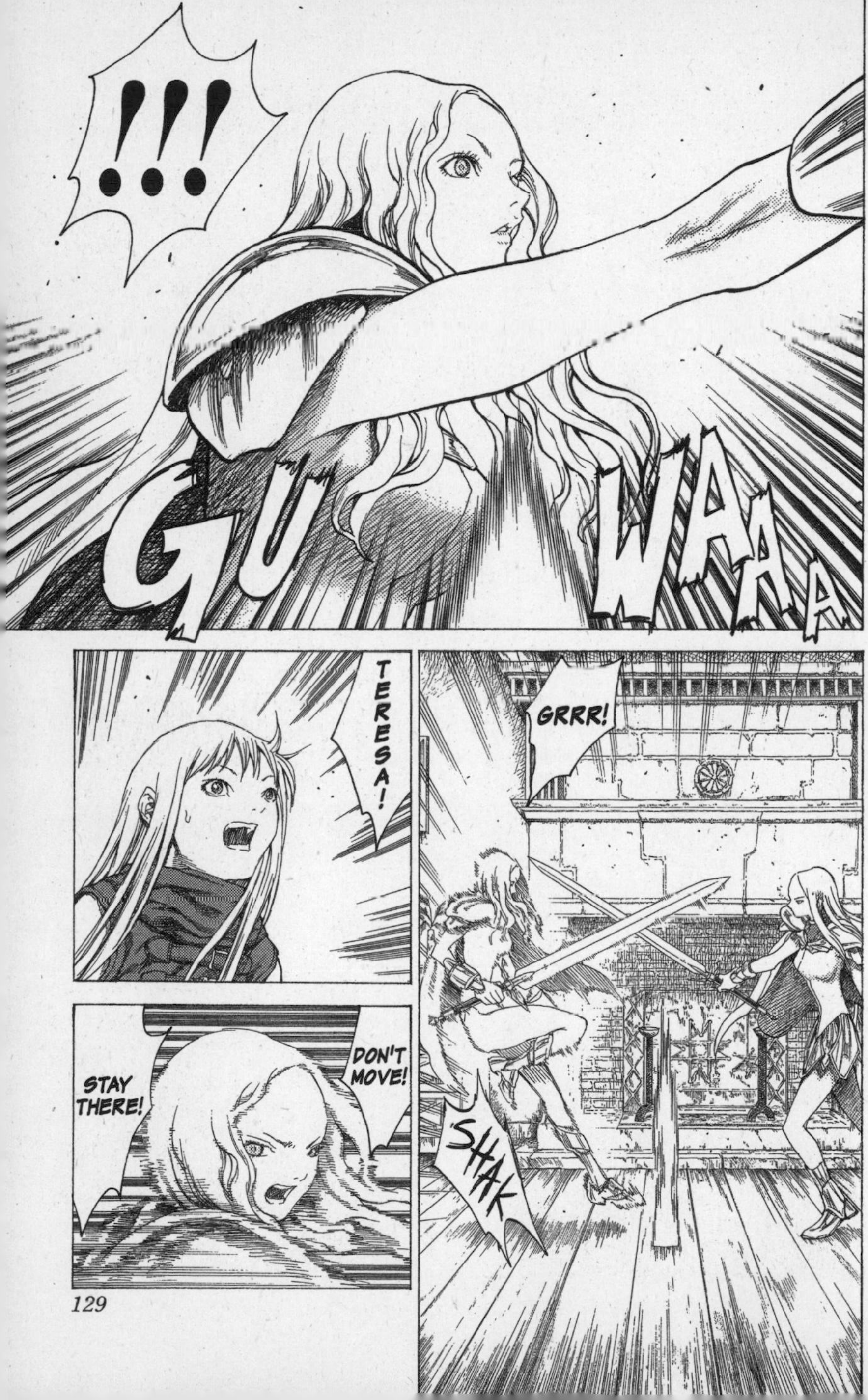
!!!
GUWAA
GRRR!
'SHAK
TERESA!
DON'T MOVE!
STAY THERE!

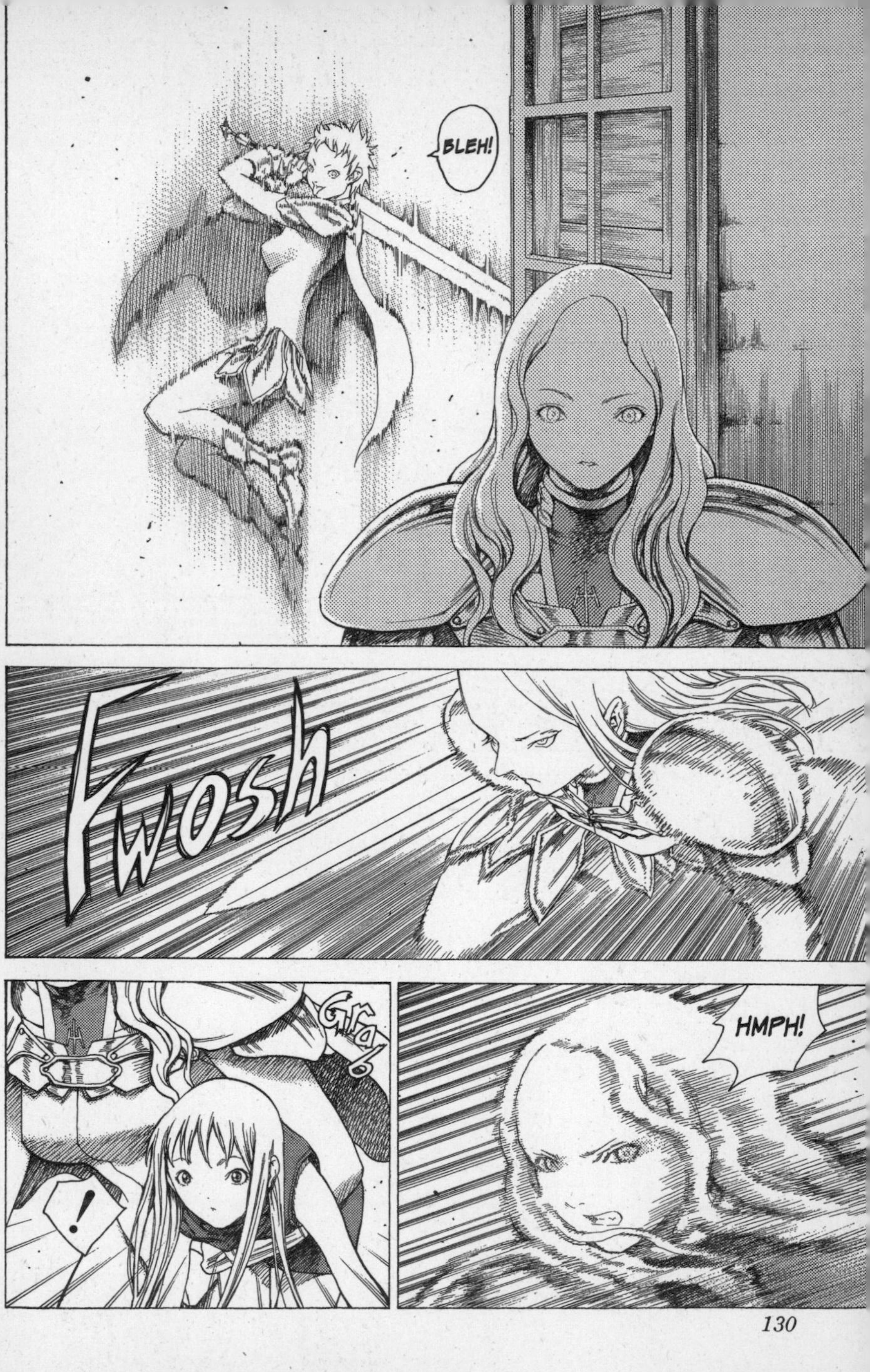
BLEH!
Fwosh
HMPH!
Grab
!

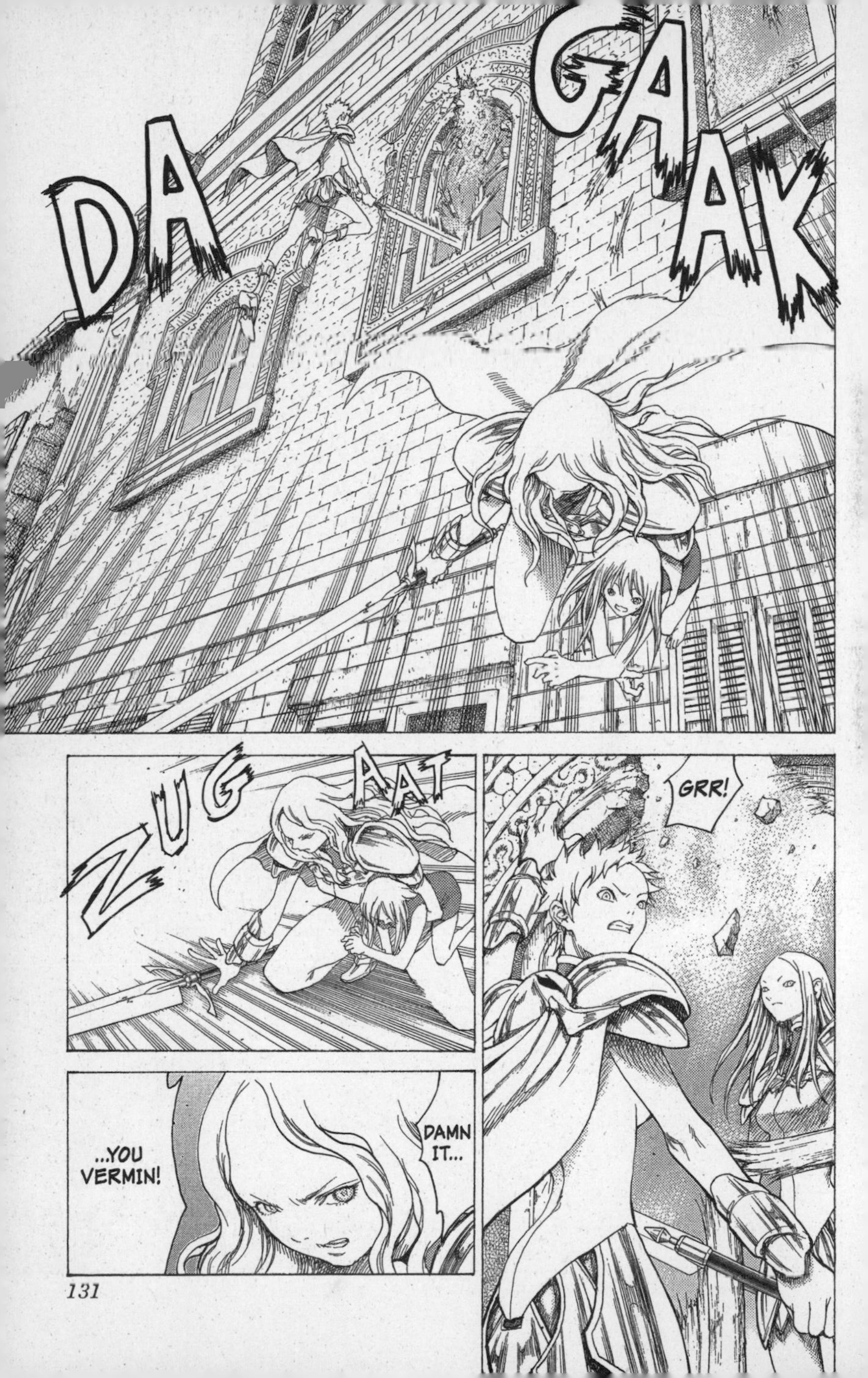
DA
GA
AK
GRR!
ZUG
AAT
DAMN IT...
...YOU VERMIN!

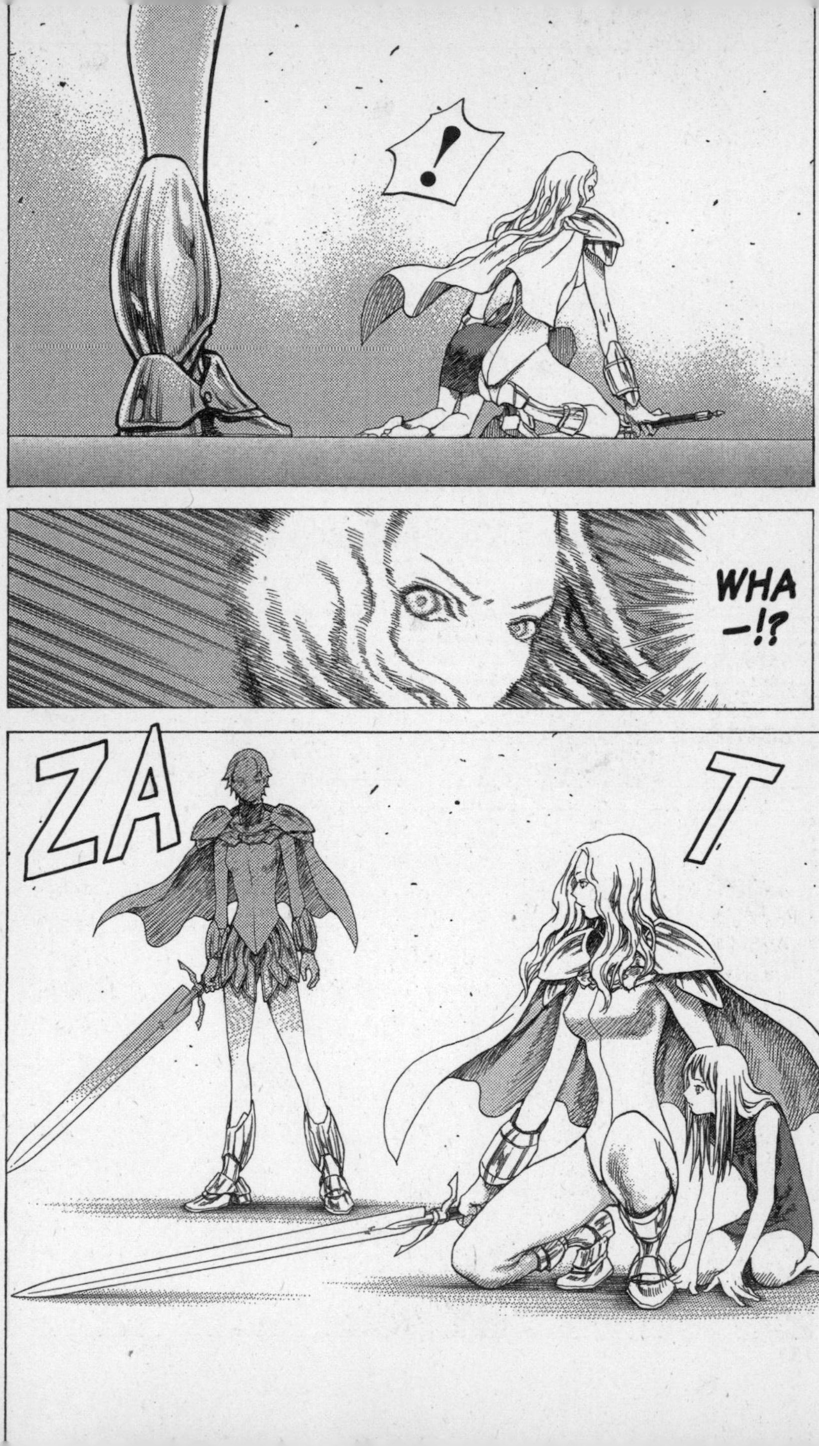
!
WHA —!?
ZA T

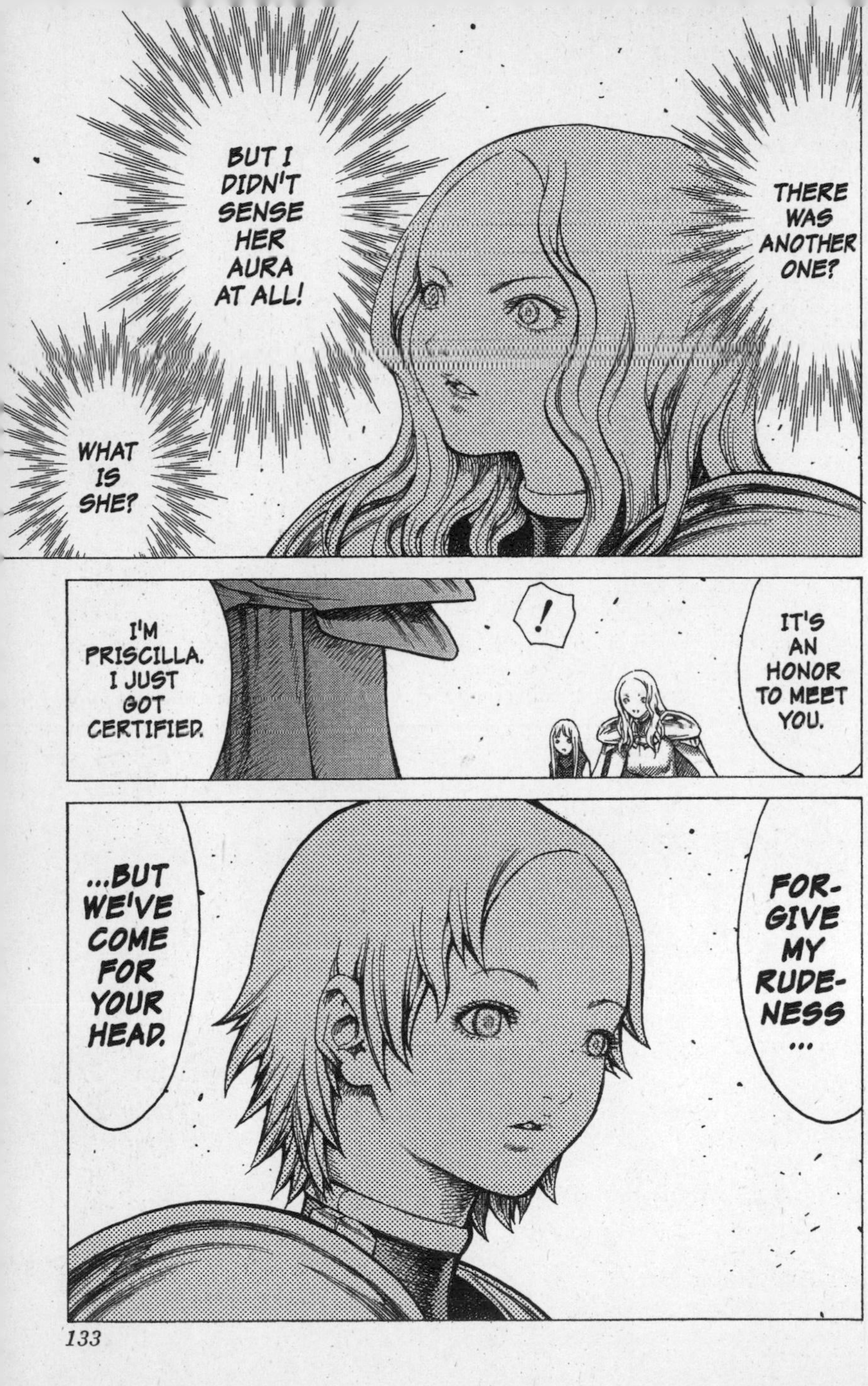
THERE WAS ANOTHER ONE?
BUT I DIDN'T SENSE HER AURA AT ALL!
WHAT IS SHE?
IT'S AN HONOR TO MEET YOU.
!
I'M PRISCILLA. I JUST GOT CERTIFIED.
FOR-GIVE MY RUDE-NESS...
...BUT WE'VE COME FOR YOUR HEAD.

クレイモア
Claymore™

SCENE 20: MARKED FOR DEATH, PART 3

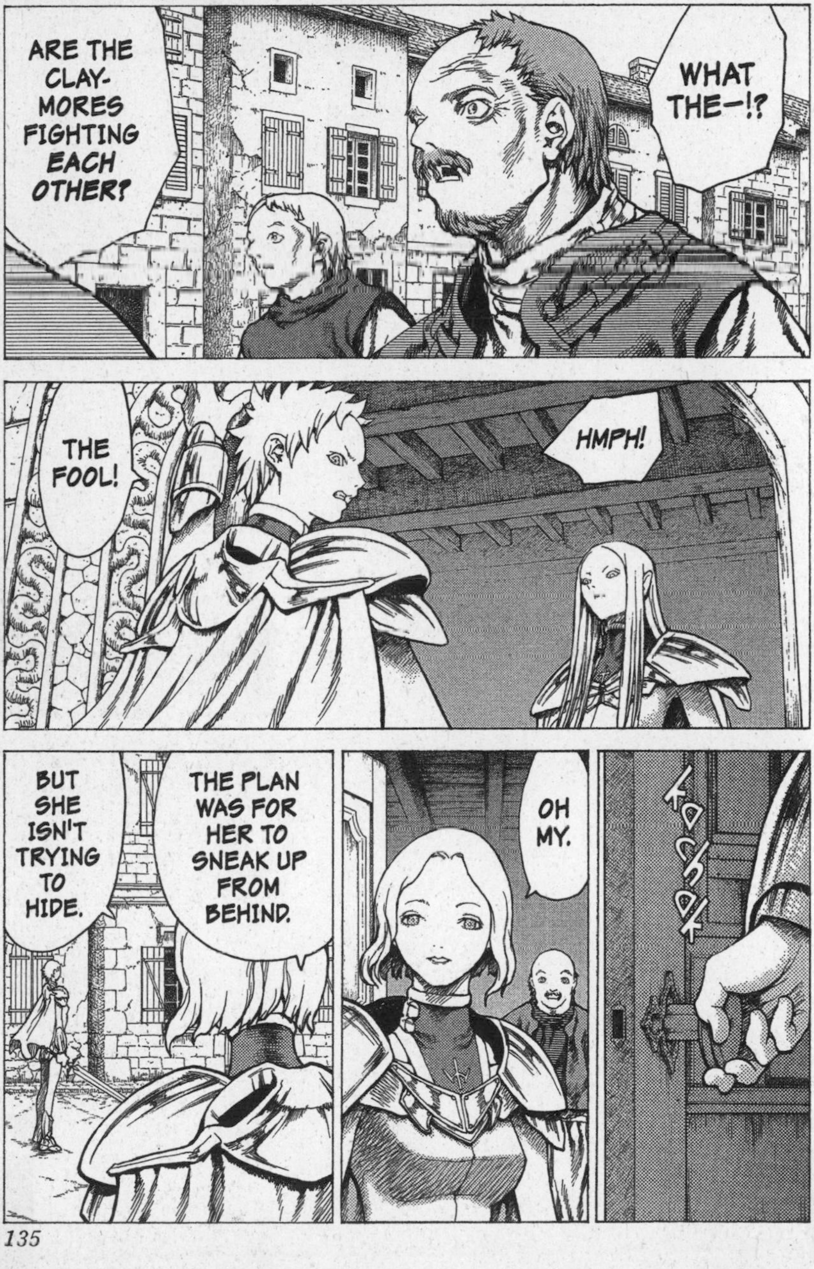

WHAT THE—!?
ARE THE CLAY-MORES FIGHTING EACH OTHER?
HMPH!
THE FOOL!
kachak
OH MY.
THE PLAN WAS FOR HER TO SNEAK UP FROM BEHIND.
BUT SHE ISN'T TRYING TO HIDE.

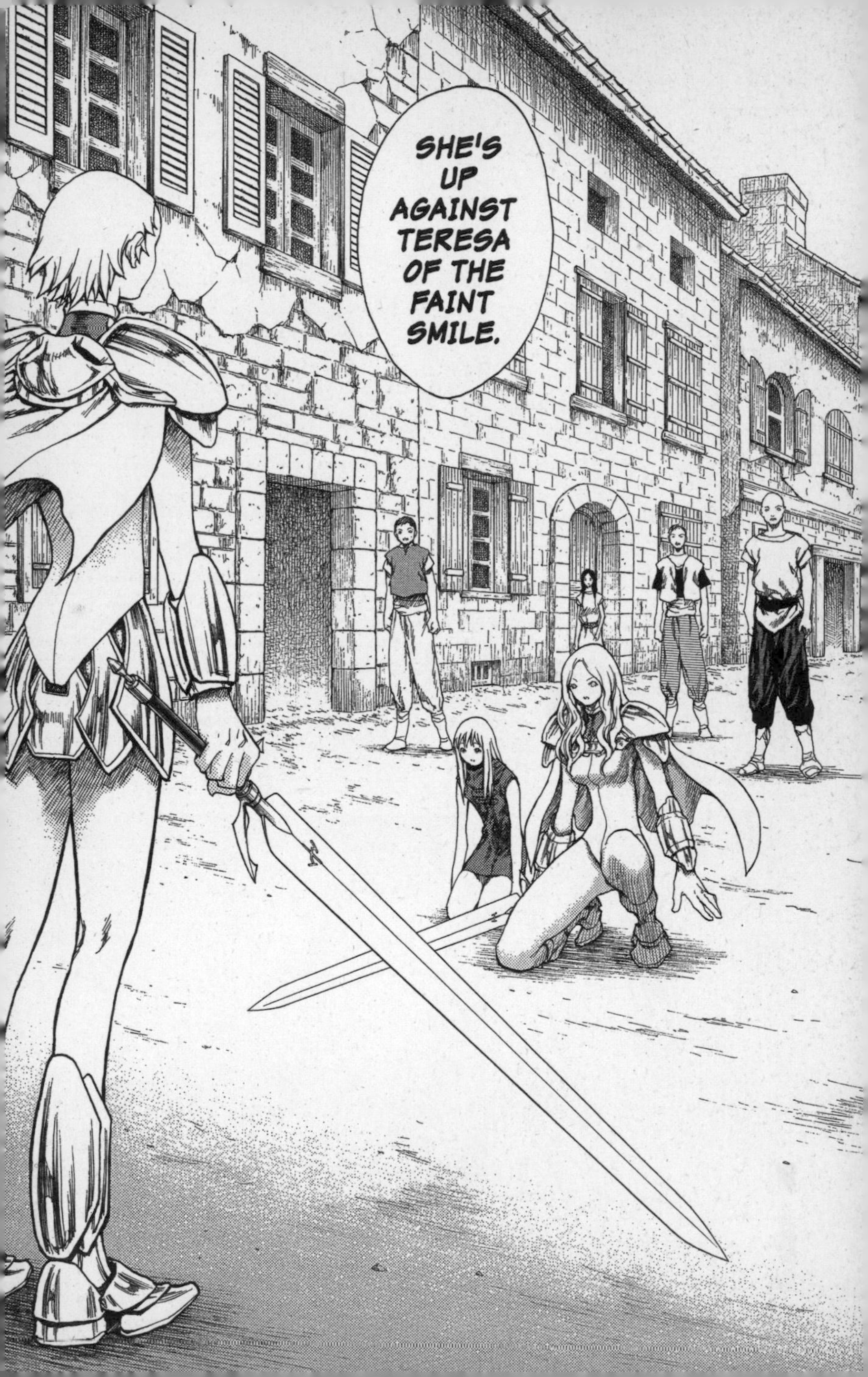
SHE'S UP AGAINST TERESA OF THE FAINT SMILE.

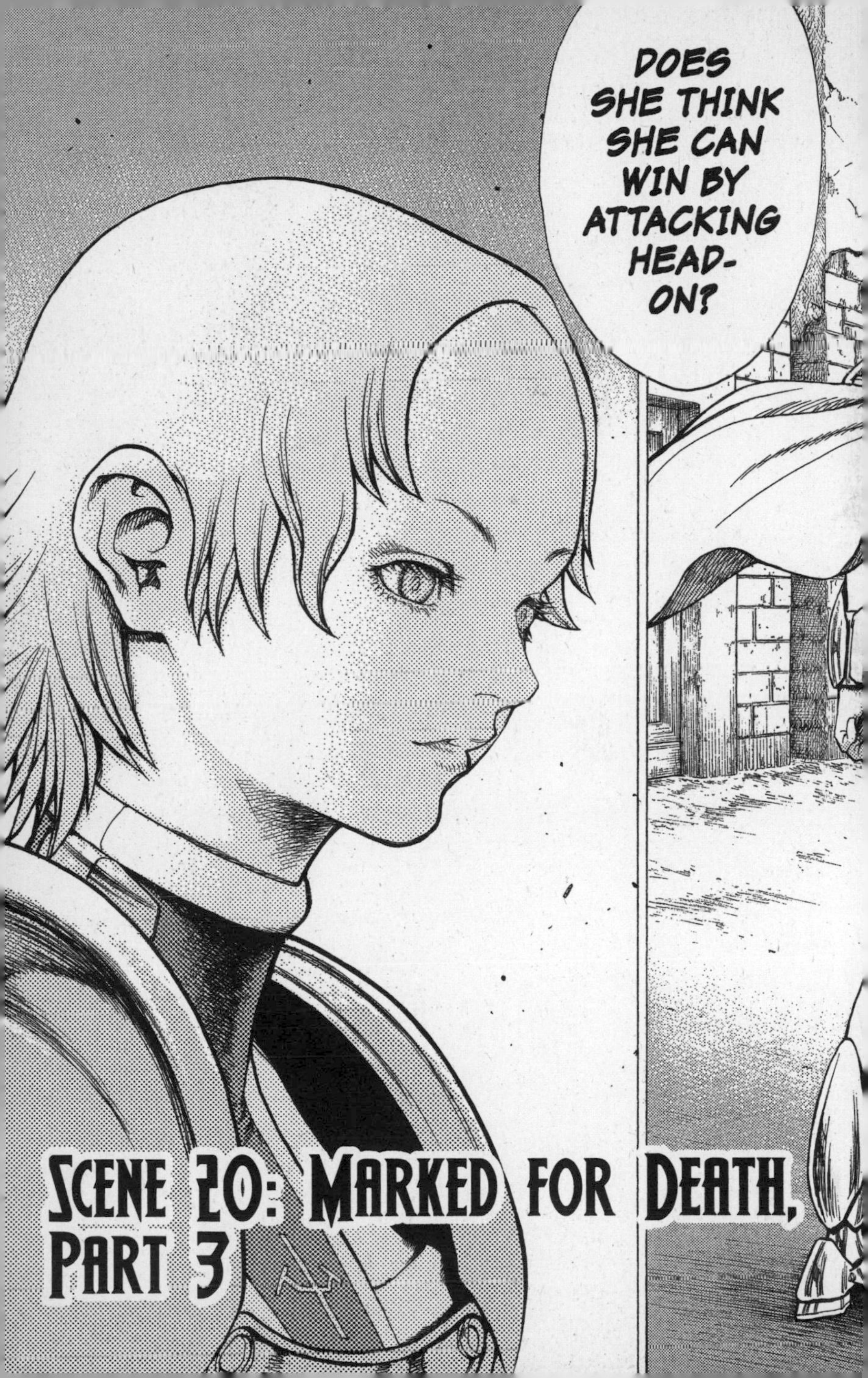
DOES SHE THINK SHE CAN WIN BY ATTACKING HEAD-ON?
SCENE 20: MARKED FOR DEATH, PART 3

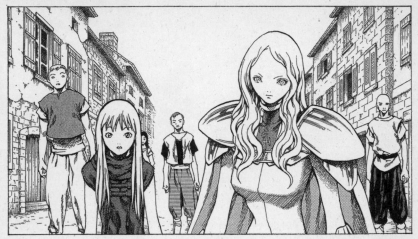

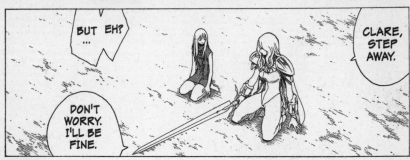

CLARE, STEP AWAY.
BUT EH? ...
DON'T WORRY. I'LL BE FINE.
BELIEVE WHAT I TELL YOU...
...LIKE I SAID BEFORE.
tmp tmp

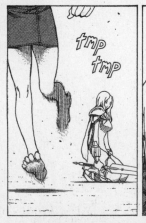

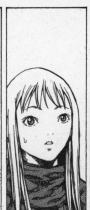

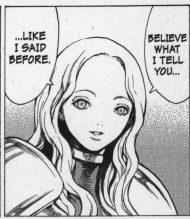

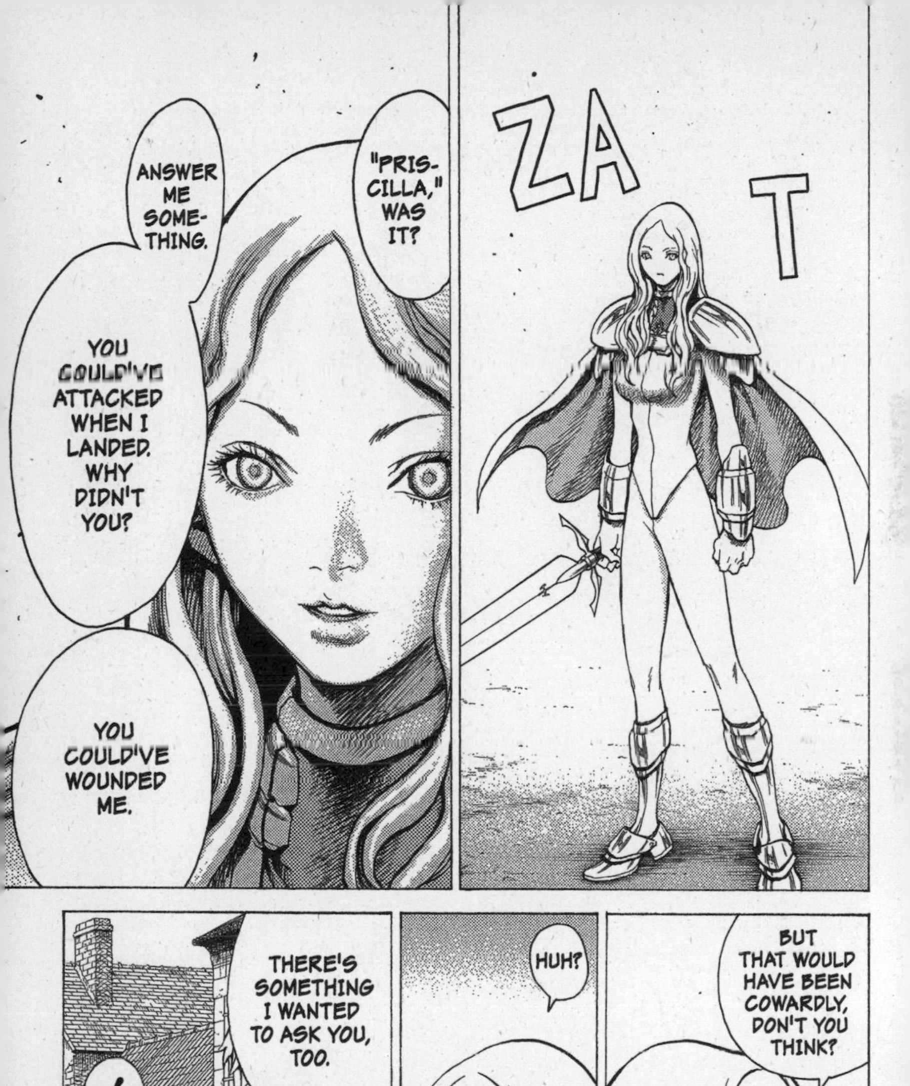
ZA T
"PRIS-CILLA," WAS IT?
ANSWER ME SOMETHING.
YOU COULD'VE ATTACKED WHEN I LANDED. WHY DIDN'T YOU?
YOU COULD'VE WOUNDED ME.
BUT THAT WOULD HAVE BEEN COWARDLY, DON'T YOU THINK?
HUH?
THERE'S SOMETHING I WANTED TO ASK YOU, TOO.
!

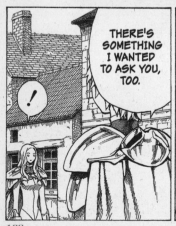

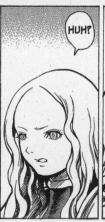

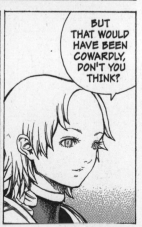

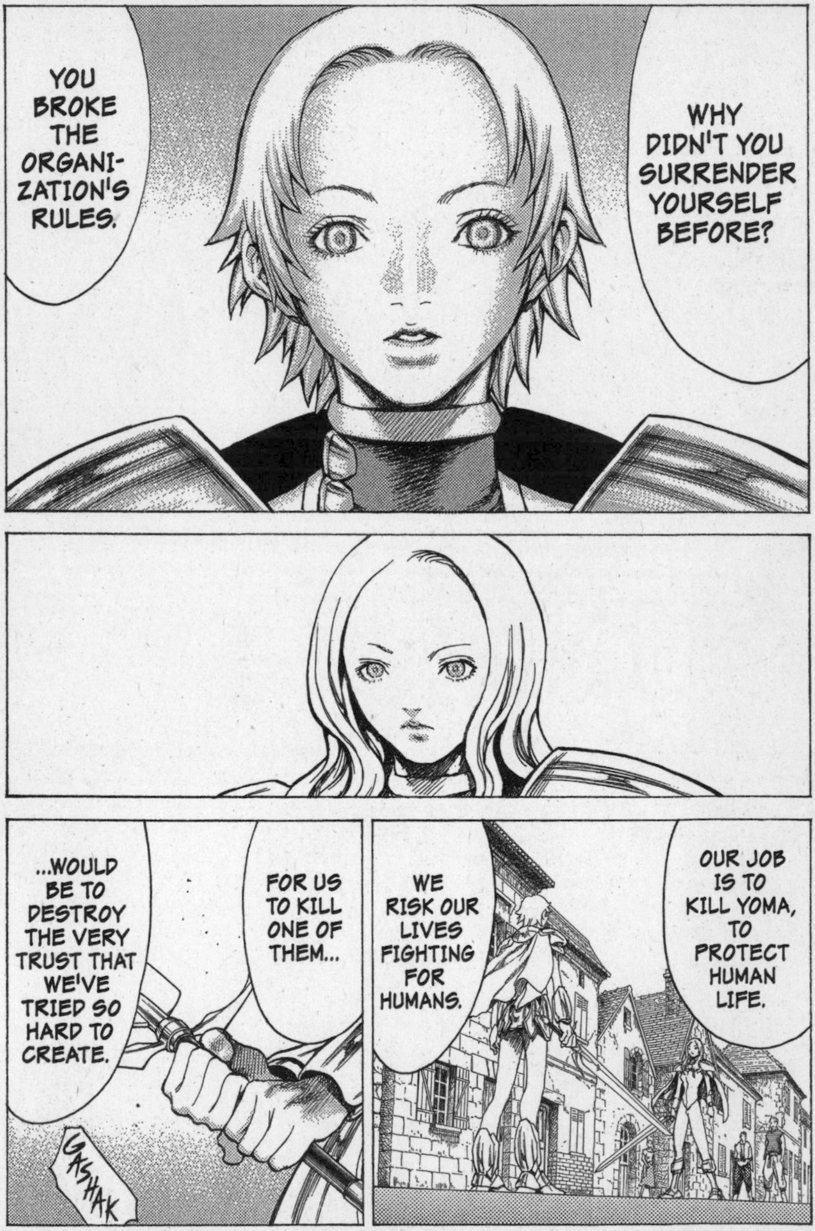
WHY DIDN'T YOU SURRENDER YOURSELF BEFORE?
YOU BROKE THE ORGANI-ZATION'S RULES.
OUR JOB IS TO KILL YOMA, TO PROTECT HUMAN LIFE.
WE RISK OUR LIVES FIGHTING FOR HUMANS.
FOR US TO KILL ONE OF THEM...
...WOULD BE TO DESTROY THE VERY TRUST THAT WE'VE TRIED SO HARD TO CREATE.
GASHAK

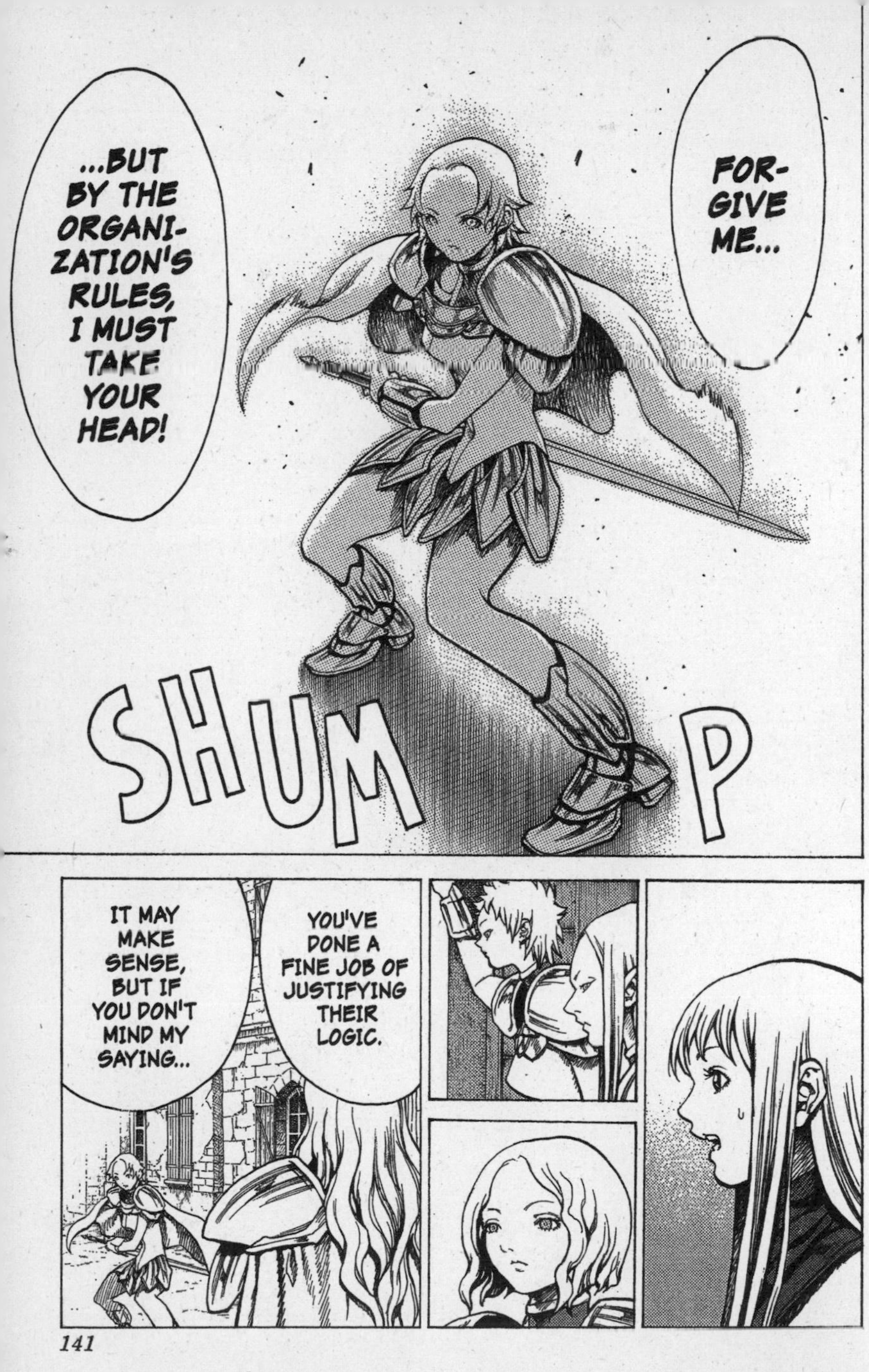
FOR-GIVE ME...
...BUT BY THE ORGANIZATION'S RULES, I MUST TAKE YOUR HEAD!
SHUMP
YOU'VE DONE A FINE JOB OF JUSTIFYING THEIR LOGIC.
IT MAY MAKE SENSE, BUT IF YOU DON'T MIND MY SAYING...

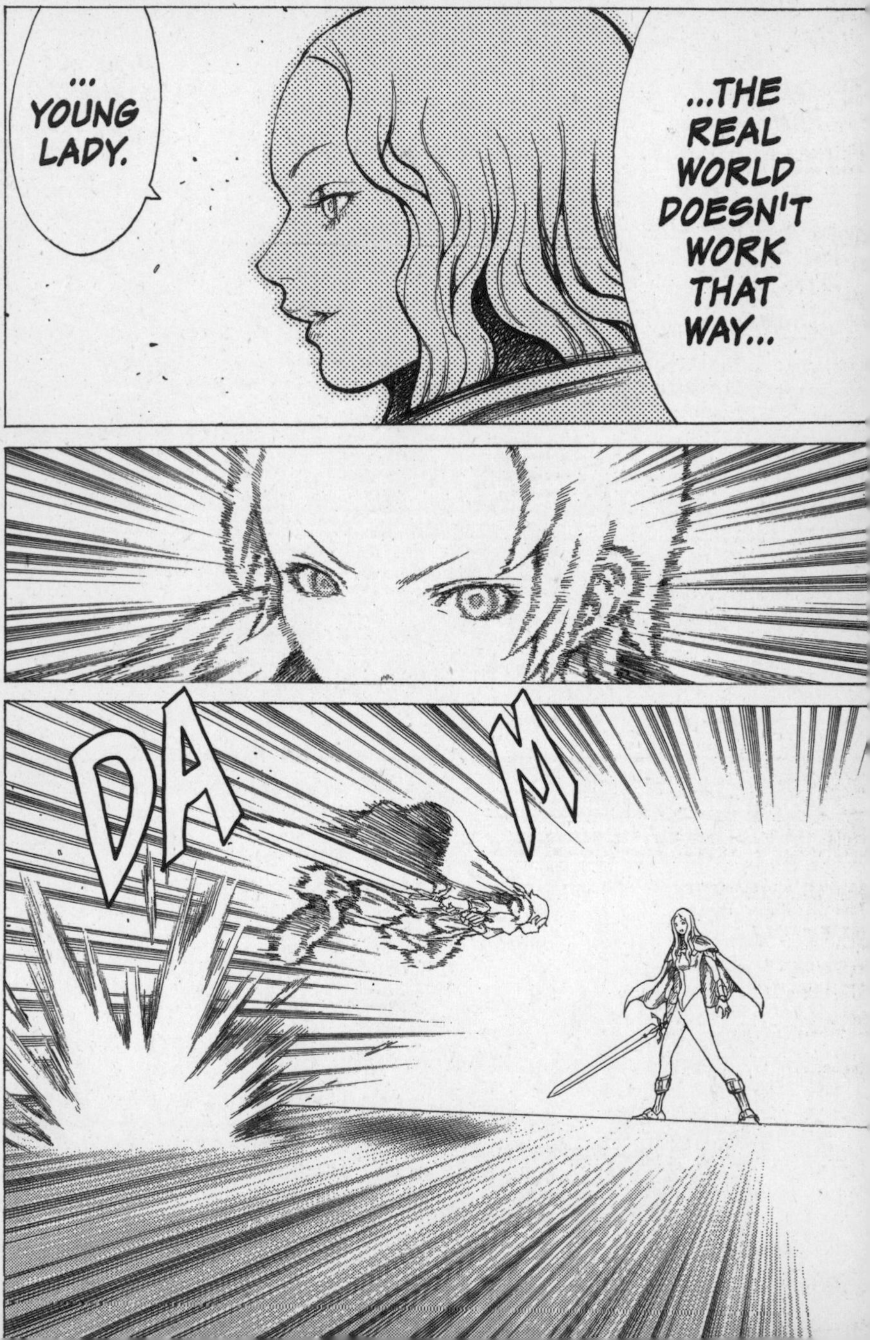
...THE REAL WORLD DOESN'T WORK THAT WAY...
... YOUNG LADY.
DAM

READ THIS WAY

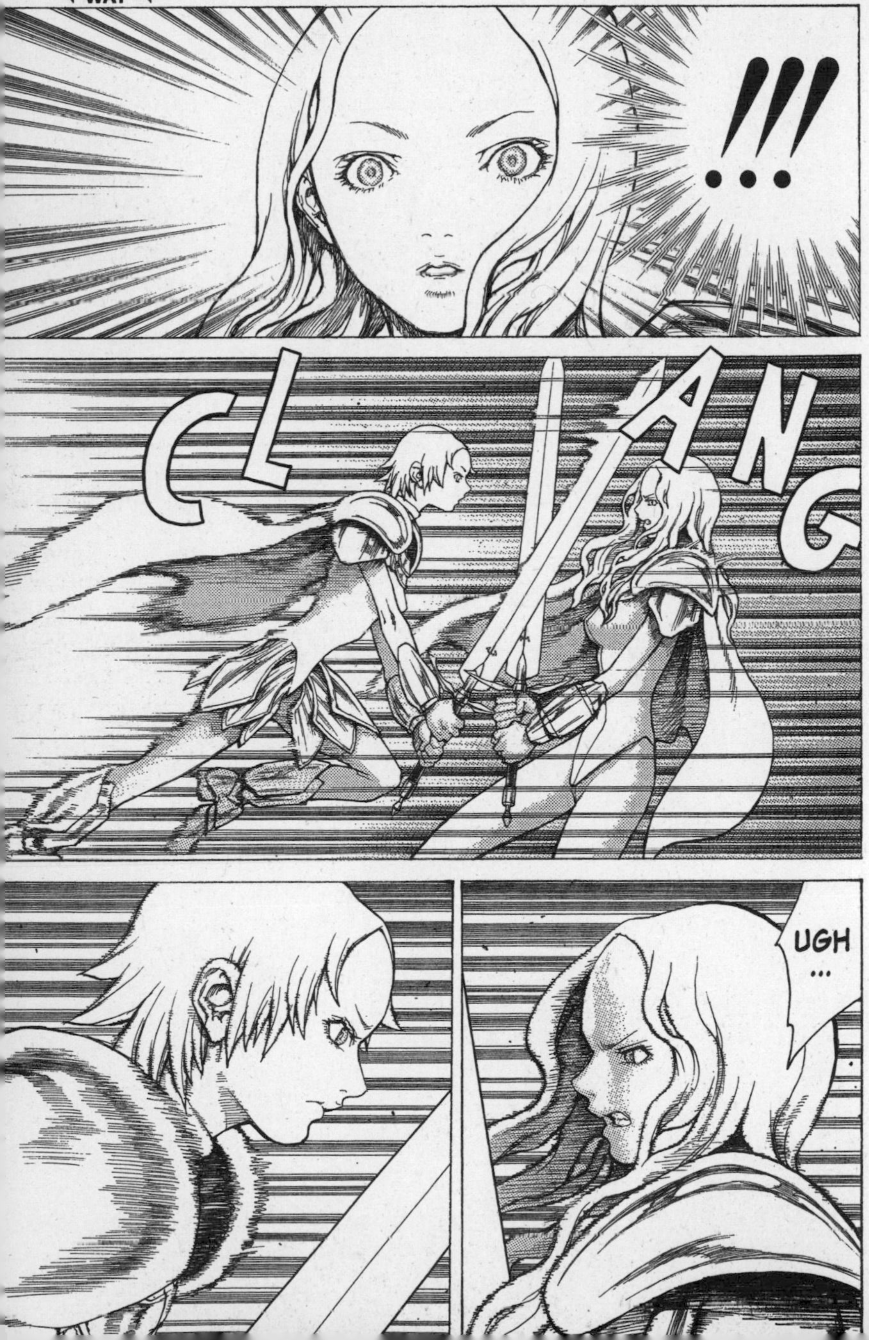
!!!
...
CLANG
UGH
...

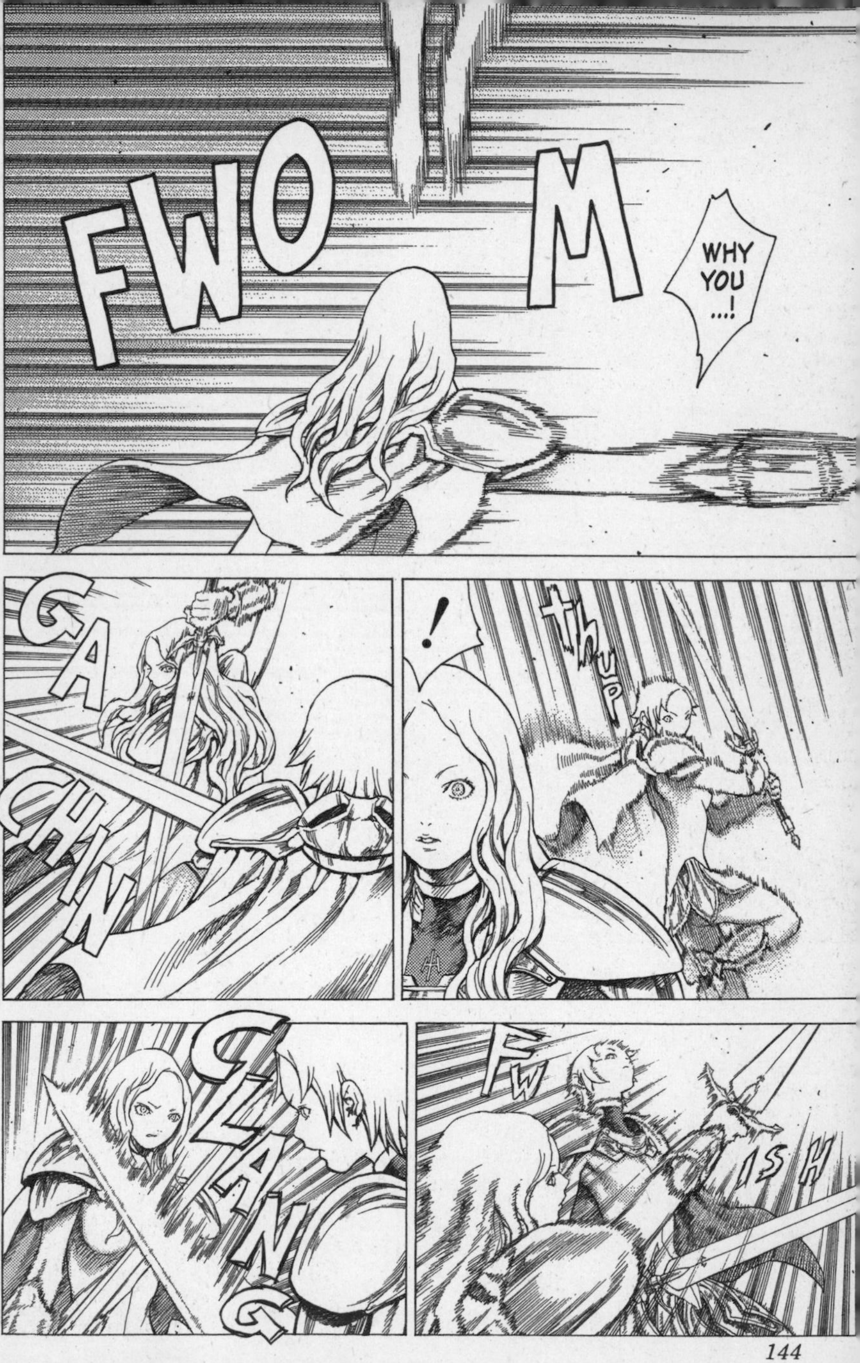
FWOM
WHY YOU ...!
!
thup
GACHINN
FwISH
CLANG

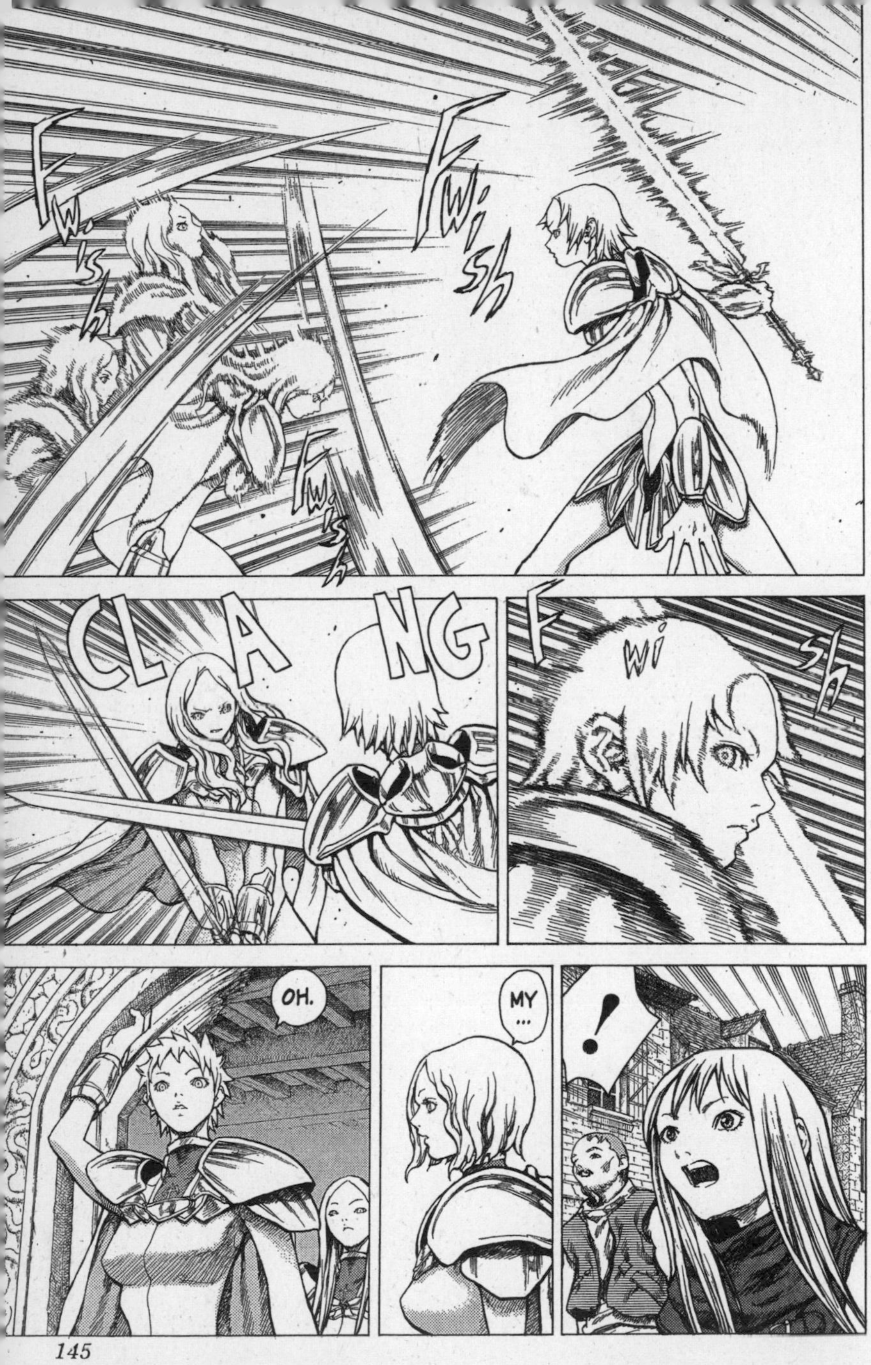
Fwish
Fwish
Fwish
Fwish
CLANG
!
MY ...
OH.

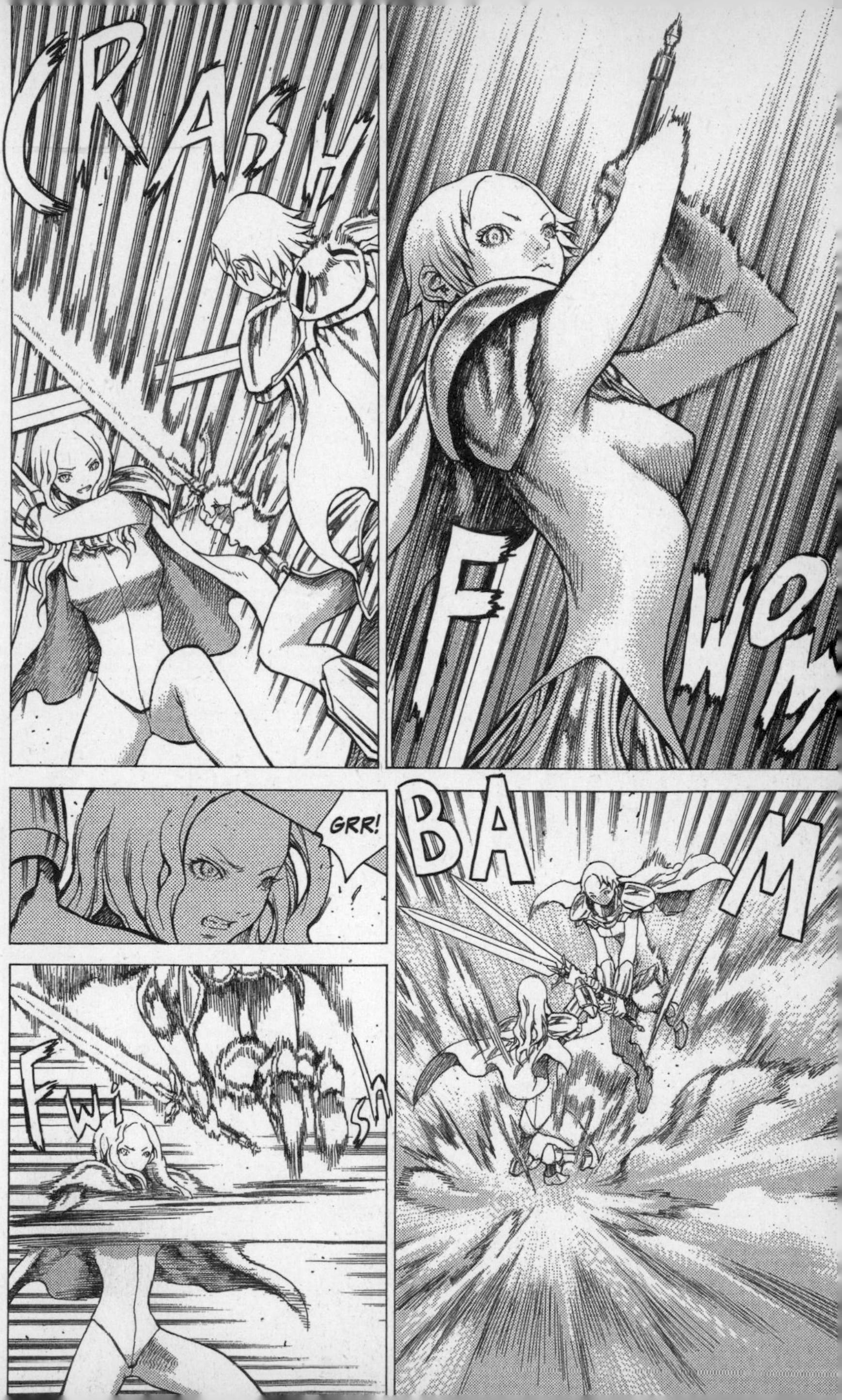
FWOMM
CRASH
BAM
GRR!
Fwish

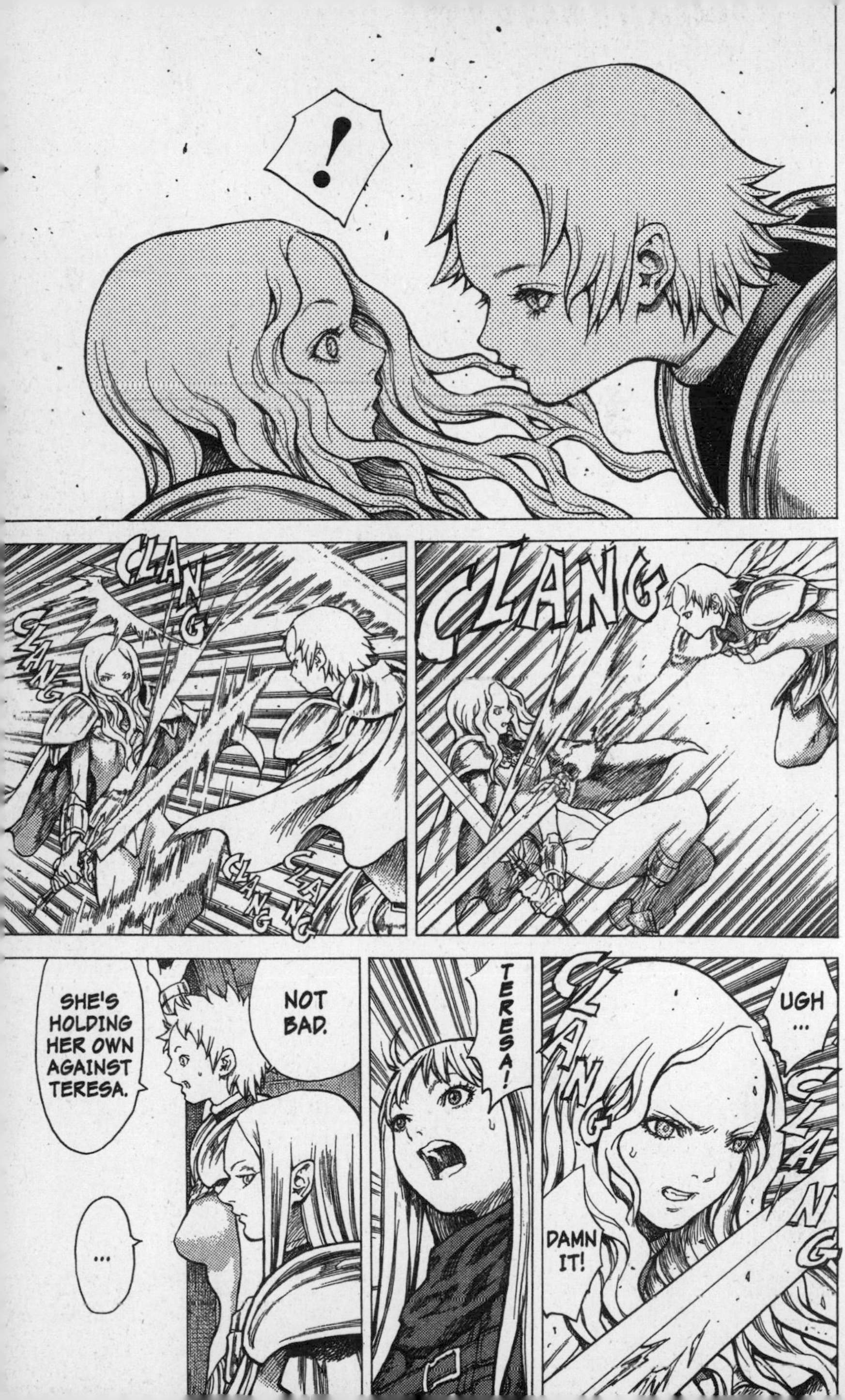
!
CLANG
CLANG
CLANG
CLANG
CLANG
UGH ...
CLANG
CLANG
DAMN IT!
TERESA!
NOT BAD.
SHE'S HOLDING HER OWN AGAINST TERESA.
...

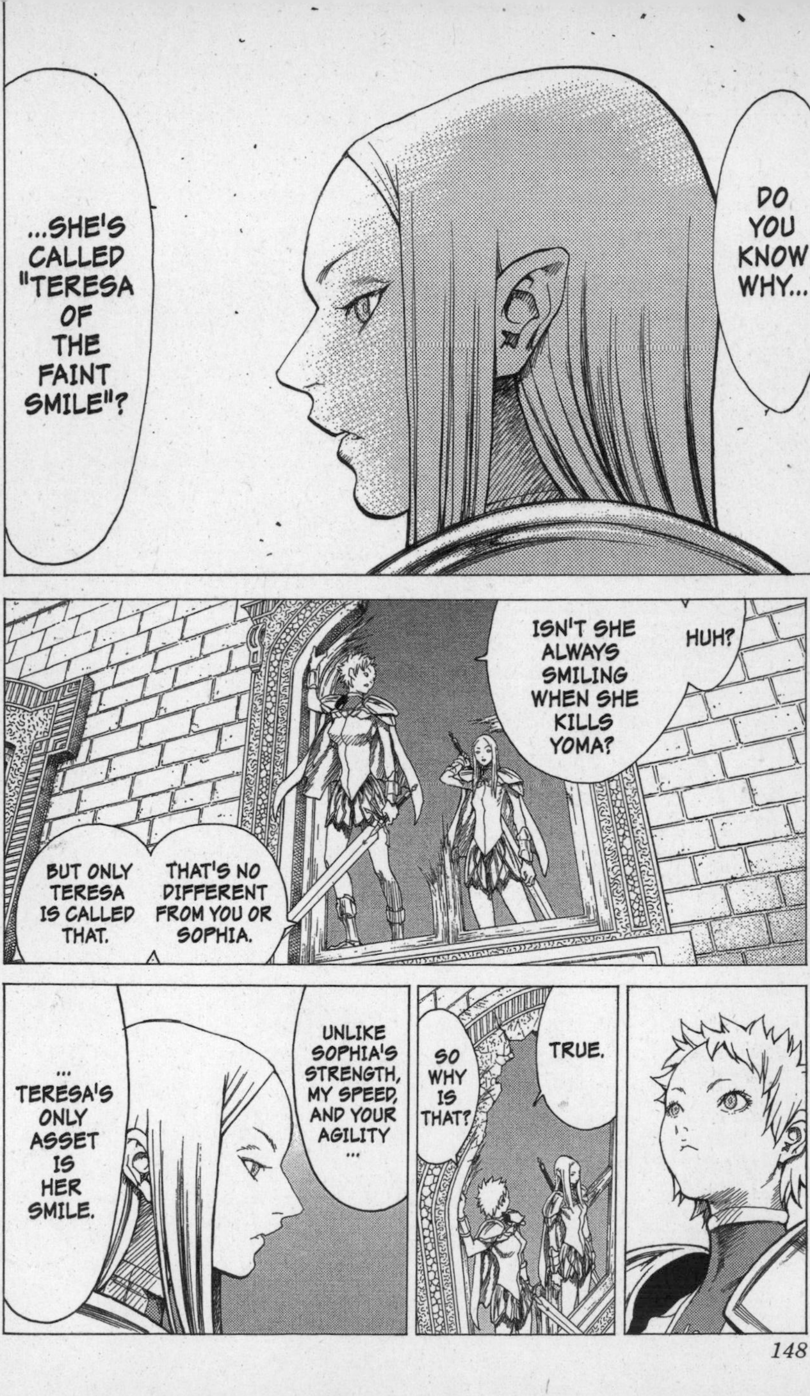
DO YOU KNOW WHY...
...SHE'S CALLED "TERESA OF THE FAINT SMILE"?
HUH?
ISN'T SHE ALWAYS SMILING WHEN SHE KILLS YOMA?
THAT'S NO DIFFERENT FROM YOU OR SOPHIA.
BUT ONLY TERESA IS CALLED THAT.
TRUE.
SO WHY IS THAT?
UNLIKE SOPHIA'S STRENGTH, MY SPEED, AND YOUR AGILITY ...
... TERESA'S ONLY ASSET IS HER SMILE.

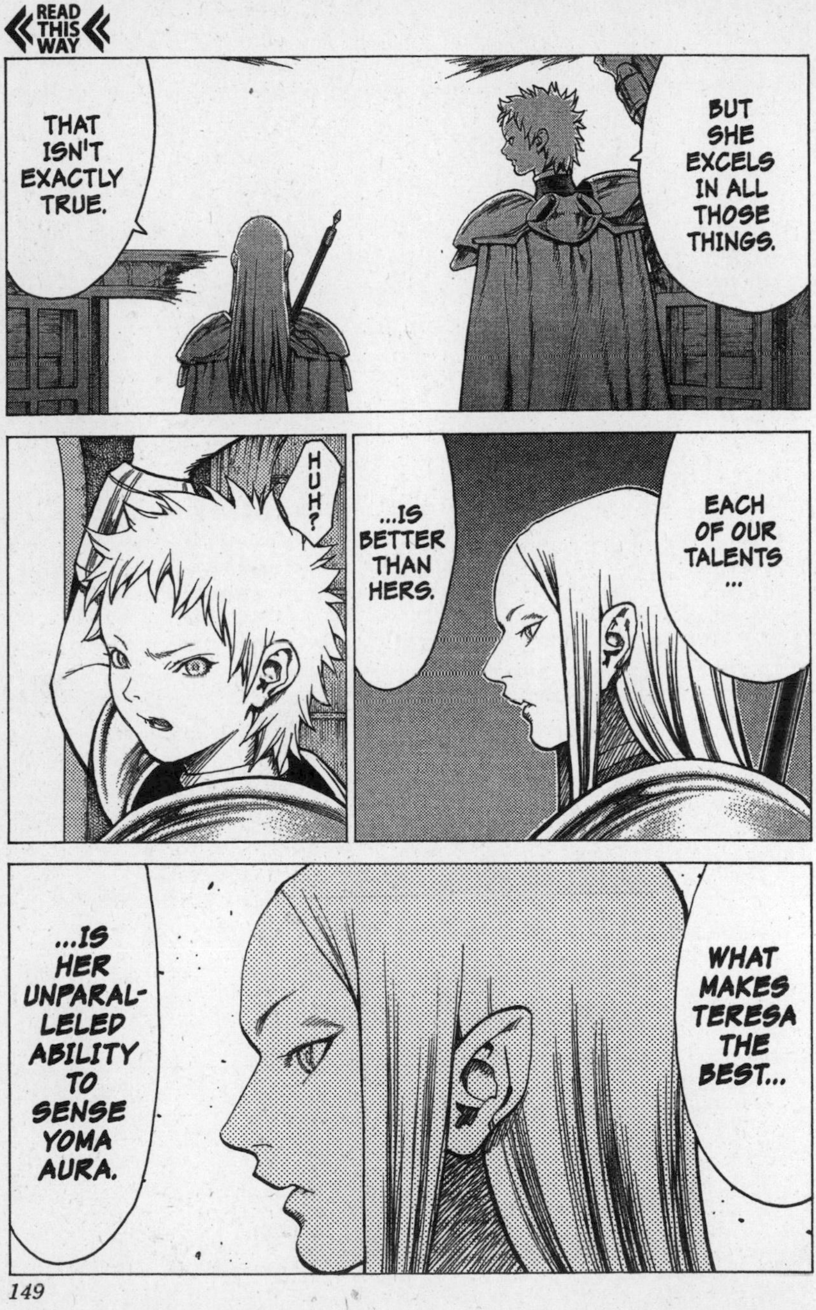
READ THIS WAY
BUT SHE EXCELS IN ALL THOSE THINGS.
THAT ISN'T EXACTLY TRUE.
EACH OF OUR TALENTS ...
...IS BETTER THAN HERS.
HUH?
WHAT MAKES TERESA THE BEST...
...IS HER UNPARAL-LELED ABILITY TO SENSE YOMA AURA.

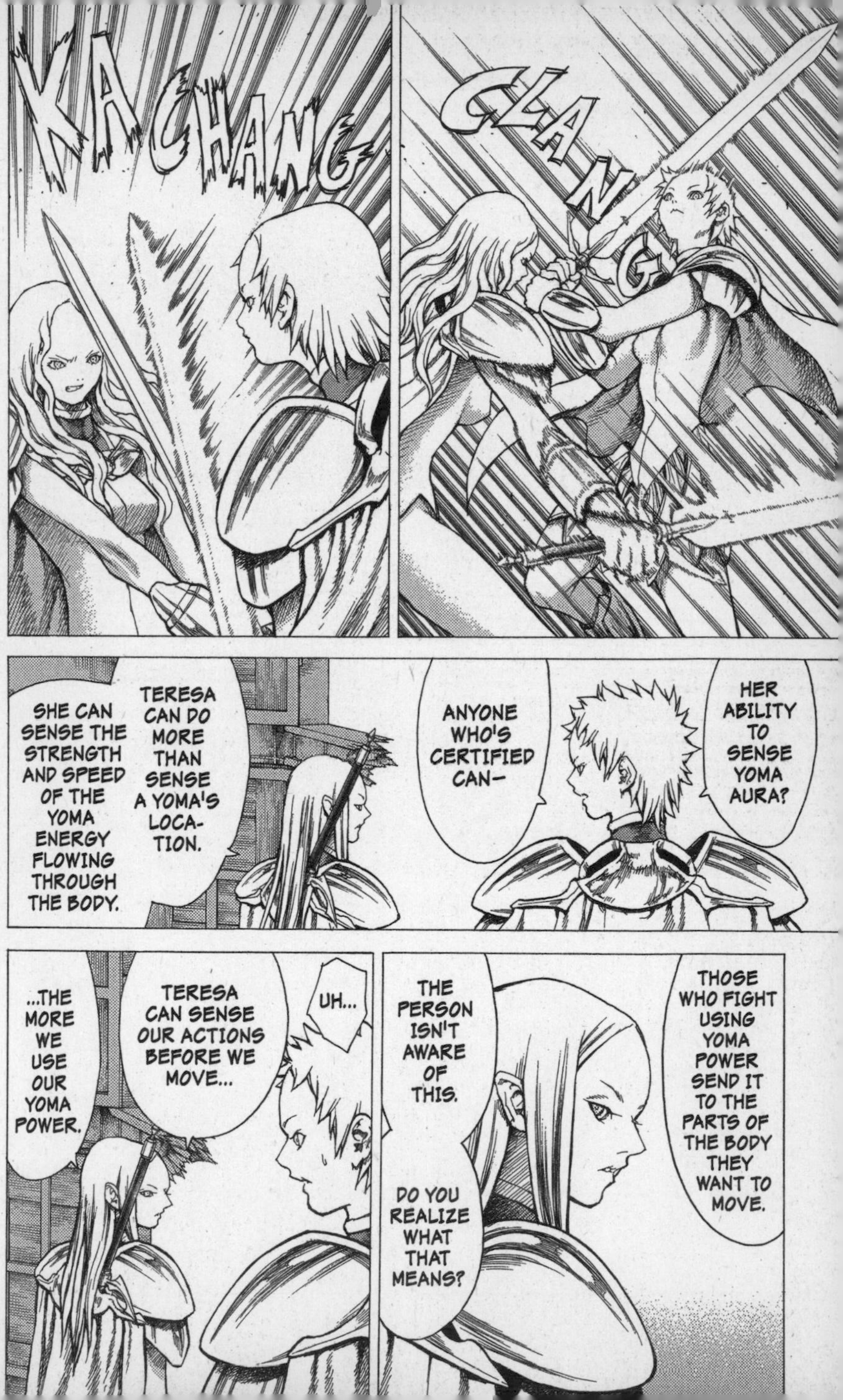
CLANG
KACHANG
HER ABILITY TO SENSE YOMA AURA?
ANYONE WHO'S CERTIFIED CAN–
TERESA CAN DO MORE THAN SENSE A YOMA'S LOCATION.
SHE CAN SENSE THE STRENGTH AND SPEED OF THE YOMA ENERGY FLOWING THROUGH THE BODY.
THOSE WHO FIGHT USING YOMA POWER SEND IT TO THE PARTS OF THE BODY THEY WANT TO MOVE.
THE PERSON ISN'T AWARE OF THIS.
DO YOU REALIZE WHAT THAT MEANS?
UH...
TERESA CAN SENSE OUR ACTIONS BEFORE WE MOVE...
...THE MORE WE USE OUR YOMA POWER.

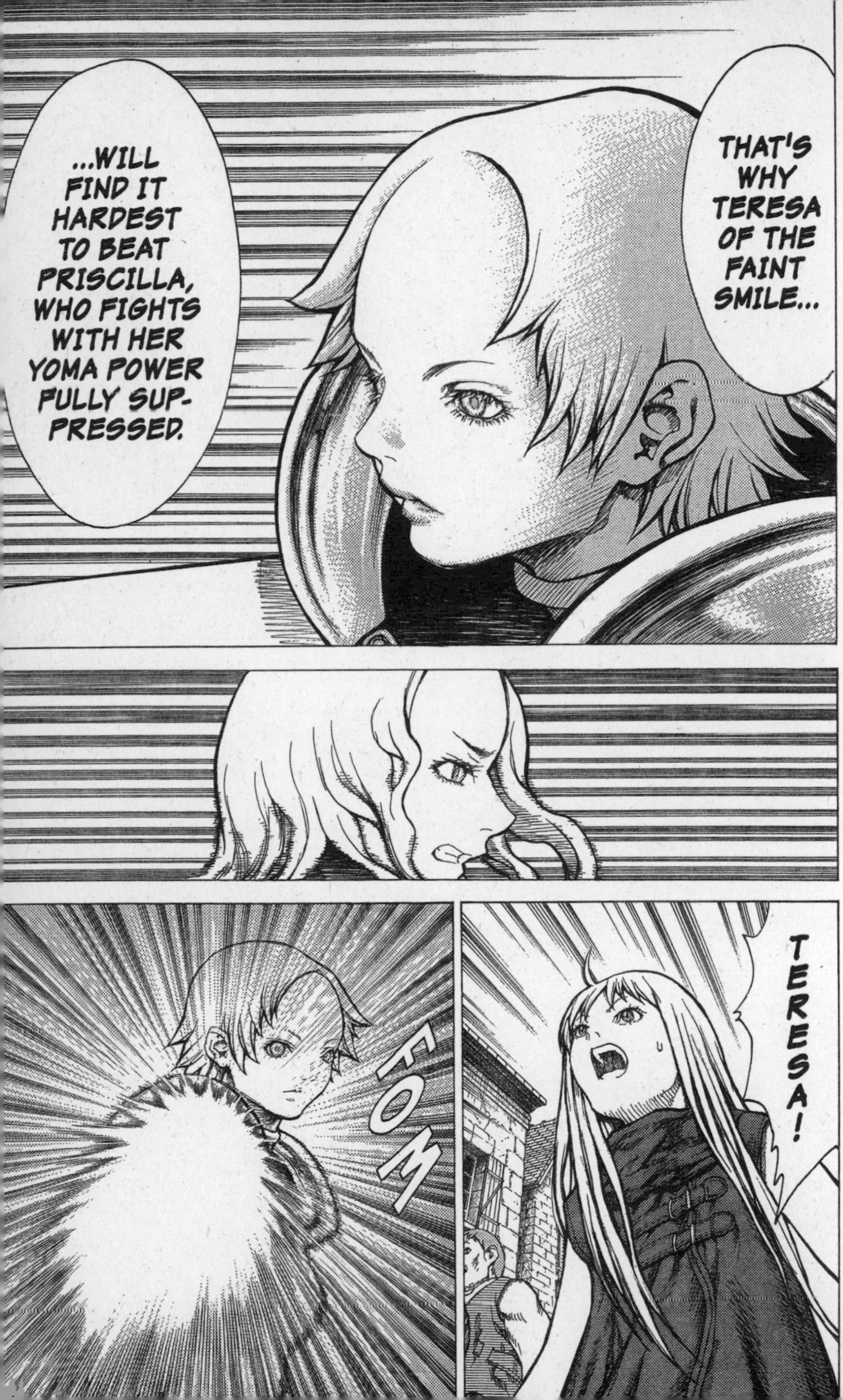
THAT'S WHY TERESA OF THE FAINT SMILE...
...WILL FIND IT HARDEST TO BEAT PRISCILLA, WHO FIGHTS WITH HER YOMA POWER FULLY SUP-PRESSED.
TERESA!
FOM

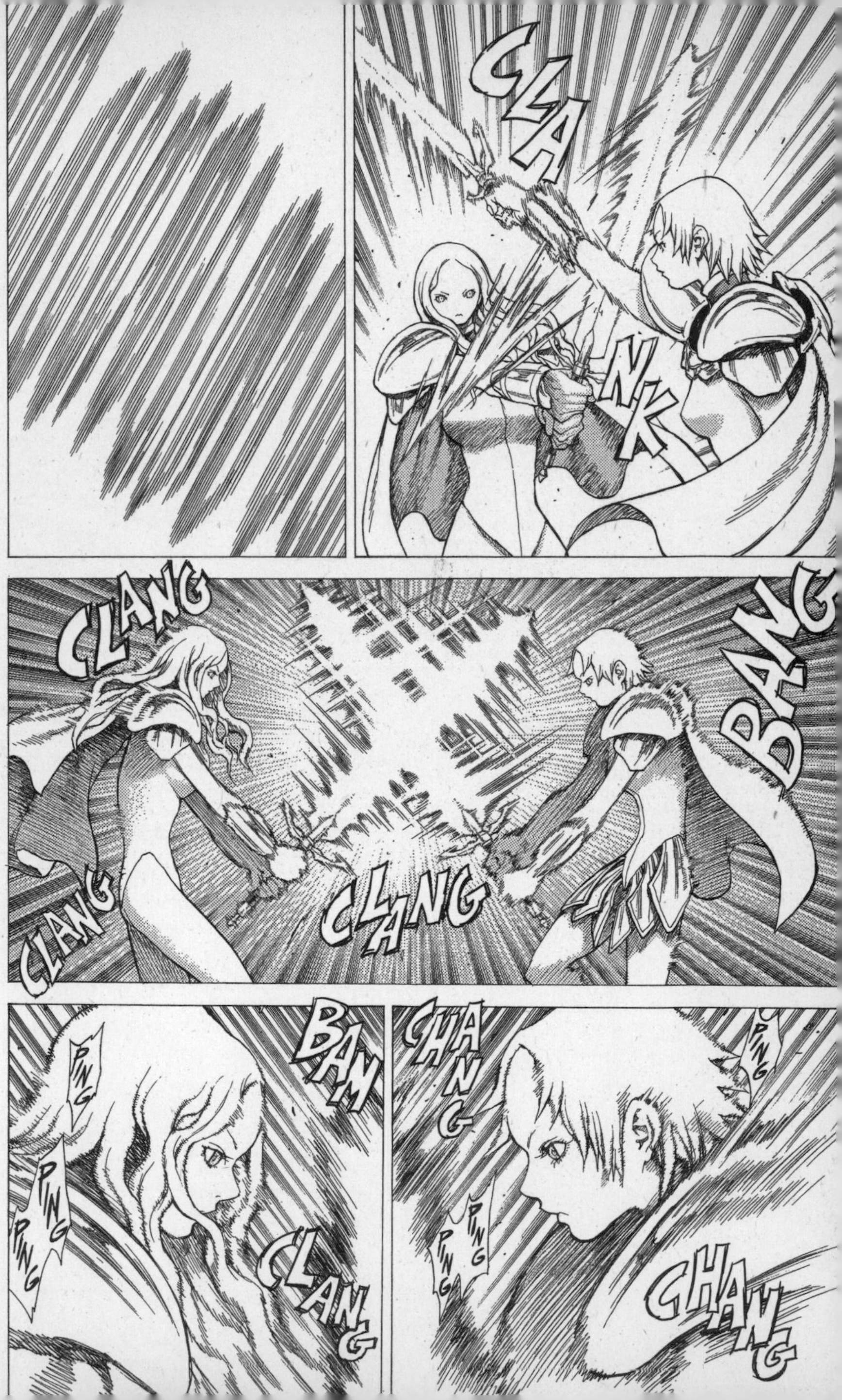
CLANK
BANG
CLANG
CLANG
CLANG
PING
CHANG
CHANG
PING
PING
BAM
PING
PING
PING
PING
CLANG

READ THIS WAY

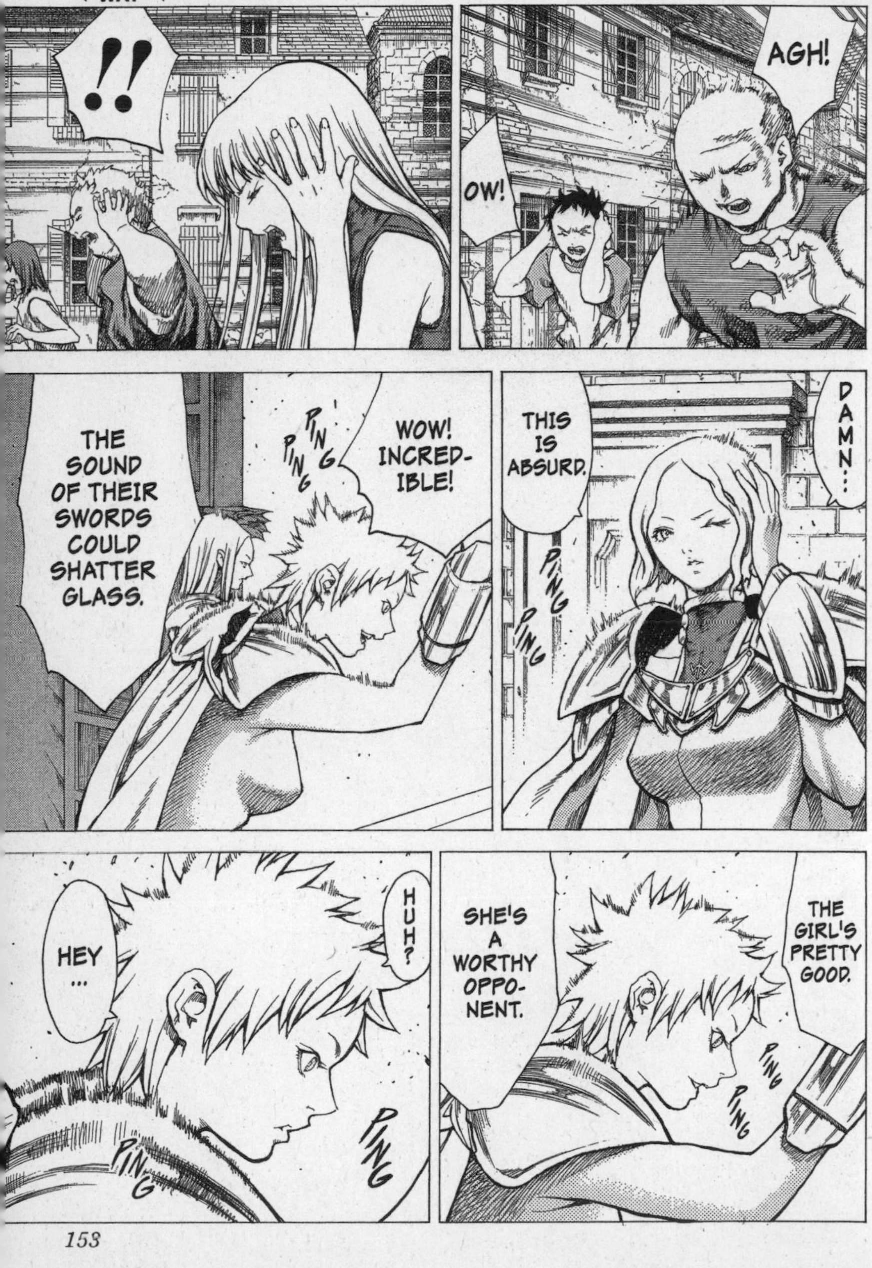
AGH!
OW!
!!
DAMN...
PING PING
THIS IS ABSURD.
WOW! INCRED-IBLE!
PING PING
THE SOUND OF THEIR SWORDS COULD SHATTER GLASS.
THE GIRL'S PRETTY GOOD.
PING PING
SHE'S A WORTHY OPPO-NENT.
HUH?
PING
HEY ...
PING

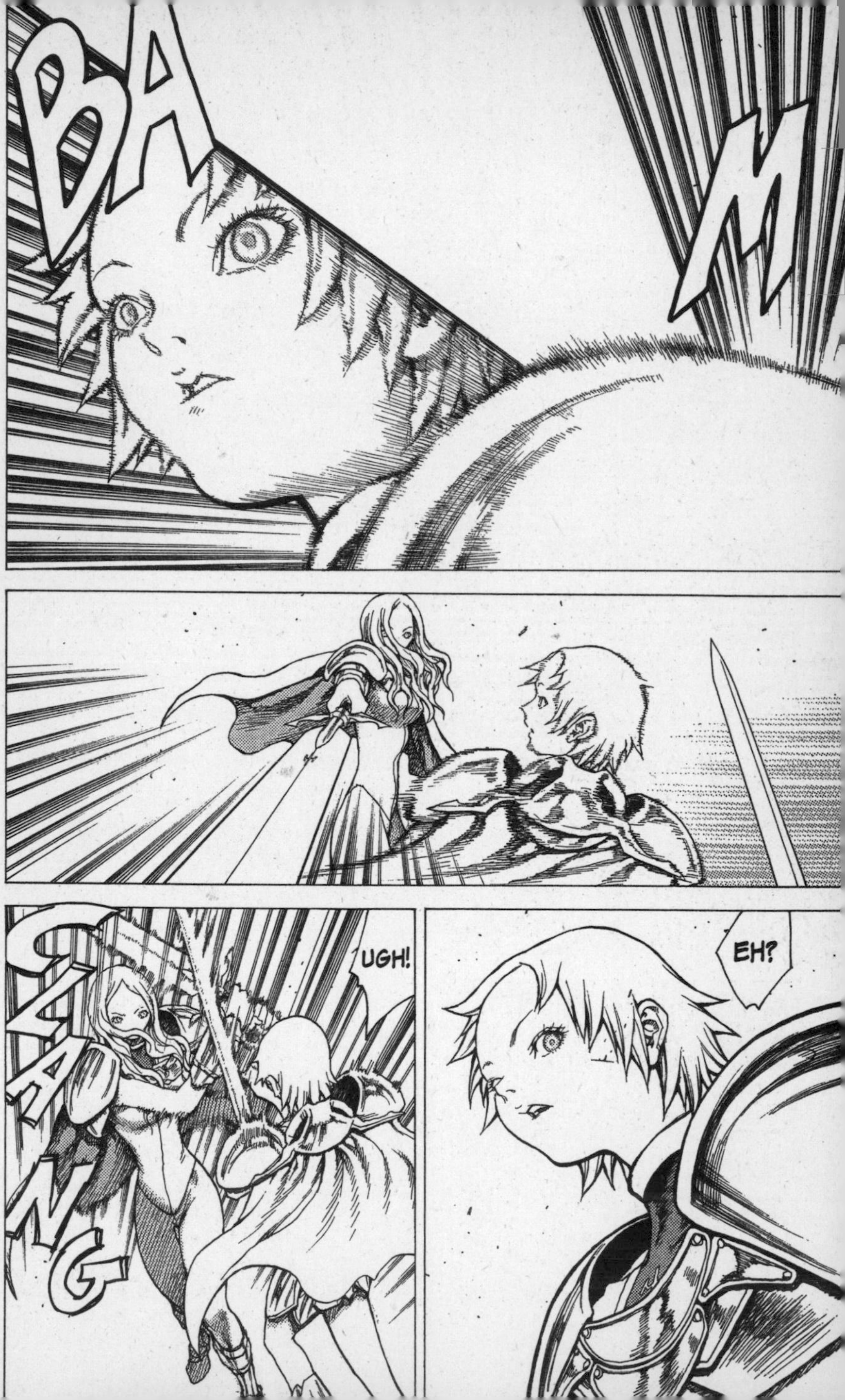
BAM
EH?
UGH!
CLANG

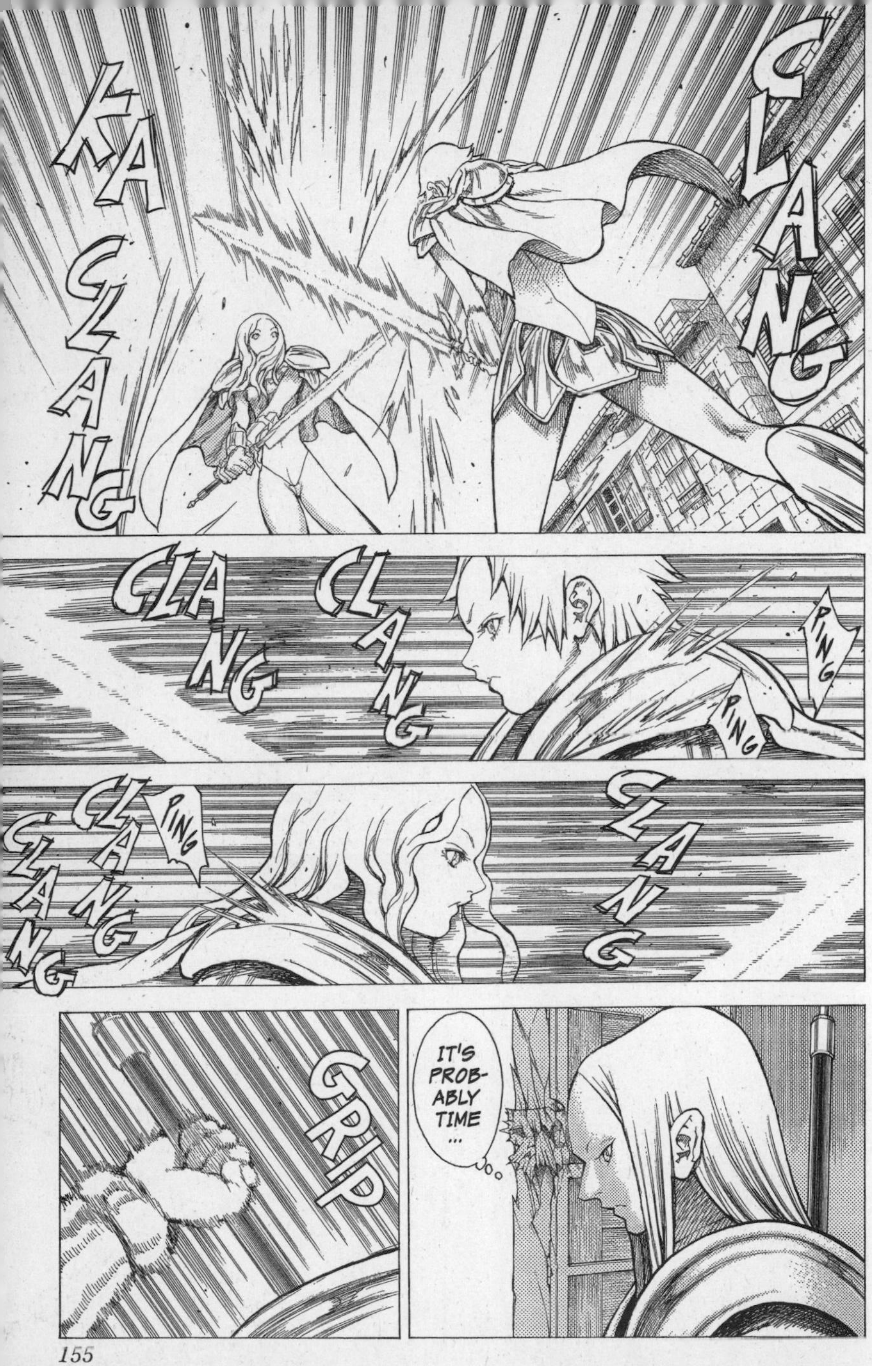
CLANG
KA CLANG
PING
PING
CLANG
CLANG
CLANG
PING
CLANG
CLANG
IT'S PROBABLY TIME ...
GRIP

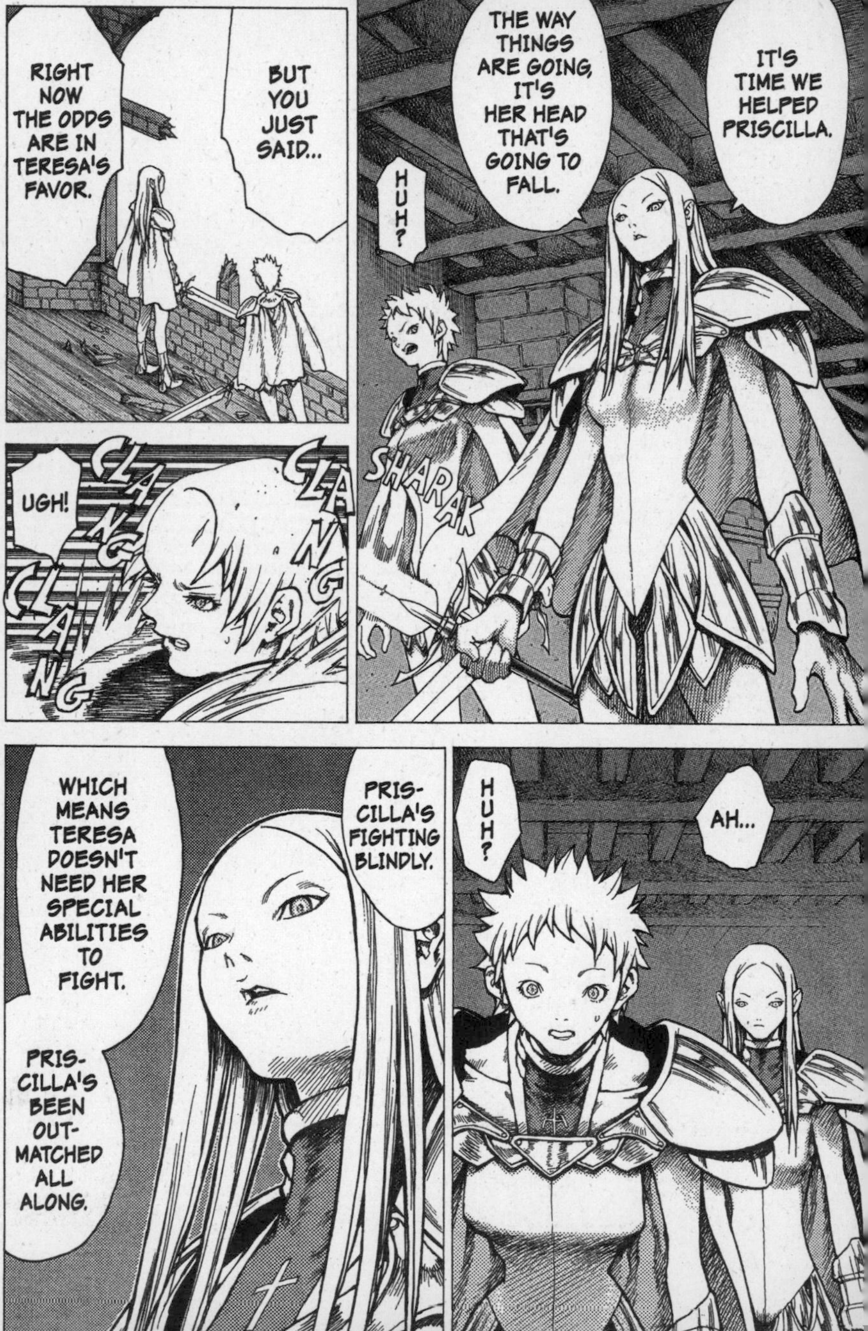
IT'S TIME WE HELPED PRISCILLA.
THE WAY THINGS ARE GOING, IT'S HER HEAD THAT'S GOING TO FALL.
HUH?
SHARAK
BUT YOU JUST SAID...
RIGHT NOW THE ODDS ARE IN TERESA'S FAVOR.
CLANG
CLANG
UGH!
CLANG
CLANG
AH...
HUH?
PRIS-CILLA'S FIGHTING BLINDLY.
WHICH MEANS TERESA DOESN'T NEED HER SPECIAL ABILITIES TO FIGHT.
PRIS-CILLA'S BEEN OUT-MATCHED ALL ALONG.

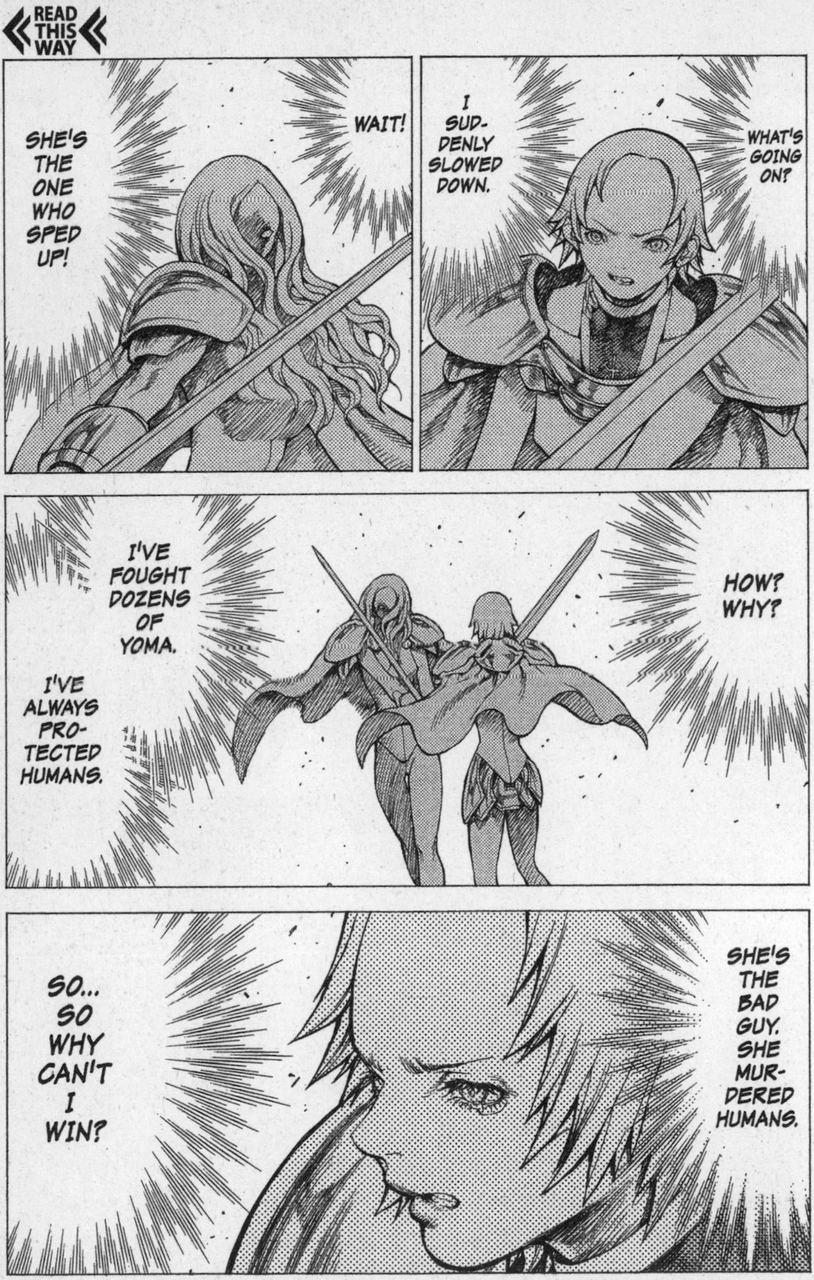
READ THIS WAY
WHAT'S GOING ON?
I SUDDENLY SLOWED DOWN.
WAIT!
SHE'S THE ONE WHO SPED UP!
HOW? WHY?
I'VE FOUGHT DOZENS OF YOMA.
I'VE ALWAYS PROTECTED HUMANS.
SHE'S THE BAD GUY. SHE MURDERED HUMANS.
SO... SO WHY CAN'T I WIN?

クレイモア
Claymore™

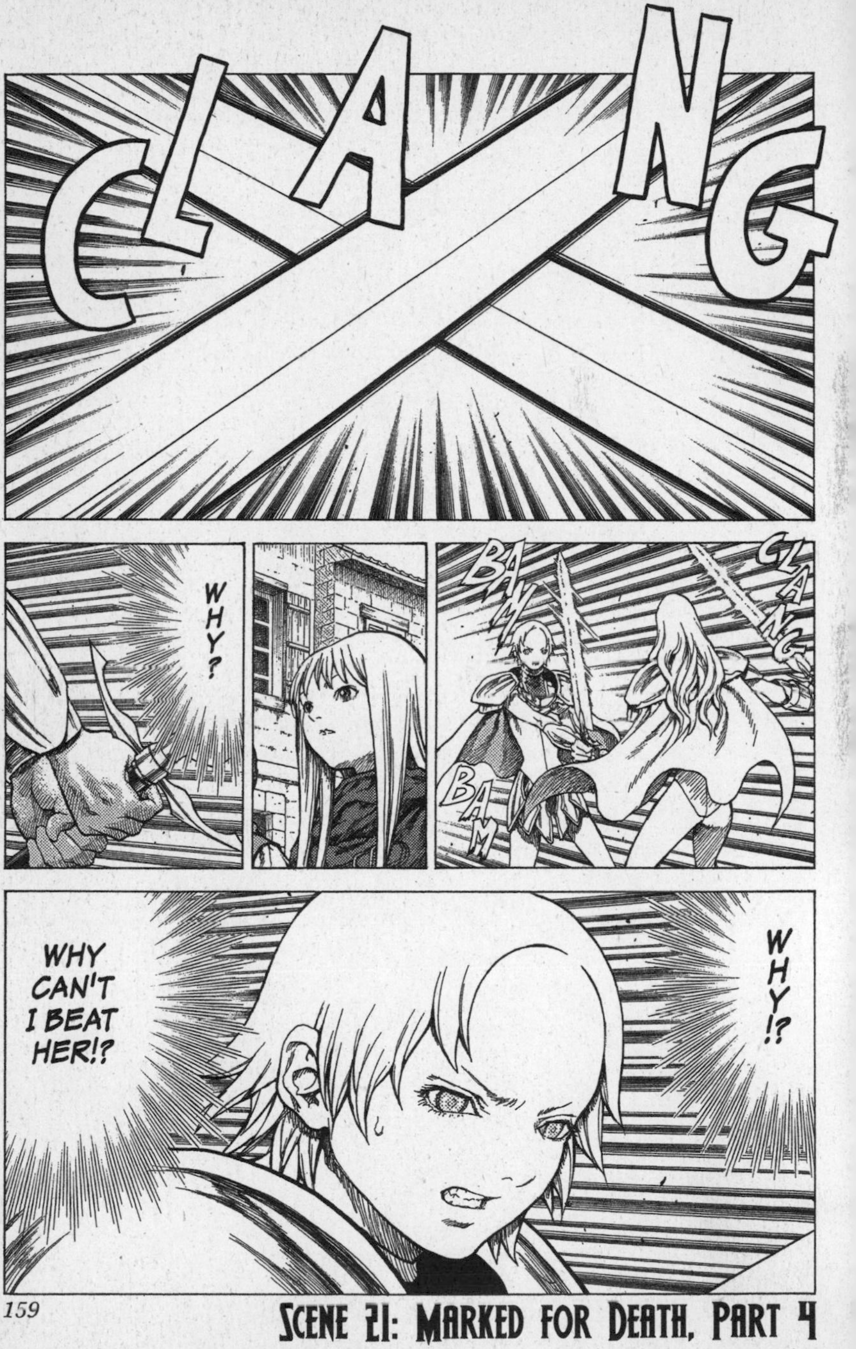
CLANG
CLANG
BAM
BAM
WHY?
WHY!?
WHY CAN'T I BEAT HER!?

Scene 21: Marked for Death, Part 4

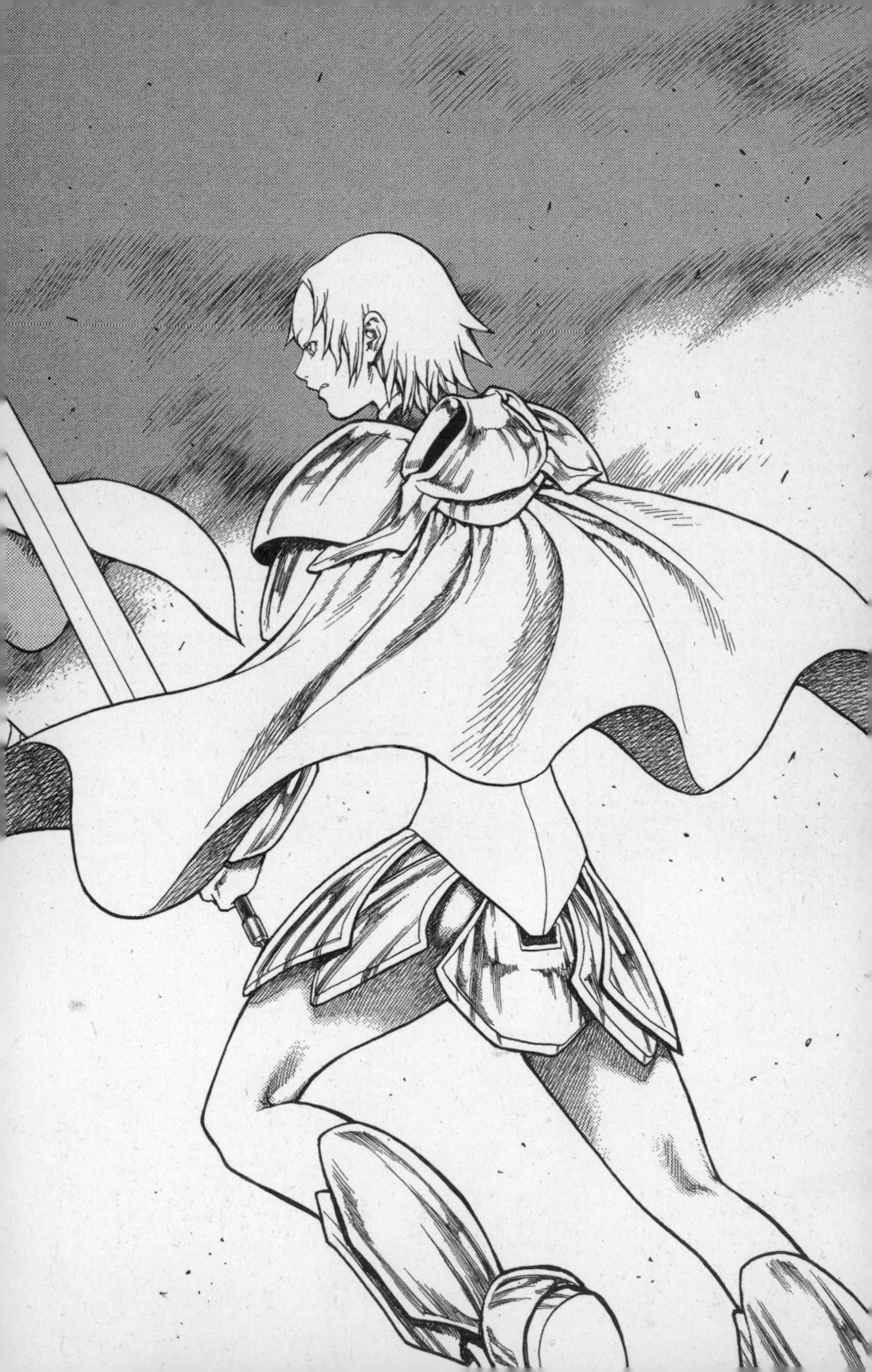

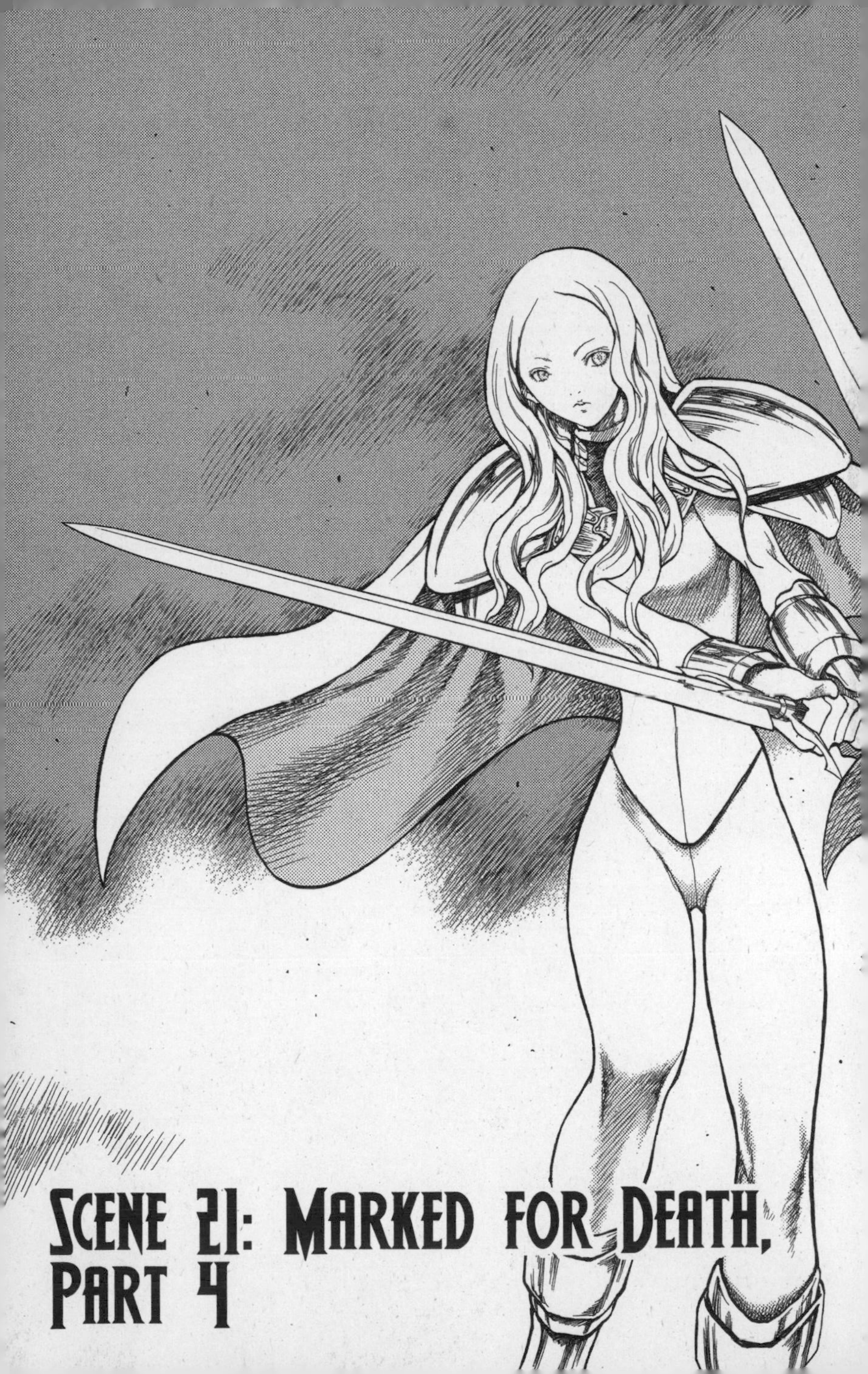

Scene 21: Marked for Death, Part 4

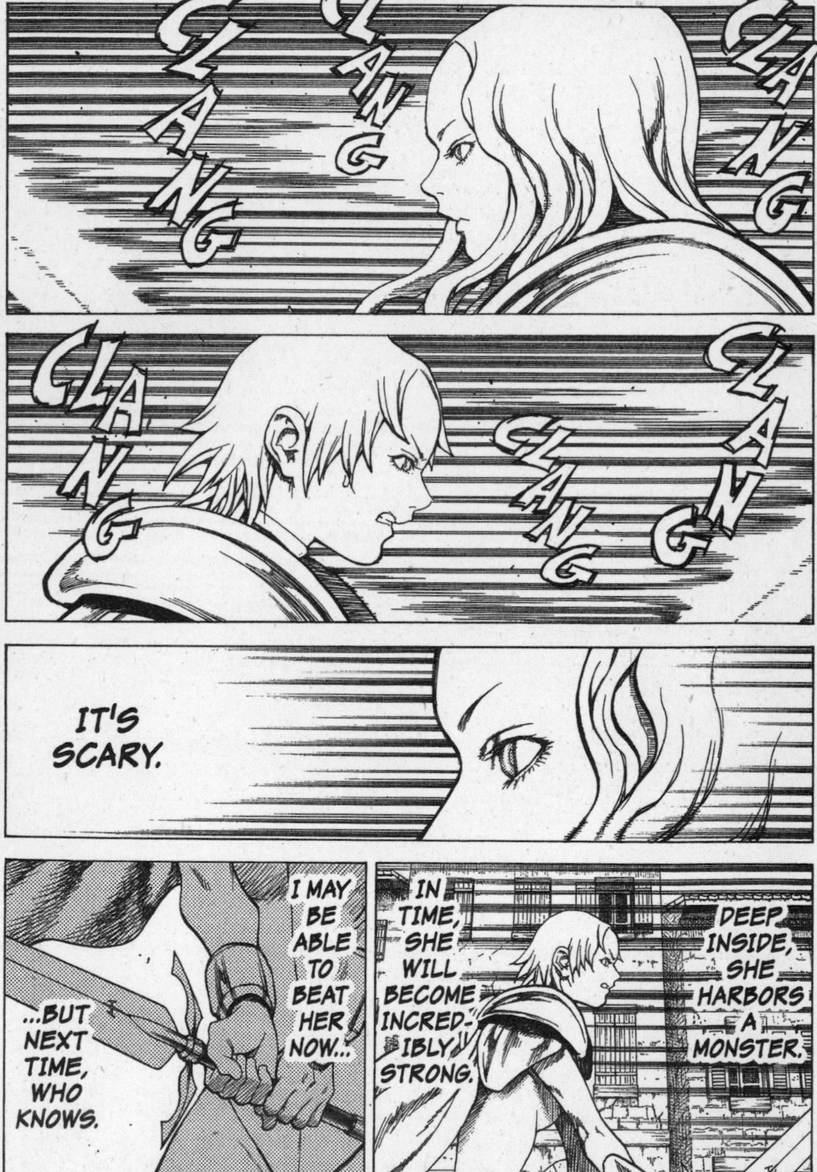
CLANG
CLANG
CLANG
CLANG
CLANG
CLANG
IT'S SCARY.
DEEP INSIDE, SHE HARBORS A MONSTER.
IN TIME, SHE WILL BECOME INCREDIBLY STRONG.
I MAY BE ABLE TO BEAT HER NOW...
...BUT NEXT TIME, WHO KNOWS.

READ THIS WAY

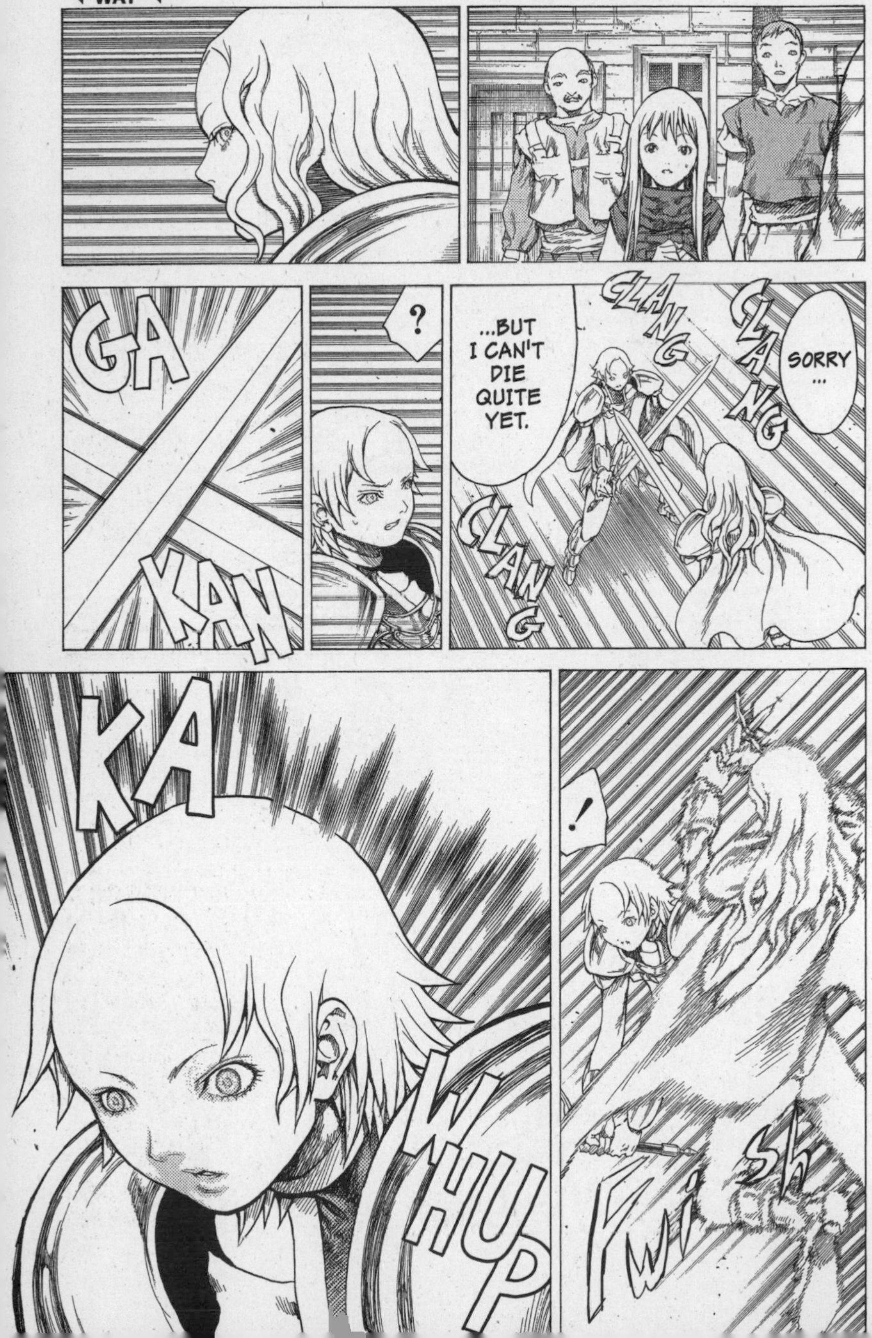
SORRY ...
CLANG
CLANG
...BUT I CAN'T DIE QUITE YET.
CLANG
?
GA
KAN
!
FWISH
KA
WHUP

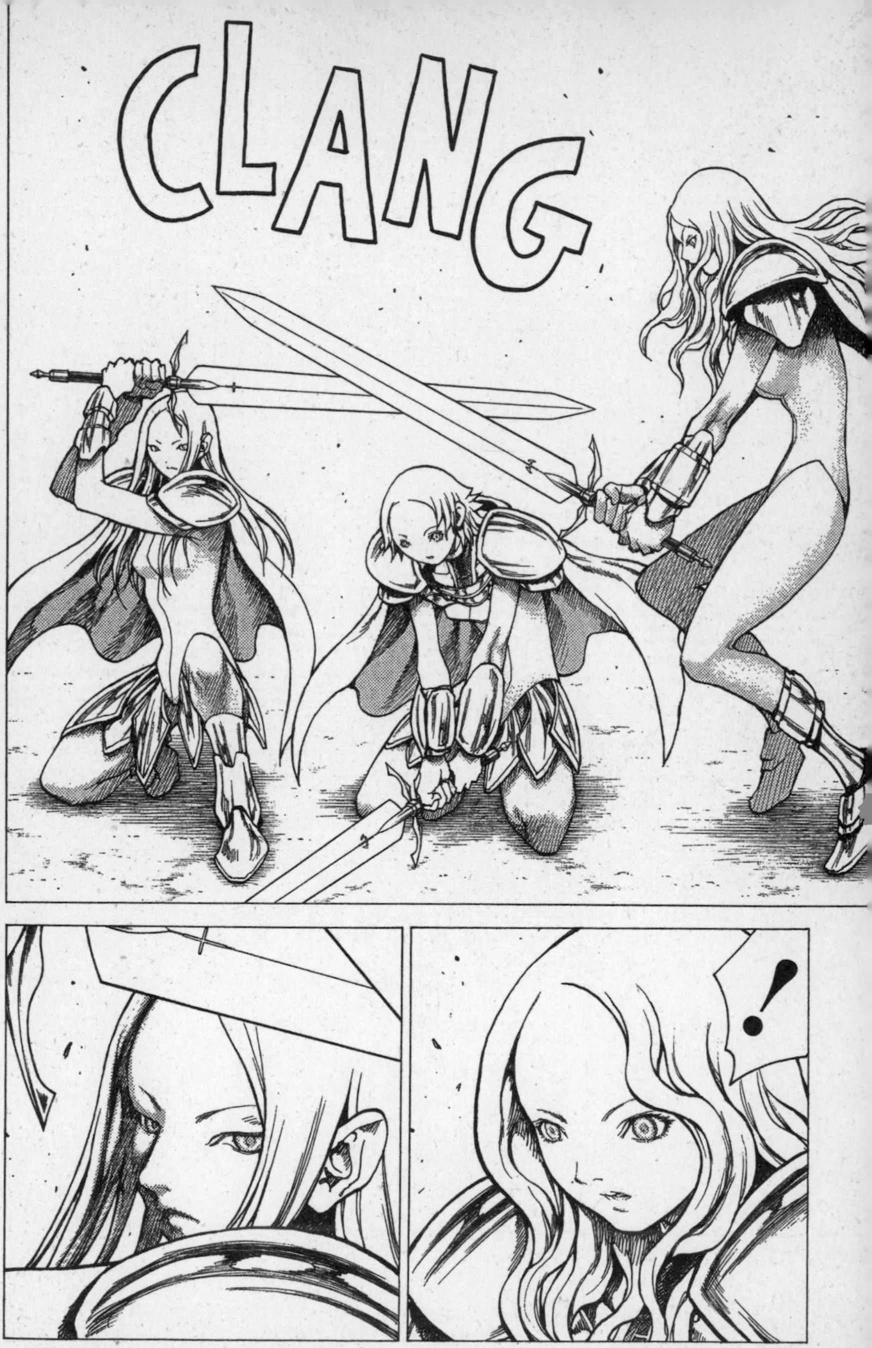
CLANG
!

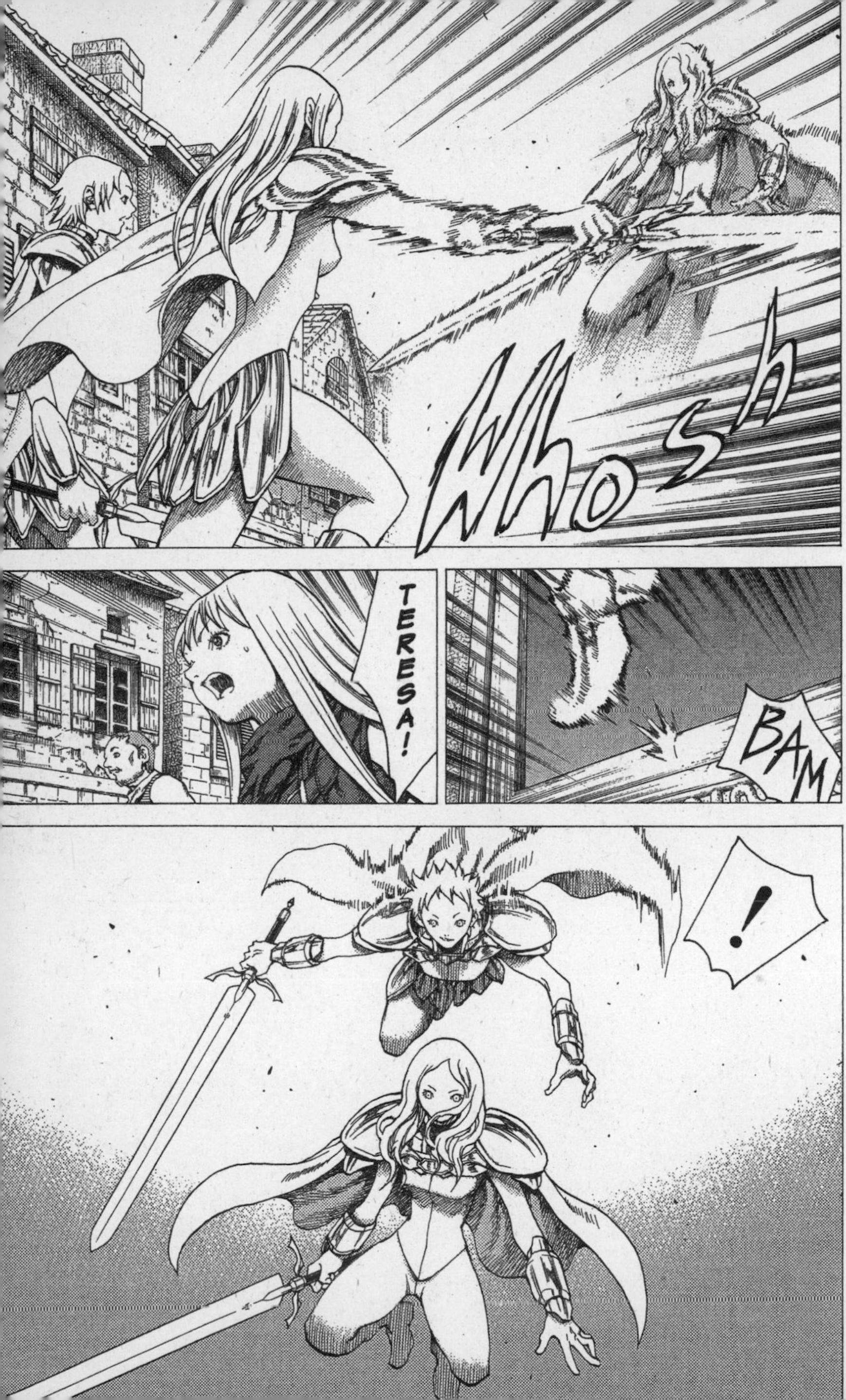
Whosh
BAM
TERESA!
!

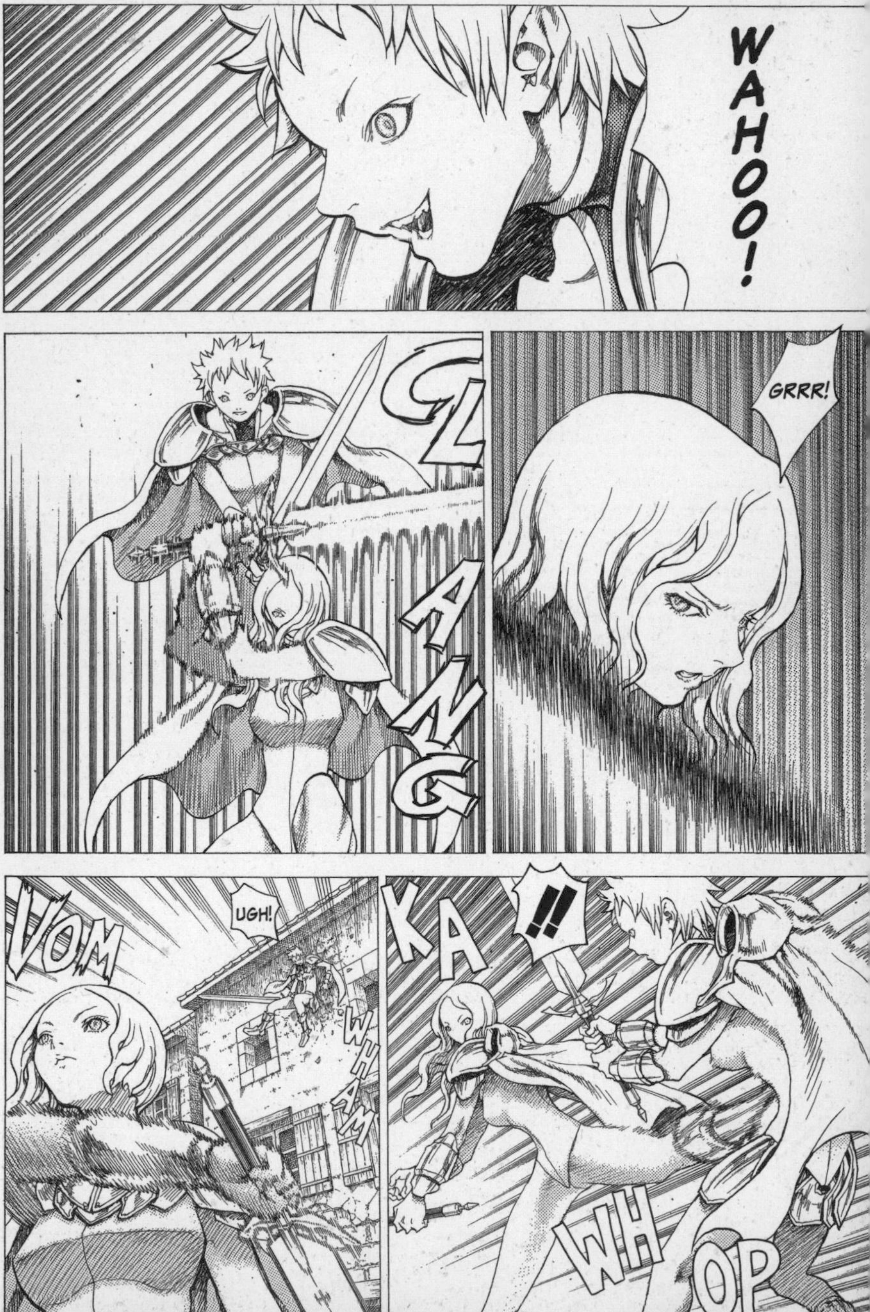
WAHOO!
GRRR!
CLANG
KA
!!
WHOOP
VOM
UGH!
WHAM

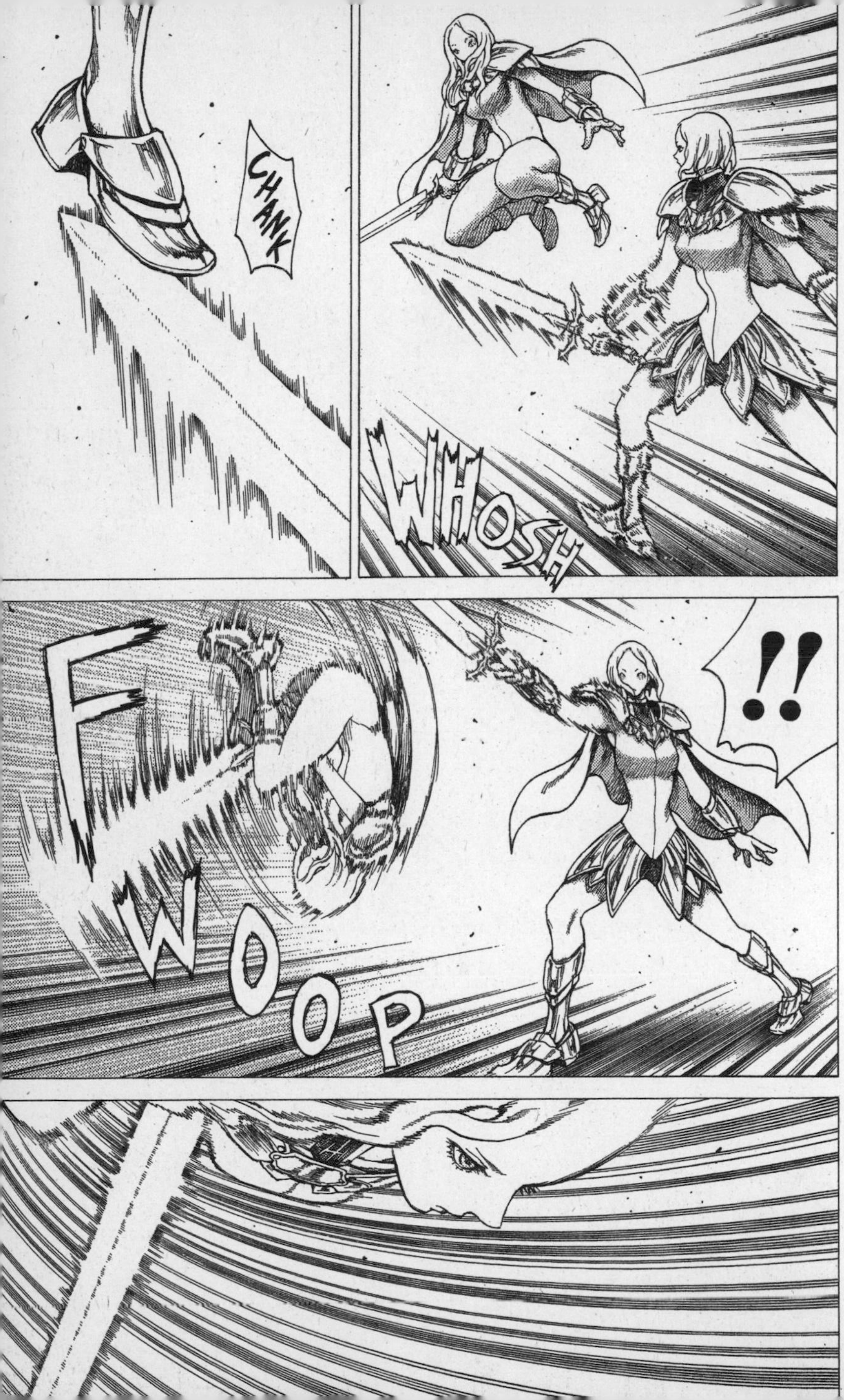
WHOSH
CHANK
!!
FWOOP

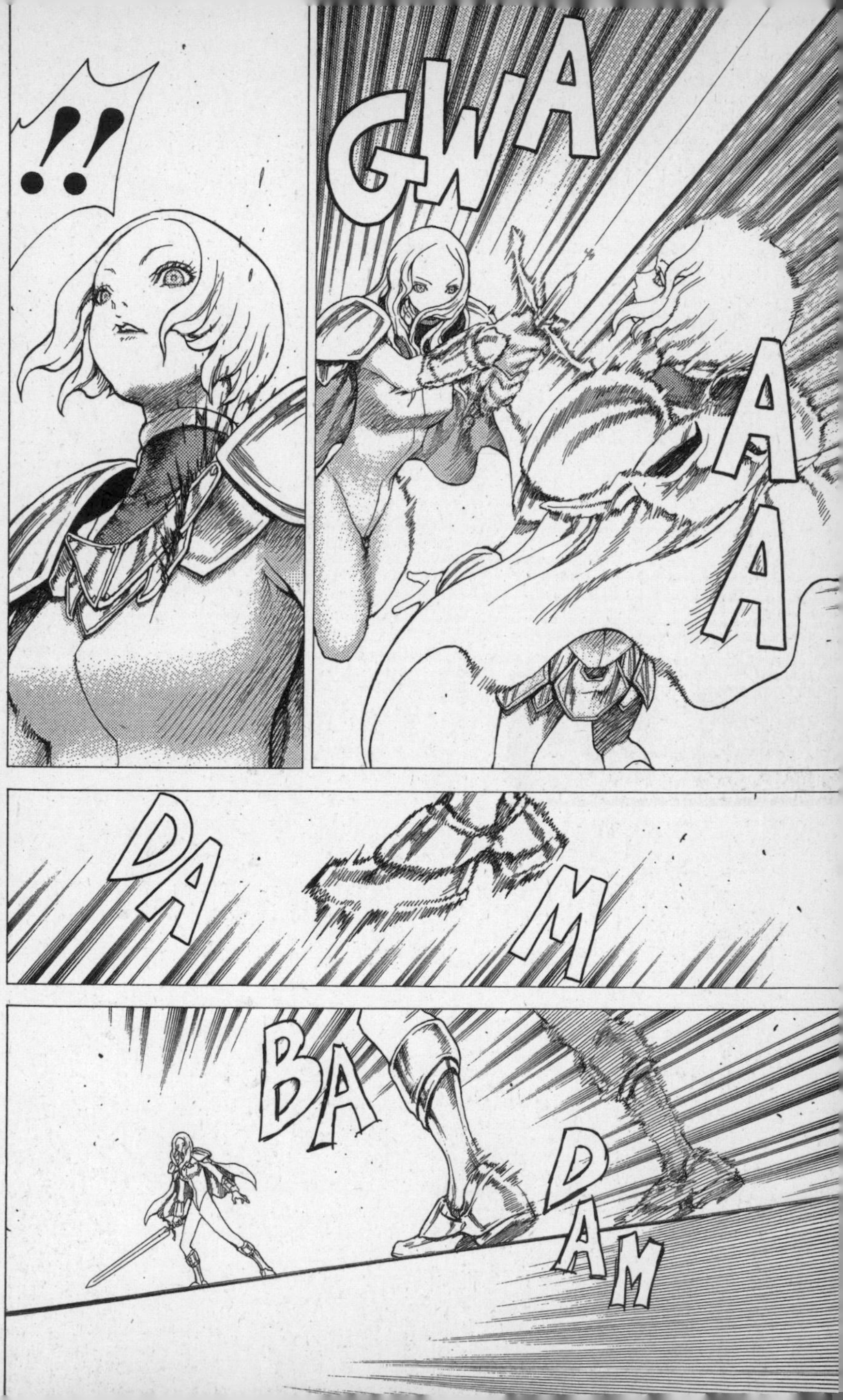
GWAAAA
!!
DAM
BA DAM
BA DAM

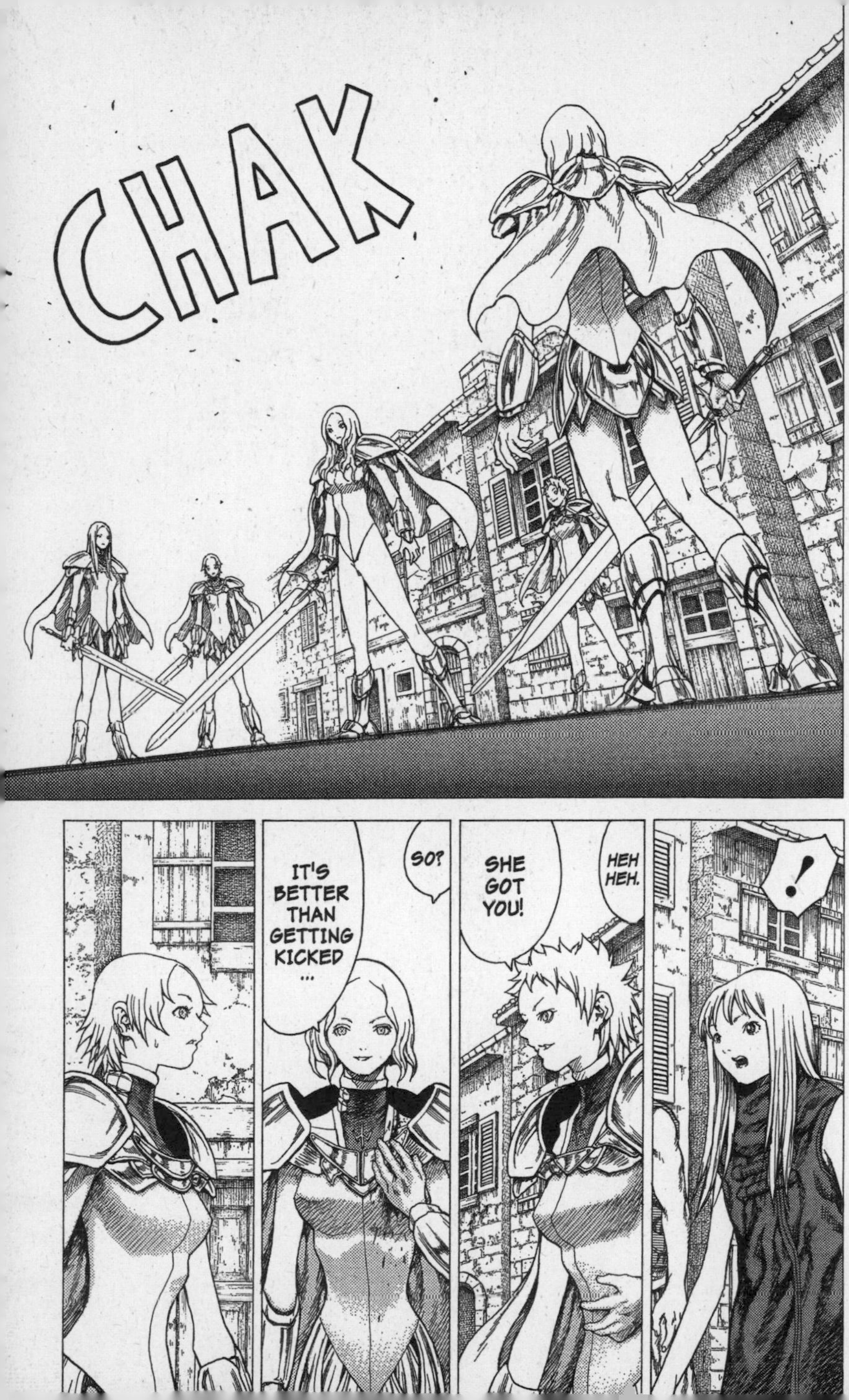
CHAK
!
HEH HEH.
SHE GOT YOU!
SO?
IT'S BETTER THAN GETTING KICKED ...

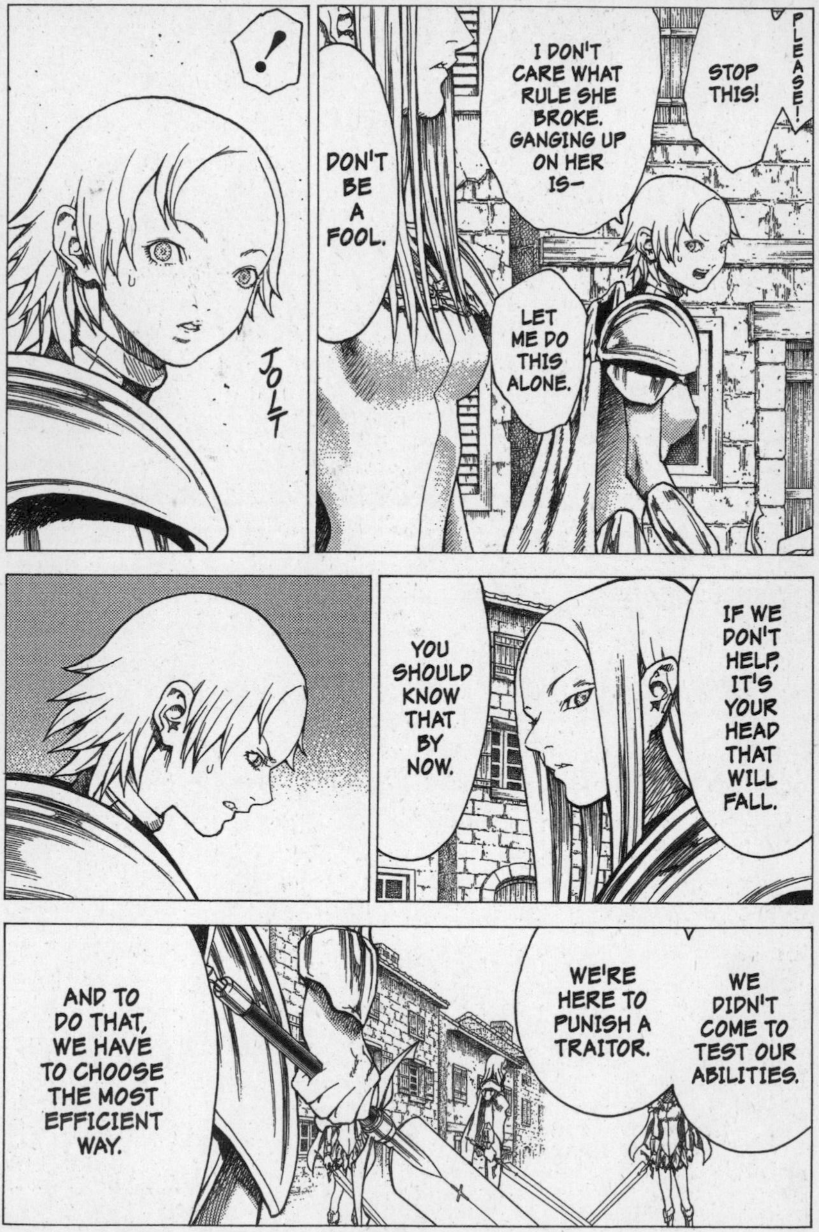
PLEASE!
STOP THIS!
I DON'T CARE WHAT RULE SHE BROKE. GANGING UP ON HER IS—
LET ME DO THIS ALONE.
DON'T BE A FOOL.
!
JOLT
IF WE DON'T HELP, IT'S YOUR HEAD THAT WILL FALL.
YOU SHOULD KNOW THAT BY NOW.
WE DIDN'T COME TO TEST OUR ABILITIES.
WE'RE HERE TO PUNISH A TRAITOR.
AND TO DO THAT, WE HAVE TO CHOOSE THE MOST EFFICIENT WAY.

READ THIS WAY

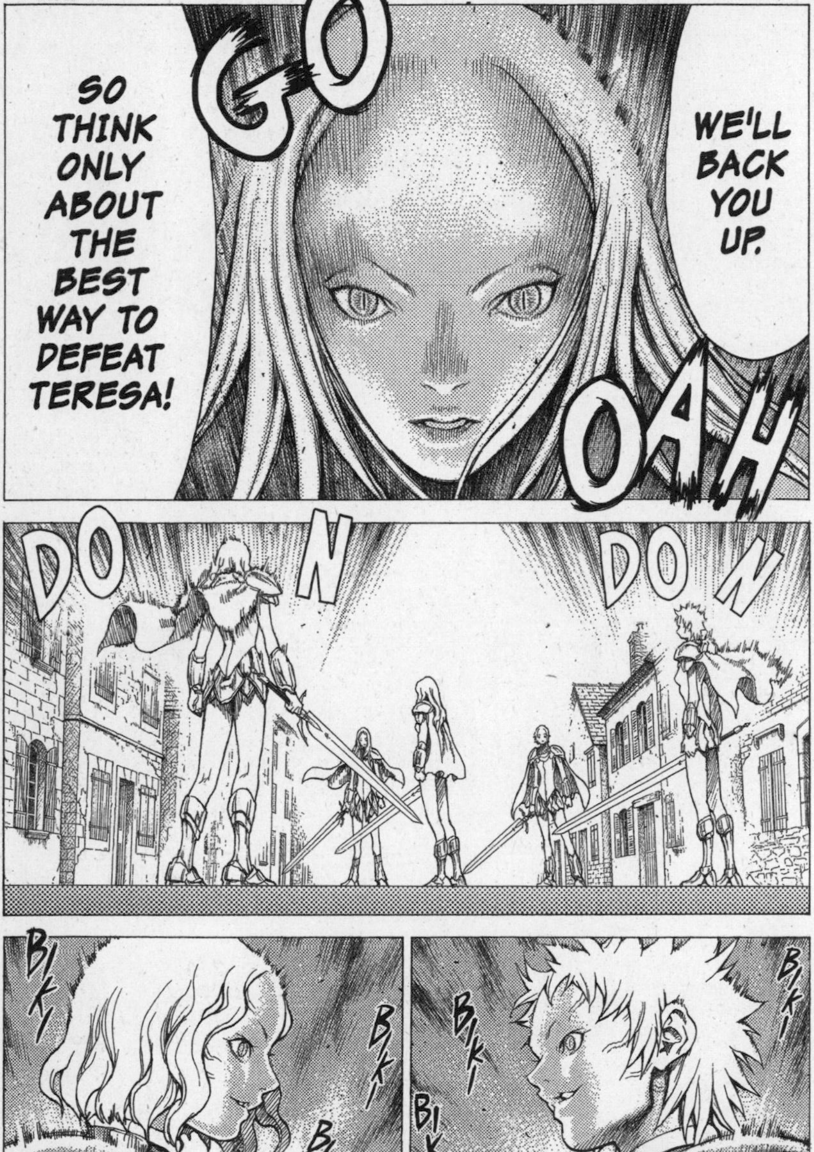
WE'LL BACK YOU UP.
GO
OAH
SO THINK ONLY ABOUT THE BEST WAY TO DEFEAT TERESA!
DON
DON
BIKI
BIKI
BIKI
BIKI
BIKI
BIKI

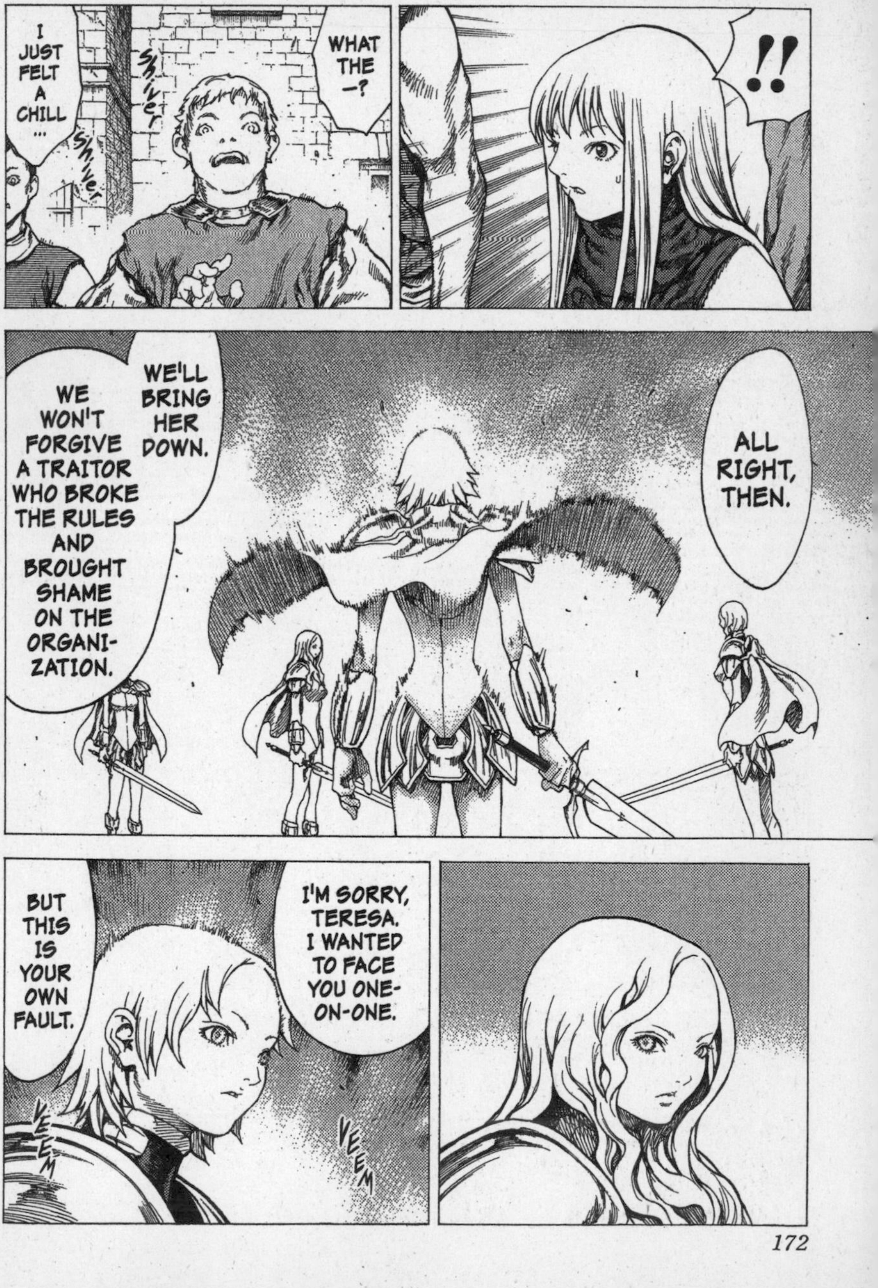
!!
WHAT THE —?
I JUST FELT A CHILL ...
shiver
shiver
ALL RIGHT, THEN.
WE'LL BRING HER DOWN.
WE WON'T FORGIVE A TRAITOR WHO BROKE THE RULES AND BROUGHT SHAME ON THE ORGANIZATION.
I'M SORRY, TERESA. I WANTED TO FACE YOU ONE-ON-ONE.
BUT THIS IS YOUR OWN FAULT.
VEEM
VEEM

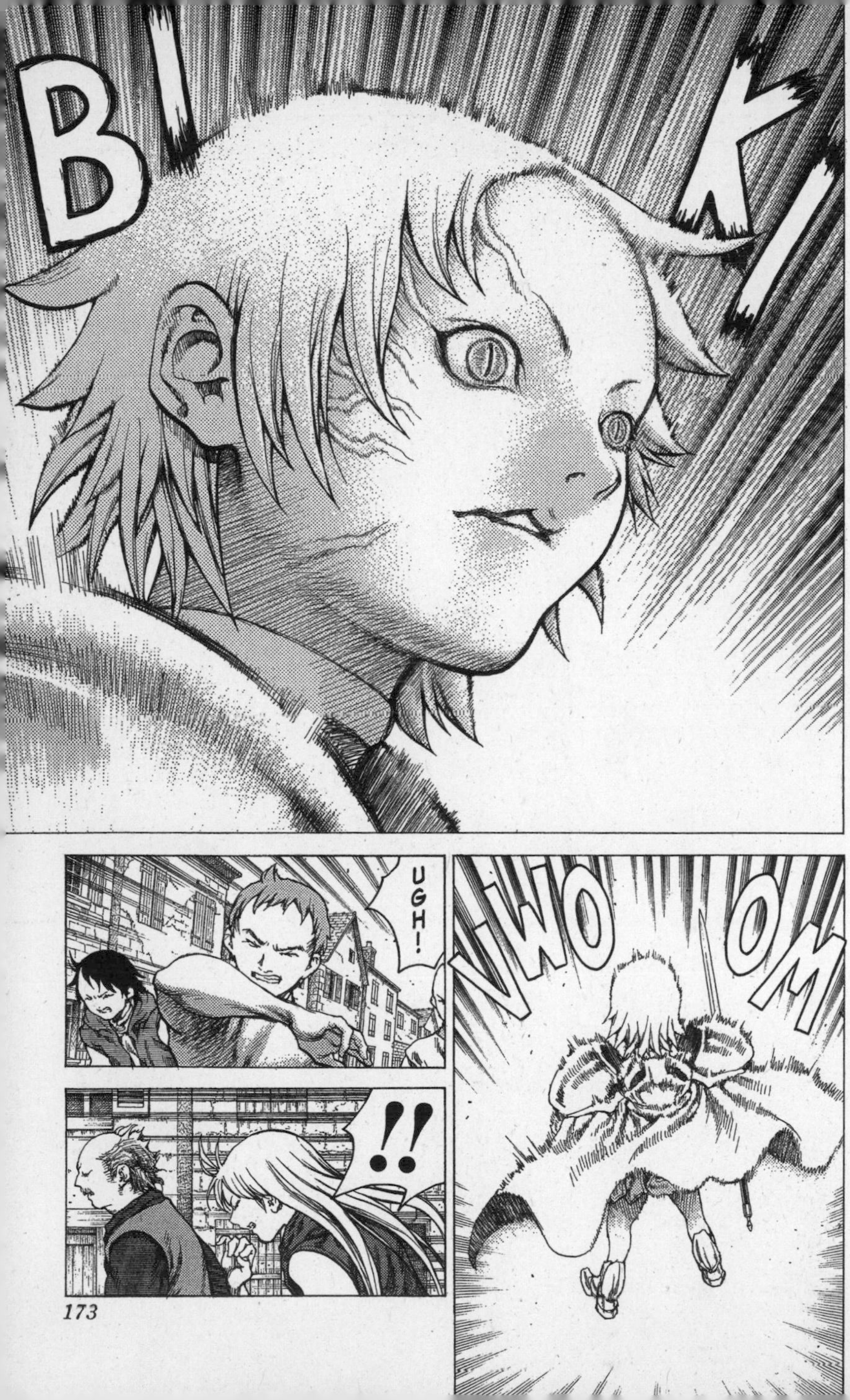
BIK!
VWOOM
UGH!
!!

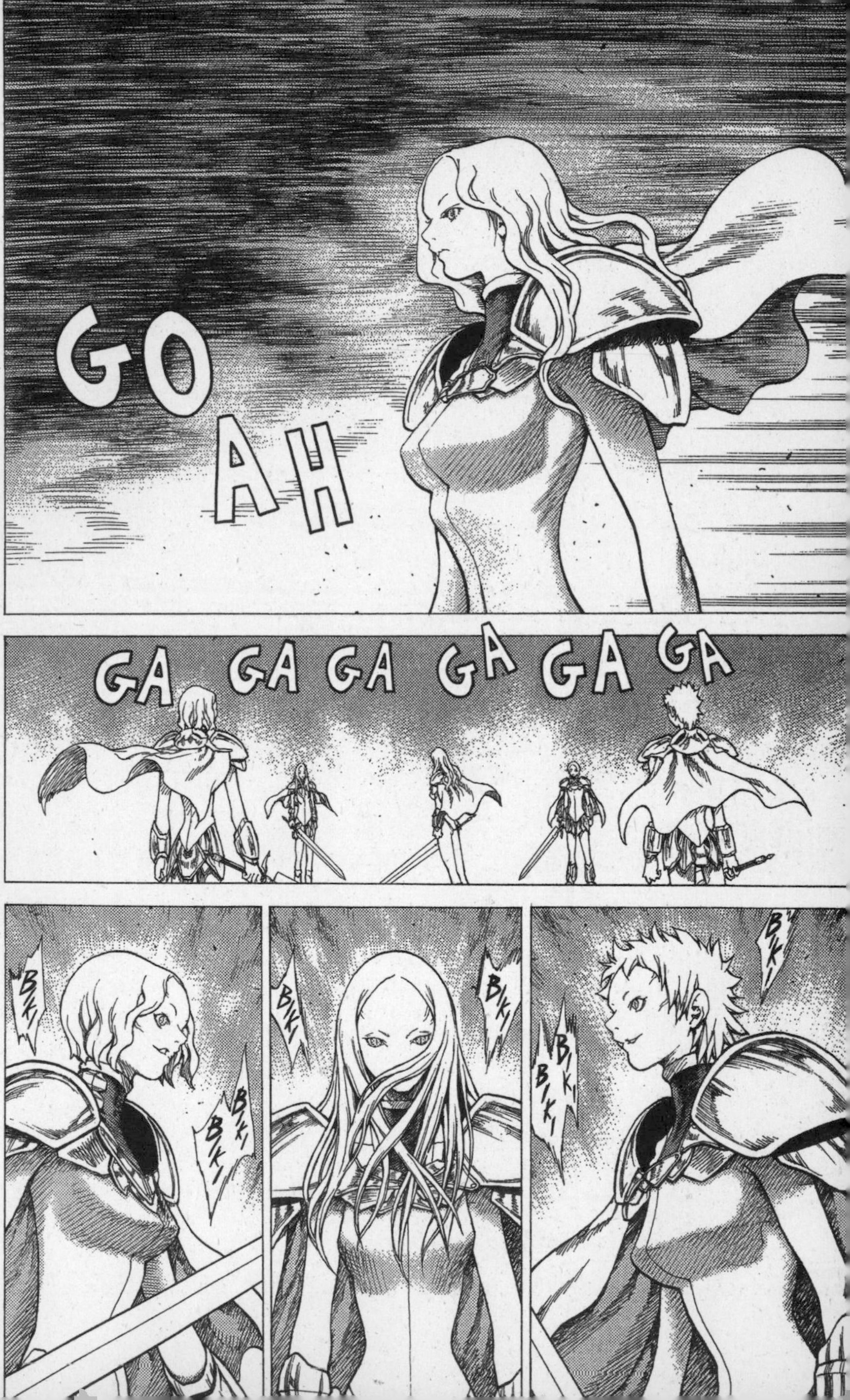
GO
AH
GA GA GA GA GA GA GA
BIKI
BIKI
BIKI
BIKI
BIKI
BIKI
BIKI
BIKI

READ THIS WAY

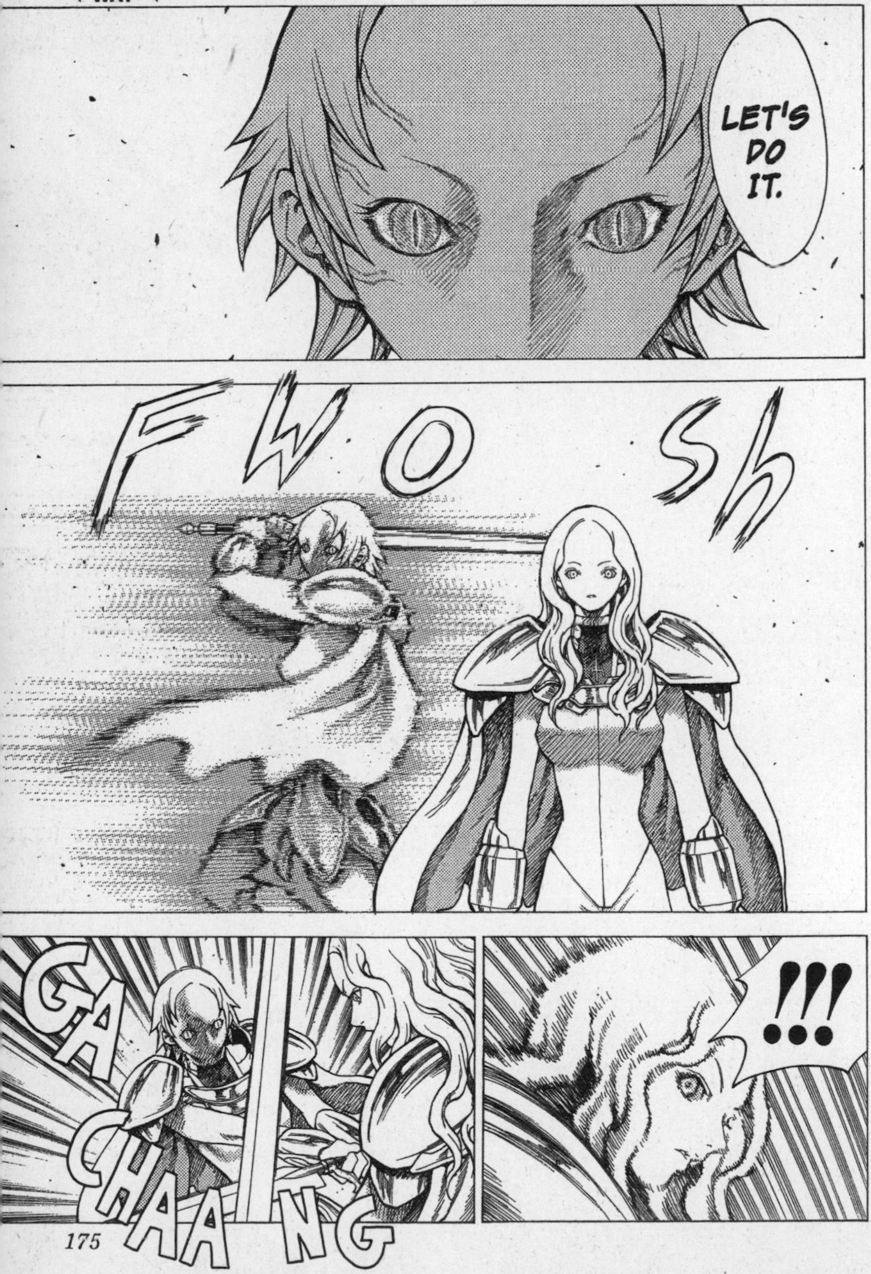
LET'S DO IT.
FWOSH
!!!
GA CHAANG

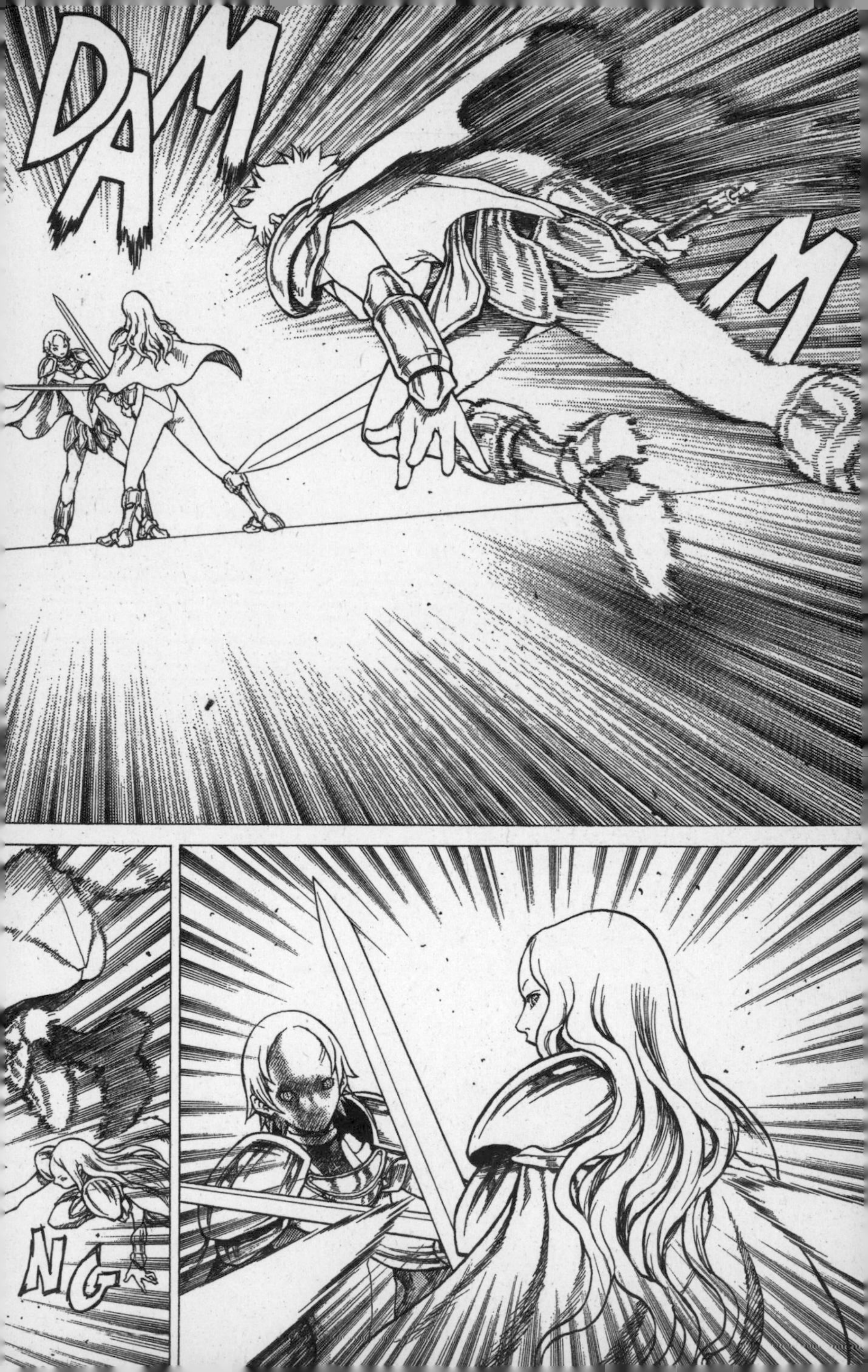
DAM
M
NG

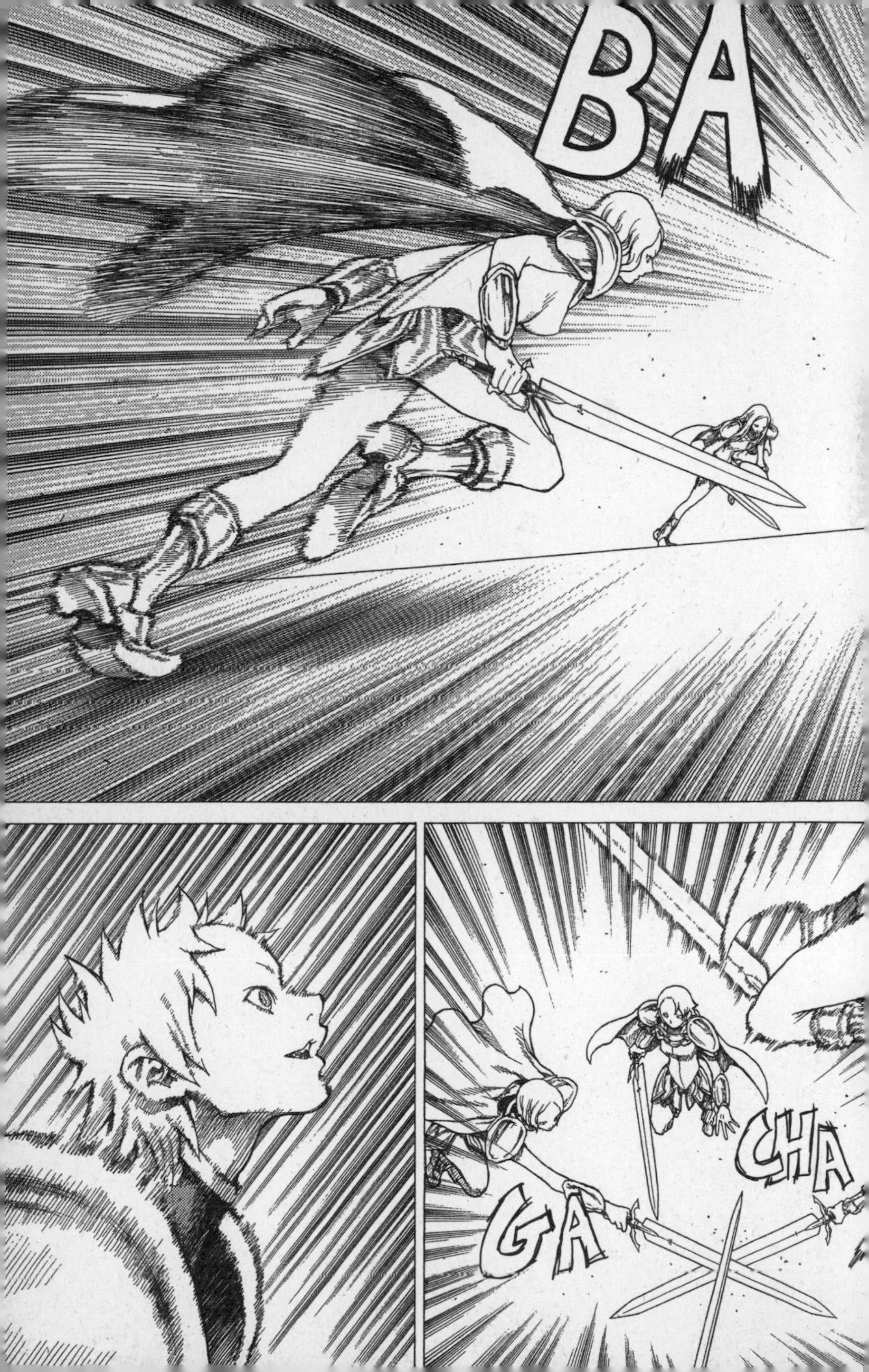
BA
GA
CHA

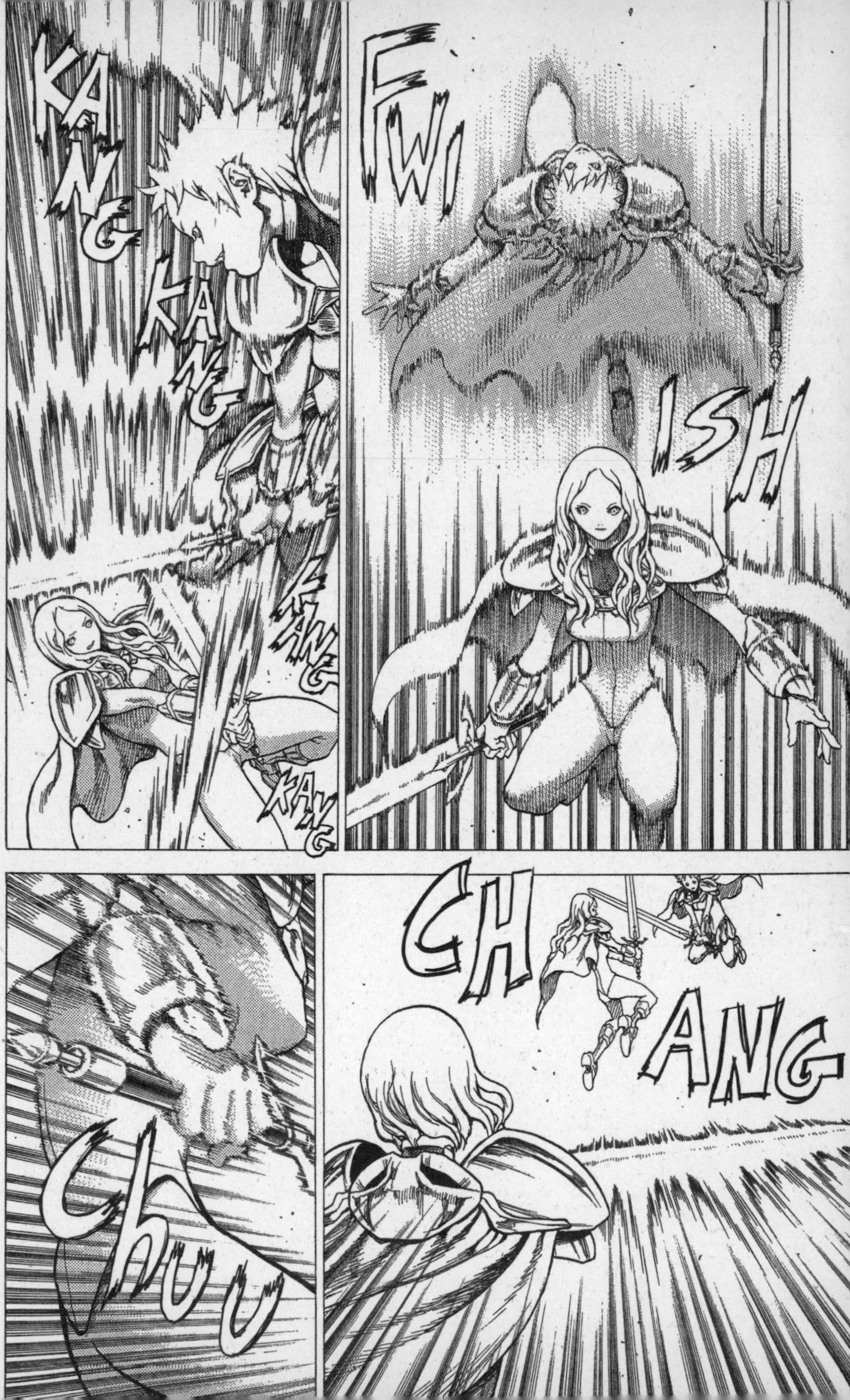
FWI
ISH
KANG
KANG
KANG
KANG
CH
ANG
CHUUU

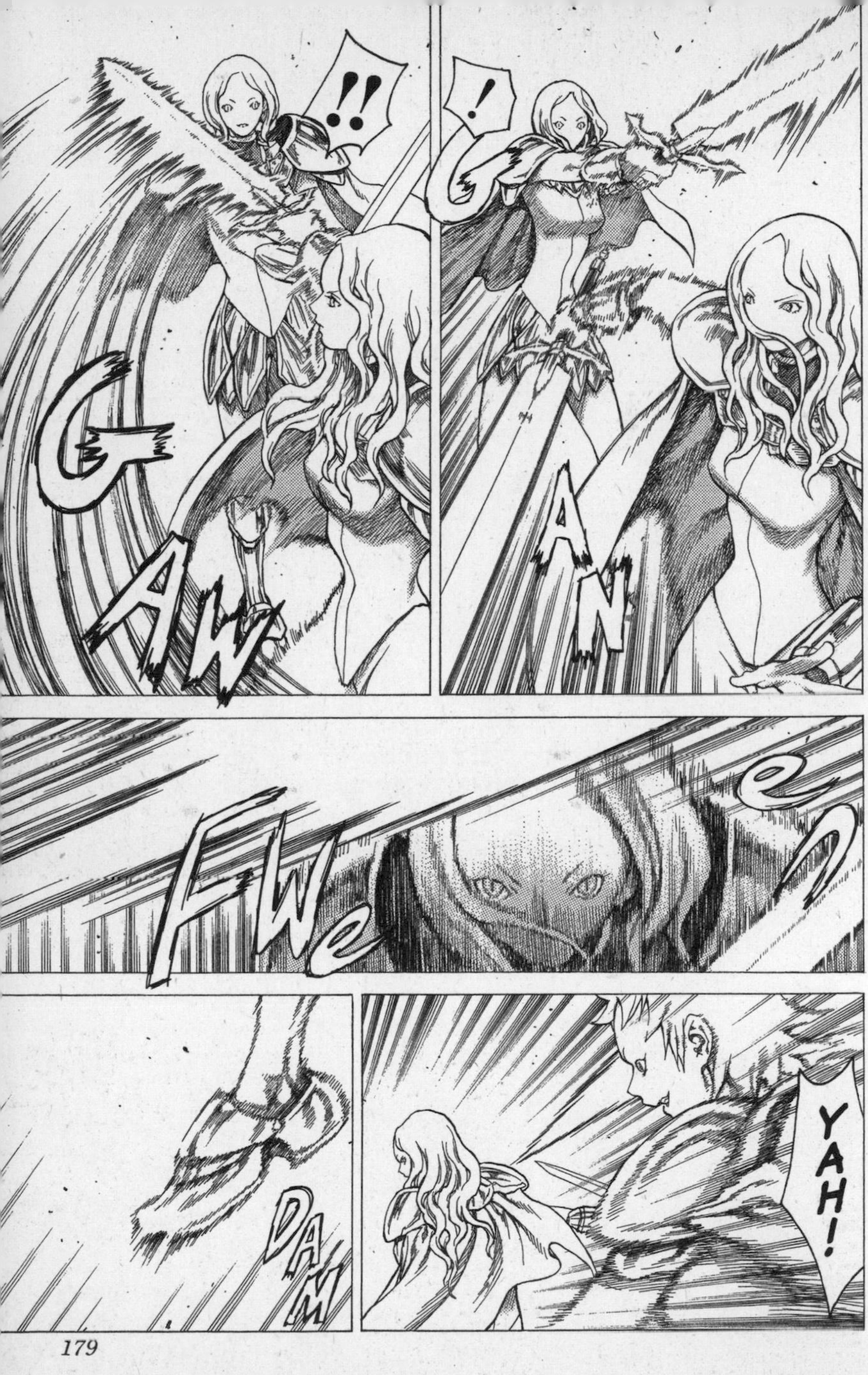
!
GAN
!!
GAW
FWeen
YAH!
DAM

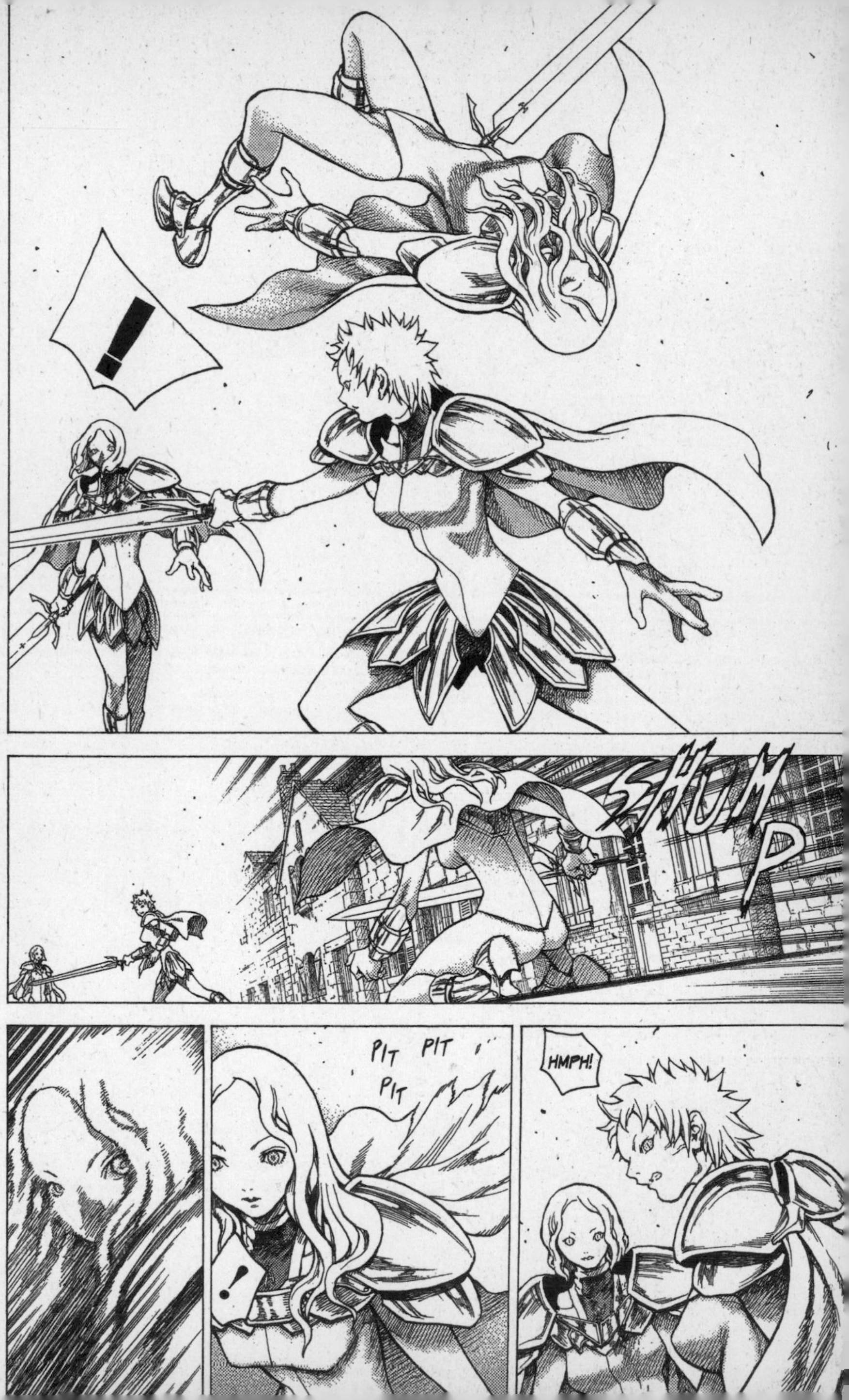
!
SHUMP
HMPH!
PIT PIT
PIT
!

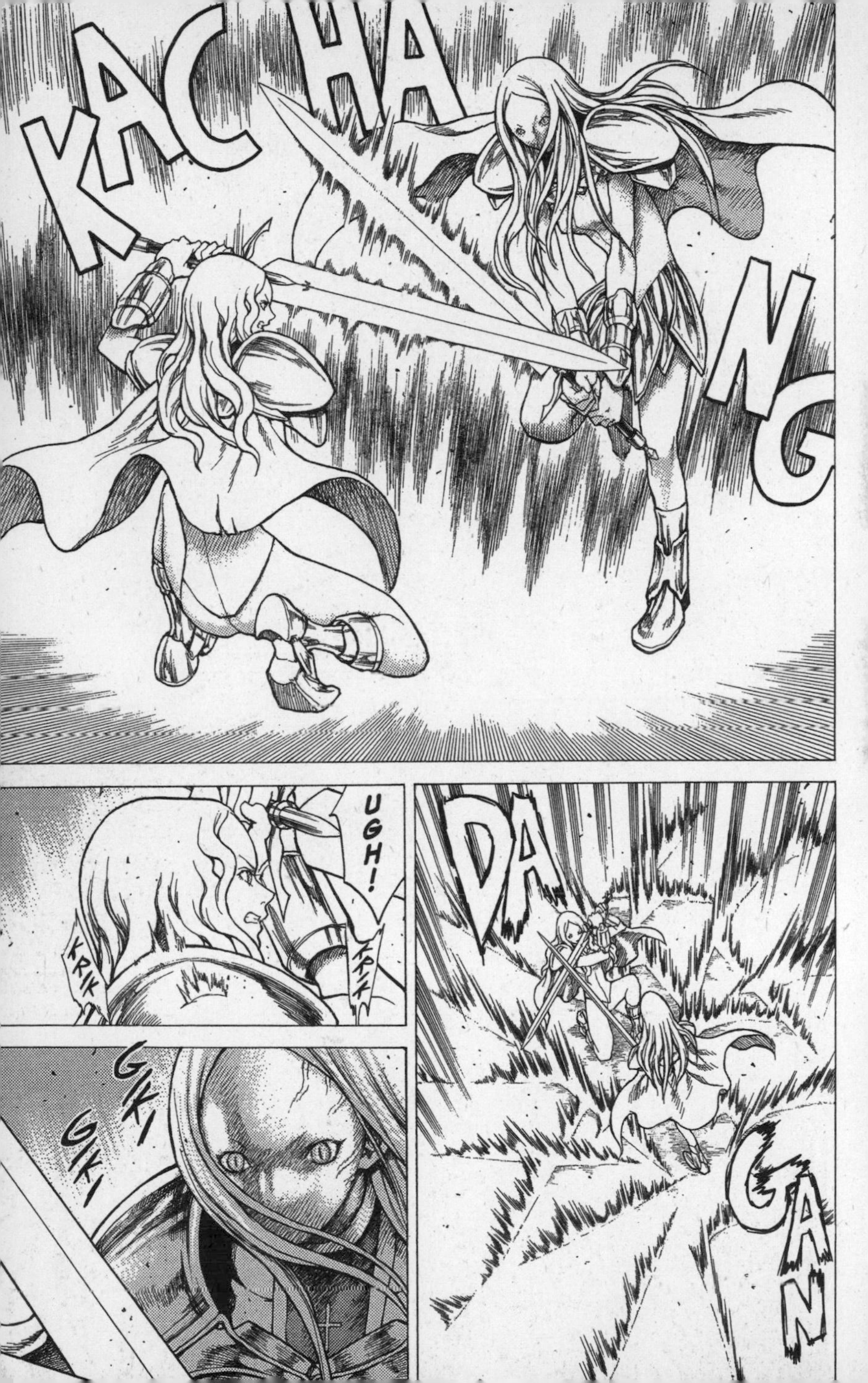
KACHANG
DA
GAN
UGH!
KRIK
KRIK
GIKI
GIKI

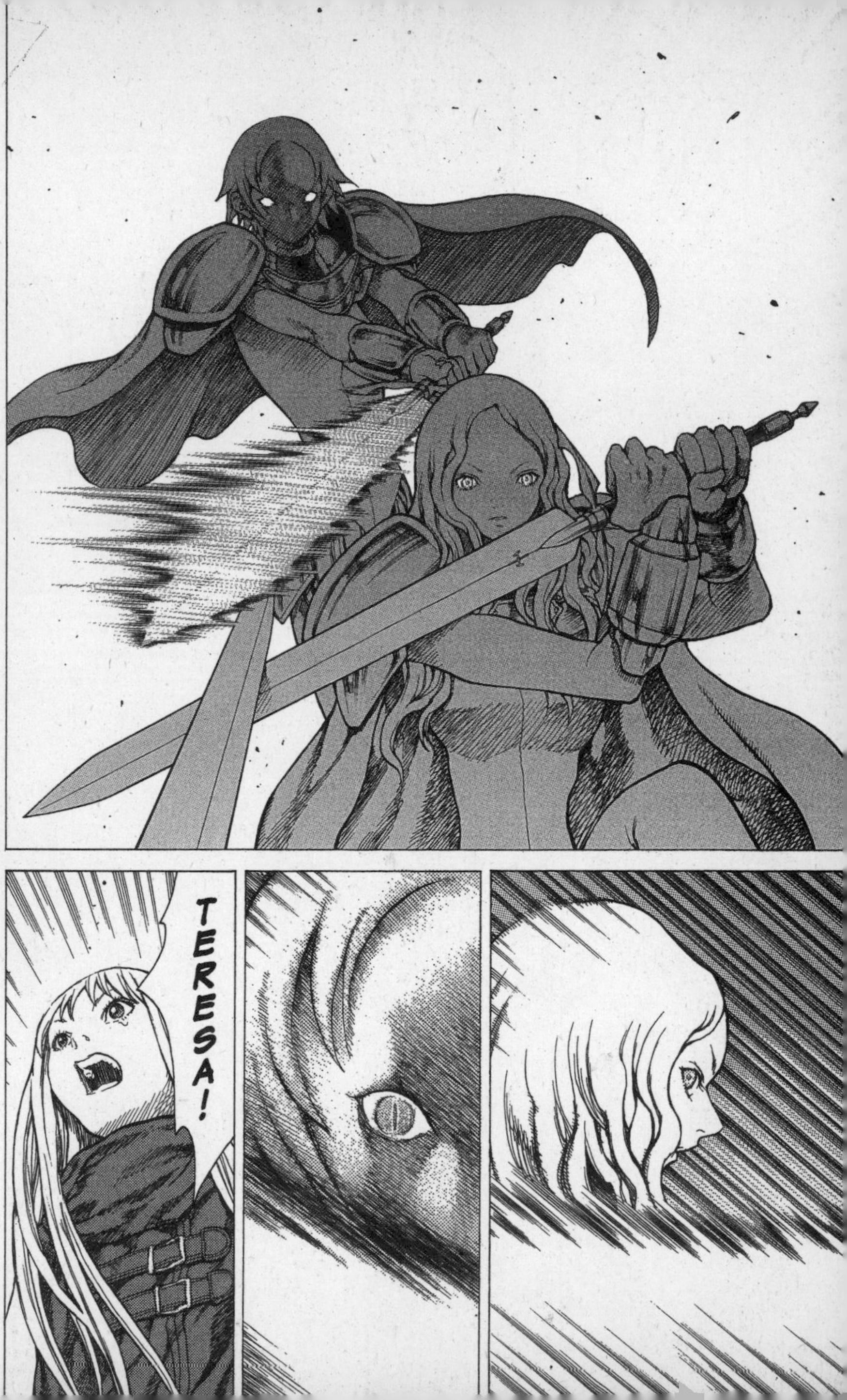
TERESA!

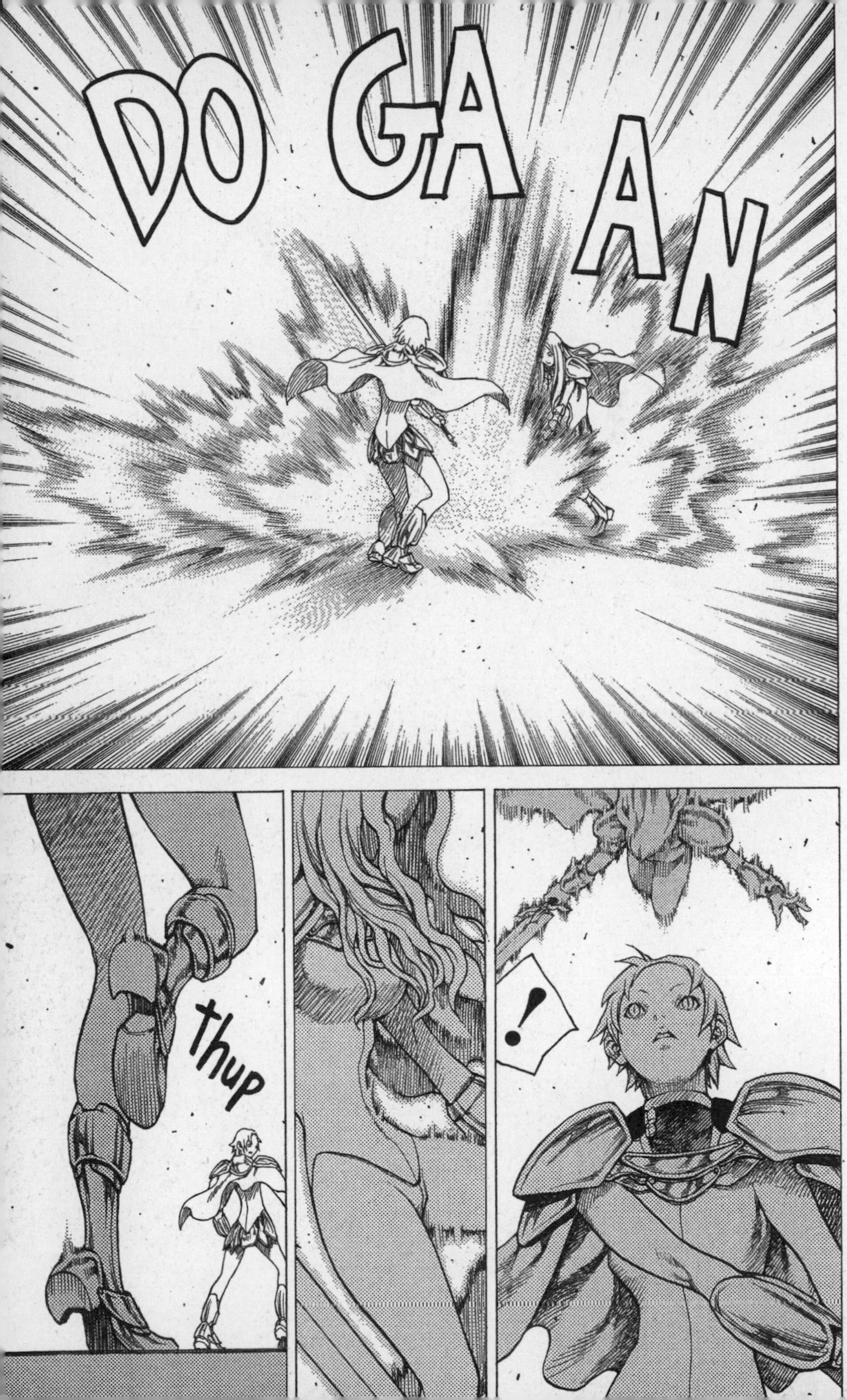
DO GA A AN
!
thup

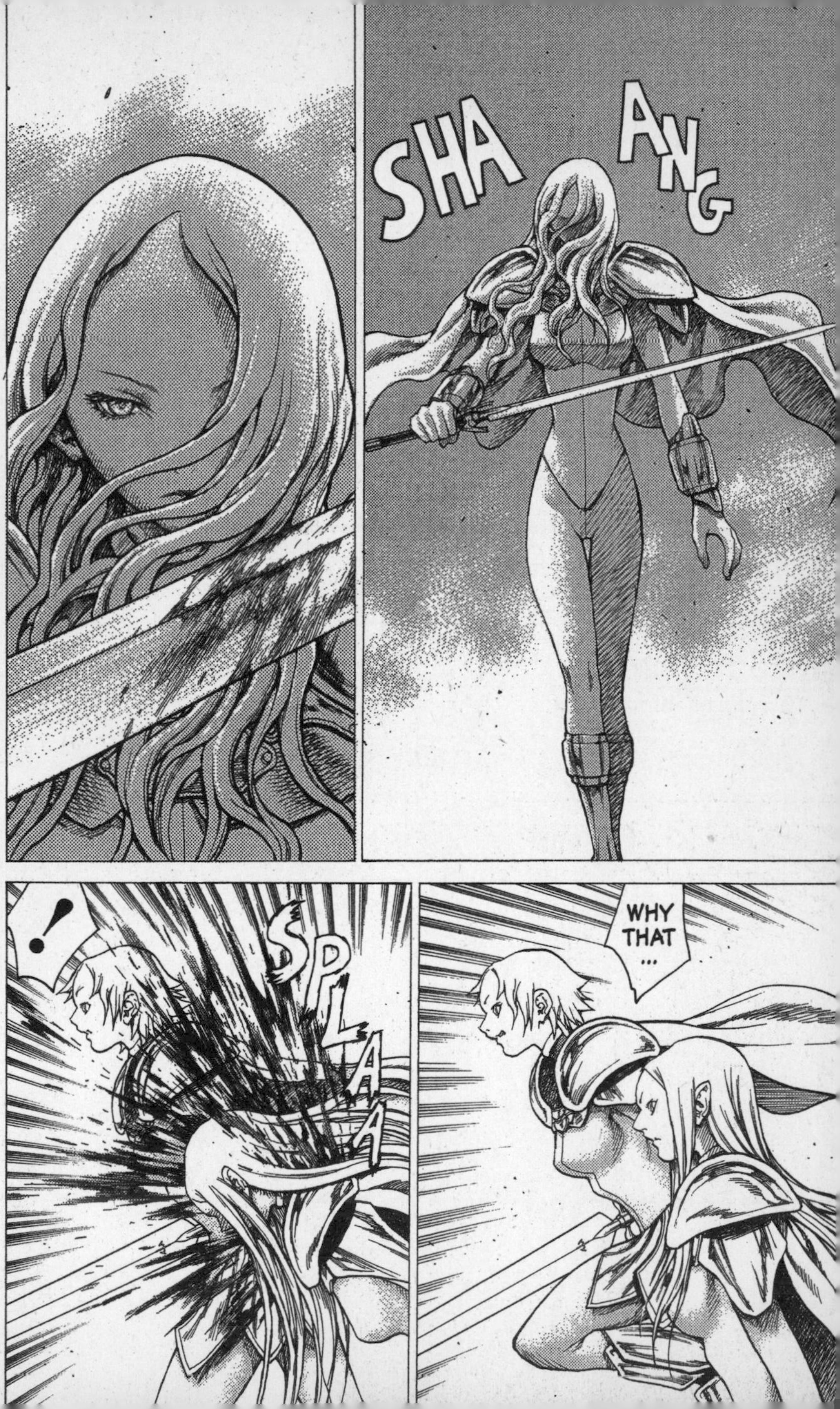
SHA
ANG
WHY THAT ...
!
SPLAA

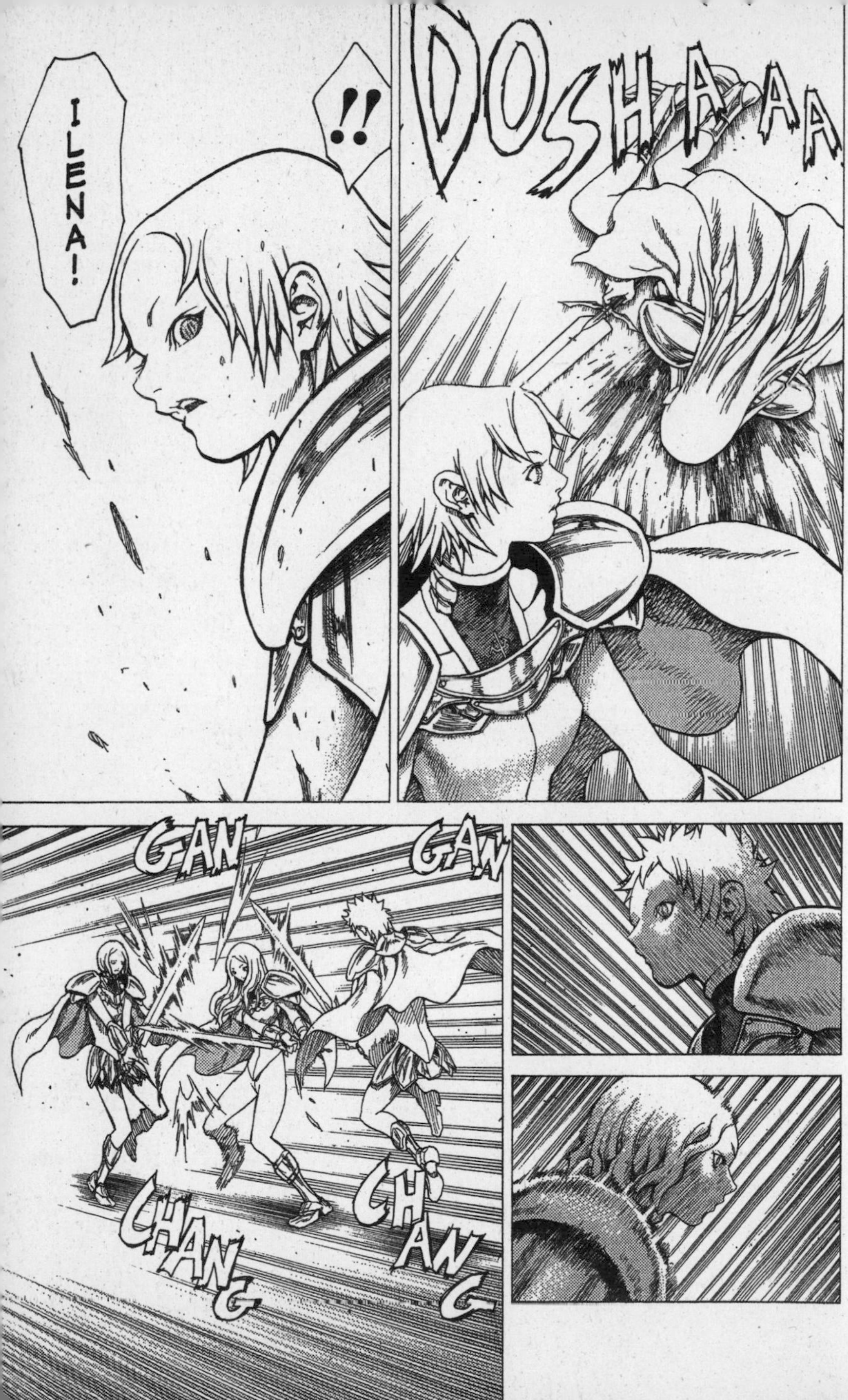
DOSHAAA
!!
ILENA!
GAN
GAN
CHANG
CHANG

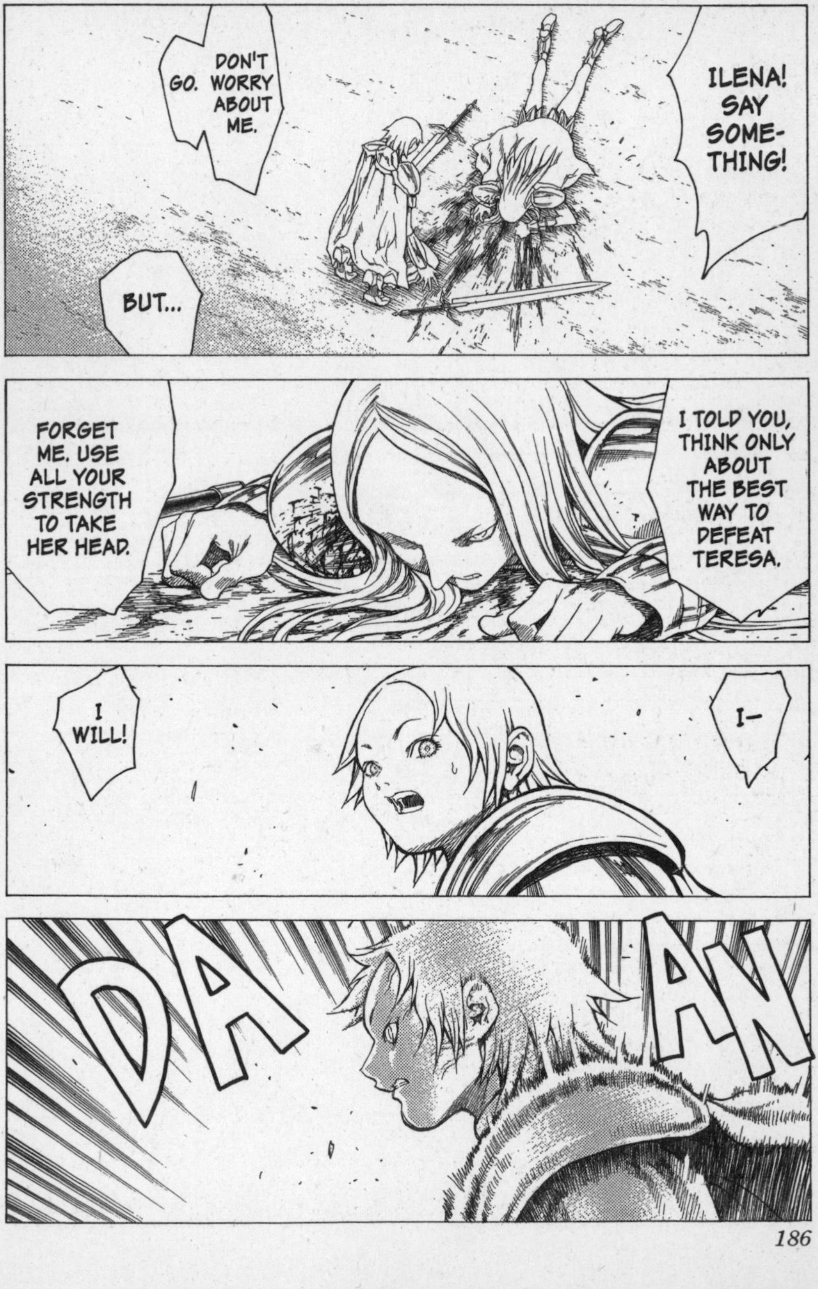
ILENA! SAY SOME-THING!
DON'T WORRY ABOUT ME.
GO.
BUT...
I TOLD YOU, THINK ONLY ABOUT THE BEST WAY TO DEFEAT TERESA.
FORGET ME. USE ALL YOUR STRENGTH TO TAKE HER HEAD.
I—
I WILL!
DA AN

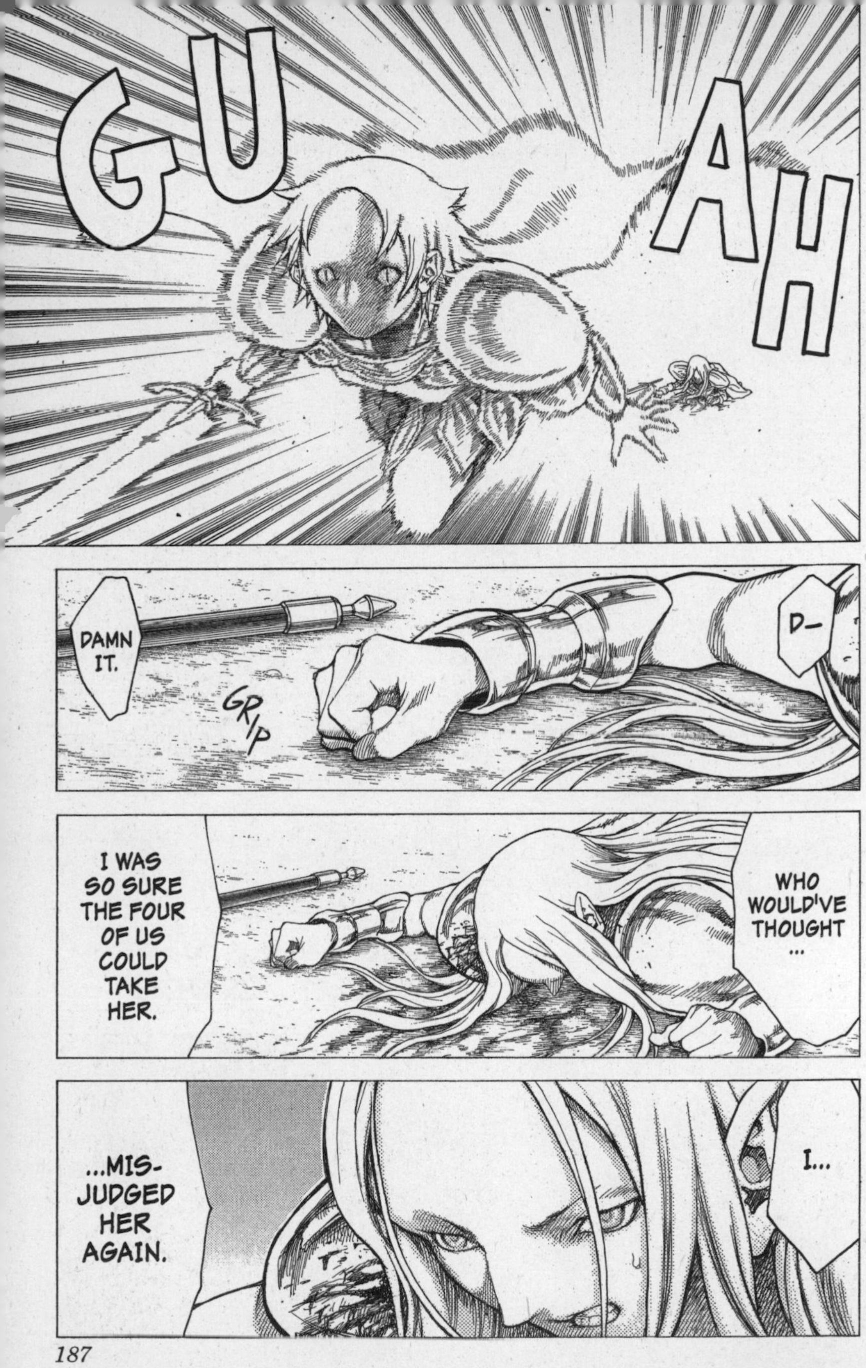
GUAH
D—
DAMN IT.
GRIP
WHO WOULD'VE THOUGHT...
I WAS SO SURE THE FOUR OF US COULD TAKE HER.
I...
...MIS-JUDGED HER AGAIN.

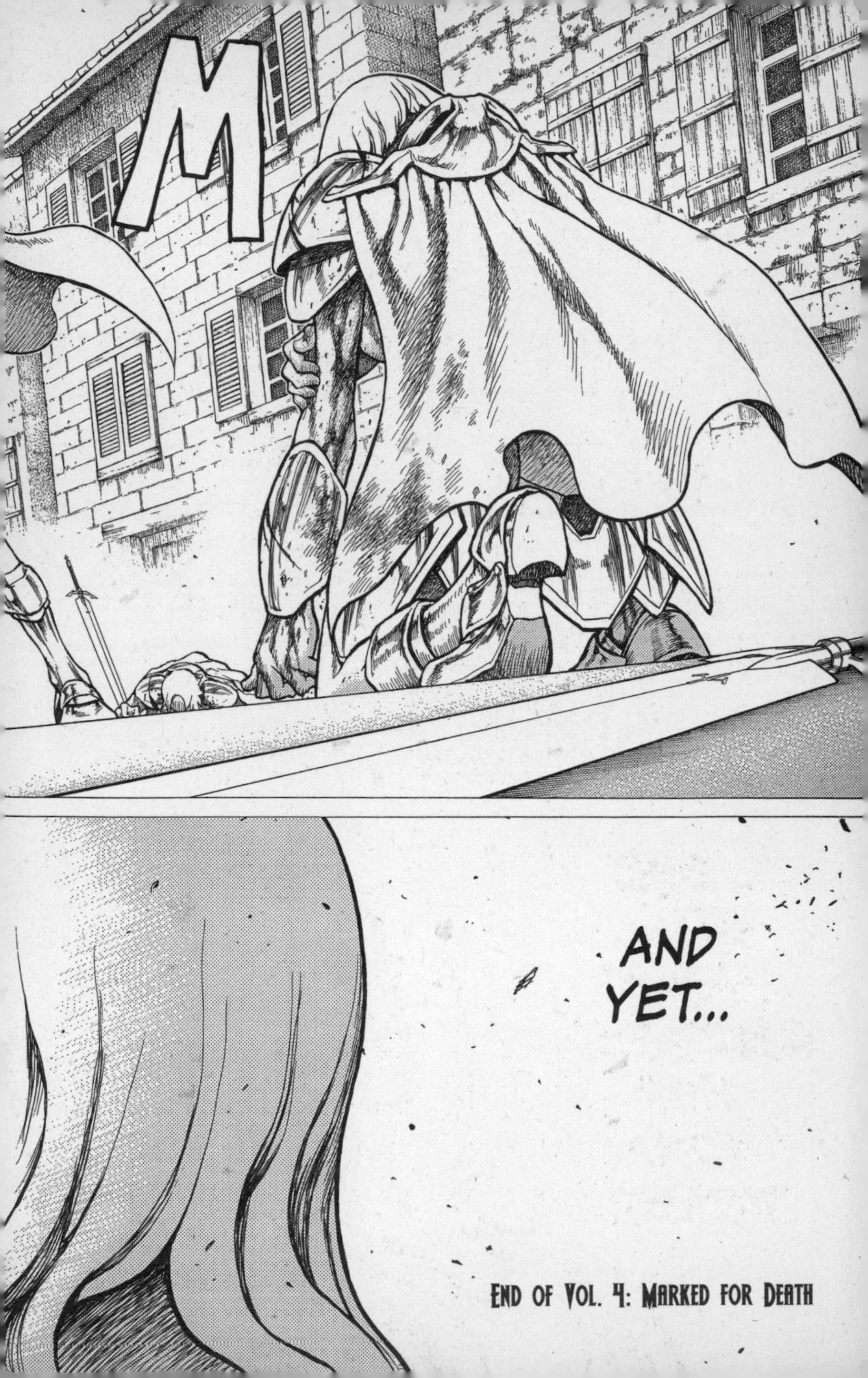
M
AND YET...
END OF VOL. 4: MARKED FOR DEATH

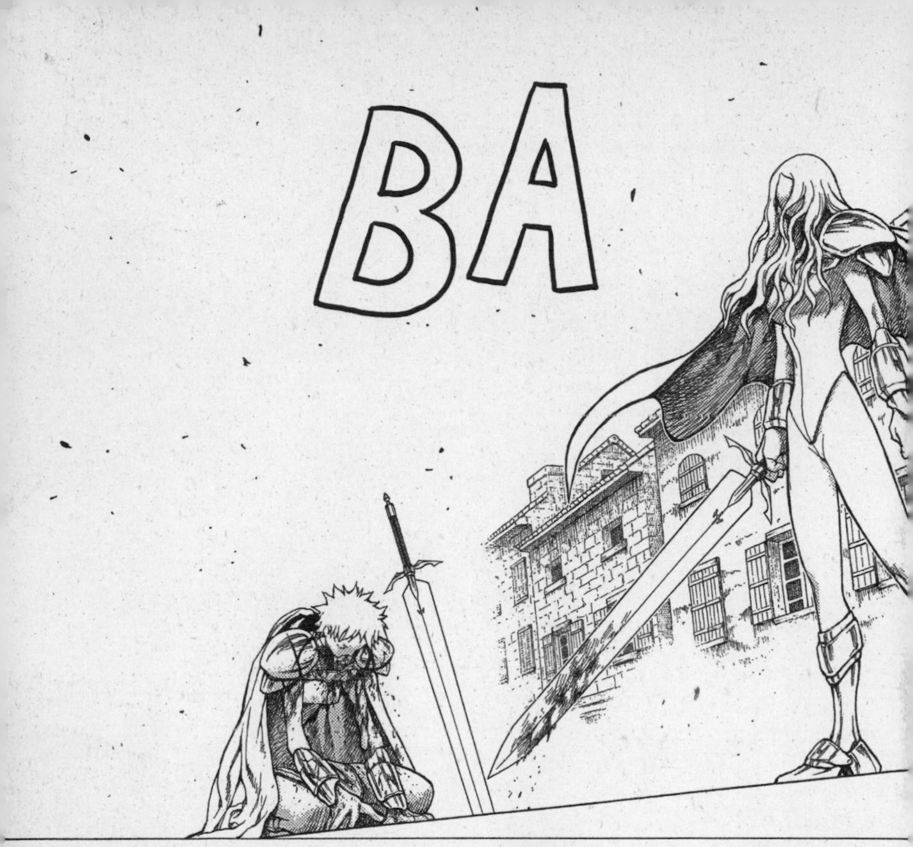
BA
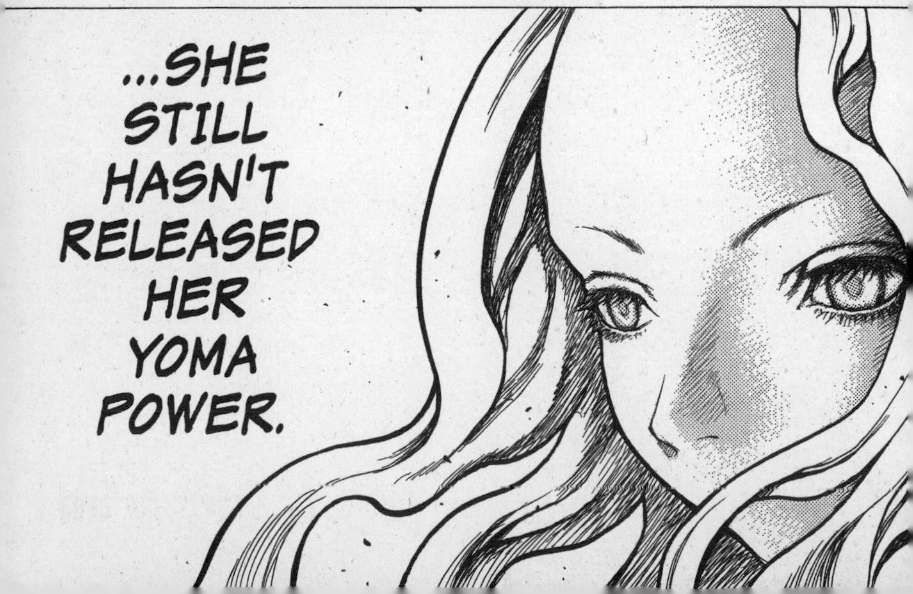
...SHE STILL HASN'T RELEASED HER YOMA POWER.

IN THE NEXT VOLUME

Teresa has defeated the Claymores who were sent kill her. But now that Teresa's human feelings have been awakened, she chooses to spare her fallen comrades rather than kill them—a move that only delays the inevitable.

Available Now

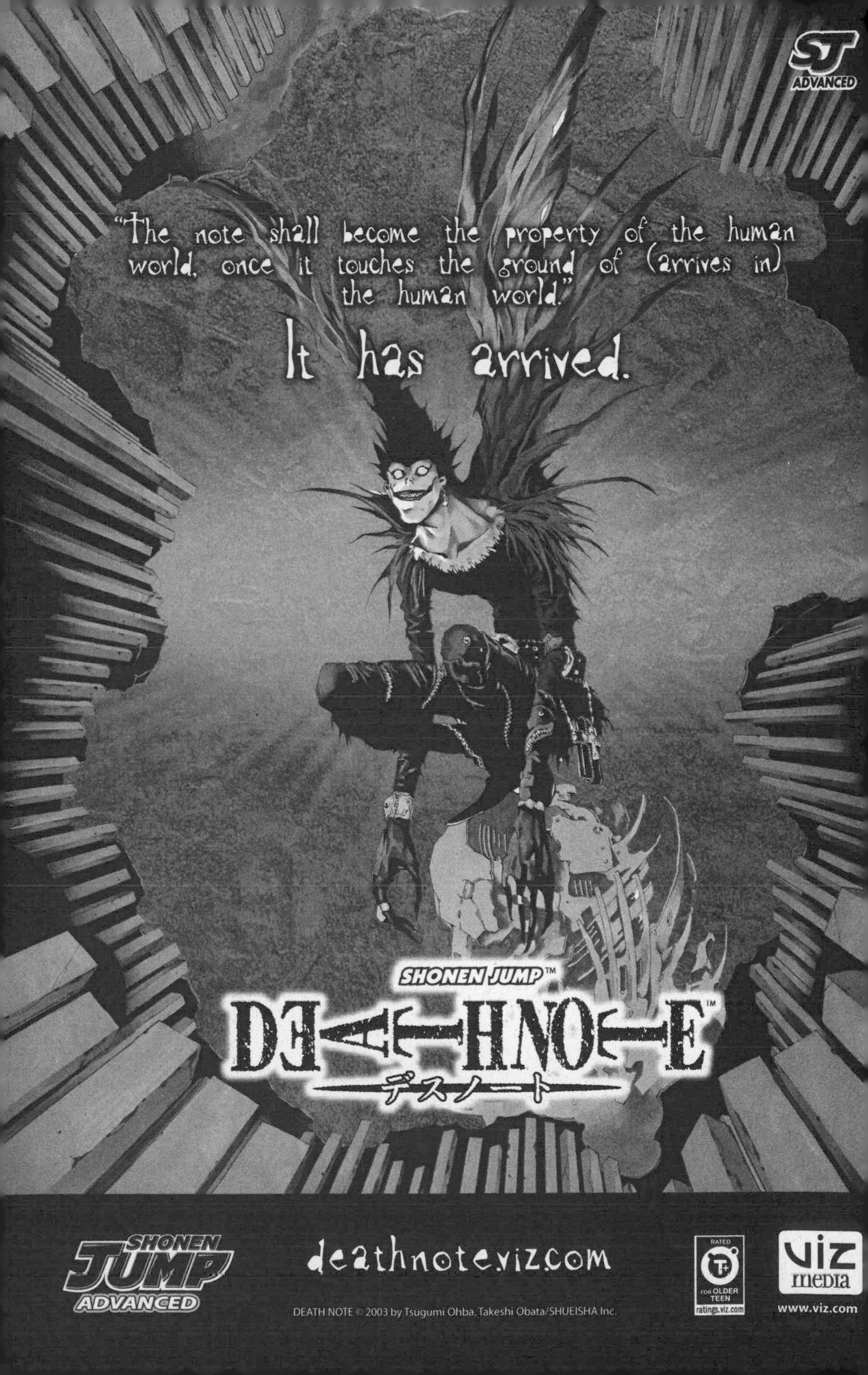
SJ ADVANCED
"The note shall become the property of the human world, once it touches the ground of (arrives in) the human world."
It has arrived.
SHONEN JUMP™
DEATH NOTE™
デスノート
SHONEN JUMP ADVANCED
deathnote.viz.com
RATED T+ FOR OLDER TEEN
ratings.viz.com
viz media
www.viz.com
DEATH NOTE © 2003 by Tsugumi Ohba, Takeshi Obata/SHUEISHA Inc.

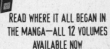
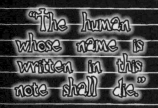

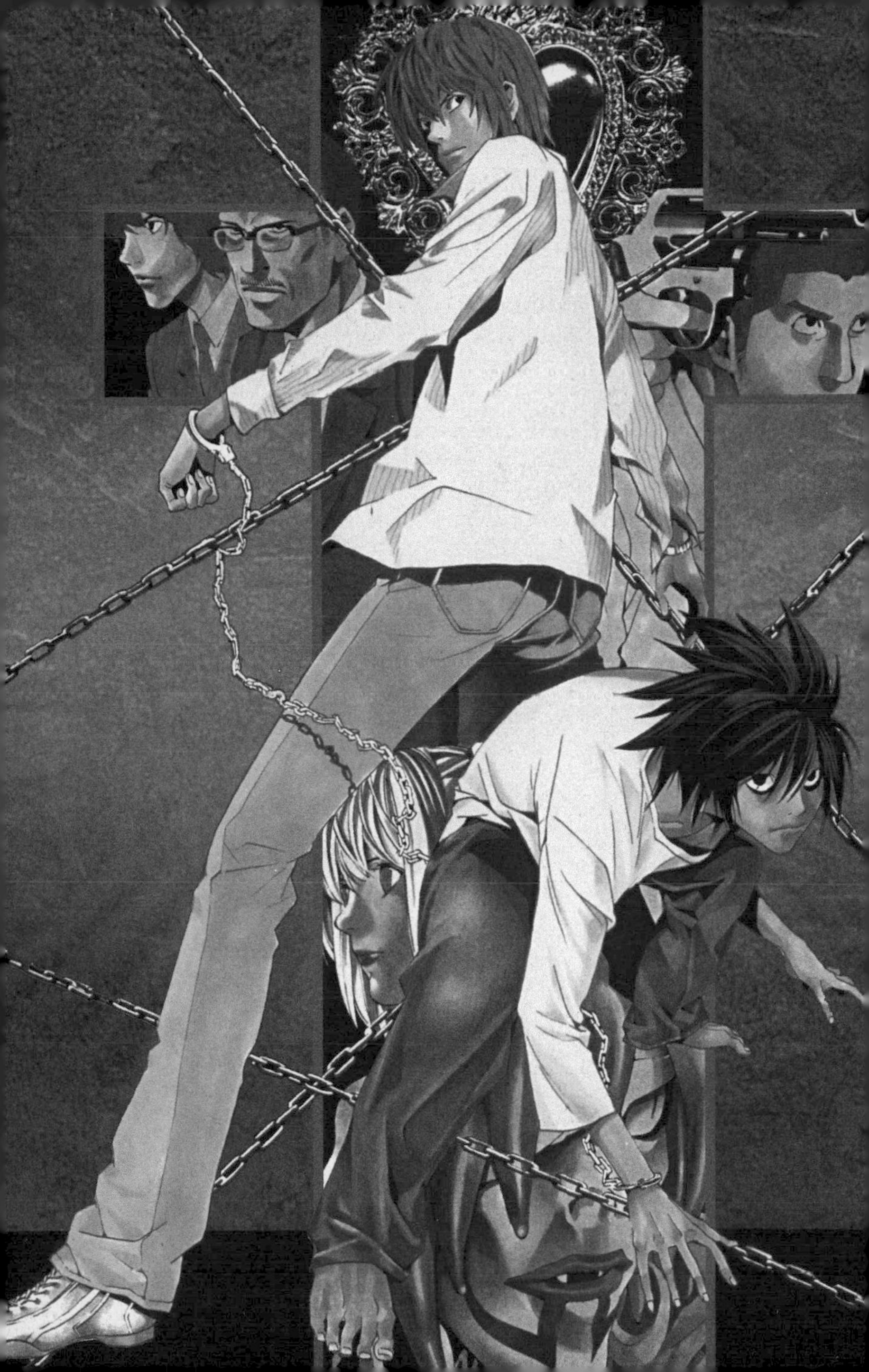

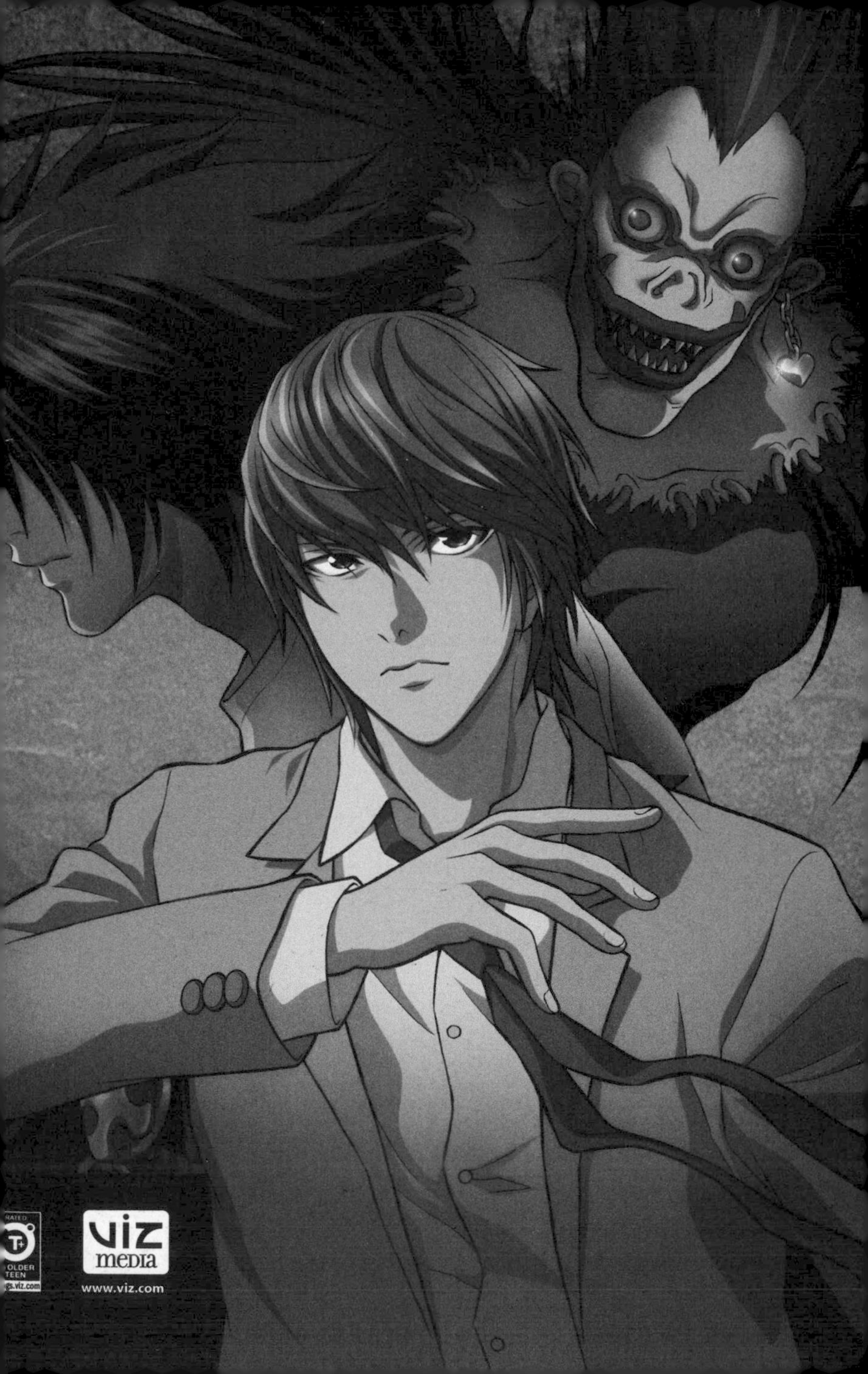
RATED
OLDER
TEEN
VIZ media
www.viz.com

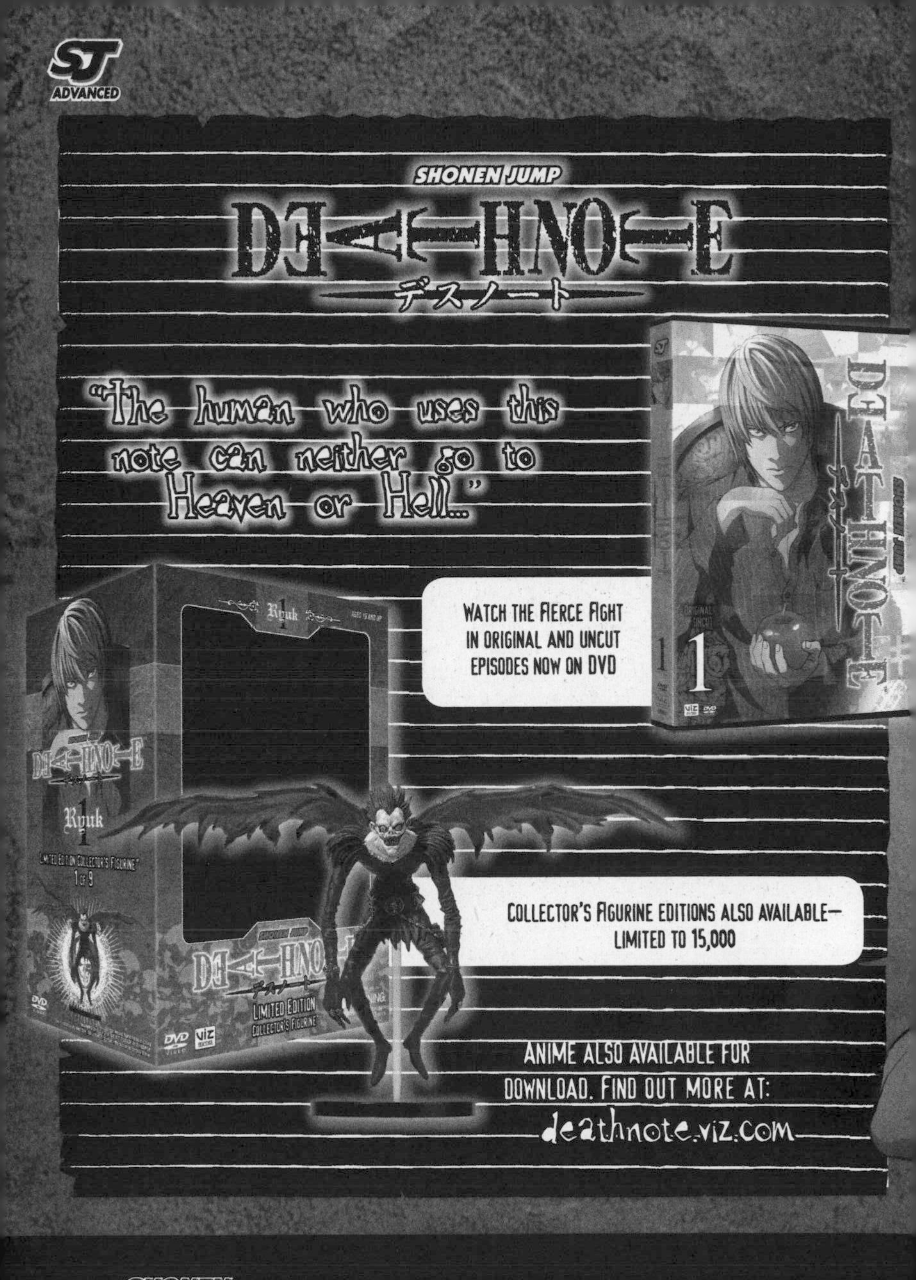
SJ ADVANCED
SHONEN JUMP
DEATH NOTE
デスノート
"The human who uses this note can neither go to Heaven or Hell..."
WATCH THE FIERCE FIGHT IN ORIGINAL AND UNCUT EPISODES NOW ON DVD
COLLECTOR'S FIGURINE EDITIONS ALSO AVAILABLE—LIMITED TO 15,000
ANIME ALSO AVAILABLE FOR DOWNLOAD. FIND OUT MORE AT:
deathnote.viz.com
SHONEN JUMP HOME VIDEO

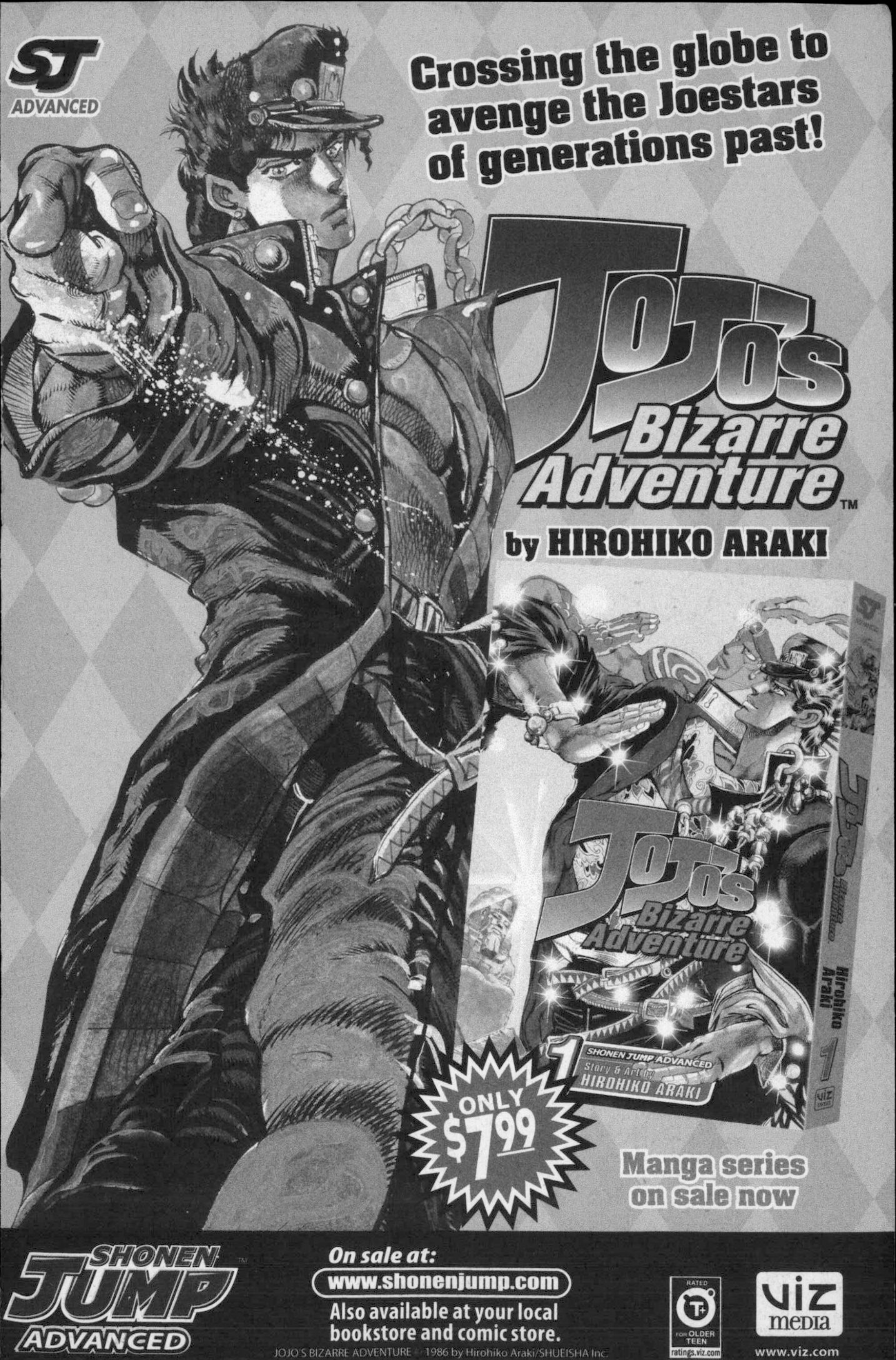
SJ ADVANCED
Crossing the globe to avenge the Joestars of generations past!
JoJo's Bizarre Adventure™
by HIROHIKO ARAKI
JoJo's Bizarre Adventure
1
SHONEN JUMP ADVANCED
Story & Art by HIROHIKO ARAKI
Hirohiko Araki
ONLY $7.99
Manga series on sale now
SHONEN JUMP ADVANCED
On sale at:
www.shonenjump.com
Also available at your local bookstore and comic store.
JOJO'S BIZARRE ADVENTURE © 1986 by Hirohiko Araki/SHUEISHA Inc.
RATED T+ FOR OLDER TEEN
ratings.viz.com
viz media
www.viz.com

The World's Greatest Manga
Now available on your iPad

Full of FREE previews and tons of
new manga for you to explore

From legendary manga like *Dragon Ball* to *Bakuman₀*, the newest series from the creators of *Death Note*, the best manga in the world is now available on the iPad through the official VIZ Manga app.

- ### Free App
- ### New content weekly
- ### Free chapter 1 previews